Nationalism, Identity and Statehood in Post-Yugoslav Montenegro

Nationalism, Identity and Statehood in Post-Yugoslav Montenegro

Kenneth Morrison

Bloomsbury Academic
An imprint of Bloomsbury Publishing Plc

B L O O M S B U R Y
LONDON · OXFORD · NEW YORK · NEW DELHI · SYDNEY

Bloomsbury Academic
An imprint of Bloomsbury Publishing Plc

50 Bedford Square	1385 Broadway
London	New York
WC1B 3DP	NY 10018
UK	USA

www.bloomsbury.com

BLOOMSBURY and the Diana logo are trademarks of Bloomsbury Publishing Plc

First published 2018

© Kenneth Morrison, 2018

Kenneth Morrison has asserted his right under the Copyright, Designs and Patents Act, 1988, to be identified as Author of this work.

All rights reserved. No part of this publication may be reproduced or transmitted in any form or by any means, electronic or mechanical, including photocopying, recording, or any information storage or retrieval system, without prior permission in writing from the publishers.

No responsibility for loss caused to any individual or organization acting on or refraining from action as a result of the material in this publication can be accepted by Bloomsbury or the author.

British Library Cataloguing-in-Publication Data
A catalogue record for this book is available from the British Library.

ISBN: HB: 978-1-4742-3518-1
       ePDF: 978-1-4742-3519-8
       eBook: 978-1-4742-3520-4

Library of Congress Cataloging-in-Publication Data
A catalog record for this book is available from the Library of Congress.

Cover image: DIMITAR DILKOFF/AFP/Getty Images

Typeset by Integra Software Services Pvt. Ltd.
Printed and bound in Great Britain

To find out more about our authors and books visit www.bloomsbury.com. Here you will find extracts, author interviews, details of forthcoming events and the option to sign up for our newsletters.

To Helen ... for the unstinting love and support

Contents

Acknowledgements	viii
List of Abbreviations	ix
Introduction	1
1 Montenegro's Twentieth Century: An Overview	3
2 The Anti-Bureaucratic Revolution and the 'January Coup' (1987–90)	29
3 From the 'War for Peace' to the 'Žabljak Constitution' (1990–92)	41
4 Fear and Flux: Montenegro's Muslim and Albanian Minorities (1992–97)	55
5 A Polity Divided: The DPS Split (1996–98)	69
6 Politics by Proxy: Orthodox Churches in Conflict (1990–2006)	83
7 From the War in Kosovo to the Belgrade Agreement (1998–2002)	95
8 The Road to the Referendum (2003–6)	111
9 Montenegro's Independence: The First Five Years (2006–11)	133
10 Progress, Protests and Political Crisis (2012–16)	151
Conclusion	169
Notes	174
Bibliography	236
Index	256

Acknowledgements

Writing a book is, of course, a rather solitary endeavour, though numerous individuals have played important roles in both its development and realization. I would therefore like to thank those who have been an integral part of my own Montenegrin experience over nearly two decades. Foremost among them are my *kum* Bojan Galić, who has been a source of great inspiration since the day I was fortunate enough to meet him. Thanks also to Snežana Galić, Jelena Galić and, of course, Kaja and Ivo Galić. Ruud Peeten, with whom I have travelled widely throughout the Balkan region, has been a constant friend and confidant; he is a genuine *bon vivant* and I have lasting admiration for his vast knowledge, indefatigable spirit and boundless optimism and enthusiasm. Neven Pajović, the son of the esteemed Montenegrin historian, Radoje Pajović, has been a true friend, a sounding board for my thoughts and observations and a participant in endless discussions about all things Montenegrin. Božena Miljić, a talented and diligent young Montenegrin scholar, helped me identify important sources at the Montenegrin National Archives in Cetinje. Mirsad Feratović, born in Plav and now residing in Brooklyn, New York, provided me with invaluable knowledge and a number of equally invaluable sources regarding Plav and Gusinje. I would also like to extend my sincerest thanks to my colleagues at De Montfort University, Leicester, and to Professor John Treadway (whose work has had a significant influence on my own), Professor Robert Donia, Professor Sabrina Ramet, Geert Hinrich-Ahrens, Dr Aleksander Zdravkovski, Nebojša Čagorović, Dragiša Burzan, Srdjan Darmanović, Elizabeth Roberts, Ivor Roberts, Kevin Lyne, Tim Judah, Boris Ristović, Milan Nikolić, Ivan and Suzanna Vukčević, Rameez Shaikh and the countless individuals I have met in Montenegro throughout long periods of conducting research. Thank you, too, to Sebastian Ballard for the maps, Rhodri Mogford at Bloomsbury Publishing for giving me the opportunity to write this book, and Emma Goode and Beatriz Lopez for making the process of publication so smooth. It goes without saying that this book could not have been written without the love and support of my family: Norma, Anita, Lawrie, Jamie, Aidan, Cherrie, Brian and, of course, Helen and Hannah – they effortlessly accept my many idiosyncrasies and are both my foundation and my greatest sources of inspiration, light and happiness.

List of Abbreviations

AA	*Albanska alternativa* (Albanian Alternative)
AEK	*Agencija za elektronske komunikacije* (Agency for Electronic Communications)
ANB	*Agencija za nacionalnu bezbjednost* (Montenegro's National Security Agency)
ANP	Annual National Programme
AVNOJ	*Antifašističko vijeće narodnog oslobodjenja Jugoslavije* (Anti-Fascist National Liberation Council of Yugoslavia)
BAF	Balkan Air Force
BIA	*Bezbednosno-informativna agencija* (Serbian Security Information Agency)
BM	*Bokeljska mornarica* (Boka Mariner's Association)
BS	*Bošnjačka stranka* (Bosniak Party)
CANU	*Crnogorska akademija nauka i umjetnosti* (Montenegrin Academy of Sciences and Arts)
CASNO	*Crnogorska antifašistička skupština narodnog oslobodjenja* (Montenegrin Anti-Fascist Assembly of National Liberation).
CDNU	*Crnogorska društvo za nauka i umjetnost* (Montenegrin Society for Sciences and Arts)
CDT	Centre for Democratic Transition
CEAC	Central European Aluminium Company
CEDEM	Centre for Democracy and Human Rights
CEMI	Centre for Monitoring and Research
CKL	*Crnogorski književni list* (Montenegrin Literary Paper)
CLRAE	Congress of Local and Regional Authorities of the Council of Europe
COE	Council of Europe
COMINFORM	Communist Information Bureau
COP	*Crnogorski oslobodilački pokret* (Montenegrin Liberation Movement)
CPC	*Crnogorska pravoslavna crkva* (Montenegrin Orthodox Church)
CSCE	Commission for Security and Cooperation in Europe
DANU	*Dukljanska akademija nauka i umjetnosti* (Dukljan Academy of Sciences and Arts)
DC	*Demokratski centar* (Democratic Centre)
DCG	Democratic Montenegro
DEMOS	*Demokratski savez* (Democratic Alliance)
DF	*Demokratski front* (Democratic Front)

DNP	*Demokratska narodna partija Crne Gore* (Democratic People's Party)
DOS	*Demokratska opozicija Srbije* (Democratic Opposition of Serbia)
DPS	*Demokratska partija socijalista* (Democratic Party of Socialists)
DS	*Demokratska stranka* (Democratic Party)
DSCG	*Demokratski savez u Crnoj Gori* (Democratic Alliance of Montenegro)
DSS	*Demokratska Srpska stranka* (Democratic Serbian Party)
DUA	*Demokratska unija Albanaca* (Democratic Union of Albanians)
DZB	*Da Živimo Bolje* ('For a Better Living' coalition)
ECM	European Commission
EC	European Community
ECDTL	European Commission for Democracy through Law
ECHR	European Court of Human Rights
ECMM	European Community Monitoring Mission
EHF	European Handball Federation
EP	European Parliament
EPCG	*Elektroprivreda Crne Gore* (Montenegrin national electricity supplier)
ESI	European Stability Initiative
EU	European Union
EUDM	European Union Delegation to Montenegro
FDI	Foreign Direct Investment
FYROM	Former Yugoslav Republic of Macedonia
GDP	Gross domestic product
GzP	*Grupa za promjene* (Group for Changes)
HGI	*Hrvatska građanska inicijativa* (Croatian Civic Initiative)
ICG	International Crisis Group
ICJ	International Court of Justice
ICTY	International Criminal Tribunal for the Former Yugoslavia
IFRM	International Federation for the Rights of Man
IMF	International Monetary Fund
IROM	International Referendum Observation Mission
ISAF	International Security Assistance Force
IZCG	*Islamska zajednica Crne Gore* (Islamic Community of Montenegro)
IZJ	*Islamska zajednica Jugoslavije* (Islamic Community of Yugoslavia)
JAT	Yugoslav Air Transport (Yugoslav state airline)
JNA	*Jugoslovenska narodna armija* (Yugoslav People's Army)
JUL	*Jugoslovenska levica* ('Yugoslav Left' party)
KAP	*Kombinat aluminijuma Podgorica* (Podgorica Aluminium Plant)
KECG	*Koalicija za Evropsku Crnu Goru* (Coalition for a European Montenegro')
KFOR	Kosovo Protection Force

KSHS	*Krajlevina Srba, Hrvata i Slovenaca* (Kingdom of Serbs, Croats and Slovenes)
LDMZ	*Lidhja Demokratike në Mal të Zi* (Democratic Alliance of Montenegro)
LS	*Liberalna stranka* (Liberal Party)
LSCG	*Liberalni savez Crne Gore* (Liberal Alliance of Montenegro)
LZCG	*List za evropski Crnu Goru* (List for a European Montenegro)
MAP	Membership Action Plan
MFA	(Russian) Ministry of Foreign Affairs
MNVS	*Muslimansko nacionalno vijeće Sandžaka* (Muslim National Council of Sandžak)
MONSTAT	*Republički zavod za statistiku Crne Gore* (Republican Statistical Office of Montenegro).
MRC	Municipal Referendum Commissions
MUP	*Ministarstvo unutrašnjih poslova* (Interior Ministry)
NAM	Non-Aligned Movement
NATO	North Atlantic Treaty Organization
NDH	*Nezavisna država Hrvatska* (Independent State of Croatia)
NDS	*Narodna demokratska stranka* (People's Democratic Party)
NGO	Non-governmental organization
NOP	*Narodnooslobodilački pokret* (People's Liberation Movement)
NOVA	New Serb Democracy
NS	*Narodna stranka Crne Gore* (People's Party of Montenegro)
ONK	*Organizacija nezavisnih komunista* (Organisation of Independent Communists)
OOACPC	*Odbora za obnavljanje autokefalne crnogorske pravoslanve crkve* (Committee for the Restoration of the Autocephaly of the Montenegrin Orthodox Church)
ORA	*Omladinske radne akcije* (Youth Action Work)
OSCE	Organisation for Security and Cooperation in Europe
PACE	Parliamentary Assembly of the Council of Europe
PBCG	*Prva banka Crne Gore* (First Bank of Montenegro)
PCG	*Pozitivna Crna Gora* (Positive Montenegro)
PfP	(NATO) Partnership for Peace
PNS	*Prava narodna stranka* (True People's Party)
PzP	*Pokret za promjeme* (Movement for Changes)
RAF	(British) Royal Air Force
REC	Republican Electoral Commission
ROM	Referendum Observation Mission
RRC	Republican Referendum Committee
RSK	*Republika Srpska Krajina* (Serb breakaway region within Croatia)
RTCG	*Radio Televizija Crne Gore* (Radio Television Montenegro)
RTS	*Radio Televizija Srbije* (Radio Television Serbia)
SAA	Stability and Association Agreement

SACEUR	(NATO) Supreme Allied Commander
SAJ	*Specijalni antiteroristička jedinica* (Special Anti-Terrorist Unit)
SANU	*Srpska akademija nauka i umetnosti* (Serbian Academy of Sciences and Arts)
SAO	*Srpska autonomna oblast Krajina* (Serbian Autonomous Region of Krajina)
SAS	British Special Air Service
SDA	*Stranka demokratske akcije* (Party of Democratic Action)
SDB	*Služba državni bezbednosti* (Montenegrin security services)
SDCG	*Socijaldemokrate Crne Gore* (Social Democrats)
SDG	*Srpska dobrovoljačka garda* ('Serbian Volunteer Guard')
SDPH	*Socijaldemokratska partija Hrvatske*
SDP	*Socijaldemokratska partija* (Social Democratic Party)
SDPR	*Socijaldemo kratska partija reformatora* (Social Democratic Party of Reformers)
SDS	*Srpska demokratska stranka* (Serbian Democratic Party)
SFRJ	*Socijalistička Federativna Republika Jugoslavija* (Socialist Federal Republic of Yugoslavia)
SKCG	*Savez komunista Crne Gore* (Montenegrin League of Communists)
SKH	*Savez komunista Hrvatske* (Croatian League of Communists)
SKJ	*Savez komunista Jugoslavije* (Yugoslav League of Communists)
SKS	*Savez komunista Srbije* (Serbian League of Communists)
SPJ	*Savez pionira Jugoslavije* (Pioneers Union of Yugoslavia)
SL	*Srpska lista* (Serb List)
SNP	*Socijalističke narodne partije Crne Gore* (Socialist People's Party of Montenegro)
SNR	*Stranka nacionalne ravnopravnosti* (Party of National Equality)
SNS	*Srpska narondna stranka* (Serbian People's Party of Montenegro)
SOE	(British) Special Operations Executive
SPC	*Srpska pravoslavna crkva* (Serbian Orthodox Church)
SR	*Stranka ravnopravnost* (Party for Equality)
SRJ	*Savezna republika Jugoslavija* (Federal Republic of Yugoslavia)
SRS	*Srpska radikalna stranka* (Serbian Radical Party)
SRSCG	*Stranka reformskih snaga za Crnu Goru* (Alliance of Reform Forces for Montenegro)
SSJ	*Stranka srpskog jedinstva* (Party of Serbian Unity)
RTCG	*Radio televizija Crne Gore* (Montenegrin State Television)
UCK/KLA	*Ushtria Çlirimtare e Kosovës* (Kosovo Liberation Army)
UDSH	*Unioni Demokratik i Shqiptarëve* (Democratic Union of Albanians)
UK	United Kingdom
UN	United Nations
UNDP	United Nations Development Programme

UNESCO	United Nations Educational, Scientific and Cultural Organization
UNGA	United Nations General Assembly
UNHCR	United Nations High Commissioner for Refugees
UOCG	*Udružena opozicija Crne Gore* ('The United Opposition of Montenegro')
URA	United Reformist Action
USSR	Union of Soviet Socialist Republics
VC	Venice Commission
VJ	*Vojska Jugoslavije* (Armed Forces of Yugoslavia)
VOPP	Vance-Owen Peace Plan
VRS	*Vojska Republike Srpske* (Army of Republika Srpska)
VZCIV	*Vjerska zajednica Crnogoraca istočnopravoslavne vjeroipovesti* (The Religious Community of Montenegrins of Eastern Orthodox Confession)
ZANVOCGB	*Zemaljsko antifašističko vijeće narodnog oslobodjenja Crne Gore i Boke* (National Anti-Fascist Council for the Liberation of Montenegro and Boka)
ZAVNOS	*Zemaljsko antifašističko vijeće narodnog oslobodjenja Sandžaka* (National Anti-Fascist Council for the Liberation of the Sandžak)
ZKS	*Zveza komunistov Slovenije* (Slovenian League of Communists)

Map 1 The Socialist Federal Republic of Yugoslavia.

Map 2 The Federal Republic of Yugoslavia.

Map 3 Montenegro (municipalities), 2016.

Introduction

On 21 May 2016 the culmination of celebrations marking ten years of Montenegro's independence was due to commence. Exactly a decade before, I had witnessed the simmering pre-referendum tensions and the subsequent celebrations in a hot, sticky Podgorica (Montenegro's capital city) as the initial results of the May 2006 independence referendum were announced, so it felt entirely appropriate to be here once again on the occasion of the ten-year anniversary of Montenegro's referendum (and thus a decade since the re-establishment of an independent status lost in 1918). In May 2006, the 'statehood question' was omnipresent and 'referendum fever' was all-encompassing; it felt to me, and I'm sure it did to others, as if Montenegro, at least for a short time, was the centre of the world. Back then, I was absolutely absorbed *in* it and entirely obsessed *with* it, to the detriment of almost everything else in my life. By the time of the independence referendum in 2006, I had already been following Montenegrin politics closely for years, had travelled widely throughout the republic, met many of the key political figures and had attended numerous political rallies throughout Montenegro prior to the referendum (including both of the large pro-independence and pro-union rallies in Podgorica), in an attempt to gauge, as best I could, the public mood. It was exhilarating to acquaint myself so intimately with Montenegro and to personally witness the potential birth (or, rather, rebirth) of an independent state.

While it had been a bitterly contested campaign and had turned out to be a close contest – and one which further widened the pre-existing cleavages that had become increasingly pronounced by the political and social flux of the late 1990s and early 2000s – Montenegro had, seemingly, made significant strides since 2006. The country had consolidated its statehood, become a member of numerous international organizations, performed respectably in sporting competitions and (in November 2015) received an invitation to join NATO while making steady progress towards European Union (EU) membership, though there was little public consensus regarding the latter. While I had visited the country many times since the independence referendum and knew the political situation wasn't entirely rosy, I was, nevertheless, quite sure that the ten-year anniversary celebrations in May 2016 would be marked with something memorable. Indeed, watching Montenegrin television and reading the local press (well, the pro-government press) in the days prior to the events, one could be excused for being in anticipation of something rather special, an event that would rekindle of the spirit and emotion so tangible, even visceral, a decade ago. It seemed fitting to be there to witness it all, but the subsequent celebrations were, frankly, a little disappointing. Perhaps the vast majority of ordinary Montenegrin citizens were now, ten years on, less interested and thus less engaged in matters political. Political stability, after all, brings with it an inevitable public disengagement with the day-to-day cut and thrust of political life, an apathy of sorts.

Having followed the first ten years of the reinstatement of Montenegro's independence closely, I was intimately acquainted with post-independence political developments, though much of my research was focused on writing (with Elizabeth Roberts) a co-authored book on the history of the Sandžak region and then a book charting the fascinating history of Sarajevo's 'frontline hotel', the Holiday Inn. A decade on from the 2006 independence referendum, it seemed an opportune time to revisit the modern political history of Montenegro, viewed now with the benefit of hindsight, experience and, crucially, some objective distance. I also had personal reasons for doing so. My first book, *Montenegro: A Modern History*, was derived from my doctoral thesis and had been published very quickly after the May 2006 referendum; it was, from a personal perspective, both rushed and, upon publication, incomplete. I never came to terms with what I believed to be a work that was both underdeveloped and hastily executed, and had long ago committed to writing another book on Montenegro (if and when the opportunity presented itself). It was my great fortune that Bloomsbury Publishing offered me the chance to do just that back in 2014. Thus, it is my hope that my acquired knowledge of Montenegro, garnered over nearly two decades of studying the country, will make this book more comprehensive, informed and, ultimately, far superior.

This book, while covering some of the same historical periods (and events therein) as the first, is a more robust and complete analysis of Montenegrin politics between 1989 and 2016, with two chapters dedicated exclusively to political developments in the decade since the 2006 independence referendum. I have included only an introductory chapter on Montenegrin history before 1989, to contextualize the main body of the text that follows. The main purpose of the book, however, is to provide a detailed account of almost three decades during which Montenegro has experienced significant political, economic and social flux – from the disintegration of the Socialist Federal Republic of Yugoslav state to the independence referendum and towards the country's seemingly inexorable path towards EU and NATO membership. The 'post-Yugoslav' in the title refers to the period after the disintegration of the Yugoslav state in May 1992, which the majority of the book focuses on (though, of course, the smaller Federal Republic of Yugoslavia, comprising only Serbia and Montenegro, existed until 2002). The chapters are essentially chronological, with each based around a critical event (or series of events) that shaped Montenegro's modern political history. These chapters address these events and are framed within a wider context of the debates over statehood, nation and identity, these themes being weaved within the text.

1

Montenegro's Twentieth Century: An Overview

On 29 December 1915, King Nikola I Petrović hastily departed the country he had led for over half a century. By then, Montenegro was embattled, close to collapse and, despite the valiant efforts of its army, facing defeat (and subsequent occupation) by the Austro-Hungarian army. He left the then Montenegrin capital, Cetinje, in the dead of night, doubtless expecting to return when circumstances allowed. Nikola, however, would never return to Montenegro and would die in exile in Antibes in France on 1 March 1921, though his remains would be reinterned in Cetinje, the capital of the Kingdom of Montenegro, in 1989. By the time of his death, Montenegro had ceased to exist as an independent country, becoming absorbed into the Kingdom of Serbs, Croat and Slovenes (*Kraljevina Srba, Hrvata i Slovenaca* – KSHS). It was a lugubrious end to the life of a man who had once sought to make Montenegro the 'Piedmont' of Serbdom, to forge a unified Serbian state with Montenegro at the core. Instead, he and his dynasty were swept away by the inexorable forces of history. By the time Nikola departed Montenegro, this small Balkan country had been an independent state for almost four decades, since the recognition of its independence formalized during the Congress of Berlin in 1878. Montenegro's trajectory towards statehood had been tumultuous and had been achieved only after centuries of struggle against Ottoman domination, during which Montenegro had remained largely (though not entirely) autonomous. Hitherto, Montenegro had essentially comprised only of four *nahije* (districts) – *Katunska, Riječka, Lješanska and Crmnička* – of *Stara Crna Gora* (Old Montenegro).[1] These areas remained essentially free from Ottoman incursions, and within this space specific Montenegrin characteristics developed. In 1796, however, Old Montenegro was unified with the *Brda* (Mountains). In these peripheries, identification with Cetinje and its environs was significantly weaker, and its people had close ties to Serbia. By 1860, Montenegro was led by Prince Nikola I Petrović, the last in a long line of the Petrović-Njegoš dynasty that had ruled Montenegro since the *Vladike* (Prince-Bishops) had been invested with power in 1516 (Vladikas had, in fact, been elected until 1697, whereupon a hereditary system replaced the pre-existing elective one, with the Vladika emanating from the Petrović clan). Nikola's predecessors, particularly Petar II Petrović 'Njegoš', had forged the foundations of a state by uniting Montenegro's fractious *pleme* (clans), regulating laws and endeavouring to centralize power in Cetinje, the de facto capital of Montenegro. By the time Nikola ascended to become prince following the assassination of Danilo I Petrović in Kotor in August 1860, Montenegro was essentially a secular principality. Nikola did much to consolidate and build upon the achievements of his predecessors and fought numerous wars of expansion, notably the Montenegrin war against the Ottoman Turks (1876–78) which included victories at Vučji Do and Fundina and led to significant territorial acquisitions.[2] In 1878, Montenegro was recognized as a sovereign and independent state at the Congress of Berlin.[3]

A long period of relative stability commenced, during which Nikola consolidated his power and Montenegro's relations with her neighbours and the Great Powers. The Petrović dynasty was based in the then Montenegrin capital, Cetinje – a small town established by Ivan Cronjević in 1482, it was graced, by the late nineteenth century, with a number of small but rather grand foreign embassies (Russian, French, British and Austro-Hungarian).[4] Nikola built a palace for himself in the town (a stone's throw away from the Cetinje monastery and the *Biljarda*) which included an adjoining royal garden.[5] The first hospital in Montenegro was built in Cetinje in 1873, while the Montenegrin state archive was created in 1895 and the town's first theatre *Zetski dom* was completed in 1898. Though achieving much in state building and being the recipient of foreign education (he had been educated in both Trieste and Paris), Nikola was an autocrat who ruled Montenegro in a markedly traditional way, dispensing 'his own personal justice under an ancient elm tree in Cetinje' and making it his business to acquaint himself with every Montenegrin of note, so that he could understand their strengths and weaknesses.[6] Nikola did much to ingratiate himself to the courts of Europe, marrying a number of his seven daughters to some of the continent's most illustrious royal families (among them his daughter Zorka to Petar Karadjordjević in 1883), earning him the title of the 'Father-in Law of Europe'. His opponents, while recognizing his endeavours and successes, regarded him as a man of the past: patriarchal, even backward. To them, Serbia, a constitutional democracy, made Nikola's Montenegro appear anachronistic. By the early 1900s, Nikola faced growing challenges from those Montenegrins who no longer regarded him as the 'First Serb' and instead supported Serbia and the Karadjordjević dynasty as the leaders of the Serb nation.[7]

He made necessary concessions when required, or as the times demanded. Indeed, after Tsar Nicholas had introduced a constitution in Russia in 1905, Nikola did likewise. However, the 1905 constitution allowed for the creation of a Montenegrin Assembly, though it had only limited powers. Within the membership of the assembly were those who opposed the autocratic rule of Prince Nikola I Petrović, who formed the *Klub narodnih poslanika* (Club of National Deputies), known more commonly as *Klubaši* (club members), who formed, in 1906, the People's Party (*Narodna stranka* – NS), which advocated greater levels of democratization and unification with Serbia. The *Klubaši* (the term was more commonly used than NS) was led by Šako Petrović and was one party which included young Montenegrins educated in Belgrade and who regarded Prince Nikola's rule as autocratic and backward.[8] There were two distinct strands within the NS: one committed to achieving their objectives through the embryonic democratic system, the other to more radical, revolutionary methods to attain their goal of Montenegro's unification with Serbia and the dethroning of the Petrović dynasty.[9] Animosity between the *Klubaši* and the Petrović dynasty was heightened during the 'Cetinje Bomb Affair' of 1907, an apparent attempt by more radical elements within the *Klubaši* and members of the Serbian *Crna ruka* (Black Hand) organization to assassinate Nikola and initiate the unification of Serbia and Montenegro. Convinced of Belgrade's complicity in the plot (the weapons used had been traced to a Serbian military store in Kragujevac in Serbia), Nikola severed relations with Serbia, and a series of trials were held to bring to account a group of alleged conspirators (including leading members of the NS) whom Nikola believed were aiming to plant the seeds of insurrection.[10] The sentences were severe but deemed necessary, given the accusations that Serbian agents had conspired to undermine the Petrović dynasty and procured weapons for that very purpose.

The NS subsequently boycotted the 1907 elections, and, in response, Prince Nikola formed, in 1907, the True People's Party (*Prava narodna stranka* – PNS), known as *Pravaši*, which was led by Lazar Mijušković. Though containing some advocates of unification with Serbia (within a federal structure), they generally supported the maintenance of Montenegro's independence and the primacy of the Petrović dynasty.[11] The PNS were the only party contesting the elections, and once in control of the Montenegrin Assembly, they passed legislation allowing Prince Nikola to be declared king and Montenegro to become a kingdom in 1910. However, while it appeared that the PNS's (and Nikola's) control was unassailable, Nikola's relentless campaign against the *Klubaši* also strengthened opposition to his authoritarianism. Indeed, tensions again reached dangerous levels during the so-called 'Kolašin Conspiracy' in 1909, an attempted coup led by a small group of anti-monarchist revolutionaries (with assistance from Austria-Hungary).[12] From their base in Podgorica, they planned to foment an uprising which would topple Nikola and secure freedom for those still imprisoned over the 'Cetinje Bomb Affair' of 1907.[13] They were, ultimately, unsuccessful but the Kolašin affair only served to further damage Serbian–Montenegrin relations and radicalize the internal political situation within Montenegro.

Regional power politics soon took precedence over merely internal matters, however, with the outbreak of the First Balkan War in 1912. Joining an alliance with Greece, Serbia and Bulgaria against the Ottoman Empire, and, in the Second Balkan War, with Serbia against Bulgaria, Montenegro gained much of the Sandžak, Metohija (including the towns of Djakovica and Peć), and gained the towns of Bijelo Polje, Mojkovac, Berane and Pljevlja, among others.[14] As a consequence, Montenegro established a common border with Serbia (dividing the Sandžak between them) and expanded into areas where many did not identify with Montenegrin statehood or identity. As Ivo Banac notes, Montenegrins, following the Balkan Wars, 'ruled over a large body of hostile Muslims, many of them Albanians, but also over highland tribes with a tradition of strong ties to Serbia'.[15] A campaign to take the town of Skadar (Shköder) in 1913, which would have incorporated a greater number of Albanians into Montenegrin territory, proved costly when the Great Powers ruled that Montenegro had to cede the town to the newly independent Albanian state.

The assassination of Archduke Franz Ferdinand in Sarajevo on *Vidovdan* (St Vitus's Day), 28 June 1914, by Gavrilo Princip, a member of *Mlada Bosna* (Young Bosnia), sparked a crisis of immense proportions, one which would soon envelope the entire European continent. In the wake of the assassination, the 'July Crisis' unfolded with

Austrian pressure coming to bear upon Serbia. Faced with war against one of the Great Powers, the Serbian government endeavoured to placate the Austrians, but were unable to do so. Upon the Austrian declaration of war, Montenegro declared its solidarity with Serbia, and on 6 August 1914 King Nikola immediately issued a decree of mobilization, despite an Austro-Hungarian inducement to cede Scutari to Montenegro if it declared neutrality. Despite early military successes throughout 1914, in particular the Montenegrin attack on the Austrians at Budva and the retaking of Pljevlja from the Austrian army, Bulgaria's entrance into the war (motivated by potential territorial gains in Macedonia, Greece and Romania) in the summer of 1915 dictated that the Serbian Army now faced further onslaughts from the east. With Bulgarian forces blocking the route to Salonika, the only option was a dangerous retreat through a hostile Albania.[16] By late 1915, Serbia had been overrun and Montenegrin forces were dangerously ill-equipped on the 'Lovćen front' and would soon be forced to make their last stand during the *Mojkovačka bitka* (Battle of Mojkovac). While Serbian troops moved in a column towards the Albanian coast where Allied transport would evacuate (to Corfu) those who survived the arduous and dangerous journey, the Montenegrin Army were increasingly pinned down by overwhelming Austrian firepower.[17] Yet their dogged determination dictated that they held their lines during fierce battles on 6 and 7 January 1916 – known as *krvavi božić* (Bloody Christmas) – and despite heavy losses asserted control over Mojkovac as the Austrians retreated. A subsequent counteroffensive by the Austrians again led to fierce fighting, and on 18 January 1916, unable to preserve their defensive lines, and faced with overwhelming Austrian military might, the Montenegrin Army had little choice but to retreat.[18] By this time, however, Cetinje and its environs had essentially fallen to the Austro-Hungarian army.

Despite attempts to sue for peace, the Montenegrin monarchy made preparations to flee. As Cetinje was encircled by Austrian troops, the royal family and the bulk of the Montenegrin government left Cetinje on 29 December 1915. After a brief time in Podgorica and Scutari, Nikola departed for Italy two days later, though he would subsequently move to France (first to Bordeaux and then Neuilly).[19] He would never return to Montenegro. The Montenegrin Army was formally dissolved on 25 January 1916, though many former soldiers waged a guerrilla conflict against the Austrian occupiers until the end of the war.[20] In the immediate period following the departure of the Montenegrin monarchy, the Austrians established a military administration, run by the Military General Governorship, which was in turn directly subordinate to the Austro-Hungarian high command.[21] Conditions were harsh under occupation, and, as a consequence of limited food supplies, death due to starvation was not uncommon.[22] Concentration camps were established, thousands were interned and the impoverished and undernourished population were expected to participate in public construction programmes (such as the construction of the Kotor-Njeguši-Cetinje road).[23] But despite the obvious superiority of the occupying forces, the Montenegrins did not simply resign themselves to passive acceptance. Opposition to Austrian occupation came in the form of *komiti:* guerrilla units who sought to inflict damage upon the Austrians whenever possible.[24]

The Austrian occupation of Montenegro ended in November 1918, but as their soldiers withdrew Serbian soldiers moved in. King Nikola, exiled in France, could do little to influence events on the ground, and following the arrival of Serbian troops, elections for the national assembly proceeded. The *Velika narodna skupština Srpskog naroda u Crnoj Gori* (Great National Assembly of the Serb People in Montenegro), known more generally as the *Podgorička skupština* (Podgorica Assembly), culminated on 29 November 1918.[25] Those in favour of union with Serbia printed their list of candidates and their agenda on white paper, while supporters of continued Montenegrin independence printed theirs on green paper. Thus, the terms *Bijelaši* (Whites) and *Zelenaši* (Greens) came to symbolize those either in favour of union or those in favour of the preservation of Montenegro's independence, a loose union with Serbia or, at the very least, the preservation of a Montenegrin 'entity' within the KSHS. A slim majority, however, voted in favour of Montenegro unifying with Serbia (and, subsequently, other Yugoslav territories), under the Karadjordjević dynasty and to depose King Nikola I Petrović-Njegoš and his dynasty.[26] On 25 November 1918 (in the northern Serbian city of Novi Sad), the 'Great National Assembly' had already proclaimed the unification of Srem, Banat and Bačka with Serbia.[27] Thus, following the Assembly of Podgorica, the Great National Assembly announced the formal unification of Serbia and Montenegro. Following these proclamations, both Bosnia & Herzegovina and Croatia followed suit, with the National Council in Zagreb declaring that those South Slavs living in the former Austro-Hungarian Empire wished to unite with Serbia and Montenegro. Thus, KSHS, later the Kingdom of Yugoslavia (*Kraljevina Jugoslavija* – KJ), was declared on 1 December 1918.

South Slav unity had finally been realized, but the seeds of its subsequent crisis were already sown. 'Yugoslavism' meant one thing to the Serbs and quite another to the Croats and Slovenes who headed the Yugoslav Committee. The former saw the new state as a fulfilment of the dream of a state for all Serbs, albeit along with a significant number of Croats, Slovenes and other minorities. For them, it was completely natural that Serbia, with its established state infrastructure, army and dynasty (not to mention their losses during the 1914–18 war), should lead the new state. The latter, however, envisaged that the new state would take the form of an equally balanced federation, a partnership of equals, within which the Croatian and Slovenian lands of the former Habsburg Empire would unite with Kingdom of Serbia. Such divergent expectations were to have a significant impact on the future of the KSHS.[28]

From his base in Neuilly, France, King Nikola I Petrović could do nothing to influence matters in Montenegro. He did, however, implore Montenegrins not to recognize the legitimacy of the outcome of the Podgorica Assembly. His supporters in Montenegro thereafter launched, on Orthodox Christmas Eve (6 January 1919), the *Božićna ustanak* (Christmas Uprising), during which the *Zelenaši* (Greens) besieged Cetinje and surrounding towns and villages and targeted those deemed guilty of crimes against Montenegro. Led by Krsto Popović[29] (who had led Montenegrin troops during the Battle of Mojkovac), their initial campaign was relatively successful, but the Greens were plagued by internecine divisions between factions which advocated full independence and those who merely wished to restore Montenegrin pride by achieving a more equal status within the KSHS.[30] Resistance to the new regime also emanated from the northern parts of Montenegro where there were significant Muslim populations. Indeed, in Plav and Gusinje local leaders sought some form of autonomy, a development that elicited a strong reaction from the KSHS authorities. Their response was unforgiving, with approximately 450 (mainly Muslims) being killed after a small uprising against the unification of Serbia and Montenegro and the creation of the KSHS.[31] In addition to the Plav and Gusinje incidents, an estimated 700 Albanians were killed in a similar crackdown in nearby Rožaje.[32] According to Mehmedalija Bojić, similar reprisals took place in Bijelo Polje, Pljevlja and Berane, although these were relatively minor by comparison.[33]

After the uprising had been largely crushed, King Nikola requested that one of the key organizers of the uprising, Jovan Plamenac, leave Montenegro and join him in France where the Montenegrin government-in-exile would be formed. In January 1919, the government-in-exile was formed and led by Plamenac; the main objective of the government was to internationalize the issue of Montenegro, appeal to the Great Powers during the 1919 Paris Peace Conference, maintain links between the government-in-exile and armed resistance groups in Montenegro and create an army-in-exile (based in Gaeta in Italy). But the course of events undermined their cause. During the Paris Peace Conference, which opened in January 1919, Montenegro was 'the empty chair', treated, according to Warren Whitney, akin to a 'conquered nation instead of an ally that had entered the war at once and made every sacrifice for the common cause' and its exiled rulers (the Montenegrin government-in-exile, based in Italy) observing developments from a distance.[34] Montenegro had its advocates, including the *Engleski Crnogorac* (English Montenegrin), Alexander Devine, who became the London-based 'Honorary Consul General' to the Montenegrin government-in-exile, though his significant endeavours proved to be in vain.[35] France formally severed diplomatic relations with Montenegro in December 1920, the United States in January 1921 and Great Britain in March of the same year; all quickly closed their embassies in Cetinje.[36] Montenegro ceased to exist as an international subject. By the time of the Great Powers' recognition of the KSHS in 1922, King Nikola had died; his successor, Danilo, abdicated soon after and the Montenegrin government-in-exile was in disarray.[37] With Queen Milena now the head of the Montenegrin royal court, matters worsened; her relationship with Jovan Plamemac was strained and the Montenegrin community-in-exile began to fragment. In Montenegro, the uprising had largely stalled, though some Green *komiti* continued to a tenacious guerrilla campaign until 1924. As the rebellion faded, Jovan Plamenac, who had led the Montenegrin government-in-exile, returned to Montenegro in 1925, having been permitted to do so by the Serbian prime minister, Nikola Pašić. The Green rebellion may have been defeated and the 'Montenegrin Question' settled, though the nature of the unification of Montenegro and Serbia in 1918 and the brutality of the civil conflict that followed remained the source of antagonism. The Assembly of Podgorica, the Christmas Uprising and the loss of statehood had collectively caused significant trauma and left many nursing grievances that would periodically re-emerge throughout the twentieth century.

Montenegro, bereft of a government and state institutions, was now fully incorporated into the KSHS. Cetinje, once the capital of an independent state, with its palaces and diplomatic residencies, was relegated to the status of provincial irrelevance, while Montenegro remained a poor region with the lowest population density in the KSHS, with no industry, few crafts and little in the way of trade.[38] By 1922, much of what was Montenegro was absorbed into the *oblast* (district) of Cetinje, one of thirty-three such districts within the KSHS. The 1920s were characterized by economic marginalization and a fragmented politics, with the Greens channelling their support towards the Montenegrin Federalist Party (*Crnogorska federalistička stranka* – CFP) and the emergent Montenegrin branch of the Communist Party of Yugoslavia (*Komunistička partija Jugoslavlije* – KPJ), led by Marko Mašanović.[39] The CFP were the only political party in Montenegro that did not have their base in Belgrade, and their political position was thus viewed with suspicion.[40] The party's theoretician, Sekula Drljević, posited that Montenegrins were of Illyrian (as opposed to Slavic) descent and that the Serb and Montenegrin mentalities were too divergent to be reconcilable.[41] It was, however, the KPJ that were making a more significant impact in Montenegro. The KPJ, unusual in the fact that they were intellectuals, students and educated youth, performed well in the 1920 elections, winning 37.99 per cent of the popular vote in Montenegro. They were, however, outlawed in 1921 by the KSHS authorities and unable to continue their political activities through democratic channels began to operate underground.[42]

The Croats and Slovenes argued that Yugoslavia should be a confederation of sorts, with power decentralized to the republican capitals. Increasingly, bitter arguments in the Yugoslav parliament between the Serbian Radical Party (*Srpska radikalna stranka* – SRS) and the Croat Peasant Party (*Hrvatska seljačka stranka* – HSS) led to violence, and, in June 1928, Puniša Račić, a Montenegrin (PNS) delegate in the assembly, shot and killed HSS delegates Pavle Radić and Djuro Basariček, and fatally wounded the party's leader, Stjepan Radić.[43] It was simply one in a series of grim incidents which led to King Aleksander Karadjordjević dissolving parliament and imposing of the '6 January dictatorship'. Intended to mitigate the intensifying political crisis, Aleksander abrogated the constitution, banned political parties, and essentially ruled by decree. Many opposition politicians were arrested and imprisoned, serving to further isolate Yugoslavia's non-Serbs. In an attempt to create a genuine Yugoslav identity, all nationalist sentiment was to be crushed and 'Yugoslavism' was to be imposed from above. As part of the Karadjordjević governments' efforts to stem the rising tide of Serb and Croat nationalism, Yugoslavia's internal borders were redrawn into nine *banovine* (districts), with Montenegro largely incorporated into the *Zetska banovina*.[44] Political parties in Montenegro (particularly the Communist Party) were targeted and brutally repressed by KSHS forces. King Aleksander's assassination in Marseille on 9 October 1934 by a Macedonian, Vlado Chernozemski (though the assassination was sponsored and organized by small group of *Ustaša*, a Croatian fascist organization that had fled Yugoslavia after the 6 January dictatorship), threw the KJ into crisis. Though the assassination did not bring forth the existential crisis that those who had planned it envisaged, on the whole it brought Yugoslavs together.[45] The new government of Milan Stojadinović did their best to build upon the unity expressed by many Yugoslavs in the wake of Aleksander's death, but faced both internal problems and a rising threat from fascism in Germany and Italy.

In Montenegro, opposition to the 6 January dictatorship (and, later, the Stojadinović government) and related political instability became more acute. Following actions taken against members of the CFP and the KPJ in Montenegro (during which there were arrests and detentions), protestors gathered for a series of demonstrations. The largest of these took place in Belveder (near Cetinje) in June 1936, during which demonstrators were fired upon by the police (killing six people).[46] In the violence that accompanied these demonstrations, eleven people were killed and forty were injured. Further demonstrations took place the following year in Podgorica and then subsequently in Berane and Danilovgrad.[47]

In the immediate wake of Stojadinović's downfall in February 1939, solutions were sought to Yugoslavia's internal problems. These negotiations would be led by the Yugoslav Regent, Prince Paul, the president of the Yugoslav government, Dragiša Cvetković and the leader of the HSS, Vladko Maček. While they sought to solve the 'Croat Question', the latter also sought to address the issue of the status of Bosnia's Muslims (the intelligentsia of which, he claimed, considered itself of Croat ethnicity). Given that his own views corresponded to this, he concluded that if indeed Muslims were in essence Croats, then Croats represented the majority in Bosnia.[48] By extension, he argued, Bosnia should be given to Croatia. However, with the signing of the 1939 Cvetković-Maček pact, the so-called *Sporazum* (Agreement), Maček accepted a compromise which ceded Croatia significant levels of autonomy and a large *Hrvatska banovina*, while dividing Bosnia & Herzegovina between Croatia and Serbia. Montenegro remained within the *Zetska banovina* and firmly within the Serbian sphere of influence. The plan, however, was never fully implemented; and while it may have contributed to taking the heat out of the Croat question in Yugoslavia, it opened up the question of the Serb minority in Croatia (among other things). The *Sporazum* represented an attempt to forge better unity between Yugoslavia's national groups (particularly Serbs and Croats), but was the precursor to collapse of the state.

Externally, too, the storm clouds were gathering. A month after Germany's invasion of Czechoslovakia in March 1939, Italy invaded and occupied neighbouring Albania; by September, Germany's invasion of Poland heralded the outbreak of war in Western Europe. In this dark international environment, Yugoslavia found herself in a precarious predicament. The KJ government, led by Dragiša Cvetković, attempted to remain neutral, hoping to maintain a distance between themselves and the fascist regimes in Italy and Germany. Indeed, both the Yugoslav government and the Prince Regent (Pavle) sought to consolidate the KJ's neutral stance and reach a level of understanding with their increasingly aggressive neighbours, a position that became increasingly tenuous. By 1940, retaining such a position became increasingly problematic. Yugoslavia was not only located in dangerously close proximity to the fascist powers, it was also surrounded by their satellites, and despite the KJ's previous efforts to placate their neighbours (such as the signing of the 'Pact of Eternal Friendship' with Bulgaria and the formation of the 'Yugoslav-Italian Friendship Society' with Italy), it was too little too late. Germany's determination to secure what (in the event of a failure to control Yugoslav territory and supply routes through it) would have represented something of a soft underbelly rendered the Yugoslav government's position untenable. Thus, the KJ leadership buckled under the strain, submitting to German demands and eventually agreeing to sign the 'Tripartite Pact' on 25 March 1941.

But while the leadership acquiesced to this agreement, many within the Yugoslav military and among wider society were outraged. Many Serbs and Montenegrins viewed the Germans as the old enemy from the First World War with whom no concessions should be given. The actions of the Yugoslav government were, therefore, essentially perceived as a betrayal. Two days later, in the early hours of 27 March 1941, a small group of embittered Yugoslav army officers executed a bloodless coup against the Cvetković government.[49] They proclaimed the young King Petar II to be Serbia's new monarch, and dismissed the Council of Regency and the Cvetković government.[50] The coup was widely supported by the citizens, who demonstrated their support on the streets of Belgrade, Cetinje, Podgorica, Split, Skopje, Kragujevac, Novi Pazar, Bijelo Polje and many other towns throughout Yugoslavia (albeit that these were concentrated predominantly in Serbia and Montenegro).[51] Defiant in the face of the imminent dangers, the crowds chanted *bolje rat nego pakt* (better war than a pact). On 27 March 1941, a few hours after the coup in Belgrade, Hitler summoned his generals and informed them of his desire to eliminate Yugoslavia as a state. 'Operation Punishment' began on 6 April 1941 with a heavy aerial bombardment of Belgrade in advance of a land-based pincer movement with troops approaching simultaneously from Austria, Bulgaria, Hungary, Romania and Italy. The new Yugoslav government capitulated under intense pressure on 17 April 1941, and the royal family, headed by King Petar II, fled the country to Greece, Jerusalem and British-controlled Palestine en route to London, where the Yugoslav government-in-exile was based for the duration of the war.[52]

The war within a war (1941–45)

Following the capitulation of the army and the departure of the royal government, Yugoslavia was partitioned among Axis powers.[53] Montenegro was occupied by German forces advancing from Bosnia & Herzegovina and Italian forces stationed in Albania (although the former withdrew almost immediately). Italy's long-held territorial ambitions on the eastern side of the Adriatic made Montenegro a natural focus of their attention. They annexed the Bay of Kotor to Italy, occupied the majority of towns in the hinterland, but ceded the areas of Ulcinj, Plav, Gusinje and Rožaje to a nascent 'Greater Albanian' entity that comprised the aforementioned areas in Montenegro, the majority of Kosovo, parts of Western Macedonia and Albania proper. While Italian interest in Montenegro was primarily strategic (the Bay of Kotor would serve as an Italian naval base), it would prove problematic and costly to occupy the hinterland; indeed, the occupation of Montenegro was an economic burden from the outset.[54] Throughout the period of Ottoman rule in the Balkans, their army frequently avoided incursions into Montenegro; the principle was simple: in rocky and barren Montenegro, a small army would be defeated and a large army would starve. It was a lesson the Italians learnt to their cost. Although the Italians could generate limited food supplies from local sources, they had to import significant stocks of food (estimated to be between 1,200 and 1,500 metric tons of food monthly) from across the Adriatic.[55]

It was a practical and logistical burden that would serve only to dilute even the most basic efficacy of their operations.

However, these problems could be overcome with good strategic and logistical planning. Convincing Montenegrins of the benefits of Italian occupation or 'sponsorship' would prove much harder. To achieve this, the Italians attempted to emphasize the important dynastic links between Montenegro and Italy. King Nikola I Petrović's daughter, Elena, was the wife of the Italian King Victor Emmanuel III, and the Italians utilized this as a justification, hoping that such sentiments would be well received in Cetinje and its environs where the loss of statehood in 1918 and the death in exile of King Nikola were bitterly lamented by many. Thus, the Italian strategy was to promise Montenegrins that their independence would be reinstated under the tutelage of Queen Elena.[56] The possible re-establishment of Montenegrin independence, even if under the aegis of the Italians, appealed primarily to a small group of Greens who, upon the arrival of the Italians, established the 'Committee for the Liberation of Montenegro'. They forged friendly relations with the Italian civil commissioner in Montenegro, Count Stefano Mazzolini, and rapidly became the primary conduit for the Italians. Despite the apparent unity, however, the Greens were factionalized, with two groups (one led by Krsto Popović, and the other by Sekula Drljević) disagreeing over the form of a future Montenegrin state. Popović's faction included some members of the CFP and a significant number of *Gaetans* – members of the Montenegrin army who had been stationed in Italy following the conflict which began with the Christmas Uprising in January 1919. They sought the re-establishment of an independent Montenegro, while leaving the possibility of joining a future Yugoslav federation open. While tentatively supporting the Italian initiative, they disapproved of the Italian annexation of *Boka Kotorska* (the Bay of Kotor) and the ceding of Montenegrin territory to Albania. Sekula Drljević adopted a different approach. Drljević was no supporter of the Petrović dynasty and was opposed to the aims and objectives of the Popović faction. Willing to cooperate with the Italians to attain independence, Drljević was keen to act as a partner to the occupying forces and join with them in defeating the communists and other domestic enemies. Drljević and his supporters rejected a reconstitution of a Yugoslav state.

In any event, the persuasive powers of Drljević convinced the Italians that establishment of an independent Montenegrin state under their sponsorship would meet little resistance. Though the proclamation was relatively well received in parts of Old Montenegro, the attempts to foster the notion of Montenegro being closely linked to Italy were not received so positively elsewhere. Moreover, even those Montenegrins who tacitly supported the Italians soon found reason to be dissatisfied, largely because, in spite of Italian promises, many Montenegrins knew that this Italian-sponsored 'independence' amounted to little more than a vassal status. Significant discomfort with Italian occupation steadily grew and incubated while the Italians pressed ahead with their plans to declare 'independence'.[57] But the sentiment for rebellion and the personnel required to carry it out existed in Montenegro. The collapse of the Yugoslav Army dictated that there were both men and munitions to bolster any potential uprising. To realize such an event, opposition to Italian occupation was harnessed from across Montenegro's political and ideological spectrum; and, indeed, the subsequent uprising on 13 July 1941 was a genuinely popular uprising, one motivated more by Montenegrin pride in their freedom than by political ideology. Well before the events of 13 July, the leadership of the KPJ recognized that Montenegro was fertile ground for rebellion and were well organized there. Throughout the late 1930s, the KPJ became increasingly active, with small cells operating throughout Montenegrin territory, with particularly strong cells in Bijelo Polje and Mojkovac.[58] Among the Bijelo Polje group was Rifat Burdžović 'Tršo', the most prominent figure in the communist movement in the Montenegrin Sandžak.[59] Burdžović had developed an acute political consciousness, one which drew him towards Marxist theory, an interest he further developed while studying at Belgrade University in the early 1930s. As a student there, he joined a growing group of young communists opposed to the '6th January dictatorship' and the Karadjordjević dynasty, such as Milovan Djilas, who was already acquainted with Burdžović (they had met during summer vacations in Bijelo Polje). Djilas recalled that Burdžović was 'a gentle and honourable man who looked as if he couldn't hurt a fly', though he later 'grew aggressive and sharp, both with the enemy and regarding discipline within the party'.[60] At the outbreak of the war on 6 April 1941, he returned to Bijelo Polje, where he established a number of communist cells. Small groups in Bijelo Polje and Pljevlja began to prepare for armed uprising against the occupying forces. Rebellion was imminent; it was simply a question of *where* it would begin.

During a meeting of the KPJ's Central Committee in June 1941, it was concluded that Djilas would be sent to Montenegro to foment armed resistance. He arrived there immediately prior to the proclamation of Italian-backed independence (on 12 July 1941). According to his wartime memoirs, Djilas claimed he could immediately sense a pervasive anger with the Italian occupiers and their plans to create an Italian-sponsored Montenegrin state. Even within the Greens, he noted, 'some of their more prominent adherents rejected all collaboration with the Italians'.[61] Indeed, both a faction of the Greens and all of the 'Whites' opposed the Italian initiative, meaning that there existed sufficient scope for an uprising. The KPJ sought to gather these disparate forces and channel their collective resentment against the occupiers and their domestic collaborators, but momentum was building independently; and on 13 July 1941, the day after the proclamation of the Montenegrin 'independence', the rebellion began.

The first attacks against the Italians took place near Cetinje, though the rebellion soon spread. One week later, much of Montenegro (with the exception of the towns of Podgorica, Nikšić, Pljevlja and Cetinje) had been liberated; between 13 July and 9 August, for example, the Montenegrin rebels had overrun and briefly held Bijelo Polje, Kolašin, Berane, Andrijevica, Danilovgrad and Šavnik.[62] The speed, gravity and efficiency of the uprising shocked the Italians, but prompted them to take a much firmer approach. In the last week of July 1941, they unleashed a series of violent reprisals in Old Montenegro; martial law was declared, strict curfews were imposed and the civilian population were forced to surrender their firearms. The uprising was thus quelled. As the Italians reasserted control, the unity among the rebels began to crack; internal factions began to quarrel. Opposition to the occupation and the will to rebel against it was uniform in the summer of 1941; ideological differences could be left aside. But the participants in the uprising gravitated towards groups with radically divergent objectives; the end of the uprising marked, therefore, the beginning of fratricidal civil war in Montenegro.

By late 1941, the Partisans moved to the 'second stage' of their revolution. Upon the orders of Tito, Djilas was dismissed and replaced by Ivan Milutinović. The Partisans regained some of the territory lost following the Italian backlash, but their return was also marked by a series of revenge attacks and executions. The more zealous among the Partisans proceeded to settle scores with 'class enemies', those deemed collaborators and wealthy landowners and those who did not share their narrow ideological vision. Subsequently known in post-war Titoist terminology as the 'Mistakes of the Left', these measures proved counterproductive, and such arbitrary 'justice' served only to weaken the Partisans in Montenegro. In the wake of the 'Red Terror', many Montenegrins turned towards other resistance groups.

Opposition to the occupation came also from the *Četnici* (Chetniks), who were led by the former Yugoslav army colonel Draža Mihailović, who had refused to accept the terms of the Yugoslav government's capitulation in May 1941. The Chetniks were established at Ravna Gora in Serbia, and were quickly growing and consolidating throughout Serb-dominated areas of occupied Yugoslavia.[63] By autumn 1941, Mihailović had effectively brought most Chetnik detachments, including those operating in Montenegro, under his command. But Mihailović despised communists almost as much as the occupation, and much of his energies were channelled into defeating the Chetniks' main domestic opponents. In Montenegro, they tapped a deep vein of resentment towards the Partisans; though while the movement grew there, it became clear that it did not constitute a homogeneous group with clear objectives. The Montenegrin Chetniks (broadly led by Major Djordje Lašić) drew their support predominantly from northern Montenegro. Only the eastern Montenegrin Chetniks, led by Captain Pavle Djurišić (who had fought alongside communists in Berane during the 13 July uprising), had direct contact with Draža Mihailović.[64] Djurišić, who controlled Chetnik forces in Andrijevica, Berane, Kolašin, Bijelo Polje and Pljevlja, adhered not to the idea of reconstituting the KJ under the Serbian royal family, but to create a homogenous Serbia (which included Montenegro), a concept embedded in Ilija Garašanin's *Načertanije* (Blueprint) but crystallized by the Chetnik ideologue, Stevan Moljević. This homogenous (Serb) territory would, it was proposed, comprise of Serbia, Montenegro, Bosnia & Herzegovina, Macedonia, Sandžak, Vojvodina, Kosovo, Metohija and Croatia south of Karlovac.[65]

The 'Red Terror' of the Partisans had shifted perceptions among Montenegrins. General A. Pirzio Biroli, the Italian military governor of Montenegro, was aware of the growing animosity towards the Partisans and offered a deal: that the Italians would not encroach into Chetnik-held areas if they would reciprocate vis-à-vis areas held by the Italians. Subsequent military and political blunders by the Partisans, such as the unsuccessful attempt to take the town of Pljevlja (in December 1941) only served to bolster the Chetniks.[66] Indeed, the Partisan attempt to do so proved a fatal error. A heavily fortified Italian garrison, Pljevlja was strategically vital to the Partisans, and key to their efforts to penetrate into the Sandžak. The resulting attack was poorly planned and executed, resulting in heavy losses. By early 1942, following the debacle at Pljevlja and subsequent setbacks, the Partisans were incrementally weakened in Montenegro.

The Chetniks were now in the ascendancy (clearly demonstrated by the decision by Draža Mihailović and the Chetnik high command to move their headquarters to Gornje Lipovo, near Kolašin), while the Partisans had all but fled Montenegro, leaving behind the areas that they had previously liberated. The Italians re-established control over Montenegro's towns, while in the less-populated and rural north of the country, the Chetniks imposed their authority. In many respects they repeated the mistakes made by the Partisans in 1941. Prison camps, show trials and indiscriminate killings characterized the period following the Partisan departure from Montenegro. Often a law unto themselves, irregular Chetnik groups focused their energies not simply on the remaining Partisans but on killing or expelling Muslims in the Montenegrin Sandžak. Djurišić, who controlled Chetnik forces in Andrijevica, Berane, Kolašin, Bijelo Polje and Pljevlja, set about consolidating control over northern Montenegro. Chetniks sought to settle scores with Muslims in the Montenegrin Sandžak, and were given orders to undertake 'cleansing actions' against Muslims in Bijelo Polje and Pljevlja region. This so-called 'Lim-Sandžak brigade' waged a vicious campaign of terror against Muslims in and around the towns of Bijelo Polje (in the villages of Donji Bihor and Korita), Pljevlja and Bukovica.[67] According to Tomasevich, Chetnik losses were nominal during this campaign, while Muslim losses were heavy, perhaps as many as 10,000.[68]

The core of the Partisan leadership, meanwhile, had established their temporary headquarters in Foča, having been driven out of the short-lived *Užička republika* (Užice Republic). But it represented only a temporary respite, and on 11 March 1942, a joint German–Italian offensive known as 'Operation Trio' (or the 'Third Offensive' in Partisan terminology) began with the express purpose of annihilating the Partisans in Herzegovina, Eastern Bosnia, Montenegro and the Sandžak. Fleeing Foča and exposed, outnumbered and increasingly encircled, they moved towards the environs of Podgorica before proceeding to Nikšić, where they made only minor gains. Calculating that an ambitious attack upon Kolašin, a heavily fortified Chetnik stronghold, may bring dividends, the Partisans attempted to do so on 16 May 1942 but were ultimately unsuccessful. With retreat the only option, they began their 'long march' through Bosnia & Herzegovina. During this time, however, the Partisans, under the banner of the 'People's Liberation Movement' (*Narodnooslobodilački pokret* – NOP), attempted to generate resistance by creating a patriotic fervour among the population, framing their rhetoric in the Yugoslav context, while appealing to the people to unite against the forces of fascism. Having wrested control in the town of Bihać, they created the political wing of the liberation movement dubbed the Anti-Fascist National Liberation Council of Yugoslavia (*Antifašističko vijeće narodnog oslobodjenja Jugoslavije* – AVNOJ). During this first meeting on 26 November 1942, the leadership of AVNOJ conveyed their blueprint for a future Yugoslav state, though plans for the realization of their stated aims were not clarified until the second meeting of AVNOJ in Jajce a year later.

In the meantime, the Partisans continued to make incremental, though not inconsiderable, gains, wresting control of several towns in Bosnia & Herzegovina (including Prozor, Gornji Vakuf, Duvno, Mrkonjić Grad and Jajce), and making their presence felt over an area extending from the western approaches to the Neretva to

Karlovac in northern Croatia. It was within this context that the Germans launched Operation *Weiss* (White) – known in Partisan terminology as 'The Fourth Offensive'. Between January and April 1943, the Germans pressed the Partisans, with the objective of encircling them, destroying them and crushing further resistance. Fleeing from advancing German and Italian forces and driven from their Bihać base, the Partisan column managed trekked through Bosnia & Herzegovina, crossing the Neretva River at Jablanica (where the bridge had already been destroyed) and engaging the Chetniks awaiting them on the other bank. Unprepared for the Partisan advance following the crossing of the Neretva, the Chetniks suffered a defeat from which they would never fully recover. Chaotic leadership, poor planning and a determined and desperate adversary combined to seal their fate.[69] The Partisans, having broken Chetnik lines of defence, proceeded towards Montenegro.

These developments had been closely monitored by the Allies, though their interest in Yugoslavia was limited; the country was not, after all, deemed to be of great strategic significance (with only occasional interest demonstrated during the Belgrade coup and the 13 July 1941 uprisings in Montenegro).[70] Gathering credible intelligence was also problematic, and the complexity and fluidity of the situation on the ground made it difficult to assess *who* were the most effective opposition to the occupiers. Seeking clarification, the British sent a number of missions to Yugoslavia. The first of these, codenamed 'Operation Bullseye', arrived on the Adriatic coast and made their way through Montenegro following the Italian suppression of the 13 July uprising 1941.[71] By then, however, many of Montenegro's towns and cities had been reoccupied by the Italian forces following the post-13 July crackdown. The mission met briefly with a small detachment of Partisans in Petrovac on the Montenegrin coast, and then moved on to make contact with Mihailović at his headquarters in Ravna Gora, Serbia.[72] Given that they were recognized as the sole legitimate resistance by the Yugoslav government-in-exile (based in London), coupled with the British mission's positive assessment of Chetnik resistance to the occupation, convinced the British government to support Mihailović. Problematically, however, the Chetniks and Partisans were investing much of their respective energies into killing each other, as opposed to undermining the occupation. British appeals to both to unite against the occupying forces met with little success, and the intelligence gathered by British Special Operations Executive (SOE) officers was often conflicting in their analysis of Mihailović and the Chetniks.[73] Only when intelligence indicated that the Chetniks were collaborating with the Germans and Italians did the British consider reviewing their policy, and thus tentatively explore the option of supporting the Partisans.

These SOE missions, the objective of which was to liaise with the Partisans, would lead to a dramatic shift in British policy. Taking the initiative, the SOE prepared the despatch of personnel into areas outside Mihailović's area of control, and to the Partisans.[74] One such area was in the vicinity of Mount Durmitor, near Žabljak, where a large group of Partisans had gathered following their escape over the Neretva River in early 1943. Having faced an Axis offensive called 'Operation Trio' in April of 1942, the Partisans had fled western Bosnia through Bosnia & Herzegovina towards Montenegro. The Partisans were fighting for their very survival, but they were taking German casualties – the priority for the British. The first SOE mission to liaise with the Partisans was a joint Special Operations Executive–Military Intelligence (SOE-MI) operation, dubbed 'Operation Typical', although it was anything but.[75] Led by Colonel Fredrick William Deakin (F.W. Deakin) and Colonel Bill Stuart, it took place in May 1943. The mission were met by a small group of Partisans at a prearranged landing zone near the village of Negobudje close to Mount Durmitor, before being taken to a meeting with Tito and the Partisan leadership near *Crno jezero* (Black Lake) nearby. Initial tension and mutual mistrust pervaded. The Partisans, while more open to cooperation with the Allies than hitherto, were cautious, with the more ideologically zealous among them deeming the British 'agents of Imperialism' who had also supported the Partisans' adversaries. According to Djilas, the initial meeting was cordial, with Tito outlining clearly to the British mission the dangers of the current situation, adding that the British would have the opportunity to decide whether it was the Partisans or the Chetniks who were fighting the Germans and Italians.[76] They did not have to wait long.

By the time the British mission had arrived, the Partisans were almost completely encircled by German forces as part of an offensive known as *Operation Schwarz* (the 'Fifth' Offensive in Partisan terminology). The British mission set out across Durmitor to acquaint themselves with the situation, and in the subsequent hours both Stuart and Deakin would witness first-hand the intensity of the conflict. In his wartime memoirs *The Embattled Mountain*, Deakin described the conflict around Durmitor as 'an epic being fought out within a cauldron.'[77] The German offensive, waged by an impressive force of over 110,000 armed men, including German, Bulgarian and Italian units, had embarked upon the latest offensive two weeks prior to the arrival of the British. Trained specifically for mountainous warfare, they were pitted against a Partisan force that numbered only approximately 18,000.[78] The German push was relentless, and in fierce fighting, Stuart was killed while both Deakin and Tito were wounded. Deakin remained with the Partisans until September 1943 throughout the 'Battle of Sutjeska', during which the Allies began limited air drops of arms, medical supplies and explosives (for sabotage operations) to the Partisans. He gained an intimate knowledge of the Partisans' capabilities and objectives, and senior figures within their leadership. The results of his reports from the field were tangible. British policy towards the resistance fighters in Yugoslavia shifted following these events, during the subsequent German offensive and the battle of Sutjeska in May and June 1943, during which the Partisans survived another significant German onslaught. The shift was underpinned both by Deakin's influence and by messages received by Churchill from other SOE missions indicating that the Chetniks had collaborated with both the Italians and Germans.[79] Subsequent missions led by Fitzroy MacLean, who would become the permanent Allied liaison to the Partisans, would lend further credence to the Partisan cause.

During Deakin's mission, in July 1943, events in Italy changed irreversibly the dynamics of the conflict in occupied Yugoslavia. Benito Mussolini's fall from power led to the capitulation of Italy in September 1943, removing the Italians out of the equation and enabling the Partisans to seize large quantities of arms, equipment and other military supplies from them. In order to fill the vacuum, German forces moved into Montenegrin territory to secure what were deemed key strategic positions (such as the Montenegrin coast). Lacking the necessary manpower, they were stretched and left significant swathes of Montenegrin territory open to penetration by the Partisans. Following the Battle of Neretva the Partisans moved swiftly into these areas, eventually asserting control over approximately two-thirds of Montenegrin territory by October 1943.[80] On 15 November, the Land Assembly for the National Liberation of Montenegro and the Bay of Kotor (*Zemaljsko antifašističko vijeće narodnog oslobodjenja Crne Gore i Boke* – ZAVNOCG) was established in Kolašin, a development endorsed by the ANVOJ leadership during their meeting in Jajce in Bosnia & Herzegovina on 29–30 November 1943.[81]

Following the AVNOJ meeting, the 'war within a war' continued unabated. In Montenegro, between February and July 1944, the Chetniks carried out mass executions of Partisans and Muslims in areas they still controlled, while in the northeast of Montenegro the notorious 21st SS Skenderbeg Division massacred over 400 of the Orthodox population around Andrijevica.[82] The Partisans continued, in the meantime, to consolidate their gains and with greater support from the Allies. Indeed, the Allies now sought to provide air support to the Partisans, and thus the Balkan Air Force (BAF), known to its members as the 'Partisan Wings', was created in June 1944 with, stated Fitzroy MacLean, a dedicated Royal Air Force (RAF) formation 'responsible the planning and coordination of all supply dropping as well as for all bomber and fighter operations in support of the Partisans'.[83] This new unit would be adaptable to developing situations across the Balkans (in Albania and Greece, for example) but would primarily be utilized for Balkan operations.[84] Based in Bari in Italy, their role was to provide aerial support and allocate resources to resistance movements in Yugoslavia, Greece and Albania. They were led by RAF air vice-marshals William Elliot and George Mills, and F.W.D. Deakin was appointed their advisor. The BAF comprised two specific branches, light bombers and special operations. Predominantly British, they also included several American, Italian, Greek and Polish units. The BAF possessed two spitfire squadrons, two Italian Air Force 'Macchi' squadrons, two Halifax squadrons (one RAF, one Polish), two Dakota squadrons (one RAF, one United States Air Force). This initial force was, in both July and December 1944, reinforced to provide a larger number of Dakota squadrons. These Dakotas were first built in 1935 and conceived as civilian aircraft (known as Douglas DC-3s) but were converted for use during the Second World War and were used extensively to transport troops, cargo, wounded and on logistical missions.[85] In total, fifteen types of aircraft were employed, flown by aircrew from Britain, South Africa, Italy, Greece, Yugoslavia (and for supply operations) America, Poland and the Soviet Union.

With the BAF thus established, operations that would provide logistical assistance to the Partisans began. The Partisans were provided with Allied arms and equipment, and were often supported by Allied air and naval attacks (though these were limited in terms of both scope and efficacy). More importantly, the BAF dropped supplies, covered lines of communications and attacked key enemy lines of communication. These efforts were pivotal in that they pinned down German units which could otherwise have been deployed elsewhere. Evacuating the Partisan wounded, who were carried by stretcher bearers, also became a key part of BAF strategy. Temporary airstrips were required to be constructed that would facilitate the evacuation of the wounded, thereby freeing those carrying the wounded to bear arms (though the stretcher bearers were often

Italian prisoners, not Partisans). Reconnaissance missions by British SOE operatives identified possible locations that could be used for evacuations, with Negobudje, Kolašin, Gornje Polje and Nikšićko Polje all identified as possible sites for landing aircraft. Through clearly not without difficulty, the construction of these proceeded to the extent that the BAF assessed that these makeshift airstrips had 'sprung up like mushrooms' in the period between April and August 1944.[86]

By then, however, the Partisans were encircled and rendered less mobile by their commitment to physically transporting their injured and incapacitated.[87] This, of course, limited the capacity of the Partisans to do much more than hold back the German onslaught. The BAF's objective, therefore, became to airlift the wounded, but in mountainous territory of the areas surrounding Durmitor the chances of finding appropriate land where a temporary airstrip could be constructed were slim. Two SOE officers (Thomas Mathias and Philip Lawson) were despatched on a reconnaissance mission to source a suitable piece of terrain upon which to construct an airfield, one which would allow for the landing of Dakota aircraft. After several fruitless expeditions, they reached the village of Brezna, located in a valley approximately thirty miles north of Nikšić. There, with the assistance of locals, they constructed a temporary airstrip in two days.[88] On the morning of 22 August 1941, the airlifts began, with the first Dakota (protected by smaller fighter aircraft) landing at 9.00 am, the first of thirty-six flights. More than wounded 800 Partisans were airlifted to Italy.[89]

The BAF were also engaged in bombing raids on German positions and retreating German units, with these particularly intense throughout *Ratweek* in September 1944.[90] Major towns and communication routes, through which the German forces were retreating, were significantly damaged. Nikšić, Bijelo Polje, Ulcinj, Pljevlja and Podgorica were all badly damaged as a consequence. However, *Ratweek* changed the dynamics and trajectory of the conflict, and by November 1944 the Partisans were in control of the majority of Montenegrin territory.[91] The last of the occupying forces left Bijelo Polje in Montenegro in early 1945, in a column heading northwest towards Slovenia and the Austrian border. With the retreating Germans was a Chetnik column led by Pavle Djurišić, who was later arrested and interned by Ustasha in the Jasenovac, where he met his death.[92] Remnants of the Montenegrin Greens also fled towards Slovenia. Sekula Drljević, who had agreed to join Djurišić in an attempt to escape towards the Slovenian-Austrian border, later betrayed a number of Djurišić's followers (though some remained with Drljević in an effort to escape). They succeeded in entering Austria, where Drljević was accommodated at a refugee camp in the town of Judenberg. In November 1945, however, he and his wife were discovered there by followers of Pavle Djurišić and were subsequently murdered.[93] Draža Mihailović was, along with twenty-three other Chetnik leaders, put on trial in Belgrade in May 1946. At the end of proceedings, he was sentenced to death; while others, among them the Chetnik ideologue Stevan Moljević, were given lengthy prison sentences of between two and twenty years.[94] On 14 March 1947, Krsto Popović, who had led the Lovćen Brigade (a quasi-paramilitary group established in Cetinje in 1942 under the aegis of the Italians), was killed in an ambush by a unit led by a Partisan fighter, Veljko Milatović (who would later become a prominent Montenegrin politician).

The war had exacted a heavy price in Montenegro. According to Radoje Pajović, at the end of four years of war approximately 14,000 Montenegrin Partisan fighters had died, while an equivalent number of Montenegrin Chetniks had been killed. In addition, he argued, more than 21,000 private homes and public buildings, 321 school buildings, 15 industrial sites and 80 per cent of Montenegro's bridges had been destroyed.[95] Šerbo Rastoder estimates that the total demographic loss (taking into account natural population growth and the displaced) between 1941 and 1945 was in the region of 103,000.[96] Some of Montenegro's main population centres were almost completely destroyed. Podgorica, which had been bombed by Allied aircraft on over seventy occasions, was reduced to rubble with much of the old town devastated.[97] Milovan Djilas described Podgorica at the end of the war as a town resembling 'an archaeological excavation' and that the citizens had 'scattered to the villages or to caves around the Morača River'.[98]

The KPJ now had to rebuild both state and society, a significant challenge in light of the gravity of the conflict. In November 1945, Federal People's Republic of Yugoslavia (*Federativna narodna republika Jugoslavija* – FNRJ), a country comprised of six federal units (Serbia, Croatia, Slovenia, Bosnia & Herzegovina, Macedonia, and Montenegro), was promulgated.[99] The president of the Executive Council of the Montenegrin republic was Blažo Jovanović, a general major in the Partisans, while Milovan Djilas became the minister for Montenegro in the Socialist Federal Republic of Yugoslavia (SFRJ) government.[100] With 36 per cent of Partisan generals (and this in the context of Montenegrins being only 2 per cent of the total Yugoslav population), Montenegro had a strong Partisan tradition and was thus well placed to play a significant role in the new state.[101] Tito made his first post-war visit to Montenegro in July 1946 to mark the fifth anniversary of the 13 July 1941 uprising. The city was, subsequently, renamed 'Titograd' in his honour.[102]

Montenegro and the Tito–Stalin split

In the early years of the existence of the SFRJ, Montenegro would be at the centre of a vortex that would shake intra-KPJ dynamics. Montenegrins were disproportionately represented within the Yugoslav communist power structure. Both during and after the Second World War, the percentage of the population which were *members* of the KPJ was higher than that of any other republic, while Montenegrins were especially well represented in the Yugoslav People's Army (*Jugoslovenska narodna armija* – JNA). Post-war regeneration and investment also brought tangible benefits, and Montenegro received a disproportionate amount of funds for industrial development in the Five Year Plan package in 1947.[103] Podgorica (Titograd), which was almost completely destroyed in 1944 as a consequence of Allied air bombings, began a lengthy period of reconstruction. The KPJ's 'Five Year Plan' was, however, intended to provide development funds for the SFRJ's poorer republics, such as Bosnia & Herzegovina, Macedonia, and Montenegro, which would assist in reconstruction efforts.[104]

Problems emerged, however, as Tito's relationship with Stalin worsened throughout 1947. During the early years of post-war rule, the Yugoslav Communists had consistently demonstrated their loyalty to Moscow by adhering to their directives. But while they remained generally ideologically aligned with the Soviet Union, their relationship with Moscow was different from that of Soviet satellites such as the German Democratic Republic or Czechoslovakia. The Yugoslav Partisans had, after all, largely achieved their country's liberation largely without Soviet military assistance, and retained, therefore, a more independent agenda. But this determination on the part of the KPJ to chart an independent course led to frictions between Belgrade and Moscow, frictions that would lead to a split. The growing chasm between Tito and Stalin was fuelled largely by the KPJ's refusal to fall into line with Soviet demands that the country should provide raw materials for the Soviet industrial programme (Yugoslavia had, by contrast, embarked upon its own process of heavy industrialization, an economic strategy at odds with the Soviet plan).[105] Furthermore, Tito expressed growing independence in the sphere of foreign policy, such as his support for the Greek Communists and his ambitions vis-à-vis Albania.[106] Stalin was incandescent when, for example, he was informed that Tito had, in August 1947, signed a customs agreement with Bulgarian leader Georgi Dimitrov, without obtaining the prior permission of the Soviet authorities. Relations further deteriorated when, without Stalin's approval, Yugoslavia entered into negotiation (the so-called 'Bled Agreement') – which envisaged a 'federation' of states, including Yugoslavia, Greece, Hungary, Bulgaria, Romania, Poland, Albania and Czechoslovakia.[107] Such developments led to Stalin summoning both Tito and Dimitrov to Moscow for discussions. While Dimitrov agreed to travel to Moscow, Tito sent Milovan Djilas and Edward Kardelj to discuss matters with Stalin.[108]

On 27 March 1948, the Communist Party of the Soviet Union sent the first in what became an exchange of letters between Moscow and Belgrade. The SFRJ was formally expelled from the Communist Information Bureau (COMINFORM) on 28 June 1948, during a meeting of the organization that the Yugoslavs did not attend. This so-called 'COMINFORM Resolution' denounced the Yugoslavs and set in motion a process whereby the SFRJ was expelled from the organization. The expulsion from COMINFORM created shockwaves throughout the SFRJ.[109] Once heralded as the leading figure in the communist world, Stalin became the sworn enemy of the KPJ's leadership. Yet, support for Stalin was strong in parts of the SFRJ, and especially so in Montenegro where many viewed Stalin and the USSR as both a protector and friend. To compound this, there were historical reasons for the high level of identification with Russia and the USSR. Montenegrins were proud of their historical connections to Russia during the eighteenth and nineteenth centuries, and the cult of Russia ran deep in Montenegro.[110] However, with the COMINFORM Resolution the dynamics changed almost overnight causing, according to Ivo Banac. 'Immense moral and psychological dilemmas among the patriarchal and Russophile Serbs and Montenegrins' and that in renouncing Stalin 'these peasant (or ex-peasant) Communists would be repudiating a part of themselves, turning their backs not only on their own inspiration but also on their relatives and kinsmen who battled and died with Stalin's name on their lips. Many could not bring themselves to take this step'.[111] The ideological split ran deep, even among families, and individuals were arrested for even expressing an interest in anything Russian. Although the tiny republic of Montenegro was far from the highly industrialized societies that Marx believed incubated the workers' revolution, support for the communism was strong. According to Banac, for example, though Montenegro was 'backward and impoverished' and 'hardly ideal terrain for the urban ideology of Marx and Lenin', it nevertheless 'became one of Yugoslavia's reddest areas'.[112] Thus, when the KPJ was 'excommunicated' from COMINFORM, a number of Montenegrins who did not wish to oppose the Kremlin chose to side with the Soviets.[113]

In any event, this rapid and fluid state of affairs was the source of significant confusion. Members of the Communist Party of Montenegro (*Komunistička partija Crne Gore* – KPCG), at that time led by Blažo Jovanović, were required to declare their support for Tito without knowing the dynamics of the ideological split, and those who voiced support for Stalin were immediately arrested and expelled from the party.[114] The fact that the KPCG appeared hesitant to report on the conditions within the party fuelled the perception among the KPJ leadership that a significant number of Montenegrin Communists could not be trusted.[115] Such suspicions were not entirely without foundation. Resistance to Tito's faction within the KPJ wasn't simply confined to a tiny number of dissenters: pro-Stalinist Montenegrins accounted for a significant minority of the Montenegrin population (despite being the smallest and least densely populated republics of the SFRJ, it was estimated that these pro-Stalinist Montenegrins were, per capita, around four times the overall average in Yugoslavia).[116] The KPCG were split over the issue, while among Montenegrin military and diplomatic representatives, a significant number were ideologically loyal to Stalin more than Tito.[117]

Tito and his security chief, Aleksander Ranković, were quick to act. The Yugoslav Secret Service (*Odjeljenje za zaštitu naroda* – OZNA)[118] applied significant pressure on individuals believed to be supporting Stalin. During the tumultuous period following the 1948 split, thousands of individuals were arrested and imprisoned within Montenegro.[119] Those deemed *ibeovci* (Stalinists) were arrested and despatched to camps throughout Yugoslavia, the most notorious being *Goli otok* (Barren Island) off Croatia's north-western coast. Of the total number of those arrested in Montenegro, 2,067 individuals faced punishment, with regular courts administering justice in 34 cases and the military in 457 cases, and 1,567 individuals were sent to camps. In this dangerous context, some within the KPCG took drastic measures. In the northern Montenegrin town of Bijelo Polje, a group led by Ilija Bulatović known as the 'Bureau of the Bijelo Polje County Committee' rebelled and took to the hills around the town.[120] Out of the eighteen Bijelo Polje rebels led by Ilija Bulatović, twelve were 'eliminated' during the period of purges.[121] Among those who escaped was Vlado Dapčević, the brother of the Partisan national hero, Peko Dapčević. Vlado himself had been a Partisan fighter during the 1941–45 war, but had accepted the COMINFORM Resolution and backed Stalin. He fled to Hungary with a fellow Montenegrin, Branko Petričević (a JNA general), and Colonel Arso Jovanović, the latter killed while trying to cross the Yugoslav-Hungarian border. Vlado Dapčević subsequently spent many years living in the Soviet Union, Cuba and then Western Europe.

The Socialist Republic of Montenegro

In the years following the COMINFORM crisis, Montenegro remained passive and the KPJ – which was renamed the League of Communists of Yugoslavia (*Savez komunista Jugoslavije* – SKJ) in 1952 – remained dominant. The KPCG were also renamed the League of Communists of Montenegro (*Savez komunista Crne Gore* – SKCG), and their new leader, Djordje Pajković, oversaw a period of economic growth and infrastructural development. Between the 1950s and 1970s, Montenegro continued its economic consolidation; indeed, a significant increase in economic efficiency was recorded between 1961 and 1970.[122] A railway connecting Nikšić and Titograd, largely constructed by the Youth Action Work (*Omladinske radne akcije* – ORA) volunteer groups, was completed in 1965, while the first phase of the reconstruction of the Port of Bar, which had been destroyed by retreating Axis powers in 1944, was completed in the same year. Continued industrialization was evident in the building of the *Obod* electronic company in 1953, the reconstruction and expansion of the Trebjesa brewery in Nikšić in the 1950s, where Montenegro's excellent *Nikšičko pivo* (Nikšić beer) was brewed, and the construction of the *Kombinat Aluminijuma Podgorica* (KAP) aluminium plant in Titograd in 1969.[123] Furthermore, the ambitious Bar to Belgrade railroad was completed in 1976, and to mark the occasion Tito arrived in Titograd on the *Plavi voz* (Blue Train), his official train, and was greeted by enthusiastic crowds. Montenegro's internal infrastructure was further developed and revenue from tourism (both domestic and international) was increasing steadily throughout the 1970s.[124] There were also significant shifts in terms of urbanization with many leaving rural areas to work in the industrial centres of Titograd and Nikšić (the urban population increased dramatically from 14.2 per cent in 1953 to 58.2 per cent in 1991).[125]

Throughout this period of increasing economic productivity, there were few manifestations of political unrest in Montenegro, though there were periodic problems within the SFRJ. There was, however, political controversy, when Milovan Djilas, perhaps the most high-profile Montenegrin within the ranks of the KPJ, was castigated for a number of articles he wrote in the daily *Borba*, criticizing the Partisan elite for their attainment of wealth and privilege in the post-war years. Warned against writing such articles, Djilas persisted and was eventually jailed for three years in 1956 for a statement he made about the Soviet invasion of Hungary.[126] While in prison he began work on *The New Class* (another critique of the Yugoslav communist system), which earned him a seven-year extension to his sentence. Though permitted to leave prison in 1961, he was jailed again the following year when *Conversations with Stalin* was published. He subsequently spent the next five years in prison, where he wrote an extensive biography of Petar II Petrović 'Njegoš' entitled *Njegoš: Poet, Prince, Bishop*, as well as the novel *Montenegro* and a book of short stories called *The Leper and Other Tales*.[127] He was eventually released in 1966.

The 'national question' which Tito claimed to have solved in the early 1960s periodically re-emerged. The SJK functionary, Vladimir Bakarić, warned in 1965 that despite claims to the contrary, it could soon again become Yugoslavia's 'question number one'.[128] Six years later the SFRJ faced its most significant internal political crisis since the 1948 Tito–Stalin split, with the advent of the *Hrvatsko proljeće* (Croatian

Spring) in 1971. Such dissent was limited in Montenegro, though Serb nationalist ideas remained under the surface.[129] The majority of Montenegrins were content with the republic's position within the SFRJ, and thus Montenegro remained an 'outpost of Titoist orthodoxy' within which Montenegrins were heavily represented within the SKJ and federal institutions generally.[130] In this context, identity issues or calls for greater levels of autonomy were practically non-existent. Indeed, according to Srdja Pavlović, 'expressions of Montenegrin identity per se were viewed as the manifestation of retrograde ideology, and, in spite of the rhetoric of brotherhood and unity it was generally assumed that Montenegrins and Serbs were one nation'. Moreover, he continues, 'the absence of voices arguing in favour of Montenegrin national and cultural distinctiveness on the public scene could be taken as proof of the general consensus on this issue'.[131]

Such issues were limited in Montenegro, the exception being the antagonism generated by the destruction of the old church and building of a new mausoleum dedicated to Peter I Petrović 'Njegoš' that adorned the peak of Mount Lovćen near Cetinje (see Chapter 6). Following the adoption of the 1974 Constitution, the SFRJ became, in essence, highly decentralized, with republics, provinces and the party 'federalised', thereby turning them into ideological bases for 'various particularisms'.[132] Montenegro essentially became, as with the other Yugoslav republics, a state within the SFRJ, and with these constitutional revisions, a stronger Montenegrin political and cultural infrastructure was forged. These developments not only gave the SKCG more political autonomy, they were also, according to John Allcock, instrumental in consolidating a greater sense of a distinct Montenegrin entity and, by extension, identity largely because 'the structure of government and party organization created and sponsored the advancement of a stratum of officials who owed their position to the existence of a republic called Montenegro, and to their ability to identify themselves as *Crnogorci* (Montenegrins)'.[133]

The Montenegrin League of Communists (*Savez komunista Crne Gore* – SKCG) was entirely Yugoslav oriented, and specifically Montenegrin institutions were established relatively slowly until the immediate period following the 1974 constitutional revisions, and, thereafter, Montenegrin institutions slowly began to crystallize.[134] Post-1974, in addition to SKCG having greater political autonomy, a number of specifically Montenegrin institutions were created. The University of Titograd was established in 1974 (it was renamed the Veljko Vlahović University in 1975), meaning that Montenegrin students could pursue higher education in Montenegro, as opposed to studying in Belgrade or Sarajevo.[135] The Montenegrin Academy of Sciences and Arts (*Crnogorska akademija nauka i umjetnosti* – CANU) was created in 1976, though the organization was originally formed three years before as the Montenegrin Society for Sciences and Arts (*Crnogorska društvo za nauka i umjetnost* – CDNU).[136] Such developments aided the consolidation of Montenegrin institutional separateness, though very much within the framework of the SFRJ. Being home to less than 5 per cent of the population of the SFRJ and producing a mere 2 per cent of the federal state's gross domestic product (GDP), the republic enjoyed an influence disproportionate with its scale and economic clout. While contributing little of economic significance, Montenegro carried one-eighth of the political muscle of the SFRJ and was the recipient of generous federal funds.[137] However, the cyclical struggle over the redistribution of these federal funds did dictate that the Montenegrins had to articulate and defend specific Montenegrin interests. On occasion, the level of support required was significant. Montenegro would, for example, be the beneficiary of significant (and much-needed) levels of federal funding following the earthquakes which wrought significant destruction in Budva, Kotor, Herceg Novi and Bar. An earthquake on 15 April 1979 took the lives of 101 people and caused significant material damage. In Kotor, numerous precious buildings and monuments were badly damaged, while in Budva, only 6 of the 200 buildings within the walls of the old town remained unscathed. A number of modern tourist hotels were also badly damaged, impacting significantly on Montenegro's tourist trade.[138]

The republic was still recovering from the damage wrought by the earthquake when Josip Broz Tito died on 4 May 1980. While his death was lamented by the vast majority of Yugoslav citizens, he had left behind a federal state within which the republics functioned increasingly independently and the national question remained unresolved. The constitutional changes had ensured peace throughout his twilight years; however, these would create insurmountable problems in the years following his death, and Tito had groomed no natural successor to lead the SFRJ in the event of his death.[139] The head of the SFRJ at the time of Tito's death was Veselin Djuranović, a Montenegrin who had held the post since 1977. His task was immense, particularly given Montenegro's small economy and its reliance on federal funds. The SFRJ's economic problems were eased, to some extent, by an American-led group of organizations called the 'Friends of Yugoslavia' that succeeded in acquiring debt relief in 1983, though the general process of economic stagnation in the SRFJ throughout the 1980s gradually eroded the legitimacy of the KPJ and the Titoist system. Any adverse economic circumstances affecting the SFRJ were likely to have a significant impact on tiny Montenegro. As the economic crisis of the 1980s began to bite, the effects became increasingly evident; indeed, by 1986, Montenegro's share of the SFRJ's foreign debt amounted to US\$850 million.[140] The evident inability to address the increasingly difficult economic conditions would generate a crisis of legitimacy for the SKCG, as it became clear that they had few levers at their disposal to stabilize the deteriorating economic situation and limited capacity to continue to meet the established and increasing economic and material needs of the society.[141] It was, therefore, within this context that popular discontent soon became widespread, manifesting itself specifically in the form of low-intensity protests and small-scale industrial strikes. Indeed, the detrimental effects of the economic crisis would converge with a political climate that would ultimately fuel destabilization throughout Montenegro and the SFRJ.

Montenegrin identity in the context of the SFRJ

The question of Montenegrin identity was essentially nullified by the republic's position within the SFRJ.[142] The question of Montenegrin identity and of Montenegro's statehood, which had predominated with the political conflicts between the *Klubaši* and *Pravaši* (and later the *Bjelaši* and *Zelenaši*) and became an issue again during the 1941–45 war, had been largely, though not entirely, 'frozen' by Montenegro's position within the SFRJ. Their different historical trajectories from the late fourteenth century onward, however, created significant differentiations, and subsequent territorial expansion had brought thousands of Serbs, Albanians and Slavic Muslims under the control of Cetinje. Thus, there existed two traditions in Montenegro, forged largely by these historical divergences: *Crnogorstvo* (Montenegrin-ness) and *Srpstvo* (Serb-ness) that reflected the differing interpretations of *who* the Montenegrins were. As Elizabeth Roberts noted, their 'religious and cultural tradition is overlapping' yet 'other important aspects of the Montenegrin experience – history, geography and the persistence at least till very recently of a clan-based society with its own value system – have made Montenegrins different'.[143] Indeed, following the Ottoman incursions into the Balkans in the late fourteenth century, Montenegro was effectively cut off from Serbia, and Montenegro thus developed its own distinct characteristics, though its leaders, such as Petar II Petrović 'Njegoš' and King Nikola I Petrović, would emphasize the close bond between Serbs and Montenegrins.

Ivo Banac succinctly described *Crnogorstvo* as 'The native – intensely Montenegrin – tradition, which maintained the separate heritage of Dioclea/Zeta, permitted the Montenegrins to suffuse themselves in the genial warmth of self-being'.[144] Conversely, beyond this small area Serb identity retained primacy. Thus, in *Stara Crna Gora* (Old Montenegro), the territory that would become the embryo of the Montenegrin state, the inhabitants developed specific characteristics that differentiated them from their Serbian kin to the north. According to Banac, the population of these areas belonged to the Serbian tradition (*Srpstvo*) within which there were 'a system of mnemonic devices by which the [Serbian Orthodox] church continually admonished the Montenegrins to remember the glories of the Nemanjić state'.[145] John Allcock noted that those who identified with a specific Montenegrin identity were in the area around Cetinje. The spatial picture of identity in Montenegro is, he argued, 'like taking a photograph in which one object is held in sharp focus in the foreground. Although one is aware of a half-focused context in which the object stands, that context remains rather undefined'. 'Montenegro proper', he continued, 'shades off into its subsequent territorial accretions which have had a weaker identification with Montenegro than with Serbia'.[146]

The Yugoslav Communists' approach to the question of Montenegrin identity was to encourage Montenegrins to think of themselves 'essentially Serbs', albeit Serbs with a distinct history and distinct characteristics. Such an approach was explained by Milovan Djilas, who argued that Montenegro, as small territory and an economically underdeveloped area, could best be saved from poverty by being absorbed into a larger political unit – Serbia, the KSHS or the SFRJ, for example. By so doing, he claimed, 'the whole question of nationality and national rights' could be avoided.[147] He acknowledged that 'Montenegro and Serbia had different paths to statehood', but that Montenegro had been given the status of a republic for political reasons, but this did not amount to a recognition of Montenegrins a separate nation per se.[148] So, though Montenegro was a separate republic within the SFRJ, Montenegrins were, according to Šerbo Rastoder, an 'ideal surrogate of Yugoslav nationality ... in their equidistance from Montenegrin and Serb nationalities'.[149] Some emphasized the importance of Montenegrin separateness, and some that Montenegrins were part of the Serbian national corpus; others saw no contraction in recognizing a distinct Montenegrin identity while acknowledging their Serb roots.[150]

Expressions of a specific Montenegrin (national) identity were relatively muted, and, according to Srdja Pavlović, 'conversations about Montenegrin sovereignty, independence and identity outside the Serb national and cultural paradigm were rare and people usually spoke about it *sotto voce*'.[151] There were occasional exceptions, such as the controversy surrounding what the SKCG regarded as growing nationalism in Montenegro – both Serbian and Montenegrin. In 1972, the so-called *Bijela knjiga* (white book) was 'published' by the SKCG, which included a series of directives required because of 'the manifestation of nationalist and other ideologically unacceptable attitudes'. Seventeen intellectuals – such as the Montenegrin writer Radovan Zogović and the linguists Vojislav Nikčević and Pavle Ilić –were diametrically opposed in their views of the Montenegrin language. The 'white book' instructed Montenegrin communists working in the press and publishing houses to maintain 'a high level of ideological alertness' when making decisions to publish authors' works.[152]

It was, however, Serb nationalism (and with it the 'Serbian Question in Yugoslavia') that was resurgent in the 1980s, and Montenegrins would again be confronted with claims and counterclaims regarding the question of their own national identity.[153] Throughout the 1980s, the argument that Montenegrins were the 'best of Serbs' and Montenegro was the *Srpska Spatra* (Serbian Sparta) became *de riguer* among nationalist intellectual circles in Serbia – and among like-minded Montenegrin intellectuals – particularly within the Serbian Academy of Sciences and Arts (*Srpska akademija nauka i umetnosti* – SANU). Montenegrins, according to this narrative, were a branch of the Serbian nation – *dva oka u glavi* (two eyes in the same head), and inseparable from one another. The Montenegrin 'nation', it was argued, was merely invented by the KPJ, who wished not only to 'tear Montenegro from its Serbian roots', but to keep Serbia weak and mitigate Serb hegemony within the SFRJ.[154]

The question of Montenegrin identity was present during the socialist era, though it was muted and far from mainstream. However, the growth of Serb nationalism in Serbia also had implications for Montenegro and for debates and conflicts over Montenegrin identity. Yet, while nationalism *would* become a key factor in Montenegrin politics in the latter years of the 1980s, it was not nationalism per se that was the main driver behind the discontent that became so acute in Montenegro in the latter half of the 1980s. The anger that would be directed towards Montenegro's political elites was the result of a number of factors, but primarily the weakening of a social and economic system that underpinned the SFRJ and the subsequent failure of both the KPJ and the SKCG to deal effectively with the economic problems that were having a negative impact upon the lives of ordinary citizens. An erosion of trust and loss of confidence in their abilities would, ultimately, create a crisis of legitimacy for both, and, in Montenegro, this discontent would lead to widespread protests in 1988 and 1989. It was this pre-existing anxiety and dissatisfaction, simmering slowly but steadily for years, that would provide Serb nationalists in Serbia and Montenegro with an opportunity to harness and channel this negative energy for their own political ends. The fundaments of the political crisis in Montenegro were not, however, of their making, though they would effectively and ruthlessly capitalize on the social and political chaos fuelled by economic crisis. In so doing, they would play a major role in the ensuing political crisis that would engulf Montenegro and the SFRJ.

2

The Anti-Bureaucratic Revolution and the 'January Coup' (1987–90)

Ovaj narod traži hljeba, zato bolja vlada treba!
    (These people are seeking bread, because a better government they need!)

Oj narode Crne Gore, spremamo se na izbore!
    (Hey, people of Montenegro, prepare for elections!)

Slobodane, Srpski sine, kad ćes doći na Cetinje? Kad ćes doći pod Lovćenom? Čekamo te sa ordenom!
    (Slobodan, you Serbian son, when will you come to Cetinje? When will you come to Lovćen? We are waiting for you with a medal!)

These three slogans characterize the social, economic and political strands that would converge to force the ageing leadership of the *Savez komunista Crne Gore* (SKCG) to capitulate following the October 1988 protests and the subsequent 'January Coup' of 1989, part of the Milošević-inspired 'anti-bureaucratic revolution'. In Montenegro, a toxic mix of economic crisis, a harsh austerity programme, rising unemployment and increasing poverty fuelled by exponential rises in the prices of basic goods created a febrile social context in which the legitimacy of the ruling elite, and the ideology it espoused, was brought into question. It was also a social and economic context where nationalism could incubate and, eventually, flourish.[1] This did not, of course, take place within a vacuum. The Socialist Federal Republic of Yugoslavia (SFRJ), by the mid-1980s, was in the midst of an acute economic crisis. Household income had dropped and inflation had risen steadily since 1970, while the unemployment rate had almost doubled.[2] Western banks and investors, which had funded the 'good times' in the 1960s and early 1970s, grew nervous about the country's ability to service its debts.[3] The Yugoslav economy laboured under a growing trade deficit, a significant balance of payments deficit and a burgeoning foreign debt, which had risen from below US$2 billion in 1970 to over US$14 billion in 1979.[4] By 1983, the International Monetary Fund (IMF) demanded that the Yugoslav government initiate 'shock therapy' and endeavour to restructure the economy in an attempt to contain the worsening crisis.

Such conditions were reluctantly accepted by a government only too aware of the potential social and political consequences that could be forged by further austerity in a context of pre-existing declines in living standards.[5] Inevitably, adverse economic circumstances for the SFRJ were likely to have a significant impact on tiny Montenegro, a poor republic and a net benefactor of Yugoslav federal subsidies.

By 1987, the year Slobodan Milošević rose to power in Serbia, it was estimated that Montenegro's share of the overall Yugoslav debt of US$17 billion stood at US$1 billion, more than the republic's annual revenues.[6] In an attempt to restructure the economy, the SKCG took drastic measures, introducing laws that allowed the government to initiate the liquidation of loss-making businesses.[7] Unviable enterprises were subject to these harsh measures as the state sought to limit manpower costs and reduce their fiscal commitments. A further austerity programme ensured that the economic pain was felt by citizens who saw the price of basic commodities increase significantly. These measures, however well intentioned, were to set off a chain of events during which small-scale protests against them evolved from localized and low-intensity demonstrations to a popular anti-government movement.[8]

In any event, the measures introduced by the SKCG would prove insufficient to deal with economic anomalies that were both deep and structural. The seeds of Montenegro's economic chaos lay in doctrinal socialist economic planning, which dictated that industrial centres should be established in underdeveloped areas. Moreover, they were often located where there existed almost no preconditions (except labour) that would facilitate economic sustainability. Such structural anomalies were compounded by the uncomfortable reality that those enterprises that were unsustainable were the republic's largest employers. The 'failing giants' of the Montenegrin economy (the Boris Kidrič iron works in Nikšić, and the *Kombinat* aluminium plant and the Radoje Dakić construction company, both in Titograd) were illustrative of the gravity of the crisis. The latter, for example, had been a profitable business, one of the most successful in Montenegro. However, it too was facing hard times by the mid-1980s, as both domestic and international clients dried up. Large contracts secured by the company in the 1970s were not renewed, as the downturn in the construction industry throughout Yugoslavia worsened. Moreover, their large international contracts were also in trouble. In the mid-1970s, the Iraqi government had awarded significant contracts to the Montenegrin firm, but as Iraq became more deeply embroiled in their war with Iran, their government ceased paying their debts to the company. It was estimated that late or missing payments led to for Radoje Dakić accumulating a deficit of around US$13 million.[9]

In August 1987, while addressing the rank and file of the SKCG, Radivoje Brajović, president of the SKCG Central Committee Presidium, told his audience that the SKCG had been very slow to act, that many within the party were resistant to change and that the 'situation was now very serious'.[10] For ordinary citizens, the economic crisis was becoming a matter of primary concern. The price of basic commodities had risen significantly, putting more pressure on households struggling to make ends meet. In July 1987, electricity prices rose by 44 per cent and by August the price of staples such as milk, bread and flour steadily increased.[11] The price of alcoholic drinks (for those who could afford such luxuries) increased by almost 50 per cent.[12] Such price rises became a regular and unwelcome occurrence. In this context, protests and work stoppages became increasingly widespread, as the gravity of the government's austerity programme and the impact on citizens became evident and, more importantly, tangible. By January 1988, the SKCG issued unambiguous statements warning that the economic situation was critical and the public should prepare themselves in earnest for 'harder times'.[13] Many were already facing the harsh economic realities. Indeed, by early 1988, more than 20 per cent of Montenegrins were living below the poverty line and in receipt of social welfare benefits.[14] For those employed, wages were often paid late, leading to workers' discontent and further work stoppages. Collectively, this blend of harsh economic conditions, unemployment and increasing poverty created social conditions within which revolutionary fervour incubated. While acknowledging the seriousness of the situation, as Miljan Radović, the president of the SKCG Central Committee Presidium, did during the SKCG's congress in May 1988, the leadership's economic strategy had neither halted the downward spiral nor assuaged a deeply concerned and agitated citizenry.[15] Increasingly, the character of the protests changed from merely challenging government policy to those that explicitly challenged the legitimacy of the SKCG that, seemingly, had demonstrated no ability to find solutions to the crisis.[16] Thus, what began as an economic crisis incrementally, but steadily, transposed into a crisis of legitimacy for the SKCG.

The problems so manifest in Montenegro were equally evident throughout the SFRJ and raised tensions between Yugoslavia's republics. The economic crisis that engulfed the SFRJ throughout the 1980s often manifested itself in arguments between republics over the distribution of federal funding. But when Slobodan Milošević ascended to power in December 1987, having unseated his long-term political ally and friend Ivan Stambolić, he explicitly utilized the issue of the status of Serbs and Montenegrins in Kosovo as his vehicle to consolidate his power.[17] Previously a taboo subject in the SFRJ, Milošević called for political change in the SFRJ, specifically to reduce Kosovo's autonomy, protect Serb (and Montenegrin) rights in Kosovo and to initiate a crackdown in the province, including against the (largely ethnic-Albanian) leadership there. The leaders in other Yugoslav republics watched these developments nervously, some among them accusing Milošević of promoting Serbian nationalism and violating the KPJ's principle of 'brotherhood and unity'. By 1988, Milošević's objective was to overturn the 1974 Yugoslav Constitution that, it was argued, was detrimental to Serbian interests. Seeking to eradicate the slightly chaotic system of 'collective presidency' bequeathed by Tito, Milošević's strategy was to control four of Yugoslavia's eight federal presidency votes. To facilitate this, he would seek to replace the leaderships of the autonomous provinces of Kosovo and Vojvodina, while undermining the SKCG in Montenegro (and, ultimately, replace their leadership). By early 1988, conditions were ripe for Milošević's 'anti-bureaucratic revolution' and for those behind it to harness popular discontent as a means of facilitating the fall of Montenegro's ruling communist elite.[18]

The majority of those who would participate in the subsequent mass protests in Montenegro were not, however, motivated by such lofty political machinations, nor did the majority support or, perhaps, understand their implications. These were, on the whole, citizens encompassing all social strata that were essentially challenging the austerity measures imposed by the SKCG, their failure to deal with the economic crisis and, to some extent, the legitimacy of the SKCG.[19] If they were led, it was by a loose association of different groups: union leaders and workers from Radoje Dakić, Boris Kidrič, *Metalac* and other struggling enterprises, students from the University of Titograd and ordinary citizens.[20] However, throughout 1988, the mood began to shift and the prevailing economic and social crisis created a set of social conditions within which Serbian nationalists in Montenegro could exploit, as they sought to use inject the toxicity of the Kosovo issue into an already-febrile context.

Throughout the 1980s, the argument that Montenegrins were part of the Serbian national corpus, a rather taboo subject since the establishment of the SFRJ, became *de riguer* among nationalist intellectual circles in Serbia, and among like-minded Montenegrin intellectuals and among the *Terazije Crnogorci* (Montenegrins based in Belgrade). Montenegrins, according to this narrative, were a branch of the Serbian nation – *dva oka u glavi* (two eyes in the same head).[21] The Montenegrin 'nation', it was argued, was 'invented' by Yugoslav communists, who wished not only to 'tear Montenegro from its Serbian roots', but to keep Serbia weak and contain Serb hegemony within the SFRJ.[22] As early as 1984, the SKCG leadership recognized the dangers. Vidoje Žarković, the then secretary of the Central Committee of the SKCG, cautioned that *bratstvo i jedinstvo* (brotherhood and unity) in Montenegro, and throughout the SFRJ, must be vigorously defended against what he described as resurgent 'retrograde nationalist forces'.[23] Yet, while nationalism *would* become a key factor in Montenegrin politics in the latter years of the 1980s, it was not nationalism per se that was the main driver behind the discontent that became so acute in the late 1980s.

Nevertheless, the issue of Serbs and Montenegrins in Kosovo proved deeply problematic for the SKCG. It was highly emotionally charged and had to be treated with sensitivity, but the stories of Serbs and Montenegrins leaving Kosovo had now become a toxic political issue.[24] The Kosovo Serbs, and their supporters in Montenegro, attacked the SKCG for their alleged inaction vis-à-vis the 'exodus' of Serbs from Kosovo, and their alleged reluctance to openly criticize the largely ethnic-Albanian leadership in the province. These claims were, of course, rejected by the Central Committee of the SKCG as both 'false and tendentious'.[25] Nevertheless, the Kosovo Serbs continued to apply pressure, organizing 'meetings of truth' in Titograd and other Montenegrin towns. With the explicit intention of mobilizing Montenegrins to declare solidarity with their ethnic kin in Kosovo, the largest of these took place in Titograd on 20 August 1988, with an estimated 30,000 in attendance. Here the tone was quite different, and the atmosphere markedly more charged. The focus was predominantly on the plight of Kosovo's Serbs and Montenegrin population and less on the ongoing economic crisis, though the latter was what underpinned much of the discontent. The Belgrade daily *Politika* noted the mix of banners held aloft during the meeting, demonstrating the convergence of the economic and the political – the usual slogans lamenting the economic situation were mixed with anti-regime messages such as 'Damn the souls of the big bosses – they have sown the seeds of dissent' alongside messages of support for the Kosovo Serbs, and even chants of *hoćemo oružije!* (We want arms!).[26]

The large gathering, in Titograd's main square (Ivan Milutinović square), was addressed by, among others, Miroslav Šolević and Svetozar Arsić Basara, two of the de facto leaders of the Kosovo Serbs, and by Montenegrins sympathetic to the Kosovo Serb cause (such as Jovan Markuš and Pavle Milić).[27] But the crowd demanded to be addressed by the Montenegrin writer Batrić Jovanović, who had previously spoken in strong support of the Kosovo's Serb and Montenegrin community.[28] He was, allegedly, inhibited from speaking to the crowd by Montenegrin security services during the rally, but was carried 'shoulder high' to the garden of the *Hotel Crna Gora* (Hotel Montenegro),[29] where he delivered a short speech to the crowd and declared that the Kosovo Serbs visiting Titograd could return home knowing they had 'the full support of the Montenegrin people'.[30] (Jovanović would subsequently give an interview to the Belgrade weekly *NIN* in which he was scathing in his criticism of the SKCG and their treatment of him during the rally.[31]) As events concluded, a long column of cars left Titograd and assembled again en route to Kosovo in Kolašin (a small town in northern Montenegro), where a further, albeit smaller, 'spontaneous' rally took place.

The organizers then began planning their next meeting, scheduled to take place in Nikšić on 18 September 1988. On a platform outside the city's municipal parliament, another of the Kosovo Serbs' leaders, Kosta Bulatović, criticized the leadership of the SKCG for not doing enough to assist Serbs and Montenegrins in Kosovo, waxed lyrical about Montenegro as the *Srpska Sparta* (Serbian Sparta) and called on Montenegrins to remember their historical obligations to their ethnic kin in Kosovo. His speech was received warmly by the crowd, among which were those holding aloft banners depicting the cross and four Cyrillic S's (*Samo sloga Srbina spasava* – Only unity saves the Serbs) and explicitly stating that *Kosovo je Srbija* (Kosovo is Serbia).[32] In the wake of the rally, the Central Committee of the SKCG stated that while the protestors had every right to demonstrate their solidarity with the 'disenfranchised Serbian and Montenegrin people in Kosovo', the rally had been 'exploited for purposes contrary to their basic intention', noting that 'certain anti-socialist and anti-communist views and attitudes were presented' and that nationalist slogans and calls for 'settling of accounts' threatened social and political stability in Montenegro.[33]

In a secret operation entitled *Akcija radak* (Operation Radak), the Montenegrin security services (*Služba državni bezbednosti* – SDB), then led by Vladimir Keković, documented the events and the radicalization of the crowds and wiretapped conversations between the main protagonists – the latter operation known as *Akcija Korab* (Operation Korab).[34] The protests, they claimed, were carefully engineered by the Kosovo Serbs, their supporters in Serbia and Serbian State Security (who had ceased to cooperate with their Montenegrin counterparts prior to the protests). Armed with this information and disturbed by the increasingly radical character of the rallies, the leadership of the SKCG now prepared themselves accordingly, not only for further protests but for the possibility of an attempted coup.

The next large rally took place on 7 October 1988, the day after the 'Yoghurt Revolution' in Vojvodina had concluded.[35] Workers from Radoje Dakić and other failing enterprises, students from schools and the university, who arrived carrying banners with the slogan *Radnici: studenti su sa vama!* (Workers: we students are with you!), and ordinary citizens, some carrying portraits of Tito, descended upon the centre of Titograd.[36] A crowd, estimated at 25,000, gathered outside the parliament building. The atmosphere was relatively calm in the early stages of the rally with numerous speakers from the Radoje Dakić *sindikat* (trade union) lamenting the fate of their company, demanding action to ensure that workers received their fair pay for their labour and reminding the Montenegrin authorities that they and their families were suffering from the ravages of austerity. They demanded the resignation of a number of officials that they deemed culpable for the current economic situation. One of their leaders, Svetozar Vukčević, also called on the protestors to demonstrate solidarity with the Serbs and Montenegrins of Kosovo, who, he said, were subject to 'genocide'.

The crowds were addressed by a number of communist officials including Vuko Vukadinović (president of the Executive Board of the SKCG), Marko Orlandić[37] (a member of the Montenegrin delegation of the Central Committee of the SKJ, who had earlier articulated the thirteen key demands[38] of the protestors), Radovan Radonjić (like Orlandić, a member of the Montenegrin delegation of the Central Committee of the SKJ) and, later, the president of the Presidency of Montenegro, Božina Ivanović, who, while being loudly heckled, argued that the Montenegrin authorities were doing everything in their power to tackle the economic crisis in the republic. The worst treatment was reserved for Borivoje Drakić, president of the Titograd Municipality Committee, whose (resignation) speech was drowned out by the jeering of the crowd. There was, however, a distinct change in the atmosphere as proceedings continued into the evening and crowds joined the protests from other parts of Montenegro.[39] Following an appeal by the Central Committee of the SKCG for the crowd to disperse (that was ignored) and shaken by the size and militancy of the crowd, they issued the police with orders to break up the demonstrations and announced that 'emergency measures' had been put in place to mitigate the growing instability.[40] Božina Ivanović appeared in front of the protestors to assure them that they were doing all they could to resolve the crisis, though he acknowledged that Montenegrins 'were facing hard times'. He also appealed to the protestors to return to work, but, once again, his appeals were drowned out.

Soon after, at approximately 6.00 am, police used batons and tear gas to disperse the demonstrators and force them out of the centre of the city.[41] Later, on the morning of 8 October 1988, workers from the Boris Kidrič steelworks in Nikšić began their journey towards Titograd to join the demonstrations. Fearing an even larger gathering in the capital and thus more trouble, Montenegrin authorities ordered the blockade of the protestors coming from Nikšić, with the police violently dispersing the protestors at Žuta Greda (near Nikšić).[42] The police also stopped protestors from Cetinje from reaching Titograd and prevented workers from other state enterprises in the capital from leaving their factories.[43]

That the character of the protests had evolved was now manifest, and the authorities were no longer dealing simply with expressions of economic discontent, but demands for social justice and, moreover, ethnic justice.[44] Now, it was not simply the Montenegrin leadership's incompetence in economic affairs that was being held to account, but their 'anti-Serb' policy and their legitimacy as a government.[45] The use of force against the demonstrators proved a significant error of judgement, undermining what remained of the moral authority of the leadership, making them appear oppressive and desperate to cling to power.[46] Students residing at the 'Rifat Burdžović Tršo' student halls in Titograd announced that they would refuse food at the halls in protest against 'the unjustified use of force by security organs' against protestors.⁴⁷ Spontaneous protests also began in Nikšić on 9 October 1988, with workers from the Boris Kidrič steelworks and students based in the town demonstrating against the use of force against their comrades. Žuta Greda had proved a pivotal moment. According to Vladisavljević, in a traditional society that was underpinned by values of bravery and courage, 'the use of force against ordinary people was seen as a sign of the moral deficiency of the high officials [of the SKCG] and of their disrespect toward the population.'⁴⁸

The protestors returned to their daily lives, but the events of 7–10 October 1988 had proved pivotal. This was now a crisis of legitimacy for the SKCG, and one which they had, seemingly, been unable to contain. Those deemed by the protestors to have been instrumental in organizing the police intervention paid the heaviest price. On 13 October 1988, Lazar Djodjić, the Montenegrin minister for interior affairs, the man that protestors identified as most responsible for the interventions, announced his resignation.⁴⁹ In the Montenegrin Assembly, the events, and the consequences thereof, were discussed in detail. Miljan Radović, presenting a report on the events to the SKCG Central Committee, painted a bleak picture, stating, 'The economic, social and political situation in Montenegro today is burdened by dangers and is threatening its internal stability and the stability of the country [the SFRJ]'.... We are faced with the most serious threat to the constitutional system and the functioning of the system, such as we have never seen since the [1941–45] war.' He went on to say, 'Anti-communist and anti-socialist forces are out in the open today. Brotherhood and unity, self-management, non-alignment, the Yugoslav People's Army, Tito's personality and accomplishments, and the system as a whole are today being most virulently attacked by anti-socialist forces, as they have never been since the SFRJ came into existence.'⁵⁰ However, in a further meeting, on 26 October 1988, the Montenegrin Assembly roundly condemned the leadership cadre in the province of Kosovo for the intensification of interethnic tension throughout the SFRJ.⁵¹

The crisis now shifted from the streets to within Montenegro's institutions; essentially a struggle ensued within the SKCG, pitting the embattled Montenegrin leadership against the 'counter elite' within the system who opposed them. The Montenegrin leadership struggled on, and despite numerous resignations the organizers of the protests insisted that the 'thirteen points' advanced at the October demonstrations in Titograd be agreed.⁵² Within the deeply divided political class, institutional opponents of the leadership began to explicitly and openly demand their entire resignation.⁵³ By December 1988, there had been no resolution to the crisis and economic situation had shown no sign of improvement (and inflation was continuing to rise).⁵⁴ The demonstrators again announced that they would schedule large rallies in Titograd on 10 January 1989.

The January protests again brought together workers from Radoje Dakić plant and the Boris Kidrič steelworks with university students and ordinary citizens.⁵⁵ The organizational board of the protests were explicit: among other demands, they called for the resignation of the SKCG Central Committee Presidium, the SKJ Central Committee from Montenegro, and the resignation of the Montenegrin Presidency and the Montenegrin Assembly. The embattled leadership came under tremendous pressure to resign en masse, with many of the songs and slogans on banners reflecting these demands.⁵⁶ Protestors received messages of support from 'all over Yugoslavia' as they awaited the outcome of the tense negotiations between the protest organizers and the leadership of the SKCG.⁵⁷ They didn't have long to wait; by midday on 11 January 1989, their demands had been met. Božidar Tadić, vice-president of the Montenegrin Assembly, was the first to appear before the demonstrators, informing them that the Montenegrin Presidency would, collectively, be resigning. Subsequent resignations were announced to the jubilant demonstrators in short order.⁵⁸ In addition to the collective resignations, Miljan Radović, the chairman of the SKCG, resigned, as did Božina Ivanović, the president of the Montenegrin Presidency – to be replaced, respectively, by Veselin Vukotić and Branko Kostić. Even those who survived the initial 'purge', such as Vuko Vukadinović, the president of the SKCG's Executive Council, would later succumb (Vukadinović was eventually replaced by Radoje Kontić).⁵⁹ At 2.30 pm, Momir Bulatović, one of the student SKCG leaders at the University of Titograd, announced that 'the people are victorious!'⁶⁰

As the speeches concluded, the 'heroes of the anti-bureaucratic revolution' walked from the steps and joined the demonstrators in celebration. Yet the *Dogodjanje naroda* (happening of the people), while ostensibly a citizen's movement with a revolutionary character achieved by mass mobilization and the will of the people, was, rather, an internal coup *within* the SKCG. It did not represent a revolution generated from *without*, but change from *within* the existing system, in that the new (and younger) counter-elite came precisely from within system ranks.⁶¹ The change in personnel, argues Srdjan Darmanović, did not, therefore, represent a revolution per se, but secession from a counter-elite within the SKCG (though popular revolt was utilized as a mechanism for achieving their objectives). After all, he claimed, almost all leading figures within the protest movement 'were members or officials of the League of Communists of Montenegro [SKCG] and Yugoslavia'. Moreover, he added, 'after the overthrow was accomplished a new political party was not created; instead the leaders of the January movement simply took over the main offices within the League of Communists of Montenegro'.⁶²

The SKCG leadership were replaced by young elites under the influence, if not patronage, of Slobodan Milošević.⁶³ Indeed, their critics argued that this 'revolution' had brought to the fore a new generation of politicians who had mentors *outside* the republic, and that being both youthful and politically inexperienced, they were more pliable than their rhetoric implied.⁶⁴ Milošević was something of an ever-present at the demonstrations, and many chants could be heard from his supporters – *Crna Gora samo pita 'kad će Slobo mjesto Tita?'* (Montenegro only asks 'when will Slobo take the place of Tito?') and *Crna Gora rodi Sloba, to je čovjek našeg doba* (In Montenegro Slobo was born, he is a man of our times). Other such chants were not untypical. However, in his study of the anti-bureaucratic revolutions, Nebojša Vladisavljević argues that the degree of control asserted by Milošević directly might be overstated. 'Without doubt', he said, 'Milošević and other high officials of Serbia strongly supported the institutional and other opponents of Montenegro's leadership … this support was reflected in sympathetic reporting on the opposition to Montenegro's leadership in the media under his control and in the disapproval of the leadership'. Certainly in the case of the incident at Žuta Greda, the outrage, fanned by the indignant tone of

Miloševič-controlled media in Serbia, severely undermined the moral authority of the leadership, making them appear, at best, out of touch with the needs of the people, and at worst oppressive, while simultaneously portraying the objectives and actions of the protestors as noble. 'This support', Vladisavljević adds, 'was important because the majority of the citizens in this small republic relied more on the Belgrade press and state television than on their own local media'. Vladisavljević acknowledges that the protests of October 1988 and 19 January 1989 did represent a coup d'état but one achieved largely as a consequence of genuine mass protest, popular discontent and the fact that the existing leadership of the SKCG was already discredited.[65]

Long live the young Montenegrin leadership!

In the immediate period after the January coup, Branko Kostić (a Milošević ally and vociferous proponent of Serb-Montenegrin unity) became president of the Presidency of Montenegro; Radoje Kontić became the chairman of Montenegro's Executive Council, while Nenad Bućin (who, unlike Kostić, was known to be deeply sceptical of the machinations of Slobodan Milošević) became the Montenegrin representative of the Presidency of the SFRJ. However, the election of a new leadership of the SKCG now became a matter of some urgency. Both Veselin Vukotić and Milica Pejanović held interim roles as party secretary (the latter for only two days in April 1989), but during the tenth congress of the party, which took place in April 1989, the matter was resolved. During the congress, many of the young 'heroes of the anti-bureaucratic revolution' from within the party took centre stage. They were keen to stress their willingness to deliver positive change and tackle the social and economic problems that had been the cause of such upheaval. What became clear is that the new generation of leaders within the SKCG were in favour of political pluralism, a significant development.[66] In any event, delegates voted for a new party leadership. New members of the eleven-man Presidency of the SKCG were elected, and a subsequent secret ballot among this body voted to elect Momir Bulatović as the party president and Milo Djukanović as party secretary. These two young leaders would subsequently become the major figures in the drama that was to unfold in Montenegro in the coming decade.

The new 'young, handsome and intelligent' (all were in their late twenties or early thirties) troika of Momir Bulatović, Milo Djukanović and Svetozar Marović (who would later become the speaker of the Montenegrin Assembly) ascended to power. Bulatović was clearly *primus inter pares*, but the leadership sought to cast themselves as a collective, bringing their new ideas and talents together.[67] Often appearing in casual attire, in sharp contrast to the stiff, formal demeanour of their predecessors, they were lauded in state-controlled media (particularly the state daily *Pobjeda* and the state television service *Telivizija Titograd*)[68] as the vanguard of the 'Montenegrin Renaissance'. But while their leadership was portrayed as progressive and dynamic (and while they promised much), they struggled to deliver solutions to the economic and social problems that had been at the root of the 1988/89 protests.[69] Instead, they played on fears of a 'return of the old cadres' and their alleged endeavours to undermine the new leadership.[70] This alone wasn't enough to stem the persistent sense of crisis in Montenegro: the basic situation for many ordinary people simply did not improve after the January 1989 protests, and in August 1989 'workers and citizens' assembled in Nikšić to appeal to the new authorities to endeavour to provide for them 'a life worthy of man' and to 'stop the collapse in the standard of living and the dizzying rise in prices'.[71]

The sense of crisis increased significantly in January 1990. During the KPJ Congress, held on 23 January and chaired by Momir Bulatović, it became clear that strains between the Yugoslav republics were reaching a nadir. That the relationship between the leaderships of the Serbian League of Communists (*Savez komunista Srbije* – SKS) and the Slovenian League of Communists (*Zveza komunistov Slovenije* – ZKS) was at breaking point was immediately evident.[72] Slobodan Milošević, who had used the mechanism of the 'anti-bureaucratic revolution' to recentralize power, was opposed by the Slovene delegation to the LCY, who advanced a number of proposals to the constitution that would render the SFRJ little more than an economic union. After heated debates and a rejection of their proposed amendments, the Slovene delegation walked out and were, after a short discussion between Slobodan Milošević and Ivica Račan – who had recently replaced Stipe Šuvar as the leader of Croatian League of Communists (*Savez komunista Hrvatske* – SKH) – followed by the Croat delegation, who said they could not accept the continuation of the KPJ without the Slovenes. Despite Milošević's subsequent attempts to carry on with the congress, it was clear, by the end of the congress, that the KPJ was finished.

In Montenegro, the SKCG were now faced with the collapse of the KPJ and their own internal struggles. Having achieved their objective of overthrowing the old guard, many of the workers, students and young rank-and-file communists who had supported them (particularly those seeking genuine democratic reform) were to be disappointed with the subsequent direction of travel.[73] Disagreements soon surfaced within the new leadership of the SKCG. Following the January 'coup', consensus ended, with two competing strands emerging: the conservative, doctrinaire wing (such as Momir Bulatović, Milo Djukanović, Milica Pejanović and Svetozar Marović) fixated on maintaining the status quo, and the more liberal, progressive wing (including Srdjan Darmanović, Ljubisa Stanković and Miodrag Vlahović) advocating a reformist agenda. A bitter internal struggle ensued, ending with the purging of the reformist forces within the SKCG.[74] Indeed, during the SKCG Titograd Communal Committee meeting in February 1990, it was clear that the conservative forces were unwilling to incorporate the ideas of the more liberal elements within. As a consequence, many within the latter group, including Srdjan Darmanović and Ljubisa Stanković, left the party citing irreconcilable differences.[75] The now dominant conservative wing of the party paid lip service to democratic reform, but the conclusion of the protracted intra-party debates was essentially that 'more parties do not mean more democracy'; thus, essentially democracy could be exercised without a multiparty system, or that one party could remain dominant within such a system.[76] Transferring the SKCG into a controlled democratic environment need not undermine the power of the doctrinaire and conservative forces that could claim democratic legitimacy while maintaining power even as stymieing the growth of political alternatives.[77]

In October 1990, the Montenegrin Assembly endorsed legislation allowing multiparty elections, leading to the emergence of a more diverse, though uneven, political landscape.[78] A plethora of small parties were created within the republic, though none of which were strong enough to challenge the SKCG (who were to contest the elections *as* the SKCG).[79] Indeed, by the elections there were twenty registered political parties in Montenegro – a rather large number for a republic with a population of less than 650,000.[80] Among these emergent parties were the Alliance of Reform Forces for Montenegro (*Stranka reformskih snaga za Crnu Goru* – SRSCG), led by Ljubisa Stanković and allied to Ante Marković's Alliance of Reform Forces of Yugoslavia, and the Organisation of Independent Communists (*Organizacija nezavisnih komunista* – ONK), a party that advocated traditional communist ideals. On the right of the still emergent and thus opaque 'political spectrum' was the People's Party of Montenegro (*Narodna stranka Crne Gore* – NS),[81] led by Novak Kilibarda (a university professor), which broadly supported a pro-Serbian agenda.[82] The Democratic Alliance consisted of two ethnic minority parties: the Party of Democratic Action (*Stranka demokratske akcije* – SDA), essentially a sister to Alija Izetbegović's party in Bosnia & Herzegovina, and the Party for Equality (*Stranka ravnopravnost* – SR), a party that advocated equality for minorities in Montenegro.[83] The Democratic Alliance of Montenegro (*Demokratski savez u Crnoj Gori* – DSCG/*Lidhja Demokratike në Mal të Zi* – LDMZ), led by Mehmet Bardhi, was formed in Ulcinj and was, essentially, a party focused on protecting the interests of Montenegro's ethnic Albanian minority.

It was never, of course, a level-playing field. The SKCG's campaign was positively glossy in comparison with that of their poorly funded opponents. Moreover, they already held power, albeit in a transitional phase, and retained control over the instruments of the state and their funds far outstripped those of other parties (leading some within the opposition to cry foul).[84] The SKCG remained by far the strongest political party, though, as the Belgrade daily *Borba* noted, 'only the party name remains the same'; the political substance was quite different.[85] Throughout the pre-election campaign, the party leadership expressed their commitment to democracy, human rights, economic efficiency and individual civil rights, under the slogan *Mi znamo kako!* (We know how!).[86] (After all, claimed Momir Bulatović, the SKCG had 'the most respected and moral people' within their ranks.[87]) They were ruthless in their criticisms of other parties, with particular invective directed at the reformists of the SRSCG.[88]

The elections, which took place on 9 December 1990, were won comfortably by the SKCG, who won 55.16 per cent of the vote and gained 83 of the 125 seats in parliament.[89] The victory ensured that the SKCG could consolidate its power base in the nascent and, subsequently, rather fragmented 'democratic' landscape. In the presidential elections, the first round of which took place simultaneously, Momir Bulatović won the greatest number of votes but did not achieve an absolute majority (he won 42.2 per cent of the vote; Ljubisa Stanković won 16.4 per cent, while Novak Kilibarda won 8.3 per cent). In the second round, contested on 23 December 1990, Bulatović won 76.1 per cent of the votes while Stanković won only 21.3 per cent.[90] The new president declared thereafter that, given the ongoing crisis in Montenegro and throughout the SFRJ, a quick and efficient formation of a government was his highest priority.[91]

Invited to do so by the Montenegrin president, Milo Djukanović formed his first government, and became Europe's youngest prime minister at the age of just twenty-nine.[92] Thereafter, on 22 June 1991, the SKCG officially changed its name to the Democratic Party of Socialists (*Demokratska partija socijalista* – DPS). A largely symbolic change, the structure of the SKCG remained largely intact, with the offices, personnel, assets and funds of the SKCG transferring smoothly to the DPS. The party's dominant position within Montenegrin political life was reminiscent of its 'conservative' Communist party predecessors, as the state's main assets were gradually put in the direct service of the ruling party.[93] And while the ideological substance of the party may have transformed, the membership of the DPS was, more or less, the same as the SKCG – a broad stratum of Montenegrin society (bureaucrats, security services personnel, company directors and Yugoslav Army veterans), though they were generally younger than their predecessors. In essence, the party was a *nomenklatura party*, comprising powerful individuals and interest groups that had an interest in maintaining, as best it could, control over political life. Indeed, far from making progress on democratic reforms, Montenegro simply shifted from one form of closed society (communist) to another (nationalist).[94] But the 'heroes of the anti-bureaucratic revolution' now had to govern, and in context of both ongoing economic chaos and a rapidly disintegrating SFRJ.[95] The challenges would be both myriad and arduous.

3

From the 'War for Peace' to the 'Žabljak Constitution' (1990–92)

The trajectory of Montenegrin internal politics was, of course, determined not only by the 'January Coup' in 1989 and the coming to power of a new generation of politicians within the *Savez komunista Crne Gore* (SKCG) (following the first multiparty elections), but by events elsewhere in the Socialist Federal Republic of Yugoslavia (SFRJ). While the new Montenegrin leadership had been resolving their internal differences and organizing the republic's first multiparty elections, events in neighbouring Croatia had moved quickly, bringing the SFRJ a step closer to disintegration, which was grist to the mill of Serb nationalists in Montenegro. Multiparty elections, held in Croatia in April 1990, had brought the nationalist Croatian Democratic Community (*Hrvatska demokrastka zajednica* – HDZ) to power. The presidential election, a closely fought contest between Ivica Račan of the Party of Democratic Reform (*Socijaldemokratska partija Hrvatske* – SDPH) and the HDZ's Franjo Tudjman (the latter backed by powerful and radical émigrés from the Croatian diaspora), ended with a narrow victory for Tudjman.[1] Croatia's Serb community, particularly those inhabiting the Krajina region, watched these developments with growing alarm. History weighed heavily on the Serb population there. The experience of the area's Serbs between 1941 and 1945 when the Krajina was part of the Ustaša-led Independent State of Croatia (*Nezavisna država Hrvatska* – NDH), during which they were subject to mass persecution, murder and expulsion, resonated strongly with them.

In response to events in Zagreb, Croatia's Serbs (the vast majority of whom were located in the Krajina) embarked upon a rebellion following the announcement of a new constitution – which relegated Serbs to the status of a 'national minority'. In December 1990, the Krajina Serbs established the Serbian Autonomous Region of Krajina (*Srpska autonomna oblast Krajina* – SAO Krajina), set up roadblocks – the so-called 'Revolution of the Logs' – and three months later declared the region's separation from Croatia.[2] An organized rebellion by the Krajina Serbs soon turned into a full-scale war, and as conflict intensified in both the Krajina and Eastern Slavonia during the spring and summer of 1991, the Montenegrin government expressed concern about the future of the SFRJ and were, generally, committed to preserving the territorial integrity of the country, they remained loyal to the Serbian president, Slobodan Milošević.

As the temperatures rose and armed clashes intensified, Serb nationalist parties in Montenegro warned that the territorial integrity of the SFRJ was now in real danger and the Montenegrin public was increasingly threatened by resurgent Croatian 'fascism' backed by the 'Fourth Reich' (i.e. post-reunification Germany) and the secessionist ambitions of both Muslims and Albanians. The sabre-rattling rhetoric became increasingly audible. In early April 1991, Novak Kilibrada of the People's Party (*Narodna stranka* – NS) issued an appeal to the Montenegrin government to arm citizens in preparation for war, and that the government had a duty to provide people with the means to defend themselves should negotiations between the Yugoslav republics fail.[3] It was in this context that, on 29 April 1991, during a meeting of the SFRJ's presidents in Cetinje, that the Croatian president, Franjo Tudjman, made a very public demonstration of the mistrust that pervaded. The atmosphere was visibly tense at the conference, as the republican presidents (Momir Bulatović, Slobodan Milošević, Franjo Tudjman, Kiro Gligorov, Alija Izetbegović and Milan Kučan) attempted to find a way out of the crisis that was engulfing the SFRJ. At the press conference at the conclusion of the meeting, the Croatian president, Franjo Tudjman, was asked by Božidar Čolović, the chief editor of Montenegrin state television (TVCG), why he was the sole republican president requiring such a robust security detail (including a bulletproof BMW) while in Montenegro. Tudjman responded by claiming that that he had information that an assassination attempt 'against me and others' (information that he claimed had been given to him by sources in the SFRJ as well as 'three European countries') was being planned in Montenegro. As the audience laughed uncomfortably, Tudjman responded by rising from his seat and walking out, pausing only to shake Momir Bulatović's hand before he departed.[4]

In the wake of the Cetinje meeting, relations between Montenegro and Croatia steadily worsened. In May 1991, the Montenegrin government also raised the stakes, accusing the Croatian government (following the killing of a Macedonian Yugoslav Army soldier in the city of Split during anti-JNA protests and the first incidents in Borovo Selo) of engaging in 'state terror' with the objective of 'realizing the sovereignty of the Croatian state by force'.[5] Undeterred by the statements emanating from Belgrade and Titograd, the Croatian government announced that they would declare independence on 8 October 1991 and would be seeking international recognition as a sovereign state. In the meantime, Slovenia declared independence on 25 June 1991, leading to a short, ten-day war between the JNA and Slovenian Territorial Defence Forces. As the JNA departed from Slovenia, however, the seemingly inexorable trajectory to full-scale war in Croatia continued. In August 1991, a Croatian government was formed under the presidency of Franjo Tudjman. This took place in the midst of a worsening conflict, with JNA barracks and facilities being blockaded by units of the Croatian National Guard (*Zbor narodne garde* – ZNG) and violent clashes breaking out in Glina, Kostajnica and, later in Osijek, Vinkovci and Vukovar in Eastern Slavonia. By then the Montenegrin authorities were warning their Croat counterparts that any attempt to forcefully secede from the SFRJ could also be answered by force. The aforementioned events in Croatia in the summer of 1991, and the way in which they were conveyed by the Montenegrin media, were met with a deep sense of foreboding and anger in Montenegro. They also had a significant impact on public perceptions of events in Croatia (and the character of the Croatian government) throughout the course of the late summer and autumn of 1991.[6] During this period, the JNA and Serb paramilitaries intensified their activities in the Krajina and the Yugoslav Navy began a de facto blockade of towns along the Croatian coast.[7]

As the war in Croatia intensified, the Montenegrin government began to warn of the need for its border with Croatia to be defended, despite the fact that the armed clashes in Croatia in the summer of 1991 were far from the Montenegrin border. Nevertheless, persistent rumours of an imminent Croat attack from Dubrovnik (an area coveted by the Serbs and Montenegrins, and one 'claimed' by many of their intellectuals) now became abundant and widely believed.[8] These warnings, however, sounded rather hollow in the context of the Dubrovnik area, which bordered Montenegro. There was a tiny Serb (or Montenegrin) minority there and the area, which had been demilitarized in 1971, possessed no JNA barracks (and thus the ZNG blockade of JNA barracks elsewhere in Croatia were not necessary in Dubrovnik). But with the Croats under increasing pressure in Eastern Slavonia, the opening of a 'second front' in the south, it was argued by advocates of military action, would hasten the Croat government's capitulation.

However, justification for such an attack, which would involve both the JNA and Montenegrin reservists, would need to be carefully engineered. With this objective uppermost, the Montenegrin leadership set about informing the public of possibility of the darkest of scenarios being realized; it was not difficult to create a sense of foreboding in Montenegro. After all, if Croatia were to secede from the SFRJ, the Prevlaka side of the entrance to *Boka Kotorska* (the Bay of Kotor) – an ethnically and religiously diverse area in which Orthodox and Catholic lived cheek by jowl – would fall into Croat hands, making any Yugoslav naval vessels there vulnerable to attack.[9] The fishing industry, so important to Montenegro's coastal economy, could also be detrimentally affected, with Croatia making claims of extended territorial waters.[10] Moreover, the towns nestling along the shores of the Bay of Kotor might be threatened. Milo Djukanović, playing on these fears, adopted a combative position, warning that 'if the Croats want war, they can have it'.[11] He then stated that the current border had been designed by 'semi-skilled cartographers' and that the time had come to 'draw the demarcation lines *vis-à-vis* the Croats once and for all'.[12] He also, rather bizarrely, stated that he would, on the basis of the Croatian *šahovnica* (the Croatian chequerboard flag), never play chess again. To justify the war, the government utilized the state-owned daily *Pobjeda* and *Radio Televizija Crne Gore* (RTCG), both of which were used as instruments for the dissemination of government propaganda.[13] These media, in particular, were used to forge 'war euphoria' and to provide justifications for an attack on the Konavle region.[14] The pages of the paper were abundant with anti-Croat propaganda, nationalist slogans such as *Prevlaka je naša!* (Prevlaka is ours!) and even stark warnings of genocidal *Ustaše* amassing at the Debeli Brijeg border between Montenegro and Croatia.[15] The paper's editorials, as part of the rather Orwellian *Rat za mir* (War for Peace) propaganda campaign, featured numerous high-profile politicians making their case for war. And it was in this column that Svetozar Marović, the deputy president of the DPS, implied that, in order to defeat evil, Montenegrins must face the prospect of going to war. Indeed, on the eve of the Dubrovnik campaign, for example,

Marović assured the Montenegrin public that it was impossible to secure peace in any other way, and it was sometimes necessary to control evil through force.[16]

Framed, therefore, as a defensive (and thus necessary) war, Montenegrins were encouraged to understand the conflict as one imposed on them and think of themselves not as aggressors but as defenders of the SFRJ, fighters against resurgent pan-European fascism, even liberators of Dubrovnik. During the autumn of 1991, according to Srdja Pavlović, 'the political leaders of Montenegro and the military brass of the JNA rationalized the aggression on Dubrovnik as a necessary move towards protecting the territorial integrity of Montenegro and Yugoslavia and preventing a potential conflict along ethnic lines' and to stop the secession of Croatia.[17] Many, though by no means all, responded to the subsequent mobilization call issued on 16 September 1991.[18] In advance of the seemingly inexorable conflict, a significant number of *dobrovoljci* (volunteers) eagerly volunteered to carry out their patriotic duty. But such enthusiasm was not, by any means, universal; and while the mobilization call was answered strongly in some areas, such as Nikšić and Ivangrad (Berane), it proved far less effective in Titograd and coastal towns (such as Bar and Kotor). In any event, those who did not respond to the original mobilization were subsequently drafted; and for those who objected, attempted to avoid the draft or made it known they had no wish to participate, significant pressure was applied.[19] In an interview for *Pobjeda*, for example, Milo Djukanović warned that those reluctant to serve in the army should be subject to a law that would involve harsh punishment for deserters, more drastic, he warned, than simply 'firing them from their jobs'.[20] It was, quite simply, dangerous to be anti-war or to resist the related mobilization, though many young Montenegrins were willing to take that risk rather than be forced into mobilization.[21]

But if life for those who opposed the approaching war (or had no intention of participating in it) was tough, it was even more difficult for Montenegro's ethnic Croats. Concentrated in the Bay of Kotor, Montenegro's (approximately 12,000-strong) Croat community was, throughout 1991 (and beyond), subject to a torrent of Serb nationalist propaganda and anti-Croat hysteria, which labelled them *petokolonaše* (fifth columnists) who wished to annex the Montenegrin coast to a 'Greater Croatia'.[22] This, of course, came amid a pervading and sinister atmosphere of 'fear and lynch law' that worsened as the conflict in Krajina intensified, exacerbated when Croatia declared independence in June 1991 and peaked when the JNA and Montenegrin reservists crossed the border on 1 October 1991. The Croat community's de facto community leader, Don Branko Sbutega, a Catholic priest and native of Kotor, became the subject of something of a smear campaign in which he was cast as the worst of *crnolatinaši* ('Black Latin' – a derogatory term for a Catholic priest)[23] who was 'irrationally anti-Serb', had strong connections in Croatia and was often alleged to be in the company of *domaći izdajnici* (domestic traitors) such as leading figures from the Liberal Alliance of Montenegro (*Liberalni savez Crne Gore* – LSCG), journalists from that party's newspaper *Liberal* or journalists from the anti-war weekly *Monitor*.[24] Under tremendous pressure, he was forced to flee to Italy in late September 1991. Other factors impacted upon the lives of Boka's Croats, including the arrival of Serb refugees from Krajina and (later) Bosnia & Herzegovina. As a consequence, Croats in the Boka attempted to distance themselves from the Zagreb government. Indeed, even the Boka

Mariner's Association (*Bokeljska mornarica* – BM), which came under increasing pressure throughout 1991, separated from its Zagreb branch, lest there be any doubt about their loyalty to Montenegro.[25] But even such attempts weren't always sufficient to ease their difficulties. A gradual exodus of Croats from the Bay of Kotor subsequently ensued, though this was facilitated by pressure imposed from outside the area, not, on the whole, from *Bokelji* (citizens of Boka Kotorska).[26]

In this febrile context, the Montenegrin Assembly declared on 20 September 1991 in Žabljak that Montenegro was the world's first 'ecological state'. While Momir Bulatović did his best to wax lyrical about the importance of the declaration, it was overshadowed, quite naturally, by events in Croatia and the looming conflict with the Croat government. Branko Kostić, now the Montenegrin member of the SFRJ presidency (Nenad Bućin had resigned from the post in March 1991), cautioned that the war was 'close to Montenegro's borders', with what he claimed were an estimated 30,000 Croatian soldiers gathering in the Dubrovnik area intent on exporting Croatia's war to Montenegro.[27] Mitar Čvorović of the NS warned that 'now is the right time to discuss the borders with Croatia, because tomorrow may be too late already', lest Montenegro 'lose very important territory'.[28] But preparations had already begun for the Croat 'attack'. The JNA and the Montenegrin irregulars began to gather in Boka, in preparation for their operation that would 'neutralise' the Croats. Images, broadcast by RTCG, showed the Montenegrin reservists being welcomed by locals there. Volunteers – including around 400 volunteers from Nikšić (fathers and sons, young women, pensioners and members of various boxing clubs) – were all seen eager to go straight to the front line to carry out their patriotic duty. They were depicted being welcomed by the people of Kotor as defenders of Montenegro. Local women provided them with freshly baked cakes.[29]

By the end of September there was significant tension on the Montenegrin–Croatian border, with 'treacherous attacks' coming from the Croatian side of the border.[30] Thus, on 1 October 1991, following alleged firing from the Croat side of the border at Prevlaka and at Dibeli Brijeg, Montenegro's troops crossed their border with Croatia, with, evidently, little regard for environmental matters. The attack was facilitated by the mobilization of Montenegrin irregulars, who were placed within the framework of the JNA's '2nd Operational Unit', commanded by Lieutenant General Pavle Strugar. The latter's motivations were driven by necessity. Indeed, for many professional soldiers, the collapse of the SFRJ would dictate not just that they would lose the privileges that they had become accustomed to, but that the very ideological principles in which they had been schooled would be defeated. The JNA's legitimacy and survival depended, therefore, on the SFRJ continuing to exist. [31] Unleashed, they rampaged through the Konavle region, descending upon Dubrovnik from two directions (from Primorje and Trebinje in Eastern Hercegovina, and from the coastal road through Herceg Novi towards Konavle and Dibeli Brijeg) and in 'multi-axis advance'.[32] The JNA, with the support of Montenegrin reservists, seized territory stretching to the town of Neum[33] in the north to the Montenegrin border, and positioning themselves on the strategic high ground (on Žarkovica and other hills), effectively surrounding the city of Dubrovnik.[34]

The Montenegrin reservists who participated alongside the JNA believed, in accordance with the pre-war propaganda, that they were in Croatia to 'liberate' the people of Dubrovnik from 30,000 'fascist hordes', though upon their arrival on Croatian territory they met almost no resistance, and none of the thousands of fanatical *Ustaše* were amassing on Montenegro's border with Croatia. With little in the way of resistance, the JNA and Montenegrin reservists swept through the prosperous region – the latter particularly undisciplined – looting and burning village after village, until they reached and occupied the small port of Cavtat near Dubrovnik (allegedly an *Ustaša* stronghold).[35] Thereafter, they began to take up strategic positions on the mountains north and east of Dubrovnik, aided also by the Jugoslav Navy (led by the Miodrag Jokić), who enforced a blockade along the coastline. As a consequence, an estimated 15,000 civilians, many of them from the Konavle area, fled to Dubrovnik to shelter either within the walls of the old town or in the many tourist hotels in the Lapad bay – though both electricity and water supplies had been seriously inhibited by JNA aerial bombardments on the city's electricity grid.[36] Montenegrin reservists 'sweeping the terrain' near Dubrovnik claimed that numerous volunteers from other parts of the SFRJ, including Muslims from Tutin (in the Serbian portion of the Sandžak) and Albanians, and foreign mercenaries (Kurds and fighters from Indonesia and Singapore, for example), were fighting alongside the Croats.[37] Those Croatians unfortunate enough to fall into the hands of the JNA/Montenegrin reservists captured along the way were treated as 'prisoners of war'; some were transferred to a camp in Bileca, while others, particularly those regarded as belonging to the ZNG, known colloquially as *Zengas*, were interrogated in Kumbor before being transported to the Morinj Camp in Boka, where they were subject to numerous forms of torture, which, according to Srdja Pavlović, included beatings, sleep deprivation, water deprivation and water boarding.[38]

In the early days of the Dubrovnik operation, the government sought to play down Montenegro's involvement in the war, with reports of a government document stating that *Crna Gora nije u ratu* (Montenegro isn't at war).[39] The combative rhetoric so evident in the Montenegrin Assembly suggested otherwise. On 4 October 1991, assembly members gathered for a debate on the political and security situation in Montenegro. Božidar Babić, the minister for national defence, began by providing an overview of events in the days that led to the invasion (in a patriotic tone) before a number of delegates gave their own impressions. Speaker after speaker then lined up to give their patriotic speeches in defence of Montenegro. Among the combative speeches were those by Mitar Čvorović of the NS, who argued that Montenegro had the right to take action against the 'programme of the Ustaha government', and Ranko Jovović, who made a brief, albeit astonishing speech in which he said, 'War is [for Montenegrins] our inspiration … in this war we are defending our honour', waxing lyrical about Montenegro as the 'Serbian Sparta' and Montenegrins as 'the pearl of the Serbian people'.[40] The SDPR leader, Žarko Rakčević, then gave a lengthy more measured speech appealing to delegates to calm the talk of war and warning them of the potential consequences for Montenegro and for the SFRJ.[41] The debates, lasting long into the evening, demonstrated the divided opinions among the delegates.

There was, then, much at stake as Momir Bulatović left Titograd to travel to the European Community (EC)-sponsored Hague Conference (held between 7 and 12 October 1991). Dubrovnik was relatively calm while the conference was taking place, though after the failure to reach agreement (see below), the assault on the city and its environs resumed. On 21 October 1991, the Montenegrin daily *Pobjeda* warned again the public that the Ustaša remained a threat around Dubrovnik, but such warnings came as the number of Montenegrin casualties increased and unity began to wane.[42] The enthusiasm of Montenegrin reservists operating in the Dubrovnik area stood in stark contrast to the increasing hesitation of the Montenegrin government.[43] Their initial fervour was slowly being replaced by growing doubts, perhaps fuelled by the realization that the Dubrovnik campaign was both a military folly and a public relations disaster for Montenegro. Images of Dubrovnik, a well-known and loved tourist destination, being shelled were transmitted across the world, creating a sense of outrage. Many of the Western journalists based at the Hotel Argentina,[44] in close proximity to the walls of the old town, wrote both of the looting of the Montenegrin troops from places such as the tiny port town of Cavtat and Dubrovnik's Čilipi Airport (which had been completely destroyed and its duty-free shop plundered) and of the shelling of Dubrovnik itself.[45] Some in Montenegro were vocal in their condemnation of the actions of Montenegrin troops, and the role of the Montenegrin government in creating 'war euphoria'. Slavko Perović, the leader of the LSCG, and many within his party were among the few courageous enough to oppose the war unambiguously and openly.[46] Those who did were subject to a relentless media campaign, cast as *izdajnici* (traitors) and placed under tremendous pressure.[47]

Realizing, albeit belatedly, the damage that had been incurred, the Montenegrin government endeavoured to make their case, denying that the old town of Dubrovnik itself had been attacked and making claims that Croats had set alight rubber tyres within the walls of the old town to give the impression that the United Nations Educational, Scientific and Cultural Organization (UNESCO)-protected old town had been shelled.[48] They argued that in the conflict Montenegro had been the victim of a well-orchestrated Croat propaganda campaign and that the war had been intended as a defense of the SFRJ, not a campaign to establish the borders of a 'Greater Serbia'.[49] The then foreign minister, Nikola Samardžić, stated that many Montenegrins considered the conflict in Croatia to be the JNA's war, not Montenegro's war.[50] Žarko Rakčević, the leader of the SDP, would later say that those who had called for war had 'led Montenegro to the beggar's stick'.[51]

The Dubrovnik campaign was becoming increasingly damaging for Montenegro. As a consequence, both Bulatović and Djukanović appeared to be keen to assert some distance from Belgrade. In September 1991, Djukanović announced preparations to declare Montenegrin sovereignty (albeit within the framework of the SFRJ), while Bulatović had tentatively suggested that Montenegrin reservists should be withdrawn from the area around Dubrovnik.[52] Neither materialized, but by early December 1991 it was estimated by the growing casualty numbers and growing perception among Montenegrin citizens that their young men were being sent to die in a senseless war. These conditions meant, according to the Belgrade daily *Borba*, that ongoing EC sanctions would 'wrap Montenegro in black'.[53] Shaken by the course of events, the Montenegrin leadership sought to distance itself from the Dubrovnik campaign. Bulatović and Djukanović became increasingly critical of parliamentary delegates who continued to support the war. The former noted that not only were potential military gains stymied by the pressure of the international community, but that he, as the president of a republic in which 10 per cent of the population was mobilized for war, was also under tremendous pressure.⁵⁴ Milo Djukanović, in stark contrast to his early combative stance, sought to draw a clear demarcation between him and those who still advocated war and further mobilization. 'All of us', he said, 'have to take responsibility for that, including those in the parliament building – [but] responsibility lies with those who are still calling for war from their warm houses and offices'.⁵⁵

The Hague Conference and its discontents

By mid-October 1991, just two weeks after the Dubrovnik campaign had begun, Bulatović and Djukanović began seeking a way out of the growing crisis and of the growing international condemnation generated by the attack on Dubrovnik. During the 'Hague Conference', organized by the EC and chaired by Lord Peter Carrington, the former British foreign secretary, Bulatović, boldly took a decision that would cause an internal political crisis and strain, significantly, the hitherto consensus between Titograd and Belgrade. The subsequent plan for future arrangements between republics of the SFRJ, known as the 'Carrington Plan', envisaged Yugoslavia becoming a loose association of independent states that would have the status of subjects under international law.⁵⁶ The position that the Montenegrin leadership would adopt seemed clear; uniformity with the Serbian line (which was to reject the plan) was, surely, a certainty. But Bulatović had other ideas, possibly driven by the growing crisis in Konavle/Dubrovnik, but perhaps influenced by the promise of a generous EC aid package and assurances that Italy, in particular, would strongly support Montenegro if it pursued a more independent path. (The Italian foreign minister, Gianni De-Michelis, claimed that Bulatović had told him that he wanted to chart an independent course from Belgrade and from those Montenegrins who were 'tied to Belgrade by ideology and politics'.⁵⁷)

At any rate, during a session in the Montenegrin Assembly immediately prior to the Hague conference (on 17 October 1992), Bulatović, as president of the republic, had essentially been given carte blanche to take the decision himself.⁵⁸ Then, during the Hague Conference on 19 October, Bulatović shocked the conference with his announcement that Montenegro would sign. The decision convulsed a Serbian leadership (and some of those within the Montenegrin delegation), many of whom simply did not expect such dissention from the Montenegrin president.⁵⁹ The impact within the Montenegrin camp was immediate. Gavro Perazić, a lawyer and one of the Montenegrin expert delegation during the conference, submitted his resignation immediately, stating that the proposal proceeded from the supposition that the SFRJ no longer existed which, he said, was 'a blatant violation of Article 2.4 of the United Nations Charter which unambiguously safeguards the territorial integrity and political independence of [member] states'.⁶⁰

Bulatović returned to Montenegro, where he faced delegates in the Montenegrin Assembly and the public, in an effort to convince them of the merits of the Carrington

Plan, while providing a justification for why he opted to sign. Though debates over the wisdom of his decision were fierce, it was essentially ratified by the Montenegrin Assembly, during sessions on 24 and 25 October 1991 (as the bombardment of the Dubrovnik area continued). There was strong support in some quarters, but to others his actions were regarded by some as nothing short of treachery. Branko Kostić, the acting president of the SFRJ (and a strong advocate of Serb–Montenegrin unity), was particularly scathing of what he described as a 'shameful capitulation'.[61] Upon his return, he attempted to persuade delegates in the Montenegrin assembly. Bulatović knew there existed strong reservations – particularly among delegates from Ivangrad (now Berane)[62] and Andrijevica in northern Montenegro – but hoped that most DPS delegates in other municipalities would acknowledge the merits of his decision.[63] He argued that acceptance of the Carrington Plan would make it possible for Montenegro to secure its own interests, the interests of others, and put an end to the war (the scales may have been tipped by the prospect of a generous EC aid package worth several million dollars). Despite objections from numerous delegates, the majority voted to uphold his decision. The Montenegrin president believed that this represented the end of the matter.[64] He was wrong. Suddenly, opinion appeared to turn sharply against him. There were demonstrations in Titograd in support of Bulatović, but, equally, were those calling for him to reverse his decision. In an emergency session of the Montenegrin Assembly called by Novak Kilibarda's NS in late October, Bulatović was lambasted for his support of the Hague document, which was cast as a betrayal of Montenegro. The session was, Bulatović later acknowledged, extremely tough, and he saw the potential for 'a major rift that would have serious consequences for peace and stability'.[65]

To compound his experience in the Montenegrin Assembly pressure was, simultaneously, applied by Belgrade, where Bulatović was 'invited' to attend meetings held with the sole objective of coercing him into reversing his decision.[66] It was, noted Borisav Jović (the then president of the Yugoslav Presidency), not too late 'for the Montenegrin Assembly or the people of Montenegro overturn the position of Bulatović'.[67] During the meetings, Milošević insisted on the insertion of a clause in the plan that would allow the republics who wished to remain in a federation to do so, thereby creating the possibility of a new Yugoslavia, consisting of Serbia and Montenegro. After the Belgrade meetings, the Montenegrin leadership returned to Titograd for consultations, and upon their return to the Serbian capital, Bulatović (and Djukanović) agreed to the amendment that stated that a 'rump' Yugoslavia could continue to exist if two or more republics wished to remain in federation. Bulatović would later claim that his change of direction was 'far from a policy of appeasement', though. On 30 October 1991, Serbia and Montenegro proposed an amendment to the Carrington Plan that would allow for those states which did not wish to secede from the SFRJ to establish a successor federal state.[68] With the Carrington Plan dead, the SFRJ continued its inexorable fragmentation. The JNA and Montenegrin reservist attacks on Dubrovnik resumed on the same day that Bulatović agreed to the amendments to the Hague document – peaking on 6 December 1991, during the so-called 'St. Nicholas Day bombardment', during which the old town of Dubrovnik was targeted, the library of the Inter-University Centre burned down and the Hotel Libertas in the west of the city badly damaged by fire.[69] (The hotel complex at Kupari, in which was located the

Hotel Pelegrin – a gem of Yugoslav modernist architecture designed by David Finci and opened in 1963 – was also destroyed by a JNA and Yugoslav Navy bombardment, as were hotels in Gruž, Babin Kuk and the Boninovo area.)

Three of the country's republics (Slovenia, Croatia and Macedonia) had applied for international recognition. Only Slovenia and Macedonia met the conditions laid down in the Badinter Commission (which published its findings in January 1992). Undeterred, Germany recognized Slovenia and Croatia's independence on 23 December 1991, thus forcing the hand of the EC into formal recognition (Greece simultaneously vetoed Macedonia's application on the basis that the name 'Macedonia' implied territorial aspirations vis-à-vis northern Greece). Thus, Slovenia and Croatia were the first two Yugoslav republics to be granted recognition by the EC in January 1992. The United States was more cautious, choosing to adopt a 'wait and see' policy, though it, too, bowed to the inevitable, recognizing the independence of both Slovenia and Croatia in April 1992. (Likewise, Bosnia & Herzegovina had been recognized as an independent state by the EC and the United States in the days following the events of 5 and 6 April in Sarajevo.[70]) By May 1992, the operations in Dubrovnik were all but over, though war would continue to rage in Bosnia & Herzegovina for a further three and a half years.

Amid the chaos, the SFRJ had essentially ceased to exist, and thus plans were made by elites in Serbia and Montenegro to establish a new state, which would become the 'Federal Republic of Yugoslavia' (*Savezna republika Jugoslavija* – SRJ), comprising approximately 44 per cent of the population and around 40 per cent of the territory of the defunct SFRJ.[71] These plans were made public (though no date for a referendum was set) in January 1992, only two months before its realization; constitutional experts took only five days to write the new constitution (the much-maligned Žabljak Constitution). Milošević's SPS played the key role in the negotiations, the DPS a secondary role.[72] Throughout the process the Montenegrin public remained largely uninformed of the development of the new constitution.[73] Similarly, opposition parties were not consulted regarding the make-up of the new state, determining that the character of the state's inception created the conditions for the gestation of dissatisfaction with the SRJ from its inception.[74]

The opposition went on the offensive, despite being under tremendous pressure since the Dubrovnik operation began. Indeed, leading opposition figures had paid a heavy price for their opposition to the war. Some left Montenegro to live in exile.[75] Nevertheless, the opposition soldiered on, and on 2 February 1992, the LSCG, in concert with a number of other opposition parties, organized a large gathering in Cetinje, where party supporters in that town were joined (despite the snow) by carloads of people from Titograd, Nikšić, Kotor, Bar and even as far afield as Bijelo Polje and Plav.[76] The mood was defiant – the crowds chanting *Sa Lovćena vila kliče, oprosti nam Dubrovniče!* (Dubrovnik, forgive us, the fairy cries from Mount Lovćen!) – though the event passed without incident.[77] Typically, the state-controlled media in both Serbia and Montenegro was deeply critical of the LSCG. The Belgrade daily *Politika* stated that the meeting had been held outside the residence of King Nikola I 'to elevate the importance of the gathering', and that the meeting was not simply attended by 'Montenegrins', but by Albanians and Muslims.[78] This was followed by a similar gathering in Titograd three weeks later. The crowd, having walked through the city, assembled outside the Montenegrin Assembly where they listened to speeches by a number of the LSCG's leading figures, including Slavko Perović, Miodrag Vlahović and poet Branko Banjević. Both of these rallies attracted big crowds, which listened to Perović tell them that the Montenegrin government was collaborating with Milošević's SPS in the debasement of Montenegro and the 'ethnic assimilation' of Montenegro by Serbs. He made clear that the LSCG opposed both the military engagement in Croatia and the forthcoming referendum.[79] But while Perović's speech resonated, many counterdemonstrations in support of the creation of the new state in front of the Montenegrin Assembly the following day were demonstrative of the widening divisions in advance of the referendum.

For those, like Perović, who had opposed the war in Dubrovnik and attempted to highlight the undemocratic nature of the process that would lead to the formation of the SRJ, everyday life could be extremely difficult. Perović was under constant pressure, as were many of those that were members of the LSCG, or who worked to produce the party's newspaper *Liberal*.[80] Likewise, those who worked for the independent weekly *Monitor* were also the subject of intimidation and, occasionally, violence. *Monitor* first appeared in October 1990, and was intended to reach the democratically inclined among the Montenegrin population. Ostensibly independent, it was partly funded by Stanislav-Ćano Koprivica, the wealthy Montenegrin businessman (and owner of the export company MONTEX) who also funded the LSCG and had significant influence over the editorial policy of the magazine.[81] The editor-in-chief was Miodrag 'Miško' Perović, who would later become the owner. *Monitor* was anti-war, pro-European and highly critical of the Montenegrin government, and produced brave and credible journalism that represented a vital counterpoint to the state daily *Pobjeda*. But such an editorial position would come at a cost. Its offices in Dalmatinska Street in central Titograd were the subject of a two bomb attacks in October 1991 during the war in Dubrovnik and its reporters and staff frequently harassed.[82] They continued, however, to be critical of the government during the 'negotiations' that led to the creation of the SRJ, despite the evident dangers.

In the meantime, and following his Hague debacle, Bulatović proposed a framework for the state-legal status of Montenegro within the SRJ. In Montenegrin Assembly sessions between 16 and 22 January 1992, he consistently argued that there was 'a minimum under which Montenegro cannot go' vis-à-vis their status within any new federation.[83] He advocated a *ni lanci, ni pasoši* (no chains, no passport) position, a compromise between virtual subordination by Serbia and outright independence.[84] Initially, he proposed a confederal model that envisaged the SRJ possessing a single market, single currency, unitary monetary policy, foreign policy (which would allow separate consular representations) and a joint defence system, albeit with a degree of autonomy. But the subsequent negotiations with the Serbian leadership bore little fruit, and his vain attempts were dubbed his *Drugi Hag* (Second Hague). He was not, however, negotiating from a position of strength; the SPS was not, after all, receptive to the idea of the equal status of Montenegro within the SRJ.[85] For his part, Bulatović claimed there was no pressure applied by Serbia and that there was, in any event, 'no need to declare the sovereignty of Montenegro, because the republic already enjoys this', while Milo Djukanović stated that Montenegro would enjoy 'full equality' in any state with Serbia.[86]

The next step towards creating the SRJ took place during a meeting in Titograd on 12 February 1992, which was attended by a Serb delegation, led by Milošević, and a Montenegrin delegation, led by Bulatović (two members of the 'rump' SFRJ presidency – Branko Kostić and Borisav Jović – were also present). The meeting adopted a 'statement'; something of a blueprint for the new state.[87] It was agreed that in order for the new state to be realized the Montenegrins would need to rubber stamp the idea through a referendum. Announced formally – through RTCG News and on the front page of *Pobjeda* – on 22 February and held on 1 March 1992 (the same weekend as the so-called 'referendum weekend' in neighbouring Bosnia & Herzegovina), it would pave the way for the establishment of the SRJ. Montenegrins were required to say 'yes' or 'no' to the question: *Do you agree that Montenegro, as a sovereign republic, should continue to exist in the joint country of Yugoslavia, on a completely equal basis with other republics who wish to do so?* But the process was somewhat flawed, and no such referendum was held in Serbia.[88] Given that the Montenegrin government formally adopted the 'Law on Referendum' only a week before the vote, the scope for public debate was limited.[89] The opposition, already dismayed by the Dubrovnik campaign, stated that they would boycott the referendum, organize rallies to oppose the creation of the SRJ, to agitate against it and to highlight Montenegro's likely subservient role within it.[90] They united under the umbrella of 'The United Opposition of Montenegro' (*Udružena opozicija Crne Gore* – UOCG), which included, among others, Slavko Perović's LSCG and Žarko Rakčević's Social Democratic Party of Reformers (*Socijaldemokratska partija reformatora* – SDPR). They did their best to highlight what they argued was an undemocratic referendum process. But the homogenized press and the campaigning clout of the DPS ensured an uneven playing field and the result of the referendum was, in essence, a fait accompli.

There were significant flaws in the referendum process, though the Montenegrin government sought to make the case that while the timescale between announcement of the referendum date and the vote was short, the matter had been extensively debated in the months leading to the referendum. With the opposition boycott, participation in the referendum was estimated as 96 per cent (though only 66 per cent if one takes into account the opposition boycott), only approximately 280,000 people – less than half the population – and, given that no referendum had taken place in Serbia, a tiny fraction of the overall population of the SRJ. And while there was no monitoring of the referendum by international organizations, some external observers were critical of the way the referendum process was executed. Citing the lack of any election monitoring, domestic or international, as evidence that the referendum process was flawed, an organization called the 'International Federation for the Rights of Man' (IFRM) sent a telegram to Momir Bulatović, criticizing the conduct of the referendum. They also claimed that those who had boycotted the referendum were 'shamed' by having their names listed on state television. Bulatović's response, published in *Pobjeda*, was to argue that the IFRM had not understood that the debates had been extensive, that there had been no such list and that the referendum was entirely legitimate. He further invited the organization to 'check all the facts'.[91] In any event, regardless of the controversies surrounding the referendum, the discussions about the structure of the new state and its constitution began. Holed-up in the Hotel Planinka in Žabljak in the town of the same name in Montenegro, a working group comprising experts and political leaders from both of the republics (essentially *nomenklatura* from both republics) discussed the parameters of the constitution and the character of state symbols. The resulting *Žabljački ustav* (Žabljak Constitution) determined that the new state would continue to be called 'Yugoslavia' and that the national anthem would remain *Hej Sloveni* (Hey Slavs), the anthem of the SFRJ.[92] The SRJ was formally proclaimed on 27 April 1992 in Belgrade, with the 'spiritual father of the Serbian nation', the writer Dobrica Ćosić, as president and Milan Panić (a Serbian-American businessman) as prime minister. From the very outset, therefore, the SRJ was an asymmetrical federation comprising two federal units of disproportionate scale, population and with two very different economies. To compound this, the United Nations (UN) began imposing sanctions on the SRJ on the same month, beginning with UN Security Resolution 757. So, despite the best efforts of the opposition, the new state was something of a fait accompli.[93]

In December 1992, more than a year after the beginning of the 'War for Peace', the SRJ president, Dobrica Ćosić, and the Croatian president, Franjo Tudjman, reached an agreement on Prevlaka, which facilitated the exit of JNA (now *Vojska Jugoslavije* – VJ) troops from the area. The area was demilitarized under UN supervision, ostensibly for a ten-year period. Just before the expiration of the UN mandate in Prevlaka, the International Criminal Tribunal for the Former Yugoslavia (ICTY) would, in February 2001, indict the 'Dubrovnik Four' (Pavle Strugar, Miodrag Jokić, Milan Zec and Vladimir Kovačević) for the 'fifteen counts of violations of the laws or customs of war' and 'one count of grave breaches of the Geneva Convention'.[94] Strugar was sentenced to seven and a half years in prison and Jokić to seven years and charges were dropped against Zec. Kovačević, born in Nikšić and known as 'Rambo', pleaded insanity and has, thus far, not faced a criminal trial. In 2008, six former JNA officers were arrested and charged with war crimes committed in Morinj camp in 1991 and 1992. Four of the six were sentenced by the Montenegrin courts for prison terms of between two and four years in July 2013.

4

Fear and Flux: Montenegro's Muslim and Albanian Minorities (1992–97)

The aforementioned political and social developments in Montenegro between 1988 and 1991 would have a significant impact on Montenegro's largest ethnic minorities (Slavic), Muslims and Albanians. And as the SFRJ disintegrated they would find themselves isolated and increasingly threatened by the nationalist hysteria that accompanied the wars in Croatia and Bosnia & Herzegovina. The years between 1992 and 1997, the focus of this chapter, were the darkest of times for Montenegro's ethnic minorities, and while there was no war per se in Montenegro, Muslims and Albanians were not only politically marginalized, but often the target of intimidation or violence, sometimes by locals, but more often by Serb or Bosnian Serb paramilitaries who used the towns in the area near the Montenegrin-Bosnian border as bases from which to cross over into Bosnia & Herzegovina. These years would, then, be characterized by fear and flux, though the fortunes of both Montenegro's Muslims and Albanians would change dramatically in 1997.

According to the 1991 census (the last conducted in the SFRJ),[1] the population of Montenegro comprised: Montenegrins (61.28 per cent), Muslims (14.57 per cent),[2] Serbs (9.34 per cent), Albanians (6.57 per cent), 'Yugoslavs' (4.25 per cent) and Croats (1.02 per cent), Roma (0.53 per cent) and a number of minorities (Macedonian, Slovene, Hungarian and German) that represented under 1 per cent of the population. Montenegro's Muslim population were concentrated largely, though not exclusively, in the municipalities straddling the border between Serbia and Montenegro: Berane, Bijelo Polje, Pljevlja, Rožaje and Plav in the Montenegrin portion of the historic Sandžak region (or *Raška*, as it is known to Serbs), which was once called the *Sandžak of Novi Pazar*.[3] There were 89,614 Muslims in Montenegro (14.57 per cent of the total population), though there were only two of Montenegro's twenty-one municiplaities that were majority Muslim – Rožaje, where 87 per cent of the population were Muslim, and Plav, where 58 per cent were likewise. There were, however, large Muslim minorities in Bijelo Polje (41.57 per cent), Ivangrad/Berane (30.2 per cent), Pljevlja (17.6 per cent) and Bar (13.76 per cent), as well as smaller Muslim communities distributed throughout the republic.[4]

Many of the areas inhabited by Slavic Muslims or by Albanians were not part of *Stara Crna Gora* (Old Montenegro) or the *Brda* (mountains) and were incorporated into Montenegrin territory only in the the latter part of the nineteenth century. Montenegro had expanded significantly in 1877 (gaining Nikšić, Bar and Podgorica – towns previously under Ottoman control); this expansion endorsed during the Treaty of San Stefano. Montenegro became an independent state a year later and later expanded into territories where the tradition of Montenegrin uniqueness and identification with Montenegrin identity and statehood was weaker.[5] Plav and Gusinje were not formally incorporated into Montenegro until 1912, though the area had been awarded to Montenegro by the Great Powers and formalized during the 1878 Congress of Berlin (which also granted Montenegro the coastal town of Ulcinj). However, in the wake of the Congress, the Albanian nationalist movement, 'The League of Prizren', fought (during the Battle of Novšiće in 1879) to prevent the handover of Plav and Gusinje to the Montenegrins. These towns would, however, become part of Montenegro as a consequence of the First Balkan War in 1912, during which Serbian and Montenegrin armies moved into and absorbed the Sandžak region (creating a common border between Serbia and Montenegro). Later, after the creation of the Kingdom of Serbs, Croats and Slovenes (KSHS), uprisings, known as the *Plavska pobuna* (Plav rebellion), against the new authorities led to bloody retributions in Plav, Gusinje and Rožaje.

In November 1924, around 600 Muslims were killed in and around Šahovići, Vraneš and Pavino Polje (Muslims in Bijelo Polje were also subject to violent attacks).[6] In Šahovići and Pavino Polje, the massacres were fuelled by the murder, on 7 November, of Boško Bošković, the governor of the Kolašin district and fervent supporter of unification, who had been ambushed on the road between Šahovići and Mojkovac. It was assumed by local Montenegrins that the perpetrators of the crime were Muslim *komiti* from the Sandžak, and the troika of Jusuf Mehonjić, Husein Bošković and Mehmed Kalić were singled out as likely perpetrators. Local Montenegrins then marched on Šahovići two days after the murder to settle scores, and in the subsequent violence hundreds of Muslims were indiscriminately killed.[7] In the wake of the Šahovići massacre, many Muslims prepared to leave the Montenegro. The violence, while most acute in Šahovići, was by no means limited to the Bijelo Polje district, or indeed to Montenegro.[8] In a final tragic twist, it emerged that those who fled Šahovići and its environs did so after a massacre that was fuelled by rumour and disinformation. It had not been Jusuf Mehonjić or any of his associates that had murdered Boško Bošković, but Montenegrins from the rival Rovci clan. These incidents initiated a large-scale emigration of Muslims from the region, with many leaving for Skopje or to Turkey.[9]

During the Second World War in Yugoslavia (1941–45), the Montenegrin portion of the Sandžak was occupied by both German and Italian troops, while becoming the epicentre of conflict between the Serb nationalist Chetniks and the communist-led Partisans. Western parts of the Sandžak – including Pljevlja – were also briefly occupied by Ustaša battalions from the Independent State of Croatia (*Nezavisna država Hrvatska* – NDH).[10] Pljevlja was also the site of the 'Battle of Pljevlja' – a failed Partisan attack on the Italian garrison based in the town in November 1941 (see Chapter 1).[11] While much of the area was carved up among different occupying forces and their quislings with different objectives, part of the present-day Sandžak was, for a time, an 'autonomous' entity, ostensibly under the control of the Land Assembly for the National Liberation of the Sandžak (*Zemaljsko antifašističko vijeće Sandžaka* – ZAVNOS), a body created in Pljevlja in November 1943 and comprising Serbs, Montenegrins and Muslims.[12] The Montenegrin towns of Bijelo Polje and Pljevlja fell under this administration, but in March 1945, ZAVNOS was dissolved and with it the idea of a separate Sandžak republic.[13] The area was again divided between the Serbian and Montenegrin republics within the SFRJ, and those parts of the Montenegrin Sandžak that were ostensibly administered by ZAVNOS were incorporated into the Montenegrin republic.

Muslims were well intrgrated into the SFRJ, particularly after the political downfall fall (in 1966) of Tito's security chief, Aleksander Ranković, who had long mistrusted Muslim (and Albanian) motives. The subsequent period of liberalization allowed Muslims to become part of the political mainstream and to express their Muslim identity. Though observance was generally low, the religious life of adherents to the Islamic faith (both Slavic Muslims and Albanian Muslims) was organized by the Islamic Community of Yugoslavia (*Islamska zajednica Jugoslavije* – IZJ), which was disbanded following the disintegration of the SFRJ.[14] (In 1994, the Islamic Community of Montenegro (*Islamska zajednica Crne Gore* – IZCG), with its seat in Podgorica, was established.) The identity of the Muslims of the SFRJ was always contested, with both Serb and Croat nationalists claiming Muslims as either 'Serbs or Croats of Muslim faith'. To overcome this rivalry, the SFRJ government opted to recognize Muslims as a separate 'nation', a process essentially completed by 1971. By then, the SFRJ had become one of the de facto leaders of the nascent 'Non-Aligned Movement' (NAM), a powerful group of countries that did not (within the parameters of the Cold War) align themselves to either the United States or the Soviet Union (USSR). The NAM, which had met for the first time in Belgrade in 1961, included a number of powerful and influential Muslim countries (such as Egypt and Indonesia), and, in this context, the status of Yugoslavia's Muslims significantly improved.[15] No longer considered a potential 'fifth column', they were treated instead as assets. (It was, after all, imperative that the SFRJ could demonstrate that Muslims were both well 'emancipated' and fully integrated into the Yugoslav social, political and economic system.)

Internally, relations between Muslims and their Orthodox *komšije* (neighbours) had generally been good since the end of the Second World War, but as interethnic tensions within the SFRJ worsened, and the ruling DPS supported Belgrade's position vis-à-vis relations with the breakaway Yugoslav republics, Muslims in Montenegro felt increasingly threatened.[16] A distinct anti-Muslim rhetoric had been evident in both Serbia and Montenegro years before the SFRJ disintegrated. Once an essential pillar of Yugoslavism and the communist mantra of *bratstvo i jedinstvo* (brotherhood and unity), Muslims were increasingly reduced to the status of *Turci* (Turks) or *Poturice* (apostates). And as the SFRJ began its slow demise, a creeping anti-Muslim discourse emerged in the Serbian and Montenegrin press (particularly *Politika*, *Politika ekspres* and *Pobjeda*), where Muslims were bluntly and indiscriminately depicted as 'secessionists', 'fundamentalists' or 'extremists', a potential *peta kolona* (fifth column).[17] It was they, according to this narrative, who had profited from the suffering of the Serbs, and who had done so while 'real' and 'proud' Serbs stayed true to their Orthodox faith. Muslims were further portrayed as closet 'Islamic extremists' who, in collaboration with their ethnic kin in Bosnia & Herzegovina, secretly nurtured a desire to recreate the 'Old Constantinople Road', forging a *zelena transverzala* (green transversal) which would link Albania, Kosovo and the Sandžak with Bosnia & Herzegovina, thereby facilitating the Islamic penetration of Europe.[18] They were, their detractors claimed, subject to the influence of radical variants of Islam (both Shia and Sunni), from that extolled by Ayatollah Khomeini in Iran to that propagated by the Muslim Brotherhood in Egypt. A synthesized, simplified variant of this argument was ever-present in the Serbian and Montenegrin media by the late 1980s, despite the obvious contradictions.

By 1989 the sharp rhetoric contained within the pages of print media became manifest in everyday life; Montenegro's Muslims began to face discrimination and, on occasion, outright hostility. In January 1989, events in Plav foreshadowed the subsequent experience of Muslims in Montenegro and mirrored, to some extent, the rising resistance to the 'anti-bureaucratic revolution' in Kosovo (the autonomous status of which would be rescinded by Milošević's government in Serbia). The 'January Coup' in Montenegro had resulted in mass resignations by the leadership of the SKCG (see Chapter 2), and, as it became clear what was taking place in Titograd, the municipal SKCG leadership in Plav did likewise. However, the municipal assembly in Plav refused to endorse their resignations, leading to something of an impasse.[19] On 25 January 1989, demonstrators, largely consisting of Muslims and Albanians from Plav and Gusinje, gathered outside the municipal assembly building denouncing Milošević's 'anti-bureaucratic revolution' and calling for 'brotherhood and unity'.[20] In response, some of the footsoldiers of the 'anti bureaucratic revolution' arrived in Plav (they were joined by local Serbs and Montenegrins) to insist that the town's leadership resign and that the municipal assembly consent to them doing so and that the inevitable outcome of the 'happening of the people' be recognized. Their arrival brought locals out on to the streets, and a tense stand off ensued. The two groups, kept apart but in the vicintiy of Plav's municipal assembly building, taunted each other across police lines. The locals voiced their support for the town's embattled SKCG leadership and the chairman of the Presidency of the SFRJ, Stipe Šuvar, while chanting *Ovo nije Srbija!* (This isn't Serbia!). The opposing group, conversely, chanted songs and slogans in support of Slobodan Milošević. Tensions rose, and police were eventually forced to intervene as the two groups clashed on the peripheries of the gathering.[21] The situation was, according to *Pobjeda*, 'relatively peaceful' the morning after, but the mistrust between the citizens of Plav and the new government in Titograd was now firmly established.[22]

Muslims and Albanians thereafter began to organize political parties that would protect their interests. In November 1990, in advance of Montenegro's multiparty elections, there existed only one Muslim (Bosniak) party of any significance, the Montenegrin branch of the Party of Democratic Action (*Stranka demokratske akcije* – SDA), formed in Rožaje and led by Harun Hadžić. The party was the sister of their Bosnian counterpart led by Alija Izetbegović, and worked closely alongside the Serbian branch of the SDA. The latter was led by a former dentist, Sulejman Ugljanin, who had become notorious for his radical rhetoric and his stated desire that the Sandžak, in the event of the SFRJ's disintegration, should become 'automomous' (or conjoined to an independent Bosnia & Herzegovina).[23] As the war in Croatia intensified throughout 1991, the *Muslimansko nacionalno vijeće Sandžaka* (MNVS),[24] which included the

SDA and a number of smaller parties, began preparations to hold a referendum on autonomy, which was eventually held on 26 and 27 October 1991 (it was deemed 'unconstitutional' by the governments in both Serbia and Montenegro). Among Muslims in the Serbian Sandžak (Serbs did not participate) the turnout was relatively high in places such as the predominantly Muslim towns of Novi Pazar, Sjenica and Tutin, lower in the ethnically mixed towns of Prijepolje and Priboj, and very low in towns such as Nova Varoš, where Muslims were in a minority. In Montenegro, the turnout was lower still. The MNVS claimed it was relatively high in Rožaje (Harun Hadžić's hometown) and in Plav (though local leaders in Plav denied that there had been anything approaching such a turnout), but acknowledged that turnout was particularly low in Pljevlja and in Bijelo Polje.

The referendum on Sandžak's autonomy was not, therefore, supported by anything like the majority of Montenegro's Muslims.[25] The SDA (and, by extension, the MNVS) did enjoy strong support from some within the community, but even SDA supporters were unconvinced by Ugljanin and Hadžić's arguments during the pre-referendum campaign. Others merely aligned themselves with the Party of National Equality (*Stranka nacionalne ravnopravnosti* – SNR), the Social Democratic Party (*Socijaldemokratska partija* – SDP) and Slavko Perović's LSCG, all of which were multiethnic, anti-war and, to a greater or lesser extent, advocates of Montenegro's independence. It was equally evident that very few Muslims in Montenegro supported the radical arguments posited by Ugljanin vis-à-vis autonomy or the MNVS proposal that the Sandžak be conjoined to Bosnia & Hezegovina. That did not mean, however, that they would remain immune to the growing tensions as war in neighbouring Bosnia & Herzegovina (where many Montenegrin Muslims had family links) approached, seemingly inexorably. Muslims in the Montenegrin Sandžak were being viewed with great suspicion by authorities in Podgorica; interethnic tensions slowly but incrementally increased, particularly in towns such as Berane, Bijelo Polje, Pljevlja, Plav and Gusinje. The growing mistrust was further fuelled in February 1992, whereupon the Belgrade daily *Politika* reported that 'Albanian extremists' in Plav and Gusinje were planning to annex that part of Montenegro, which would then be absorbed into a 'Greater Albania'. It was also claimed that 'Muslim extermist missionaries' from Novi Pazar, Sarajevo, Rožaje, Bijelo Polje, Skopje and Prishtina (in Kosovo) were arriving in numbers to help defend their Muslim *braća* (brothers).[26] The report went on to say that non-Muslims (Serbs and Montenegrins) were 'gripped with fear' as a consequence of these developments.[27] And such fears, whether founded or baseless, played a considerable role in the fracturing of interethnic relations in Montenegro. These were aided not just by the negative media reports about 'Islamic extremism', and clandestine annexation plans, but by the statements (or the interpretation of them) emanating from the leadership of the Montenegrin SDA. Following the referendum, Harun Hadžić, the party's leader, had stated that 'if Montenegro is annexed to Serbia' Montenegro's Muslims would be 'forced to seek autonomy'.[28] Though possibly just political rhetoric to be understood within the parameters of political debate, such remarks were interpreted by non-Muslims as a threat.

In the midst of this political sabre-rattling, there were tangible consequences for ordinary Muslims, whether they cared for politics or otherwise. Those working within the state sector suffered the most. Large numbers were made redundant in the spheres of law enforcement, education and the state bureaucracy.[29] And as the political climate worsened, social bonds weakened to be replaced with mutual mistrust. In this darkening context, implied or veiled threats soon transformed into intimidation and physical attacks. In this regard, March 1992 presented a pivot. Collectively, the independence referendum in Bosnia & Herzegovina, the related 'war of the barricades' in Sarajevo and the brutal attacks upon Muslims by Željko 'Arkan' Ražnjatović's paramilitary group 'The Serbian Volunteer Guard' (*Srpska dobrovoljačka garda* – SDG) in the Bosnian towns of Bjeljinja and Zvornik in March 1992 sent a wave of fear among Muslims in Bosnia & Herzegovina and throughout Muslim communities in the Montenegrin and Serbian Sandžak.[30]

The outbreak of war in Bosnia & Herzegovina, following the events in Sarajevo on 5 and 6 April 1992, fuelled tensions in Montenegrin towns and villages located near the Bosnian border. The atmosphere darkened; fear and mistrust pervaded. In June 1992, as the war raged in cities close to the Bosnian-Montenegrin border (such as Foča), Montenegrin police claimed to have broken an 'arms smuggling ring', who, they alleged, were bringing weapons from Kosovo and Albania into the nothern Montenegro towns of Plav and Gusinje.[31] Such allegations further marginalized the Muslim poulation and increased tensions, which were particularly acute in towns such as Pljevlja (the location of the beautiful Husein Paša mosque) and to a lesser extent in Berane and Bijelo Polje, where relations between Serbs (and Montenegrins) and Muslims worsened nevertheless.[32] In Pljevlja, the gradual separation and growing hostility between Serbs and Muslims had been evident for some time before the outbreak of war in Bosnia & Herzegovina.[33] To add to the growing distrust and divison at the local level, Pljevlja, a town traversed by numerous Serb paramilitary en route to the war in Bosnia & Herzegovina, became the site of numerous crimes against Muslims. Some of the ensuing violence and intimidation that Muslims experienced there was meted out by those from other parts of Montenegro and from Serbia – including units loyal to Vojislav Šešelj, the leader of the Serbian Radical Party (*Srpska radikalna stranka* – SRS)[34] – though it was a local extremist who engineered the violence in Pljevlja.[35]

A collection of small paramilitary formations had been brought together by (and were under the command of) 'Šešelj's man' in the town – Milika Čeko Dačević, an SRS 'activist' from the village of Odžaci near Pljevlja, who had previously fought in Vukovar, Foča and Goražde. In the summer of 1992, he and his men began to intimidate Muslims – who his men referred to as *Turci* (Turks) – with the express objective of forcing their silent departure and to steal their assests. The pattern of intimidation was thus: Muslim workers would be sacked from local enterprises, Muslim businesses would be boycotted and people sidelined, even by their Serb or Montenegrin neighbours (who had been warned by the paramilitaries not to engage with Muslims). If this was not sufficient to persuade the town's Muslims to leave, their property and businesses would then be attacked (twenty-five were attacked between June and August 1992); the final phase would involve both psychological and, on occasion, physical violence. Frequent gunfire and the sound of paramilitaries signing Chetnik songs or shouting Chetnik slogans was the menacing aural backdrop to the climate of fear pervading the town.

By way of response, Pljevlja's Muslims, frightened by the dark social environment they were inhabiting, avoided public spaces (where they may encounter aggression), particularly Serb districts or restaurants and bars frequented by Serbs, and retreated into their homes, their families – into themselves.[36] Some, at least those brave enough to speak out, complained that the Montenegrin police were doing nothing to dissuade the perpetrators. But while there was undoubted legitimacy in these grievances, the police were poorly armed and operated knowing that any attempt to tackle the paramilitaries (who were armed with sophisticated, modern weapons) could end in disaster.[37] In early July 1992, the situation in Pljevlja appeared to be calming. But on 1 July 1992, villages in the Bukovica area (near Pljevlja) were attacked by Serb paramilitaries,[38] leading Muslim villagers (around 800 of them) to flee for their lives.[39] Simultaneously, the situation throughout Montenegro appeared to be worsening. Indeed, following an increase in violent incidents throughout Montenegro, Harun Hadžić, the leader of the Montenegrin SDA, appealed to Momir Bulatović to provide a personal guarantee for the security of Muslims who, Hadžić claimed, had been subjected to attacks in Bijelo Polje, Berane, Nikšić and Podgorica.[40]

The events in Pljevlja (and certainly Bukovica) went largely unreported at the time, and the Montenegrin government did little of substance to tackle the problems caused by the presence of the paramilitaries. They were, however, forced to take an interest in events in Pljevlja after the situation threatened to spiral out of control during an attempted 'coup d'état' by Dačević's paramilitaries. The town's police, who had previously appeared unable to protect the Muslim population of Pljevlja, arrested Dačević for his actions – the response was precisely as they had feared. In the wake of the arrest, his armed militia threatened to turn their guns towards the town's remaining Muslims unless he was released, and a dangerous stand-off ensued. This alarming situation was deemed sufficiently serious for the new president of the SRJ, Dobrica Ćosić, and the Montenegrin president, Momir Bulatović, to visit the town in an attempt to find a resolution.[41] In the office of the mayor of Pljevlja, they attempted to negotiate with Dačević and, conversely, sought guarantees from local Muslim leaders that they would not 'continue to seek autonomy', but such was the fear among Muslims in Pljevlja that no one dared utter the word.[42] Bulatović, for his part, argued that the Montenegrin government had an obligation to stem the kind of mutual interethnic hostility playing out so violently in Bosnia from becoming a reality in northern Montenegro; 'We have', he said, 'made enough of such errors in the past'.[43] Satisfied that they had achieved their objective, Ćosić and Bulatović left the town, giving assurances that Muslims would be protected and that Yugoslav Army (*Vojska Jugoslavije* – VJ) units would patrol Pljevlja and surrounding areas.[44] Yet prior and subsequent events suggested that these promises were rather hollow.[45] Afraid of their lives, many departed fearing repercussions emanating from Dačević's arrest. Many were convinced that the fate of the Muslim village of Bukovica, near Pljevlja, was additionally demonstrative of the inability of Ćosić, Bulatović and the VJ to rein in the paramilitaries.[46]

Throughout the war in Bosnia & Herzegovina, and despite the cooling of tensions in Pljevlja, other criminal acts against Muslims were perpetrated. The worst of these took place on 27 February 1993, though it was carried out not by Montenegrin citizen of Dačević's ilk, but by members of a Bosnian Serb paramilitary group from Višegrad known as *Osvetnici* (Avengers) – an informal volunteer unit that was also part of the *Belo orlovi* (White Eagles) paramilitary group. Led by cousins Milan and Sredoje Lukić, members of this notorious gang (which had engaged in a murderous rampage against Muslims in Višegrad in the summer of 1992) entered Štrpci, a village nestled on the border between Bosnia and Montenegro, and demanded that train No. 671 'Lovćen', which was en route to Bar (on the Montenegrin coast) from Belgrade, be stopped when it reached the platform.[47] As the train was bought to a halt, a number of Lukić's group climbed aboard the train, identified and seized eighteen Muslims and one Croat, before spiriting them across the border to Višegrad, where they were subsequently murdered near the village of Preljevo and their bodies thrown in the Drina River.[48] In October 1993, a parliamentary commission was established in the Montenegrin government, led by the SDP member of the Montenegrin Assembly, Dragiša Burzan. Though their work was initially met with some resistance, they did much to illuminate, and bring to public attention, the grim events of February 1993.[49]

There were also further isolated incidents throughout Montenegro. Pljevlja, for example, remained tense after the events of July and August 1992, though the kind of incidents seen in the town during the summer were not repeated. Pavle Bulatović's replacement as interior minister, Nikola Pejaković, acknowledged that Pljevlja had become a 'critical location' allowing paramilitaries to travel from the SRJ into Bosnia & Herzegovina, but argued that the situation was 'not an expression of local interethnic tolerance'.[50] The arrest of Čeko Dačević by Montenegrin police on 22 September 1992 led to a trial in the Bijelo Polje court (during which time he was elected as an SRS deputy in the Federal Parliament of the SRJ).[51] Astonishingly, he was acquitted of the charges against him (that he engaged in 'terrorist activities') and was thus free to return to Pljevlja. In the meantime, attacks against Muslims in the Pljevlja area continued, with reports of intimidation and violence against individuals and damage to religious buildings, including the Husein Paša mosque which was targeted on Orthodox Christmas Day 1993 (the automatic gunfire allegedly emanating from the nearby Hotel Pljevlja).[52] Later, in May 1993, while Dačević's appointment as 'Vojvoda' was being celebrated by the party leader, Vojislav Šešelj (who had visited the town for an SRS rally), his supporters shot at a van carrying Muslim civilians, four of whom were injured, in the village of Zenica near Pljevlja.[53] And while Dačević was swiftly arrested (again) by the police, he was freed soon after, having been provided with an alibi by witnesses who claimed Dačević was drinking with them in a local *kafana* (bar) at the time of the shootings.[54] In the same month, there were also incidents in Nikšić, where a mosque was blown up and Muslim houses were targeted by Serb nationalist extremists (the random shootings led to the unintended death of 36-year-old Branka Djukanović).[55]

On 13 July 1993 (the fifty-second anniversary of the anti-fascist uprising against the Italian occupation of Montenegro), Željko Ražnjatović' (Arkan), who was accompanied by his wife, the popular turbo-folk singer 'Ceca', bodyguards, supporters and a small number of Serbian Orthodox clergy, took a trip through Plav and Gusinje following a meeting of his political party, the Party of Serbian Unity (*Stranka srpskog jedinstva* – SSJ), in Andrijevica. Visiting the town on the invitation of Damjan Turković (himself from Plav), the head of the security centre in Berane, Arkan's convoy of cars and jeeps passed through the area, its members behaving in a highly provocative manner, chanting anti-

Muslim slogans such as *Ili se krstite, ili se seliste* (be baptized or re-locate) and nationalist slogans such as *Ovo je Srbija!* (This is Serbia!). The entourage stopped in the centre of Plav and 'dined' noisily at the Muslim-owned *Gradska kafana* (City Bar) before departing the town, leaving the Muslim population feeling frightened and vulnerable.[56]

While life had been extremely difficult for Montenegro's Muslims in places like Pljevlja, Plav, Gusinje, Berane, Plužine, Nikšić and Podgorica throughout 1992, the situation was even worse for those Bosnian Muslims (and for Bosnian Serbs escaping the military draft) who had fled to Montenegro seeking sanctuary. As the war in Bosnia & Herzegovina escalated throughout April and May 1992, thousands (particularly from Foča) crossed the border into Montenegro, many to Muslim-majority towns such as Plav and Gusinje, many others to the coastal towns of Herceg Novi, Bar and Ulcinj, where many had worked in the tourist or construction trade before the war. Several hundred arrived later in Podgorica, where they sought immediate shelter in the mosques in the city's Stara Varoš district.[57] They believed they would be safe there, but it was a dangerous illusion. It was to prove, in the words of the Montenegrin investigative journalist, Šeki Radončić, a 'fatal freedom'.[58] In May 1992, there began a process, initiated by the Montenegrin interior minister, Pavle Bulatović, whereby Bosnian Muslim refugees were hunted down by the police (with the assistance of Serb refugees known as 'bloodhounds') in Herceg Novi, Bar, Ulcinj, Podgorica, Plav and Gusinje, processed at local 'security centres', taken to Plužine near the border with Bosnia & Herzegovina and then deported either to Foča or to Bratunac.[59] In so doing, the Montenegrin police responsible for executing the orders (Damjan Turković, and others) sent many to their deaths – they were delivered into the hands of forces loyal to the Bosnian Serb leader, Radovan Karadžić (himself a Montenegrin, born in a small village of Petnjica near Šanvik).[60] The bodies of some of those deported were recovered many years later in mass graves. Those who were key players in the deportations went unpunished. Pavle Bulatović became the SRJ's interior minister before becoming Montenegro's defence minister in 1993, while Damjan Turković was promoted to head of the Berane Security Centre, where he would continue to use his power to intimidate Montenegro's own Muslim population. Momir Bulatović stated (and has always maintained) that the deportations were 'a tragic mistake' and that they were ended as soon as he was informed of them.

While those deported from Montenegro to Bosnia & Herzegovina were jailed or murdered in the latter, there were occasional murders in Montenegro itself, though not carried out by Montenegrin citizens.[61] On 6 July 1992, three members of one family (Hasan Klapuh, his wife, Feriha, and daughter, Sena) were murdered and their bodies thrown into the Piva canyon near the border town of Plužine. They had paid to be driven from Foča to Podgorica by a group of Bosnian Serbs – who were part of the Foča-based 'Dragan Nikolić' unit of the Army of Republika Srpska (*Vojska Republike Srpske* – VRS) – but never reached the Montenegrin capital. Instead, they were driven through the border post at Sćepan Polje into Montenegro before the car they were travelling in stopped at the Obrad Cicmil bridge near Plužine. There, Hasan Klapuh was shot in the head (killing him instantly); his wife and daughter were also shot. Thereafter, all three were thrown into the nearby Piva canyon, though both Feriha and Sena Klapuh were still alive at the time. After the murders, the group 'celebrated' in a *kafana* in Plužine before travelling back across the border towards Foča.[62]

However, Montenegrin police were forced to act, after the bodies of the three were found by a highway maintenance worker (who had followed the trail of blood). In a landmark war crimes trial, five members of the group – Zoran Vuković and Radomir Kovac, both of whom were later indicted and sentenced by the International Criminal Tribunal for the Former Yugoslavia (ICTY), Janko 'Tuta' Janjić, Zoran Simović and Vidoje Golubić – were sentenced for crimes committed in Foča.[63] The latter was the only one present during proceedings (having been arrested in Plužine in August 1992 while visitng his wife and daughter), and he was sentenced to eight months in prison, having made the case that he tried to stop the killing of Feriha and Sena Klapuh. He acknowledged, however, that he had been unable to assert control over Janjić, who Golubić claimed, threatened to kill him if he did not 'keep quiet' (Golubić acknowledged during the trial that he was frightened of Janjić, who had gained significant notoriety in Foča as a hardened, ruthless criminal).[64] The other four were sentenced (in absentia) to twenty years each, though they remained in Foča and never served the sentences handed down for the murder of the Klapuh family. The trial stemmed the traffic of armed Bosnian Serbs crossing the border into Montenegro, and, after Slobodan Milošević's break with Radovan Karadžić and the Bosnian Serb leadership after the failure of the Bosnian Serb Assembly to ratify the Vance-Owen Peace Plan (VOPP), the border between Montenegro and Bosnia & Herzegovina was patrolled by the European Community Monitoring Mission (ECMM), making it far harder for armed individuals or groups to cross what had once been a rather porous border.[65]

Amid such horrors, the pressure increased on Montenegro's Muslims/Bosniaks – particularly on the leadership of the Montenegrin branch of the SDA. Accusations that Muslims/Bosniaks from Sandžak were engaged in preparing an insurrection abounded, and in June 1993, charges were raised against the SDA leadership in Serbia. As a consequence, the Serbian SDA leader, Sulejman Ugljanin (who had endeavoured to internationalize 'The Sandžak Question'), fled Serbia and temporarily relocated to Turkey.[66] Other members of his party were arrested and faced a judicial process knowns as the 'Novi Pazar trials'. In Montenegro, in January 1994, during the so-called *Akcija Lim* (Operation Lim), twenty-six members of the Montenegrin SDA (among them Harun Hadžić (the SDA leader from Rožaje), Hakija Muratović and Isad Skenderović (party functionaries in Berane), and Ibrahim Čikić from Bijelo Polje (who was charged with, 'in the event of war', plotting to blow up bridges – despite being partially sighted) were arrested.[67] Others were arrested by the police in Bijelo Polje, Rožaje and Pljevlja, albeit without formal charge.[68] The so-called 'Bijelo Polje Group' (their trial took place in the town) were collectively charged with conspiring to undermine the territorial integrity of the SRJ by clandestinely and unconstitutionally organizing the forceful secession of Sandžak.[69] The trial took place in a highly charged and politicized context; the war in neighbouring Bosnia was raging, and news of Muslim atrocities against Serbs (in some cases of which volunteers from the Sandžak were implicated) increased hostility towards Muslims throughout Serbia and Montenegro. Such conditions effectively negated the possibility of anything resembling a fair and balanced judicial process.[70]

At the conclusion of the trial, and after a series of controversies (including a hunger strike by the accused), twenty-one members of the Montenegrin SDA were sentenced to a total of eighty-seven years imprisonment.[71] Those imprisoned included SDA members of the Montenegrin Assembly, as well as Harun Hadžić, the party's leader. But as the *Monitor* journalist Esad Kočan sardonically remarked, the haul of weapons gathered as a consequence of 'Operation Lim' was rather limited, adding that 'when any festival is celebrated in Podgorica, more shots are fired from weapons of different calibres, in front of the police themselves than the SDA leaders could, at this pace, have collected in a hundred years.'[72] The jailed SDA members claimed not only that they had been subject to torture while serving their 'sentences', but that they had been framed by the Montenegrin police.[73] Fearing for their lives, some Muslims resorted to buying weapons, despite calls by local Muslim political leaders not to do so, lest they be 'framed' by the Montenegrin police. In November 1994, however, Montenegrin police arrested nineteen Muslims/Bosniaks for allegedly attempting to procure arms through 'illegal channels'.[74] However, the imprisoned Montenegrin SDA members were subsequently pardoned (and awarded financial compensation) by Momir Bulatović, in 1996, by which time the political landscape was on the cusp of dramatic change, although it would take another year for the catharsis to become manifest.[75]

In the meantime, pressure on Montenegro's Muslims/Bosniaks eased somewhat after the signing of the Dayton Agreement in November 1995 (which brought the war in neighbouring Bosnia & Herzegovina to an end), but it was later internal (Montenegrin) developments that brought the Muslim/Bosniak community and their political representatives back into the political mainstream. In the meantime, however, tension remained and occasionally resurfaced.[76] The town of Plav, located in an area of tremendous natural beauty and peppered with its ornate mosques (the minarets constructed of wood), seemed an unlikely place for an outbreak of football violence.[77] But on 26 May 1996, during a Montenegrin *druga liga* (second division) football match in Plav between the local team FK Jezero and KF Komovi from Andrijevica, *Plavjani* (citizens of Plav) witnessed significant crowd trouble and a heavy-handed police intervention. As the supporters of FK Komovi arrived in Plav, the atmosphere darkened.[78] During the game, nationalist slogans were chanted by both sets of supporters and the temperature rose inexorably towards the end of the game.[79] A brawl between players fuelled crowd trouble, which led to an intervention by an interior ministry (*Ministarstvo unutrašnjih poslova* – MUP) special unit led by Damjan Turković, then head of the security centre in Berane.[80] The police entered the part of the stadium occupied by the *Hajvani* (supporters of FK Jezero), and as they scrambled to safety, the force of the crowd caused a fence to collapse crushing many underneath. The police then continued to harass FK Jezero supporters outside the ground (which is located within the town) and throughout the centre of Plav, rounding up the 'perpetrators' of the unrest and subjecting them to beatings.[81] In the wake of the events, the FK Jezero captain, Branko Rakočević, claimed that the normal crowd had been supplemented by 'hired fans' who were there specifically to cause trouble and that the entire violent manifestation had been organized by MUP in advance of the game.[82]

While tensions remained, the Muslim/Bosniak population of Montenegro were to experience something of a change in fortunes. In early 1997, intra-elite conflicts within the ranks of the monolithic DPS inexorably led to a split that would fundamentally alter the dynamics of Montenegrin politics (see Chapter 5) and have significant consequences for Muslims/Bosniaks in Montenegro. The SDA would split over whether to engage in the election process, allowing for Djukanović faction of the DPS to gain greater power and leverage in places such as Rožaje, where support for the SDA had traditionally been strong. Djukanović, who would become one of the two central figures (the other being Momir Bulatović) in the DPS drama, had long been suspected of secessionist tendencies by pro-Serb parties and pro-Serb factions within the DPS. Prime Minister Djukanović had been pragmatic, and he had already sought to give the impression that he would work pro-actively to improve the situation for Muslims/Bosniaks in the Pljevlja area by giving assurances to the UN's special rapporteur to the former Yugoslavia, Elisabeth Rehn, that his government would endeavour to develop the economic infrastructure of the Bukovica area (near Pljevlja) and open a new police station to improve the security situation.[83] By then, of course, Djukanović had already begun plotting his challenge to Bulatović and Milošević, and his flirtation with Muslim/Bosniak leaders (whose support he would later need) predated the intra-party crisis that would engulf the DPS in 1997.[84] Thereafter, Montenegro's Muslims/Bosniaks (and Albanians) would prove a vital ally for Djukanović in his political battles with both Bulatović and Milošević.[85]

Montenegro's Albanian community

Relations between the state and Montenegro's Albanian community were conducted in a less hostile, but no less problematic, atmosphere. The Albanians of Montenegro were (after those in Kosovo, Macedonia and Southern Serbia) the fourth largest grouping of ethnic Albanians in the SFRJ.[86] They comprised, according to 1991 census, 7.1 per cent of the population and were concentrated in areas bordering Albania proper: Plav, Gusinje, within the Tuzi/Malesija area of the Podgorica municipality, and the Albanian-majority coastal town of Ulcinj. The majority of Albanians in Montenegro are Muslim, with a smaller percentage (around one-third) adhering to the Catholic faith.[87] Many of the Albanian regions of Montenegro became incorporated into the then independent Montenegrin state during the reign of Prince (later King) Nikola I Petrović in 1878, following the Congress of Berlin, and, later, as a consequence of the 1912–1913 Balkans Wars (whereupon Plav and Gusinje were also incorporated into Montenegro). The Albanians of Montenegro speak the *Gheg* dialect of Albanian (as do their ethnic kin in northern Albania), though almost all also spoke 'Serbo-Croat', the official language of the SFRJ. In that Yugoslav state, Albanians were defined as a 'nationality' but not as a 'constituent nation', though the status of Albanians was generally good – particularly in the wake of the 1974 constitutional revisions, which gave Kosovo a significant level of autonomy. In Montenegro, the Albanian population was well established: Radio Titograd broadcast an Albanian-language programme (and there were, albeit unrealized, plans for an Albanian-language TV programme), and the Albanian-language weekly *Koha* (Time) was published in Titograd from 1978 onward (though its largest readership was in Ulcinj).[88]

Initial problems between the Montenegrin leadership and the republic's Albanian community emerged in the early 1980s, following the student demonstrations and subsequent riots in Kosovo in 1981, during which some demonstrators called for

Kosovo to be given the status of a republic within the SFRJ. The impact on Montenegro's Albanians was significant, and in the subsequent crackdown, two teachers (one from Plav, the other from Ulcinj) were expelled from the SKCG and put on trial for disseminating 'hostile propaganda'.[89] And with rising Serb nationalism in the 1980s, Albanians in Kosovo, Southern Serbia (Preševo and Bujanovac) Macedonia and Montenegro grew increasingly concerned about their status and, later, their security.[90] Throughout the 1980s, Montenegrin Albanians began to leave the SFRJ, attempting to seek work as *gastarbeiters* (guest workers) in West Germany or the United States.[91] While relations were, at times, tense, the Albanians of Montenegro were not subject per se to the kind of treatment Montenegro's Muslims had experienced in places such as Pljevlja, Plav, Bijelo Polje, Berane and Gusinje (though Albanians in the latter were the subject of allegations that they had been involved in providing logistical support to their ethnic kin in Kosovo). Albanian grievances were, on the whole, focused on the alleged suppression of their (Albanian) flag and the use of national symbols which they asserted represented attempts to rob them of their identity. Moreover, they claimed, they were under-represented in all state and public institutions.[92] Nevertheless, with the advent of multiparty elections in Montenegro in 1990, exclusively ethnic Albanian parties emerged, the first of which was the Democratic League of Montenegro (*Demokratski savez u Crnoj Gori* – DSCG/*Lidhja Demokratike në Mal të Zi* – LDMZ). Though formed in Titograd (Podgorica), the party was most active in the predominantly ethnic Albanian coastal town of Ulcinj. It was led by Mehmet Bardhi (as president) and soon established itself as the main ethnic Albanian party in Montenegro. DSCG/LDMZ also played a key role within the umbrella organization known as 'The Democratic Forum of Albanians'. Together with the SDA they united under the title of the *Demokratska koalicja* (Democratic Coalition) to contest the 1990 elections, in which they gained 10 per cent of the popular vote.[93]

There were issues to contend with, however. As the SFRJ disintegrated, there were tensions in the Montenegrin–Albanian border area, particularly around the *Prokletije* (Damned) mountains. Since the fall of the communist regime of Ramiz Alia (the successor to the long-serving leader of communist Albania, Enver Hoxha) in Albania in December 1990, the border had been subject to incursions as Albanians (from Albania) used a number of routes to cross (the border) into Montenegro.[94] There were an increasing number of incidents, mainly robberies, in the border area, forcing the Montenegrin president, Momir Bulatović, to state that serious measures were being taken by his government to deal with the smuggling of people and arms.[95] In March 1992, one Montenegrin border guard was killed and one seriously injured while patrolling the area. While this incident was regarded by the Montenegrin government as a failure by their Albanian counterparts to manage their own border, and was not a source of significant tension between the Montenegrin government and the Albanian population in Montenegro (nor was it used to increase tensions in the areas near the border), it was demonstrative of ongoing problems.[96] In the same month, however, rumours began circulating alleging that the DSCG were planning to organize a referendum on autonomy, similar to that previously organized by the MNVS in the Sandžak in October 1991.[97] By this time the military operations in the Dubrovnik area had begun, and Albanians also felt the impact of this. According to Jovan Nikolaidis, this period 'was marked by an exodus of young Albanians [from Montenegro] who sought asylum throughout Europe'.

At the same time, he said, 'Armed Serbian volunteers on their way to the Dubrovnik front gathered in the city of Ulcinj. Bursts of machine gun fire delivered by drunken soldiers disturbed its citizens throughout the nights – [but] they kept silent and endured.'[98]

Yet while rumours of an alleged referendum on autonomy were largely unsubstantiated (though the leader of the DSCG, Mehmet Bhardi, did not deny outright such plans), the leadership of the DSCG had actively encouraged its supporters not to participate in the Montenegrin referendum (on the formation of the SRJ) on 1 March 1992 (they also boycotted the May 1992 SRJ federal elections).[99] The party, in essence, were not advocating a 'Greater Albania' solution to the problems of the Albanian communities in the SRJ, but they did support an independent Montenegro (on the basis that such a state would provide greater minority rights for Montenegro's Albanians). This position and the widespread Albanian boycott of the referendum led to an impromptu 'visit' to Ulcinj by Vojislav Šešelj and his *Beli orlovi* paramilitary group during which they 'strolled' through the city and surrounding villages, intimidating Albanians and providing Serbs and Montenegrins with arms – after which Albanians joined the DSCG in significant numbers.[100] In a potentially explosive political climate, the DSCG considered their options, and perhaps understanding that being overly assertive might lead to greater conflicts they published and released a document entitled 'The Memorandum on the Special Status of Albanians in Montenegro'. The memorandum's central claim was that the Albanian minority (both Muslim and Catholic) was politically marginalized and that Albanians faced discrimination in all areas of public life, even in parts of Montenegro where they represented either a relative or absolute majority.[101] The memorandum was, however, widely condemned in Montenegro, and lambasted in the Serbian press.[102] And despite receiving significant public attention, it was shelved after the failure of Albanian parties to win seats in the 1994 Montenegrin parliamentary elections, although the issues raised within it were briefly revived in the wake of these elections, as the DSCG/LDMZ again argued that discrimination continued.[103]

The second Albanian party to emerge was the Democratic Union of Albanians (*Demokratska unija Albanaca* – DUA/*Unioni Demokratik i Shqiptarëve* – UDSH), formed in Ulcinj in November 1996. The DUA, led by Ferhat Dinosha, pledged to recognize the territorial integrity of Montenegro and stated their willingness to respect the Montenegrin state. Simultaneously, however, it called upon the Montenegrin government to recognize the equality of the Albanians as constituent people. However, as political dynamics changed with the DPS split in 1997, Albanians played a key role in ensuring the victory of Milo Djukanović in the subsequent presidential elections and the post-split (Djukanović-controlled) DPS in the parliamentary elections in 1998. Since then, ethnic Albanian parties have benefited from specific arrangements which acknowledged the 'special' status of Albanians, ensuring the participation of Albanian deputies in the Montenegrin parliament.[104] The Albanian community would prove a staunch ally of Djukanović throughout the 1998/99 war in Kosovo and, thereafter, allies in the DPS-led independence project, which would culminate in the Montenegrin independence referendum of May 2006.

5

A Polity Divided: The DPS Split (1996–98)

Milo, Sveto, Milica – su za Jugoslavija a ne za diktaturu!
(Milo, Sveto, Milica – they're for Yugoslavia but not for the dictatorship!)

Milo – Turčine, Sveto – lopove!
(Milo is a Turk, Sveto is a thief!)

These competing slogans (heard throughout the intra-party crisis that emerged in 1997) perfectly sum up the divisions that would split the DPS. By then the bonds that held the monolithic ruling DPS were becoming weaker, and tensions increasingly manifest. Moreover, while the period between 1990 and late 1996 was essentially marked by relative consensus between the two ruling parties in Serbia (the SPS) and Montenegro (the DPS) on the functioning of the SRJ, the period thereafter (following the cathartic split within the DPS) was marked by serious political conflicts between these hitherto allies.[1] In the wake of the signing of the Dayton Agreement in late 1995, which brought the war in neighbouring Bosnia & Herzegovina to an end, some within the DPS began to incrementally distance (and, ultimately, disassociate) themselves from the policies of Slobodan Milošević and the SPS. Problematically, however, there existed no consensus within the DPS vis-à-vis the future political orientation of Montenegro. Despite the increasing dissatisfaction, the DPS had settled into a period of unchallenged dominance and any conflict with Milošević would almost certainly shatter the comfortable co existence that had become the normal state of affairs. Yet the lack of consensus about the future orientation of the party (and of Montenegro) could not be concealed indefinitely. This emergent bifurcation would result in increasingly heated intra-party debates and, eventually, function as a kernel for a struggle that would engulf the party, divide it into two factions, cause bitter political struggles and set Montenegro on a different political trajectory.

The basis of the intra-DPS conflict was the emerging difference of opinion about Montenegro's status within the SRJ. Some within the party, particularly those close to Milo Djukanović, had long denied allegations that they were dissatisfied with Montenegro's 'junior partner' role within the federation (denying, moreover, that they were in favour of greater autonomy for Montenegro within it). But Djukanović's occasional trips to the United States in the early and mid-1990s had become the source of rumour and speculation: In short, had the Montenegrin prime minister been offered him a deal by the United States to pursue Montenegro's separation from Serbia?[2] Had they promised him something in exchange for agreeing to do so? Djukanović, of course, consistently refuted such allegations and denied that any such conversations had taken place, stating in the Belgrade weekly *Vreme*, for example, that 'there is not a single reason to believe such a promise, which, indeed, no-one has made'.[3] The speculations and allegations continued, however. While visiting the United States (including a trip to the Pentagon) in November 1995, it was alleged that Djukanović and Svetozar Marović had offered the port of Bar to NATO peacekeeping forces in Bosnia & Herzegovina.[4] Thereafter, in May 1996, Djukanović was again in the United States, this time on a (seemingly) much higher-level visit. He visited the White House, the Congress and had meetings with representatives from the World Bank and the International Monetary Fund (IMF). He was also alleged to have met with the billionaire businessman and philanthropist George Soros, again fuelling speculation about the motives of the Montenegrin prime minister.[5] Whatever, the substance of the discussions Djukanović may have had in the United States, it was clear that some within the DPS were openly engaging with the United States and, thus, moving further away from Milošević. And they were doing so without broad party consensus.

The shift in Djukanović's rhetoric was increasingly evident. In a speech to the Montenegrin Assembly in July 1996, he hinted at his new course, emphasizing the importance of establishing better relations with its regional neighbours and with the international community, particularly the United States (while implying that by being part of the SRJ, Montenegro was blackened by association).[6] In essence, he posited that Montenegro's best interests would be served by moving closer to the European Union (EU) and the United States, signalling that it may do so within or without the structure of the SRJ – this would, of course, lead to conflict with Slobodan Milošević. While causing convulsions among some within the DPS, it was a message warmly received by the United States, which saw Djukanović as an important factor in their endeavours to undermine and weaken Milošević from the SRJ's peripheries. A Montenegrin leadership opposed to Milošević would, after all, be a useful tool for US regional objectives – to attempt to unite and bolster the Serbian opposition within Serbia itself (including Bosniak parties in the Sandžak),[7] to offer support to Ibrahim Rugova (the de facto leader of the Kosovo Albanians) in Kosovo and to encourage the Montenegrin government to distance itself from Belgrade.[8]

Djukanović's pro-Western rhetoric was matched by his increasingly critical comments about Milošević. Indeed, a small number of key DPS members close to Djukanović became more vocal in their condemnation of him in the wake of the November 1996 Serbian elections, during which the Serbian opposition accused Milošević of electoral fraud (an alleged fraud that Djukanovic, whose relationship with Milošević had been deteriorating since the beginning of 1994, called 'the last straw').[9] Such a development further destabilized increasingly strained relations *between* the SRJ's republics while simultaneously increasing tensions *within* the DPS. Such tensions were manifest when, on 30 January 1997, Zoran Lilić, the then president of the SRJ, visited Podgorica in an attempt to improve the rapidly deteriorating relations between Serbia and Montenegro. Upon arrival in Podgorica, Lilić was met by protestors (organized, he claimed, by Djukanović) who 'threw tomatoes and other such things' at the convoy carrying his delegation.[10] His experience in Podgorica was doubtless unpleasant, but it was simply a portent of things to come.[11]

Cleavages were now becoming visible within the upper echelons of the DPS, a reality clearly manifested by the dynamics between erstwhile allies, the Montenegrin president, Momir Bulatović and the prime minister Milo Djukanović. In the wake of the 1996 Serbian elections, a 'difference of opinion' regarding how official Podgorica should react to the events in Serbia became increasingly evident. While Bulatović continued to support Milošević, Djukanović saw an opportunity to exploit Milošević's weakness – and he now embarked upon the biggest gamble of his relatively short political career. Long excluded from Milošević's inner circle, in essence persona non grata, Djukanović's relations with the Serbian president (and his wife, Mira Marković) were, at best, strained.[12] Djukanović had often exchanged barbs with Marković and just as frequently criticized her party 'Yugoslav Left' (*Jugoslovenska levica* – JUL) party, which he stated were a party 'devoted to an ideologically retrograde and abstract society', a remark that elicited a sharp response from Marković, who, in response, labelled Djukanović a 'smuggler employed as a prominent politician'.[13] So while the pretext for a conflict between Djukanović and Milošević had already been established, the alleged electoral fraud following the November 1996 elections in Serbia would be the fuse.

The conflict did not become 'open' until Djukanović expressed his support for the *Zajedno* (Together) coalition and their anti-Milošević protests, which were taking place throughout Serbia in the wake of the November elections. Both Milo Djukanović and his close ally Svetozar Marović saw the *Zajedno* protests as the beginning of the end for Milošević and sought to capitalize on his perceived weakness.[14] But while Djukanović's early statements may only have implied support for the protestors, there was little ambiguity in his very public pronouncements that Milošević himself was, politically speaking, a spent force. As the *Zajedno* protests in Belgrade and other Serbian cities were putting pressure on the Milošević regime, Djukanović calculated that the opportune moment had been reached. Utilizing the widely read Belgrade political weekly *Vreme* as the forum, he unambiguously asserted that Milošević was 'a man of obsolete political ideas, lacking the ability to form a strategic vision of the problems this country is facing, surrounded by unsuitable individuals who are following the time-tested method of many authoritarian regimes'.[15] Milošević immediately 'returned the serve', accusing Djukanović of being in the service of foreign interests.[16] This was followed by a focused and orchestrated campaign by media loyal to Milošević. Djukanović was cast as a traitor and a criminal, deeply involved in illegal activities (in particular his alleged involvement in lucrative cigarette smuggling and his links with the Italian mafia) during the height of the UN-imposed sanctions. Broadly, Milošević sought to portray Djukanović as an individual without morals – an opportunist, interested primarily in consolidating his power and 'capturing' the Montenegrin republic. By way of response, Djukanović sent a letter offering his explicit support to students in Belgrade, who were the bulwark of the *Zajedno* protests.

In Montenegro, Djukanović's controversial actions had caused convulsions within the DPS, the membership of which was, in the main, cautious about engaging in open conflict with Milošević. While Djukanović's and, to a lesser extent, Marović's statements had clearly fuelled a worsening conflict with the Serbian president, the Montenegrin president, Momir Bulatović, chose not to follow the same path of conflict, perhaps expecting that the Serbian president would overcome the crisis, as he had done in the past. Publicly, the leadership of the DPS retained a superficial visage of unity, with Djukanović claiming that although there had been a worsening of relations between him (and his closest allies) and Milošević, there was no significant schism within the DPS itself. Bulatović, Marović and himself were, he said, 'in full agreement on all of the most important strategic issues'.[17] But despite the rather hollow and unconvincing rhetoric of unity, the split was becoming increasingly manifest.

By March 1997, it appeared that the party was on the verge of a bitter split.[18] Intra-party relations had become so strained that on 24 March, during the first meeting of the *Glavni odbor* (Main Board) of the DPS since Djukanović had publicly denounced Milošević, a vote was called among board members to decipher the future direction of the party.[19] This meeting – held ostensibly to discuss matters pertaining to wider political, economic and social issues – instead became an intra-party debate on the implications of Djukanović's position vis-à-vis Milošević.[20] The majority of members of the main board were, at least initially, unconvinced of the wisdom of generating an open confrontation with Milošević.[21] As a result, Djukanović was lambasted by a number of his DPS colleagues for comments he made in *Vreme* and during a recent visit to Washington D.C. Opposed by the majority, Djukanović stated his case, reiterating the need for the Montenegrin government to distance themselves from Milošević.[22] Bulatović (who later confessed that he had been instructed by Milošević, and was obliged to 'remove' Djukanović) decided that the time was ripe for a showdown, and following lengthy discussion the main board voted on whether to remove Djukanović. On this occasion, Bulatović's pro-Milošević stance was convincingly confirmed (of the ninety-nine members, sixty voted in favour, seven voted against and twenty-two abstained). This was, seemingly, an overwhelming endorsement of Bulatović's position within the DPS and Djukanović's weakness. Djukanovic argued that the debate (and thus the final result of the vote) became skewed by the perception (engineered by the Bulatović faction) that the Montenegrin president was *for* Yugoslavia, while Djukanović was *against* it – this was not, he claimed, representative of the reality.[23] Nevertheless, Djukanović, undermined by the course of the debate and the subsequent outcome of the vote, resigned as vice president of the DPS.

The matter, it appeared, had been brought to an end, and at the conclusion of the meeting of the main board Momir Bulatović announced that the party remained committed to maintaining the status quo in Montenegro's direction. There was, he said, 'no alternative way, no alternative programme or solution', adding that 'a referendum [on independence]' was simply 'out of the question'. We are, he said, 'continuing along the path we have embarked upon'.[24] Yet, the seemingly convincing endorsement of Bulatović's policy was, however, not as convincing as it may have appeared. Among the seven members of the DPS main board that had voted for Djukanović (and the twenty-two that had abstained) were some of the most powerful individuals in the party.[25] Crucially, Vukašin Maraš,[26] the chief of Montenegro's state security (*Služba državne bezbednosti* – SDB), and Svetozar Marović, speaker of the Montenegrin Assembly and the vice president of the DPS, backed Djukanović.[27] Over the subsequent months, they would prove key factors in convincing wavering DPS members (and even those who had initially voted for Momir Bulatović) that their best interests, and the interests of Montenegro, would be best served by supporting Djukanović. As an intense (and largely hidden) internal-party power struggle ensued, a number of influential party members came under pressure to change their positions. Between April and June 1997, Djukanović forged a powerful coalition of individuals with significant establishment interests, while wresting control (or attempting to maintain control) of the SDB, state media (while reaching out to the opposition).[28] But there were also setbacks during these endeavours: foremost among them Bulatović's attempts to pass legislation that would mean that the SDB were under a 'triple lock' control system in which the president (as well as a cross-party independent board) would have more oversight into their activities. Bulatović also succeeded, following his victory in the 24 March vote on the question of the DPS's 'Yugoslav platform', in the enablement of Milošević's proposal to amend the SRJ's constitution (Articles 97 and 98) which would eradicate the requirement of the SRJ Assembly to approve the election of federal president (thus making it possible for Milošević to become SRJ president).[29]

Weeks of political conflict followed, and in many respects Bulatović had the upper hand, in that he still controlled state media (RTCG and *Pobjeda*). But, as a battle for control of state media ensued, that grip would weaken significantly.[30] Indeed, in July 1997, Bulatović's ally and editor-in-chief of Montenegrin state television, Vladislav Ašanin, was forced out by the organization's management board. This was followed by more pressure and back-room deals in advance of the critical DPS main board meeting on 11 July 1997. It was the last time the party would assemble as the monolithic party that had held power since 1990. The primary purpose was to confirm the party's candidate for nomination for the presidency. Both Bulatović and Djukanović were bidding to be the candidate, though the DPS could only nominate one candidate. The meeting was marked by hostility between pro-Bulatović and pro-Djukanović factions from the outset, with both sides set to make their cases for their respective candidates. The meeting (involving all of the DPS Main Board), however, ended before it began. Having had their demand that the media be present throughout the session be rejected, Bulatović and his supporters walked out. Thus, their departure left the remaining sixty-two members of the main board (just one member short of the required two-thirds majority) in the chamber to continue with the business at hand.[31] And at the close of the session, the remaining members of the main board motioned that Bulatović be removed from his position as president of the party and replaced by Milica Pejanović-Djurišić. Djukanović, seemingly defeated following the 24 March meeting, had wrested control of the DPS with the support majority of the party's main board. Bulatović and his allies now prepared their next move, but the key question remained – who were the DPS now? And who would keep control over party mechanisms and, of course, retain the DPS 'brand'?

The 1997 presidential campaign

While Djukanović was confirmed as the DPS candidate for the presidential elections, Bulatović announced that he, too, would be contesting the election as a DPS candidate. His first rally, in Kolašin in early August 1997, drew relatively large crowds.[32] This rather unusual 'pre-election infrastructure' (normally each party could only put one candidate forward for election) was permitted by Montenegro's Republican Electoral Commission because the DPS was registered as both a republican party (in Montenegro) and at federal (SRJ) level – thus Djukanović was the candidate for the former, Bulatović for the latter.[33] But although both candidates were from, ostensibly, the same party, they offered two entirely different political programmes. Djukanović's wing of the DPS took the early initiative, reaching out to opposition parties – Slavko Perović's LSCG, Novak Kilibarda's NS (who had run together as the coalition *Narodna sloga* in the 1996 parliamentary elections), the SDP, and the SDA, DSCG and DUA.[34] Collectively, they drafted an *Agreement on Minimum Principles for the Development of Democratic Infrastructure in Montenegro*. Signed on 1 September 1997, the agreement had two primary functions: to guarantee 'transparent, free and fair elections in the future', while simultaneously establishing the formation of an anti-Milošević (and anti-Bulatović) 'political alliance'.[35] Supporters of neither Djukanović nor Bulatović, the party leadership of the LSCG had vociferously opposed the DPS throughout the early 1990s. However, following the DPS split, some within the LSCG were open to supporting Djukanović, believing that he may be able to deliver the LSCG's core objective – independence.[36] Liberals in Cetinje tentatively and cautiously backed Djukanović. Their understanding would be relatively short-lived, but for the purposes of the elections, the LSCG broadly supported Djukanović. Moreover, neither the LSCG or NS (or, indeed, the SDP or smaller Albanian and Muslim/Bosniak parties) put forward candidates for the election.[37] In the meantime, Bulatović initiated and organized a parallel DPS conference, largely consisting of party members from his heartland in northern Montenegro.[38]

Of the twenty-one municipalities in Montenegro, the Djukanović wing was confident that they were dominant in sixteen, while Bulatović and his bloc, though he could rely on additional rhetorical and logistical support from Milošević, dominated in only five municipalities.[39] But the campaign was about personality as much as political orientation.[40] Bulatović sought to portray himself as an 'ordinary guy' who would appeal to middle- and lower-ranking members of the DPS, older conservative voters and the ideologically inflexible. He cast himself as the binary opposite of Djukanović, who he portrayed as ruthless, scheming and serving foreign masters who wished to separate Montenegrins from their 'brothers' in Serbia.[41] Djukanović, conversely, sought to portray himself as a modern, progressive, European-style reformer, and a man who would go to Belgrade 'not for a point of view, but with a point of view'. This assiduously cultivated 'westernising' and 'reformist' image was, despite the obvious contradictions, nurtured by Western governments, and the real substance these claims were not investigated too closely as long as Milošević remained in power in Serbia. Thus, presenting two quite different approaches, styles and ideological platforms, their support bifurcated into two groups (though both were rather stereotyped): Bulatović's supporters were largely older, less-educated voters from the north of Montenegro or the republic's rural areas, while Djukanović garnered most of his support from younger, urban, educated Montenegrins.[42] While portrayed as a struggle between two fundamental positions (the status quo bloc, largely conservative, orthodox and 'anti-European' vs. advocates of a 'pro-European', progressive and democratic politics), the division between these blocs manifested itself, not only as a conflict between the so-called 'value systems' but between the advocates of preserving the SRJ and those advocating greater levels of Montenegrin independence (even outright independence).[43]

The cleavages in Montenegrin society had distinct geographical characteristics. The core of Bulatović's support, for example, was largely drawn from the towns and villages in the north, where the Orthodox population were more conservative and regarded themselves primarily as Serbs (though his bloc remained powerful in Podgorica).[44] One such bedrock was the town of Berane. Situated on the Lim River, Berane (known between 1946 and 1992 as Ivangrad) was, during the existence of the SFRJ, a relatively prosperous industrial town but had fallen upon hard times. Once, one of the most developed industrial centres in Montenegro, Berane, had been severely affected by the economic collapse in the late 1980s and the UN sanctions of the 1990s. The devastated economy, now oriented primarily towards agriculture, a decaying post-industrial infrastructure and high levels of unemployment had left evident scars on the town. Bulatović knew he could count on the majority of the Serb population of the town, as the people there were 'closer to Serbia than to Montenegro'.[45] And such sentiments were shared by the majority in the municipalities of Andrijevica, Mojkovac, Kolašin, Pljevlja, Plužine and Šavnik (and in the coastal municipality of Herceg Novi).

While the north of Montenegro was predominantly (though not exclusively) Bulatović territory, the picture was more complex in central and coastal areas of Montenegro. In 'Old Montenegro' and much of the coast, the population were less emotionally attached to Serbia and more inclined towards a sense of distinct Montenegrin identity. Nowhere was this more the case than Montenegro's historical capital, Cetinje, but such tendencies were also increasingly pronounced (and thus support for Djukanović relatively strong) in Kotor, Bar, Plav, Rožaje, Ulcinj, Tivat and Budva. The situation in Montenegro's two biggest cities – Podgorica and Nikšić – was even more complex, with these key centres largely divided between supporters of Bulatović (and, by extension, Miloševića) and Djukanović. Nikšić was Djukanović's birthplace, but many *Nikšićani* saw themselves as a people with historical roots in *Stara Hercegovina* (Old Herzegovina) and had strong links with Serbs across the borders in the Drina Valley and the eastern Herzegovinian areas of Bosnia & Herzegovina. In this regard, Djukanović was always careful not to emphasize on a commitment to outright independence, knowing that such explicit statements may be counterproductive.[46] Podgorica was equally difficult to predict. Montenegro's capital had been a relatively small town until it was (under the name of Titograd) reconstructed after the Second World War. The city had older, well-established areas such as *Stara Varoš* and *Drač*, built during the Ottoman period; but many of the city's newer areas – such as *Blok pet* (Block five), *Blok šest* (Block six) on the west side of the Morača River and *Stari aerodrom* (Old Airport) on the east side – were built largely between the 1960s and 1980s and were populated by families that had migrated into the city from rural (predominantly northern) areas.[47] *Podgoričani* (citizens of Podgorica) could vote either way, and nothing was certain; thus, the election hinged on the ability of both blocs to mobilize support in these two cities, and both invested significant energy in their respective attempts to do so.

As it transpired, the result of the two-horse race (the other candidates were largely symbolic) on 5 October 1997 turned out to be exceptionally close. In the first round, Bulatović was victorious, winning by a narrow margin of only 2,267 votes with a 75 per cent turnout.[48] In the end, Bulatović won in fourteen municipalities, while Djukanović' won in only seven. The margin was, however, insufficient to declare an outright victory, and a second round of voting was required. In the interim between the 5 and 19 October elections, the Djukanović camp made significant efforts to overturn the small margin, organizing an energetic house-to-house campaign which would, they hoped, facilitate a significant enough swing. This, coupled with Djukanović's impressive performance during a live 'TV duel' with Bulatović (held the week before the second round), proved pivotal.[49] In the second round of the elections, held on 19 October 1997 (during which the turnout was 73 per cent), Djukanović reversed the first-round results, crucially winning the *bitka za Nikšić* (the battle for Nikšić) while improving his share of the vote in other municipalities.[50] Aside from Nikšić, the overall winners in each municipality remained as per the first vote, with Djukanović winning majorities in Kotor, Ulcinj, Plav, Cetinje, Bar, Rožaje and Tivat, while Bulatović retained the traditionally more rural, conservative and pro-Serb oriented municipalities of Andrijevica, Berane, Danilovgrad, Pljevlja, Bjelo Polje, Herceg Novi, Budva, Mojkovac, Kolašin, Plužine, Šavnik and Žabljak (he also narrowly won in Podgorica).[51] The final margin of Djukanović's victory was 5,884 votes, sufficient, this time, to declare victory.

Upon the announcement of the results, however, the Bulatović camp immediately cried foul, claiming that there were significant irregularities during the election process, citing, among other factors, intimidation of members of the Montenegrin electoral commission and the intervention of Western powers. The Organisation for Security and Cooperation in Europe (OSCE), which had monitored the elections, rejected these accusations outright, stating that the final results of the elections accurately reflected the will of the electorate and met with democratic standards.[52] Nevertheless, while Djukanović and his allies began to celebrate in the government building in Podgorica in the early hours of the morning of 20 October 1997 (the Montenegrin weekly *Monitor* described it at the *jutro Crnogorske nade* – the morning of Montenegrin hope),[53] Bulatović persisted in his claims that the election process had been subject to coercion by both internal and external actors.[54] He appealed to his supporters to protest against the alleged fraud, and almost immediately demonstrations by Bulatović's supporters took place in front of the Montenegrin Assembly on 21 and 22 October 1997 (though the numbers present were estimated to be in the region of only 6,000, far below the kind of numbers that were sufficient to cause concern to Djukanović).[55] Almost simultaneously, however, Milošević tightened the noose around Montenegro, closing the SRJ's common border with Albania while imposing a de facto blockade on the border between Serbia and Montenegro.⁵⁶ Bulatović argued that the blockade was needed to stem the 'illegal activities' of Djukanović's DPS, telling a gathering of his supporters in Nikšić the week after the elections that 'the Montenegrin government advocates the opening of the border towards Albania and Croatia only in order to make smuggling easier – in other words, in order to easily bring narcotics and arms into the country'.⁵⁷ Such language and posturing demonstrated that Bulatović had no intention of recognizing the result of the election and retiring quietly from the Montenegrin political scene.

The return of the 'politics of the streets'

As Djukanović's presidential inauguration (scheduled to be held in Cetinje on 15 January 1998) approached, Bulatović made it clear he did not recognize the legitimacy of the result of the presidential elections and would not cooperate in facilitating a seamless transfer of power. He began to mobilize his supporters with the aim of creating mass demonstrations. Boldly stating that these protests were being initiated *u ime naroda* (in the name of the people), he claimed he could bring 100,000 protestors onto the streets of Podgorica.⁵⁸ The protests represented an attempt to return to the 'politics of the streets', the very same methods that had been used to undermine the leadership of the SKCG and bring him (and Djukanović) to power during the 'happening of the people' between October 1988 and January 1989.⁵⁹ Three days before the Podgorica protests, Momir Bulatović told the main board of his faction of the DPS, that on Monday 12 January at 5 minutes to 12 (in front of the Montenegrin Assembly), they would begin the *Veliki narodni miting* (Great People's Meeting) in protest against the 'illegal' government.⁶⁰ Djukanović, by way of response, played down the threat represented by Bulatović's supporters dismissing them bluntly as 'illiterate peasants' who could not 'adjust themselves to the realities of the modern world'.⁶¹ Such dismissals belied, however, the danger to stability that these demonstrations could potentially generate. And while the outcome would be different, Montenegro would pass through its most acute internal political crisis since the 'January Coup' in 1989.⁶²

On 12 January 1998, protestors began to gather, as per Bulatović's instructions, to be greeted by the former RTCG newsreader, Emilo Labudović, who did his upmost to rouse the demonstrators, who would remain rooted in front of the Montenegrin Assembly for three days. The crowd listened to speeches from a number of speakers, who took it in turns to denounce Milo Djukanović and his allies in the DPS, and carried banners emblazoned with messages such as *Jugoslavia je naša sudbina!* (Yugoslavia is our destiny!), *Rušimo vlast, branimo čast!* (Destroy the government, defend our honour) and *Policija, vi ste naš sinovi!* (Police, you are our sons!), alongside others declaring Milo Djukanović a 'Turk' (*Milo Turčine!*) and Svetozar Marović a 'thief' (*Sveto lopove!*).⁶³ The protests were, at least initially, good humoured and largely peaceful. By the third day, however, the frustration was apparent. On the evening of the 14 January 1998, a 'peaceful walk' led by Bulatović and his ally, the ex-NS deputy, Božidar Bojović, descended into violence. Having protested outside the RTCG building (on the basis that the station had been biased against Bulatović), the crowd reached the Montenegrin Assembly.[64] There, Bulatović addressed them, claiming that as the authorities had refused to engage in talks with them about 'electoral fraud' they should relocate to outside the government building (known colloquially as 'the two coffins') a few hundred metres away to confront them directly. As they did so, there was an immediate change in atmosphere.[65]

As the crowd reached the doors of the government building, they began to throw stones at the windows and doors of the building in an attempt to enter. Their actions were, however, halted by police, who used tear gas to quell the increasingly violent demonstration. Scuffles continued in the immediate environs of the building, and during the disturbances shots were fired by both police and demonstrators (and a number of explosive devices thrown at police).[66] Several prominent government ministers were trapped inside the building while the violence intensified.[67]

The police intervention had ensured that a bloody showdown was averted, and in the cold light of morning, both sides blamed each other for the chaos. Bulatović, increasingly on the defensive, described events as 'a brutal police intervention against the citizens who were protesting because of the theft of the elections', hoping that the outrage caused by the violence would lead to a 'Žuta Greda' moment akin to the one that had so undermined the legitimacy of the SKCG in October 1989.[68] He was also disappointed with the lack of support given by the Yugoslav Army (*Vojska Jugoslavije* – VJ), which he had hoped would intervene in the event of police action against the demonstrators.[69] Thus, far from achieving their objective, the demonstrations turned out to be counterproductive for Bulatović. Almost immediately, the international community, too, condemned the actions of him and his supporters. Robert Gelbard (the US special envoy to the Balkans who was in Montenegro for Djukanović's presidential inauguration) blamed Milošević for inciting and encouraging the demonstrations, while describing Bulatović's role in them as 'absolutely outrageous'.[70] The strategy of using street politics and the 'Great People's Meeting' had, therefore, been a terrible miscalculation for Bulatović and his supporters. In the meantime, at 5 pm on 15 January 1998, Djukanović's inauguration went ahead without problems in Cetinje, in the presence of diplomats, a number of leading opposition politicians from Serbia and members of the Montenegrin government. The anthem of the SRJ was replaced by the unofficial Montenegrin anthem *Oj, svijetla majska zoro* (Oh, Bright Dawn of May). Only the SRJ president, Montenegrin Radoje Kontić, was among SRJ officials in attendance.[71]

With Bulatović recovering from his failure to engineer a political stasis, the Djukanović faction of the DPS gained the momentum and used it to consolidate their position of strength in the immediate weeks and months. Seizing the opportunity presented by the post-protest fall-out, they made preparations for the parliamentary elections.[72] However, he wanted to ensure that his faction of the DPS retained the party 'brand'. As the ruling party in Montenegro since 1990, the party name carried weight, and retaining it would provide both continuity and legitimacy (the faction that could retain the original party name was more likely to be perceived to be the legitimate successor to the previously monolithic DPS). In a period of significant flux, retaining the brand was crucial. Both Djukanović and Bulatović coveted it and claimed it, but in March 1998 the High Court of Montenegro ruled that Bulatović's DPS (on the basis that *their* DPS was not registered in Montenegro, but at the level of the SRJ) must give up their claim on the party name.

In the wake of the court's ruling, Bulatović and members of the powerful and influential 'Podgorica Lobby' (former high-profile DPS members who for years had been critical towards Djukanovic) formed the Socialist People's Party of Montenegro (*Socijalističke narodne partije Crne Gore* – SNP).[73] In advance of the May 1998 elections, their first party congress took place in the Morača sport's centre in Podgorica and, according to Bulatović, was attended by 'over ten thousand people, members and sympathisers of the party'; the party's motto was *Ljudi za instinu* (People for Truth).[74] The SNP appealed directly to those who had supported Bulatović throughout the DPS crisis, the party's split and the subsequent presidential elections. Thus, their support base was composed largely, though not exclusively, of older and voters from lower social and educational strata, and those from the north of Montenegro. Their agenda remained firmly grounded in Bulatović oft-conveyed conviction that there was 'no alternative' to the SRJ. He also emphasized the importance of Serbian–Montenegrin unity; the terminology of 'brotherhood', 'fatherland' and, of course, 'Yugoslavia', was commonplace. The focus of their invective was almost exclusively Milo Djukanović and his allies – those who had 'stolen the elections' and were 'fostering separatism' – despite the new government's non-committal position vis-à-vis Montenegro's independence. Nevertheless, the SNP leadership party aimed to persuade voters of what they perceived to be the separatist and anti-Yugoslav character of Djukanović's DPS. They were, on the whole, preaching to the converted; thus, their support base had limited social and ethnic parameters from the outset. So, while the SNP enjoyed the support of much of the Orthodox population in the north of Montenegro, they immediately marginalized Montenegro's Muslims/Bosniaks, Albanians or those who advocated Montenegro's independence – and few of those shared the same emotional attachment to Bulatović and Milošević's particular form of Yugoslavism. The SNP claimed that they were subject to police harassment throughout their campaign, and during both their rallies in Nikšić (on 14 and 21 May 1998) tear gas canisters were thrown outside the meeting hall where they took place.[75]

A more cautious and inclusive, if ambiguous, platform was adopted by the 'new' DPS in their pre-election campaign. Initially, Djukanović remained wary of aligning himself with pro-independence parties like the LSCG, whose agenda was, for now at least, regarded as too radical. The DPS rhetorically supported existing SRJ structures, while simultaneously emphasizing their inability to cooperate with Milošević. Instead, they forged close links with Zoran Djindjić's Democratic Party (*Demokratska stranka* – DS), and sought an alliance with university professor and leader of the (traditionally pro-Serb) NS, Novak Kilibarda. Although this awarded Djukanović's DPS with an aura of being a 'pan-Yugoslav' party, it created a division within the NS, many high-profile members of the party refused to work with the 'separatist' Milo Djukanović.[76] But at this stage there was little suggestion of an openly pro-independence platform being adopted by the DPS. While distancing the DPS from the Milošević regime in Belgrade, Djukanović simultaneously acknowledged Montenegro's commitment to Montenegro's role *within* the SRJ. The party's slogan

Nikad sami, uvijek svoj (Never alone, always its own) was a succinct way of conveying this ambiguous position. The SDP leadership, albeit for different reasons, faced similar dilemmas with the upper echelons of the party divided over entry into a coalition with the DPS, largely because as a pro-independence and anti-war party, their leaders had suffered persecution from the ruling authorities in the early 1990s. The leader of the LSCG, Slavko Perović, who had tentatively supported Djukanović prior to the second round of the 1997 presidential elections, refused to cooperate further with the DPS (the LSCG would run alone, though not all within the party were convinced of the wisdom of doing so).[77]

In any event, for those who chose to join the coalition, intra-party disputes were smoothed out, and the DPS–SDP–NS coalition (led symbolically by Djukanović) was established.[78] Named 'For Better Living' (*Da Živimo Bolje* – DŽB), those in the coalition were frequently referred to (most especially in the pro-SNP daily *Dan*) as the party of the *Boljevići* (those who live better), a snappy critique of the DŽB's rather glossy and expensive election campaign.[79] The campaign itself took place within a tense political environment, and while there were no major incidents a bomb scare at the final DŽB rally in Podgorica on 28 May 1998 caused some of the crowd to disperse in panic.[80]

In the subsequent elections, the DŽB coalition won by a significant margin. Collectively, the DŽB coalition and the pro-independence LSCG took over 60 per cent of the votes cast (53.8 per cent and 6.4 per cent, respectively); Momir Bulatović's SNP took just over one third (37.2 per cent). The DŽB coalition won forty-two seats in parliament; the SNP won twenty-nine.[81] Setting the tone for the period ahead, Djukanović hailed the DŽB triumph as 'our penultimate victory; our final victory will be scored when democracy wins throughout Yugoslavia'.[82] The government that would be formed by the DŽB coalition (DPS members taking many of the key roles) thereafter sought to consolidate their image as the 'democratic option', by defining themselves as multiethnic, democratic and progressive – the binary opposite, they argued, of the SNP.[83]

The SNP suffered, ultimately, the consequences of negative campaigning, central to which was the targeting of Muslims/Bosniaks, Albanians, Croats and pro-independence Montenegrins who they blamed vocally and directly for 'separatism', and their campaign material, including billboard advertising, was also published entirely in Cyrillic script (aimed squarely at those Montenegrins who regarded themselves primarily as Serbs). Moreover, their strategy of polarizing the electorate and casting the contest as an essential struggle between good and evil and portraying the SNP as loyal patriots and DŽB as separatists and *izdajnici* (traitors) backfired. But while Bulatović and the SNP had failed to win the parliamentary elections, he would remain an important figure in Montenegrin politics, albeit using the mechanisms of the SRJ to assert his political power. In June 1998, largely due to the patronage of Milošević, Bulatović took over the position as prime minister of the SRJ from fellow Montenegrin, Radoje Kontić (who had become persona non grata with Milošević following his decision to attend Djukanović's presidential inauguration). Kontić (who had lost a vote of confidence in the SRJ parliament) claimed that he and his cabinet had been forcibly removed from their posts to make way for Bulatović, raising concerns among the new DPS-led government in Montenegro that Bulatović's appointment had been engineered to facilitate his continuing engagement in Montenegro's affairs.

Upon receiving news of Bulatović's appointment, the Montenegrin government responded swiftly to what they regarded as an attempt by Milošević to out-manoeuvre them. In a letter to Momir Bulatović, Milica Pejanović-Djurišić outlined the Montenegrin government position on Bulatović's appointment, stating, 'We do not accept you [Bulatović] as prime minister' and, further, 'we see your appointment to such an important position as another attack on the constitutional order and equitable position of Montenegro in Yugoslavia'. Upon taking the post of SRJ prime minister, Momir Bulatović was obliged (as per Milošević's instructions) to give up the leadership of the SNP.[84] He was replaced as party leader by his namesake (but not relation), Predrag Bulatović. As former vice president of the SNP, Predrag Bulatović was a member of the 'moderate' wing of the party and was, albeit not significantly, more inclined towards engagement and dialogue with Djukanović and the DPS. Indeed, while Momir Bulatović raged against the DPS from Belgrade (denouncing them as 'unelected' and Djukanović as a prime minster 'imposed from abroad'), Predrag Bulatović called for constructive dialogue between the SNP and the DPS. Regardless of these sentiments, however, relations between the SNP and DPS would continue to degenerate as problems mounted for the Montenegrin government in the period following the May 1998 elections. Pressure from Serbia was increasing daily and the growing crisis in Kosovo threatened to hold serious implications for Montenegro's internal security. Already strained, relations between Belgrade and Podgorica worsened dramatically when the Montenegrin government announced that they supported dialogue with the Kosovo Albanians and, should there be armed conflict, they would not participate but declare neutrality.[85] It was the SDP, part of the new governing coalition, that were the first party to explicitly state their desire that the Montenegrin government should draw a clear demarcation by refusing to allow Montenegrins called up by the VJ to participate in any armed conflict in Kosovo. The SDP's new leader, Ranko Krivokapić, argued that young Montenegrins should not be subject to conscription on the basis that 'Montenegro is an inexhaustible reserve for the [Milošević] regime where new recruits are concerned – they will be used as cannon fodder'.[86]

It wasn't only the issue of Kosovo that increased the cleavage between Serbia and Montenegro. That the latter's burgeoning independent status was becoming more evident was already evident in the realm of economic policy. In a move that was greeted by outrage in Belgrade, the Montenegrin government achieved independence in the monetary sphere by adopting, in 1999, the Deutschmark (DM) as their formal currency (in place of the Yugoslav Dinar). In so doing, they not only gained monetary independence but consolidated control over the spheres of customs and foreign trade.[87] The Montenegrin government, in essence, had incrementally moved towards a form of 'functional sovereignty' – a strategy which would secure greater economic independence which would, subsequently, lead to a de facto, if not de jure, independence.[88] The crisis in Kosovo, which had simmered throughout 1998 and early 1999, would overshadow these economic developments.

6

Politics by Proxy: Orthodox Churches in Conflict (1990–2006)

Montenegro's divisions were not merely played out in the traditional political party arena or limited to the parameters of academic or public debate. The emergent intra-Orthodox conflict between the Serbian Orthodox Church (*Srpska pravoslavna crkva* – SPC) and the Montenegrin Orthodox Church (*Crnogorska pravoslavna crkva* – CPC) over 'autocephaly' (a term used to describe a church's autonomy), while ostensibly an ecclesiastical matter for the respective churches, 'shifted on to political ground', becoming something of a proxy struggle. It became a distinct and symbolically important strand of the myriad and pre-existing political conflicts over identity, nationhood and statehood.[1] Orthodox churches in Southeast Europe have been intimately entwined with the region's dominant post-communist ideology (nationalism), with these religious institutions being actively engaged in national politics.[2] An important factor in this politico-religious character is the structural organization of Orthodox churches. With no centralized structure within Orthodoxy, churches structured along national lines have significant autonomy and thus developed distinct national characteristics. In so doing, they often become a symbol of the national being, inextricably linked with national identity and thereby politicized. In Southeast Europe (and in the former SFRJ, in particular) the social and political climate of the 1990s dictated that Orthodox churches have, in some instances, explicitly aligned themselves to nationalist political parties or governments that have sought to create ethnically homogenous states.[3] But these apparent symbols of the nation (and thus national unity) have often been burdened by internal splits, factionalism and 'schisms'. In that regard, one of the most striking examples is the case of the SPC in Montenegro and their conflict with the CPC.[4]

In the early 1990s, the SPC had been one of the primary mechanisms for underpinning what the Serbian identity of the Montenegrins was, their clergy conveying the narrative that Montenegro was the 'second Serb state', and the *Srpska Sparta* (Serbian Sparta) and Montenegrins were 'the best and purest of Serbs'. As a challenge to this narrative, however, the canonically unrecognized CPC, supporters of which claimed it had been autocephalous until it was forcibly absorbed into the SPC in 1920, was re-established with the dual purpose of undermining the power of the SPC in Montenegro and bolstering perceptions of Montenegrin separateness. Of course, while Orthodox Christianity (in the form of both the SPC and the CPC) was the dominant religion in Montenegro, the Roman Catholic Church and the Islamic community (other registered religious communities include the Seventh-day Adventist Church, Jehovah's Witnesses and the Evangelical Church) also co-existed with it. And while relations are generally good between the Orthodox churches (the SPC and CPC) and other religious communities in Montenegro (since the reign of King Nikola I), relations *between* the Orthodox churches, from the re-establishment of the CPC in the 1990s, has been both fraught and politically charged. The cornerstone of the SPC-CPC conflict is the question of autocephaly, though rhetorically underpinned by this factor, is not one simply based upon such strictly ecclesiastical, spiritual or historical matters. It was, and remains, essentially a political conflict that goes to the heart of the question about the identity of the Montenegrins. Cloaked in religious terminology, it is, simultaneously (and perhaps primarily), a proxy conflict primarily about *identity* – one fought between those who define themselves as Montenegrins and are advocates of Montenegro's independence and those who define themselves as Serbs (albeit from Montenegro) and Montenegro as a 'second Serb state'.

While it has much deeper historical roots, the current conflict can be traced back to a distinct 'pivot' during the early years of the existence of the Kingdom of Serbs, Croats and Slovenes (*Kraljevina Srba, Hrvata i Slovenaca* – KSHS), which was established on 1 December 1918. The previous month, during the so-called 'Podgorica Assembly', Serbia and Montenegro had united in advance of wider Yugoslav unification. But the contested nature of the Podgorica Assembly led to an armed conflict between the *Bjelaši* (Whites), who supported unification with Serbia, and *Zelenaši* (Greens), supporters of Montenegro's exiled King Nikola I, who sought the preservation of a semblance of independence within the KSHS. In the latter years of this conflict, the Metropolinate of Belgrade sought a union of all South Slav Orthodox churches; after all, they argued, Serbs and Montenegrins were branches of the same (Serb) nation; they had united politically and should unite under the umbrella of a unified church. Immediately after the creation of the KSHS, Regent (later King) Alexander Karadjordjević assisted in the organization of a conference of episcopes, which expressed a wish that all Serb churches be unified.[5] The following year, on 26 May 1919, a second 'conference of bishops' was held during which preparations for unification of the churches were made; the decisions of the conference were confirmed by the decrees of Aleksander and Serbian government on 17 June 1920. By decree, on 30 August 1920, they proclaimed the 'unification' of the churches. Regent Aleksander Karadjordjević simultaneously proclaimed the formation of the Serb patriarchy and that the head of this patriarchy (Dimitrije I) bear the title 'Serb Patriarch of the Orthodox Church of the Kingdom of Serbs, Croats and Slovenes'.

Following the unification of 1920, therefore, the Serb Patriarchate was the sole Orthodox body in Montenegro. Thereafter, the SPC played an instrumental role in consolidating the Serbian identity of the Montenegrins, casting Montenegrins as the 'best and purest of Serbs', descendants of those Serbs that had migrated to the rocky hinterland of Montenegro in the wake of the Battle of Kosovo in 1389. There, according to this narrative, they settled in the rocky crags of *Stara Crna Gora* (Old Montenegro), where they struggled to keep the flame of Orthodoxy and Serb identity alive while struggling to survive in a harsh, unforgiving environment. Montenegro was cast as an island of Serb freedom amid a sea of Ottoman repression. Montenegro thus plays a pivotal role in the preservation of Serbian identity.[6] Myriad symbols and myths have been embellished by the SPC in order to consolidate this collective national (Serb) identity with a sense of a shared history, community and destiny, and thus children baptized in Montenegro were predominantly, until the re-establishment of the CPC, baptized into the SPC.[7]

Despite contested nature of the Podgorica Assembly and the subsequent *Bjelaši - Zelenaši* conflict, dissention within the Orthodox clergy was rare. (There were some exceptions – the Archimandrite Nikodim Janjušivić, for example, kept the CPC in Detroit for several years after unification.) Montenegrin bishops voted unanimously to unite with the SPC, and leading voices of unification became Serbian patriarchs – both Varnava I and Gavrilo V (a Montenegrin, born Gavrilo Dožić) were born in Montenegro (though the former was born in 1880 in Pljevlja, which was then part of the 'Sandžak of Novi Pazar', an administrative district within the Ottoman Empire) and became Serbian patriarchs in 1930 and 1938, respectively.[8] Gavrilo V remained patriarch until 1950, though he was incarcerated by the Nazis in 1941, first in Serbia and later in the Dachau concentration camp in Bavaria, Germany.[9]

During the existence of the SFRJ, the KPJ ensured that the activities of the Serbian patriarchate remained low key. The KPJ, while not taking an extreme position on the freedom of religious worship (as was the case in neighbouring Albania), promoted instead 'civic religion' in which the principle of *bratstvo i jedinstvo* (Brotherhood and Unity) replaced traditional forms of religious practice. Young people, who would have once been baptised by the church, were now members of the 'Union of Pioneers' (*Savez pionira Jugoslavije* – SPJ), a secular movement which promoted communist ideals. This was part of what the SPC saw as an onslaught against them, and they formed a perception that they were being suppressed by the communist authorities. The imprisonment of the Metropolitan Arsenije of Montenegro in 1954 served only to reinforce this. The SPC's leadership also became increasingly anxious about 'regime-driven schism', a position seemingly vindicated by, given the KPJ's perceived nurturing of ecclesiastical separatism, a policy the party had promoted strongly during the early post-war years (particularly with regard to the creation of a separate Macedonian Orthodox Church, which was eventually realized in 1958).[10] But despite the challenges facing the SPC, they, albeit quietly, continued to pursue the argument that regardless of Montenegro's status as a republic within the SFRJ, Montenegrins were, in essence, Serbs. The SPC often argued that attempts to attack the unity and integrity of the church were led by the KPJ's alleged policy of 'encouraging of separatist priests in Montenegro'.[11] In 1970, the then Serbian Patriarch German II left little doubt how he perceived the identity of the Montenegrins, stating that they were simply 'Serbs by another name'.[12]

The most serious conflict between the SPC and the SKCG, however, reached a zenith in 1972, fuelled in large part by the latter's decision to dismantle the small Orthodox chapel on top of Mount Lovćen.[13] The chapel, which had been constructed in 1855 to house the remains of the Montenegrin *Vladika*, poet and writer, Petar II Petrović 'Njegoš',[14] had been destroyed by the Austro-Hungarian Army in 1916, but was rebuilt and formally reopened (and dedicated to Njegoš) with great aplomb by Aleksander Karadjordjević in September 1925. However, in the 1950s the SKCG sought to replace the existing structure with a 'secular' mausoleum (thereby recasting or 'secularising' Njegoš) designed by the Croat sculptor, Ivan Meštrović, who at that time lived in the United States.[15] It took over two decades to realize the project, during which the SPC consistently argued that the destruction of Njegoš's chapel was an attack upon both their identity and their integrity by the Montenegrin authorities.[16] Yet despite such objections, the SPC's influence was limited while the KPJ (and, in Montenegro, the SKCG) held power; thus, the project for the new mausoleum was executed and the small chapel destroyed.

Amfilohije Radović and the SPC in Montenegro

As nationalist sentiment among Serbs throughout the SFRJ increased following the rise to power of Slobodan Milošević in 1987; however, the SPC tentatively supported the so-called 'anti-bureaucratic revolution'. Between 1987 and 1990, they slowly re-emerged as a more potent spiritual (and political) force in Montenegro, becoming even more so following the election of Amfilohije Radović as head of the 'Metropolitan of Montenegro and the Littoral' in 1990 following the retirement of Metropolitan Danilo. Born Risto Radović in 1938 in Bare Radovića in the Morača area of Montenegro, Amfilohije was well suited to the task – he understood the mentality of the Montenegrins and, equally, understood the underlying social currents in Montenegro. His career began at Sava's Seminary and then at the Theological Faculty of Belgrade University (where he later taught after completing a doctorate in Greece). After a spell as Bishop of Banat in the 1980s, he was elected as the Metropolitan of Montenegro and the Littoral in December 1990.[17] His appointment coincided with a wider mobilization of Serbs throughout the SFRJ, a process in which the SPC enthusiastically engaged. Amfilohije oversaw a reinvigoration of the SPC in Montenegro, from his base at the imposing Cetinje monastery, originally built in 1484 during the rule of Ivan Crnojević.

Amfilohije energetically embarked upon a programme of building of new monasteries (the largest being the 'Cathedral of Christ's Resurrection' in Podgorica) and the rebuilding of old churches adorned with 'Serb' saints and symbolism. He increased the number of SPC priests, monks, nuns and the faithful, and increased the number of Montenegrins baptised into the church (the SPC also endeavoured to 're-Christianise' the population using the corpses and bones of saints to mobilize the faithful and heal spiritual wounds).[18] The relics of St Basil were cut and sent to monasteries of the SPC outside of Montenegro, while in new churches in Montenegro fragments of 'martyrs' from the Ustaša-run Jasenovac concentration camp were exhibited to remind worshippers of more recent historical sufferings of the Serbs.[19] Amfilohije's programme also included the opening of a theological school in Cetinje, a publishing house, *Svetigora*, and (later) a radio station *Radio Svetigora*.[20] And despite a lukewarm relationship, at this stage, with the Montenegrin government, he continued to lobby energetically for religious instruction (by the SPC) to be compulsory in

Montenegrin schools. Collectively, Amfilohije's endeavours did much to consolidate the power of the SPC in Montenegro.

Amfilohije had strong views on Montenegrin identity (and statehood); they were unambiguous and they would, ultimately, lead to an inexorable conflict with a Montenegrin government that were moving towards a policy of independence from Serbia.[21] He regarded the Montenegrin nation as an invention of 'separatists' and 'communists' who were endeavouring to tear Montenegrins from their historical roots and, more broadly, divide the Serbs of the Balkans. He also viewed those advocating the restoration of the CPC as a 'heretical and schismatic' group waging a continuing war against the SPC (he openly referred to Montenegrin autocephalists as *crnolatinaši*, a derogatory term normally reserved for dogmatic or fanatical Catholic priests).[22] Indeed, in an interview for the Belgrade weekly *NIN*, Amfilohije denounced the nascent CPC as a 'political entity', and their supporters as 'Godless' people from 'non-church circles' who had 'been raised in a completely anti-church spirit'. 'These are people', he added, 'who rarely went to church, a considerable number of them are unbaptised, and they have only an elementary knowledge of theology ... they are displaying their interest in the church in the same way as the communist party during the past fifty years, using methods characteristic of it'.[23]

But Amfilohije, too, demonstrated that his talents extended beyond the realm of the spiritual. He initially supported the policies of the Serbian president, Slobodan Milošević and later became a vociferous supporter of the Serb nationalist cause during the wars in Croatia and Bosnia & Herzegovina. He played the *gusle*[24] (choosing verses from the epic poem, 'The Battle of Mojkovac') for Montenegrin troops on the Dubrovnik front in 1991[25] and often praised the Bosnian Serb leaders Radovan Karadžić and Biljana Plavšić (the latter of whom he described as a 'Kosovo maiden'). He invited the Serbian paramilitary leader, Željko 'Arkan' Ražnatović, and his paramilitary group *Tigrovi* (the Tigers) to 'protect' the Cetinje Monastery from the CPC supporters who had gathered on King Nikola's Square on *badnjak* (Orthodox Christmas Eve) 1992.[26] He also acted as an arbiter in intra-party conflicts within and interparty conflicts between Serb political parties in Serbia, Bosnia & Herzegovina and Montenegro. Indeed, Amfilohije's political influence increased, and while his relationship with the Pale-based Bosnian Serb leadership remained strong, his relationship with Milošević soured after the Serbian President's break with the Bosnian Serb leadership following the rejection by the Bosnian Serb Assembly of the Vance Owen Peace Plan (VOPP) in May 1993. Thereafter, Amfilohije became one of Milošević's fiercest critics and continued in his support of the Pale clique.[27] In August 1995, while Croatian forces were conducting the latter stages of 'Operation Storm' in the Serb breakaway region within Croatia (*Republika Srpska Krajina* – RSK) and the Bosnian Serb Army (*Vojska Republike Srpske* – RSK) were losing territory as the result of NATO airstrikes and a joint Muslim–Croat offensive in Bosnia & Herzegovina, Amfilohije addressed the Montenegrin Assembly, berating delegates there for their continued support of Milošević and demanding that they reverse their decision to impose sanctions on the Bosnian Serbs.[28] Amfilohije's opposition to Milošević meant that he found common ground with Milo Djukanović when the DPS split into pro- and anti-Milošević factions in 1997, but it was to be a relatively brief marriage of convenience.

The re-emergence of the Montenegrin Orthodox Church

While Amfilohije was revitalizing the SPC in Montenegro, those advocating Montenegro's independence sought to re-establish the CPC as a part of an endeavour to aid strengthen and consolidate a distinct Montenegrin national identity.[29] These supporters of an autocephalous CPC claimed that the SPC had little influence over events in Montenegro during the long period in which Serbia proper had been occupied by the Ottoman Turks.[30] Over time, they argued, Montenegro had, from 1603, developed its own peculiarities distinct from the SPC, and that they had, in any event, become independent of the Patriarchate of Peć in 1766.[31] They also argued that the CPC had been autocephalous de facto and de jure thereafter and that this had been acknowledged in the Montenegrin Constitution of 1905 and had been forcibly and illegally absorbed into the SPC in 1920.[32] The issues of autocephaly occasionally arose thereafter. In June 1945, for example, a small group of Orthodox priests, led by the Montenegrin Partisan veteran Petar Kapičić, held an assembly in Nikšić, during which they requested from the communist authorities that the Montenegrin Orthodox Church be re-established, though disagreements on the issue among the Montenegrin communist cadres ensured that this never materialized.[33]

With regard to contemporary matters, the CPC sought to portray the newly anointed Amfilohije as a dangerous fundamentalist intent on imposing the SPC on all Montenegrins of the Orthodox faith.[34] His three years of being Metropolitan in Montenegro were, according to those who supported the re-establishment of the CPC, part of an assimilatory 'anti-Montenegrin campaign'.[35] It was an argument well received by those parties that advocated Montenegro's independence, and thus the issue of the autocephaly of the CPC was one that politicians and parties with a pro-independence agenda could utilize. Indeed, the re-establishment of the CPC was openly supported by pro-independence parties, the most influential of which was Slavko Perović's Liberal Alliance of Montenegro (*Liberalni savez Crne Gore* – LSCG).[36] Their support for the re-establishment of the church was part of a broader strategy that would help them reach their stated objective of re-establishing a sovereign and independent Montenegrin state.[37] The issue of the CPC's autocephaly was a near constant in the LSCG's magazine *Liberal*, which was published for the first time in 1990. The party was particularly strong in Cetinje, the heartland of *Stara Crna Gora* (Old Montenegro) within which there was a strong sense of *Crnogorstvo* (Montenegrin-ness), though it was, paradoxically, the base of the SPC in Montenegro.[38] As early as 1989, messages such as *Živjela crnogorska autokefalna crkva* (Long live the Montenegrin Autocephalous Church) began to appear in the town,[39] and by June of that year the LSCG had organized a conference in Cetinje with the objective of debating the subject of the CPC's autocephaly. In November 1990, in Cetinje, a group called the *Odbora za obnavljanje autokefalne crnogorske pravoslanve crkve* (Committee for the Restoration of the CPC'S Autocephaly), led by the organizer's first president, Dušan Gvozdenović, soon announced their intention to re-establish an autocephalous Montenegrin church and that the church would hold its first *badnjak* (Christmas Eve) celebrations in Cetinje.[40] On 6 January 1991, an 'All-Montenegrin National Synod' was held, during which their commitment to restore an autocephalous CPC was stated: a church that would serve to unite Montenegrins through the worship of specifically Montenegrin saints, and, by extension, aid their wider objective of establishing an independent state, with the church acting as the central pillar of a distinct Montenegrin national identity.[41]

Those advocating the re-establishment of an autocephalous CPC quickly became more assertive, and on both *Badnjak* and *Petrovdan* (St Peter's Day – 29 June) 1991, their supporters gathered in Cetinje carrying banners adorned with slogans such as *Amfilohije, Vi nijesti naš mitropolit!* (Amfilohije, you are not our Metropolitan) and *Hoćemo da smo Crnogorci i u krštenicama* (We want to be baptised as Montenegrins). At the nearby Cetinje monastery, the SPC faithful, including leading figures from pro-Srbian parties in Montenegro (such as Novak Kilibarda, the leader of NS), gathered – a meeting described by *Liberal* as 'a gathering of Chetniks under Orlovi Krš'.[42] In a heated atmosphere, speeches by Dušan Gvozdenović and Jevrem Brković were interrupted by violent clashes with both police and supporters of the SPC, during which a number of people were injured.[43] This set the tone for subsequent manifestations. In January 1993, the Badnjak celebrations took place as usual, albeit in a tense atmosphere, with an estimated 6,000 to 7,000 people in attendance.[44] Tensions, however, could not be contained indefinitely. In August 1993, for example, supporters of the CPC gathered outside the plot where the foundation stone for the Cathedral of Christ's Resurrection in Podgorica was being symbolically laid by Metropolitan Amfilohije to express their objections.[45] Soon after, on 29 September 1993 supporters of the CPC (led by Božidar 'Boba' Bogdanović) interrupted a meeting of the Montenegrin Academy of Sciences and Arts (*Crnogorska akedemija nauka i umjetnosti* – CANU) and SANU in Cetinje attended by Amfilohije, which was held to commemorate the life and poetic works of Petar II Petrović Njegoš, and jostled and insulted the Montenegrin president, Momir Bulatović, after the meeting in front of the *Biljarda* (once Njegoš's home, now a museum).[46] In the aftermath, those deemed responsible for disturbing the meeting were hunted down by police; cafés and bars were searched and twenty-four people were arrested.[47]

The CPC then began the next phase of its re-establishment, registering initially as a non-governmental organization (NGO), under the name of *Vjerska zajednica Crnogoraca istočnopravoslavne vjeroipovesti* (The Religious Community of Montenegrins of Eastern Orthodox Confession). Soon after, it was announced that a Montenegrin-born Antonije Abramović (who had been born in 1919 in Dobrota in the Bay of Kotor), a clergyman of the American Orthodox Church in Toronto, was to be anointed as the 'Metropolitan' of the CPC.[48] On 31 October 1993, the CPC's supporters gathered in King Nikola's Square to celebrate Abramović's consecration. His first 'sermon' took place, in the absence of a church large enough to hold the gathered crowd (the LSCG magazine *Liberal* claimed the crowd reached approximately 10,000), on an 'altar under an open sky' whereupon celebratory gunfire could be heard above his speech.[49] Though appearing mildly uncomfortable in his new environment, Abaramović soon settled in, establishing his headquarters in a house on the outskirts of Cetinje, the so-called *Vladičanski dom* – a rather modest headquarters, at least in comparison to the imposing Cetinje monastery. From there he began to agitate for autocephalous status for the CPC.⁵⁰ In his first major interview for *Liberal* in November 1993, under the headline *Naš svetac je u ropstvu* (Our saint in slavery) he set out his objectives – in essence to promote the CPC – while railing against the 'occupation' of Montenegrin churches by the SPC.⁵¹

The SPC, conversely, sought to discredit Abramović. In addition to the accusations that he was merely a puppet working in the service of greater political interests, rumours were abundant regarding his alleged lack of moral fibre, and the SPC sought to capitalize on the numerous ambiguities regarding Abramović's past and his personal idiosyncrasies; some critics questioned whether Abramović had, in fact, ever been consecrated as a priest.⁵² The SPC, however, acknowledged that he had, during the 1950s, spent time in Kosovo with the bishop of Ras and Prizren, Gojko Stojčović (later the Serbian Partiarch 'Pavle' between 1990 and 2009), followed by a spell as abbot of Savina in Herceg-Novi, but had been asked (in the early 1960s), allegedly, to leave the SPC, due to 'homosexual activity'.⁵³ The SPC further claimed that Abramović fled to Greece before migrating to Canada, where he remained until 1993, whereupon he returned to Montenegro to lead the 'uncanonical' CPC. Despite these accusations, Abramović led the CPC through its early development and led the ceremony with relative efficacy, and was the central figure when, on King Nikola's Square in Cetinje, the 'Autocephalous Montenegrin Orthodox Church' was formally proclaimed.⁵⁴ And he was energetic in his efforts in attempting to persuade the Montenegrin government of the legitimacy of the CPC's claims. He claimed to lament the 'moral collapse of the SPC' and that 'everyone says that we [the CPC] are on a good path', and that Montenegrins were justified in their quest for their own autocephalous church.⁵⁵ He frequently appealed to the Montenegrin government to recognize the legitimacy of these demands, and in June 1996 he wrote to Milo Djukanović setting out the historical claims of the church, the historical injustices imposed upon it.⁵⁶ Soon after, however, Abramović fell into ill-health, eventually dying in November 1996. He was buried in Cetinje thereafter.⁵⁷

After a short impasse, Abramović was succeeded by Miraš Dedeić, known to the CPC faithful as 'Metropolitan Mihailo'. He was appointed by the Montenegrin Synod in January 1997 and was subsequently, on 15 March 1998, ordained as a bishop by Patriarch Pimen of the breakaway 'Bulgarian Alternative Synod' in Sofia. He was formally ordained 'Metropolitan' by the CPC in October 1998. From the outset, the SPC were as unrelenting in their criticism of the Metropolitan (who the SPC referred to simply as 'Dedeić') as they had been of his predecessor. According to the SPC, Dedeić was simply another discredited priest who had 'sold his soul' working in the service of Montenegrin separatists. He had always, they argued, been viewed with deep suspicion by his fellow Orthodox priests while he was a student; some claimed he was a fraud who had demonstrated little commitment to the faith. And, indeed, Dedeić appeared to have something of a chequered past: alleged 'unclerical behaviour' on Dedeić's apparently led to him being de-frocked, ex-communicated and finally anathematized by the Ecumenical Patriarch in Constantinople. Rejecting accusations about his past, Dedeić, of course, preferred to divert attention towards the CPC's claim that they had existed as an independent entity since 1603, an autonomy, which, they claim, had been recognized in 1766 by both the Holy Russian Synod and the Patriarchy of Constantinople.⁵⁸ He cast the SPC as occupiers who had imposed themselves upon Montenegro after the CPC had been forcibly dissolved against both the 1905 Montenegrin constitution and canon law.[59] He was also vocal about what he regarded as the forcible absorption of the CPC into the Serbian Patriarchate in 1920 (which, he would consistently claim, represented a theft of Montenegro's identity, an imposition of Serb identity in Montenegro and an occupation of the CPC's sacred buildings).[60]

In the churches and on the squares

Montenegro's ruling DPS considered the CPC–SPC conflict an ecclesiastical matter, and they remained largely disengaged.[61] However, the political flux in Montenegro from 1997 would give the issue new momentum. The DPS split became the crucial fault line in Montenegrin politics (see Chapter 5), and in the immediate period following Djukanović's inauguration as Montenegrin president in Cetinje in January 1998 (during which Djukanović had received blessings from Amfilohije), the conflict between the SPC and the CPC increasingly served as a point of reference for expressing national identity and attitudes towards the state, and in essence the continuation of political struggles by proxy.[62] Djukanović may have received blessings from Amfilohije before his inauguration as president in January 1998, but the Montenegrin president's shift towards an increasingly independent position in subsequent years determined that their understanding was fleeting. Thereafter, Amfilohije would become one of his most vocal opponents as he continued to consolidate the position of the SPC in Montenegro.

The bitter public exchanges between the SPC and the CPC extended beyond the matter of unification to arguments over the ownership of Montenegro's religious buildings and related property (such as the remains of St Peter of Cetinje and the right hand of St John the Baptist, both kept in the SPC-administered Cetinje monastery). The CPC began to assert their claim to 650 churches across Montenegro which had been 'requisitioned' in 1920 and were being administered by the SPC. 'We only want', Dedeić consistently argued, 'that which is ours'.[63] Thus, between 1998 and 2000, the CPC claimed to have had gained, by plebiscites held among parishioners, legitimate possession of a number of churches which had previously been run by the SPC, the majority of these being located around Cetinje and Njeguši in what was *Katunska nahtja* (symbolically the very heart of Old Montenegro).[64] Emboldened, the CPC set about reaching their stated objective of repossessing more churches administered by the SPC; on occasion this required that controversial actions be undertaken. In December 2000, for example, supporters of the CPC attempted to take possession of the Vlaška church in Cetinje, a building with much historical significance.[65] Their objective was to stop the SPC renovating the church (thereby, claimed the CPC, eliminating evidence that the church was originally Montenegrin). In protest against the attempted 'appropriation' of the church by the CPC, an SPC priest, Radomir Nikčević, barricaded himself inside the building and embarked upon a hunger strike by way of protest.[66] After appeals by the Montenegrin prime minister, Filip Vujanović, the crisis did not end in the 'Christmas bloodshed' that Amfilohije had warned of.[67] It was, however, a clear signal that the SPC–CPC conflict had the potential to lead to greater violence.[68]

Arguments over ownership and control of religious buildings were, however, merely one strand of a multifaceted conflict. Amfilohije's opponents continued to accuse him of endeavouring to 'provoke' the Montenegrin government and the CPC.[69] Amfilohije, conversely, did likewise, arguing that the Montenegrin government were, not by accident but by design, allowing the CPC to undermine the authority of the SPC. Tensions between supporters of the respective churches became most acutely manifest during festivals and religious holidays, in particular during the aforementioned 'burning of the Yule log' on Orthodox Christmas Eve. The SPC, which held its ceremony outside the Cetinje monastery, protested vehemently that this 'Serbian tradition' had been hijacked by the CPC, which held its own parallel ceremony merely a stone's throw away on King Nikola's square.[70] The first of these parallel events took place in 1991, and they would subsequently become a key annual date in the conflict between the SPC and CPC.[71] While ostensibly religious gatherings, they became more akin to quasi-political meetings, marked by the presence of nationalist symbols, slogans and banners and, often, they were marred by low-intensity violence and, occasionally, police interventions. Supporters of the SPC carried banners and flags adorned with Serbian national symbols, SPC iconography and portraits of Slobodan Milošević and King Aleksander Karadjordjević. The faithful of the CPC would, conversely, carry flags and banners displaying symbols of the Petrović dynasty, including the Montenegrin cross with 'H.I' – King Nikola I Petrović – a copy of the famous *barjak* (banner) carried by Montenegrins during their victorious battle against the Ottoman Army at Vučji Do in July 1876, as well as Montenegrin state symbols. The rival groups used traditional means of intimidating each other, singing nationalist songs, fist fighting and, occasionally, the firing of handguns (albeit only in the air).[72] And while Cetinje was the epicentre of such events, they were by no means confined to this small town. In Berane, a traditional stronghold of the SPC, a number of violent incidents took place as the CPC attempted to hold their own Badnjak celebrations in the town. Six months later, followers of the SPC were forbidden from holding ceremonies in the village of Njeguši (the birthplace of Petar II Petrović 'Njegoš), near Cetinje.

In the midst of these conflicts, the Montenegrin government sought, at least publicly, to defuse tensions between the churches, although their position was often ambiguous. Following the 'registration' of the CPC in January 2000, Milo Djukanović courted controversy in 2000 by sending, for the first time, Easter greetings to the CPC as well as the SOC (the latter subsequently accusing him of encouraging separatism).[73] This led to a split between Djukanović and Amfilohije, who had, since the DPS split in 1997, been on relatively good terms.[74] Thereafter, the Montenegrin government frequently implied support for the CPC's quest for autocephalous status, but adopted a seemingly neutral position, largely because the church issue was one, which divided his own party. Conversely, Svetozar Marović, the then Speaker of the Montenegrin Assembly and (at that time) a close ally of Djukanović, condemned the CPC for attempting to seize two relatively isolated churches on an island in Lake Skadar. Given the obvious intra-party differences over the issue of the CPC's claim for autocephaly, their position remained opaque. But as relations between ruling elites in Belgrade and Podgorica cooled as it became evident that the Montenegrin government would pursue independence, the conflict between the SPC and the Montenegrin government (who the SPC alleged were promoting 'false churches' and 'false priests' as part of their quest for independence) intensified.[75]

In October 2004, relations were strained again when two staff members from *Radio Svetigora* were attacked by a 'group of youths' in Cetinje. A press statement from the SPC in the wake of the attack implied that the Montenegrin government had created a political and social context in which such attacks were becoming commonplace, particularly in Cetinje. Moreover, they argued, reports of intimidation, gathered over years, had led to no formal charges being brought.[76] Tensions between the SPC and CPC (and the SPC and the Montenegrin government) were further exacerbated by the appearance, in June 2005, of a small tin church on the peak of Mount Rumija near the town of Bar. Mount Rumija has traditionally been a place of pilgrimage for Montenegro's main religious communities (Orthodox, Catholic and Muslim). Every August, pilgrims from these faiths climb to the peak in honour of St Vladimir, who died fifty years before the 'Great Schism' of 1054 (whereupon Christendom was divided into eastern and western branches). The tradition is a symbol of inter-religious and interethnic cooperation, and had continued throughout the most difficult of times. But less than a year before Montenegro's independence referendum (held on 21 May 2006), the SPC, with the help of a helicopter flown by the Army of Serbia and Montenegro, placed a prefabricated tin church on the peak. Its appearance angered those who argued that Rumija was a symbol of inter-religious harmony and was immediately interpreted by pro-independence parties and organizations (such as the CPC) as a threat to those who wished to pursue independence – the SPC marking 'their' territory in Montenegro.[77] Rumours (that turned out to be unfounded) circulated that the SPC might also place similar structures on other peaks in Montenegro: Bjelasice (near Kolašin), Komovi (near Andrijevica), Lovćen (near Cetinje) and Durmitor (near Žabljak).[78] The CPC argued that this was, once again, proof of the SPC's misuse of religion for political ends.

Indeed, in advance of the May 2006 referendum, Amfilohije played a significant role in the 'Movement for a Joint State of Serbia and Montenegro' and was often considered a more effective articulator of Montenegrin Serb interests than the de facto leader of the bloc, Predrag Bulatović (the SNP leader). In the weeks and months prior to the referendum, the SPC–CPC conflict continued, though it was largely obscured by pre-referendum political campaigning. In April 2006, Amfilohije railed at the CPC for attempting to force their way into the St Nikola church in Bajice, near Cetinje, stating explicitly that he believed the Montenegrin government to be supporting the actions of the CPC. Yet the issue of the CPC was only a marginal theme in the respective (pro- and anti-independence) campaigns, though it carried significant symbolic weight nevertheless. In any event, the CPC would use Montenegro's seemingly inexorable path to independence to argue that their church, too, should be a pillar of any independent Montenegrin state.

7

From the War in Kosovo to the Belgrade Agreement (1998–2002)

Events following the DPS split and the subsequent presidential elections in 1997 and the inauguration of Milo Djukanović as Montenegro's president in January 1998 had served only to further damage relations between Belgrade and Podgorica. Meanwhile, Djukanović continued to ingratiate himself to the US and Western European governments. In April 1998, as the crisis in neighbouring Kosovo was unfolding, he visited Rome, Paris and London – followed by a trip (by invitation of the US State Department and the US Congress, to Washington D.C.). After several rounds of meetings, he addressed diplomats, journalists and carefully selected guests at the Mayflower Hotel, where a reception was held in his honour. He went to significant lengths to make the case that Montenegro was a democratic state impeded in its democratic transition only by its partner in the SRJ, Serbia.[1] He did not mention Kosovo in his speech, but the issue loomed large nevertheless. As armed conflict between the Kosovo Liberation Army (*Ushtria Çlirimtare e Kosovës* – UÇK/KLA) and Serbian security forces escalated, the Montenegrin government sought to distance themselves from the approaching maelstrom, declaring neutrality and advocating dialogue with the Kosovo Albanians (albeit in conjunction with the European Union (EU)). But the attacks by the KLA and the retaliations by the Serb police were driving an inexorable spiral of violence, which worsened throughout 1998. While the Montenegrin government endeavoured to distance themselves from events in Kosovo, they simply could not avoid being significantly impacted by the worsening conflict just across the border, not only because thousands of Kosovo Albanian refugees were fleeing the worsening conflict and seeking shelter in Montenegro (particularly because of fighting around Peć), but because the VJ were alleging that weapons were being smuggled by the KLA through Montenegro – at the border crossing at Božaj (near Tuzi), between the Albanian border and Plav/Gusinje and across Skadar Lake.[2]

The Montenegrin government were all too aware that as an integral part of the SRJ and home to parts of the SRJ's military infrastructure, they would be targeted as part of any NATO bombing campaign. They cautioned against baiting NATO, who had warned, in October 1998, of the possibility of airstrikes against the SRJ. During a meeting of the SRJ's 'Supreme Defence Council', held in Belgrade on 4 October

1998, the Montenegrin representatives expressed concern over developments in Kosovo and the possibility that a conflict there could result in NATO taking military action against the SRJ. Djukanović claimed that such concerns were dismissed by Milošević, who was sceptical about NATO's threat to bomb the SRJ.[3] The Serbian president considered the international community's warnings to be hollow rhetoric and that Kosovo was an internal matter, and the NATO alliance a paper tiger.[4] In any event, a ceasefire brokered by the US Special Envoy, Richard Holbrooke, and signed in 1998 temporarily ended hostilities. But Milošević's assessment (reached in spite of the advice of VJ General, Momčilo Perišić, that a conflict with NATO was unwinnable) that the Western military alliance would not act if hostilities resumed was a dangerous miscalculation. Throughout 1998, the situation on the ground in Kosovo deteriorated, and the international community focused their attention on events unfolding there. With the then US secretary of state, Madeleine Albright, denouncing the Milošević regime as 'the last powerful obstacle to the integration of the Balkans into a democratic Europe', it was clear that Kosovo would be the focus of international attention. Indeed, after months of brinkmanship, mutual threats and failed negotiations (the much-feted 'European Dayton') at Rambouillet, France, in February 1999 (which Milošević did not attend), NATO began a bombing campaign against the SRJ. It would last seventy-eight days; far longer than leaders of the Western alliance had dared to predict.

On 24 March 1999, the NATO bombing campaign against the SRJ commenced. Military targets were hit throughout the SRJ, including Montenegro. Momir Bulatović, the SRJ's president, announced a state of emergency, a move interpreted in Podgorica as a means of undermining Montenegro's institutions and facilitating a takeover by the VJ.[5] Djukanović called on Montenegrins to remain calm, show restraint and remain united.[6] While the NATO bombing campaign had significantly less material impact on Montenegro than on Serbia (where the physical damage and civilian casualty rate far exceed that experienced in Montenegro), the targeting of Montenegrin territory was essentially 'secondary and selective', with NATO bombs primarily aimed at VJ assets within Montenegro (Podgorica airport in the Golubovci area and the airstrip in Berane), not, on the whole, aimed at the civilian infrastructure.[7] Aware of the potential for instability, Milo Djukanović made an immediate appeal for 'calm and unity'.[8] Likewise, the speaker of the Montenegrin Assembly, Svetozar Marović, cautioned political parties had to put their differences aside, as Montenegro was 'more important than any political party'.[9] Nevertheless, from the commencement of what became a seventy-eight-day bombing campaign, the internal social, political and security situation in Montenegro steadily worsened. On 1 April 1999, Djukanović met with Orthodox, Muslim and Catholic religious leaders in Montenegro (Amfilohije Radović, Idris Demirović, Zeff Gashi and Ilija Janjić, respectively), appealing to them to help calm tensions. (Their statements were published verbatim in *Pobjeda* the following day.[10]) A joint statement released following the meeting implored all Montenegrin citizens of different faiths to remain united, emphasizing the need to preserve 'civic peace and ethnic and religious tolerance in Montenegro and Yugoslavia' and that this was 'the most important obligation of all our citizens'.[11] But with every bomb that fell on Montenegro that became more challenging.

Targeting Montenegro, whatever the military rationale, created a dangerous situation for the Montenegrin government.[12] They feared their grip on power would be significantly weakened with every NATO bombing operation that targeted Montenegro. The British defence minister, George Robertson, later acknowledged the realities on the ground in Montenegro and the challenges faced by the government, but argued that 'it was necessary to take out some of the air defence capabilities of Yugoslavia that were based in Montenegro', as well as 'huge petroleum facilities that could not be allowed to continue [to function]'.[13] Djukanović appealed to NATO to take seriously the risk that the targeting of Montenegrin territory could have upon his government's ability to preserve peace and stability. 'Every bomb that fell on Montenegro', he later said, 'threatened to weaken my government.'[14] The issue of whether or not to target Montenegro became one, which strained the NATO alliance. Wesley Clark, NATO'S Supreme Allied Commander (SACEUR), wanted to increase the targeting of what was essentially civilian infrastructure in Serbia and also wanted to hit targets in Montenegro. While Montenegro was ostensibly neutral, Clark claimed that NATO were 'becoming increasingly concerned' about the VJ 'air base' in Podgorica, but were 'stopped at every turn by concerns, especially by the French, that we [NATO] would undermine the tenuous grip on power by Montenegro's Western-inclined president, Milo Djukanović'.[15] Though he was broadly supported by the NATO secretary general, Javier Solana, there were political considerations to take into account. Solana knew that Clark was aware of a 'supply route to Milošević through Montenegro', but he acknowledged that 'Montenegro was not part of Milošević's coalition ... so we had problems with that'.[16] And it was indeed the French president, Jacques Chirac, who forcefully argued that targeting Montenegro would be counterproductive for NATO. Doing so would, he argued, 'play into Milošević's hands' by 'weakening President Djukanović, who, by and large, represented some kind of opposition to Milošević'.[17] Following a subsequent telephone exchange between Chirac, Djukanović and US President Bill Clinton, it was concluded that the strategy of targeting Montenegro was potentially damaging to the interests of the NATO campaign.[18] Thereafter, Montenegro largely ceased to be targeted by NATO, though there were further casualties. Six people, including three children, were killed on 30 April 1999 on a bridge over the Lim River (which was hit by ten NATO bombs) in Murino, a small village on the road between Andrijevica and Plav.[19]

The promise of more limited bombing did not, however, ease tensions on the ground. This was ominously manifest in the tense stand off between the VJ and Montenegrin police. Milošević sent equally unambiguous signals. The moderate VJ general, Radoslav Martinović (a Montenegrin), was replaced by the more hawkish Milorad Obradović (also a Montenegrin). Consequently, rumours abound that a coup d'etat against Djukanović was imminent.[20] Fears of a military coup were fuelled by statements emanating from Belgrade. The Serbian deputy prime minister and SRS leader, Vojislav Šešelj, warned that any attempt by the Montenegrin authorities to use the cloak of the NATO campaign to seek independence would 'end in blood'.[21] Responding to the speculation and threats, Djukanović warned that if it was to be attempted, it would lead to 'the most tragic and violent conflict so far in the former Yugoslavia'.[22] NATO also continued to provide rhetorical support for Djukanović, by stating that 'any move against him and his government will have grave consequences' for Milošević.[23]

Key to control over the social and political climate in Montenegro was control of the media. RTCG, the republic's TV broadcaster, was under the control of the DPS, and it became a crucial instrument for conveying the government's message that the NATO campaign was targeting the Milošević regime, not ordinary citizens in Serbia and Montenegro. It became a matter of some urgency for Belgrade, in the context of a 'state of war' to bring Montenegrin media under the control of the VJ. They attempted to do so in the early weeks of the NATO campaign. Djukanović claimed that representatives of the VJ came to Podgorica to attempt to persuade his government to 'censure TV because of the state of war. I later met with him and told him that this would not be allowed'. Following this exchange, Djukanović claims that his government 'found out about a military plan [prepared by VJ] to take over the RTCG building' but that they army abandoned the idea 'because they realized we were ready to defend democratic institutions in Montenegro and that we were ready for a direct confrontation [with the VJ] if they tried this'.[24]

During the NATO bombing, however, the VJ had regularly attempted to provoke Montenegrin authorities. Towards the end of May 1999, the VJ essentially blockaded the Port of Bar, while Momir Bulatović, the president of the SRJ, spoke at a rally in Podgorica whereupon he implored the Montenegrin government to place the police under the control of the VJ 'for the benefit of the whole SRJ and its citizens'. The tensions between the VJ and the police and quasi-paramilitary groups loyal to the Montenegrin government increased. Indeed, there were a number of scenarios in which a single shot fired could have sparked a far more serious conflict. According to a report by the European Stability Initiative (ESI), 'for a period of time [during the NATO bombing], VJ troops adopted an aggressive posture', with tension particularly acute in the Debeli Brijeg area and in the environs of Cetinje, sometimes 'conducting house-to-house searches and threatening political allies of Djukanović'.[25] Indeed, on 31 May 1999, on the outskirts of Cetinje, the VJ blocked the road between the town and the coast, erecting roadblocks and restricting movement. Such developments were sufficient for the citizens of the town to feel under siege.[26] Within hours of the VJ erecting roadblocks outside Cetinje, protestors gathered outside the municipality building demonstrating against the roadblocks and the attempts by the army to enter the town. The protestors called on the VJ to leave, emphasizing that they sought a peaceful resolution, though they warned that *Cetinje će braniti Cetinjani* (Cetinje will defends citizens of Cetinje). A tense stand-off then ensued between the VJ and the local Cetinje paramilitary formation, the Lovćen Guard (named in honour of the 'Lovćen Brigade', a paramilitary group established by Krsto Popović in Cetinje in 1942 under the aegis of the Italians), led by Božidar 'Boba' Bogdanović, a Montenegrin police reservist who had been a leading figure in the Cetinje 'resistance' throughout the 1990s (see Chapter 6).[27] The VJ was, seemingly, rather shocked by the determination of Bogdanović and his men, but they succeeded in arresting him and two of his fellow militias. The arrests sparked what threatened to turn into an armed rebellion by members not only of the Cetinje militia, but the police and even ordinary citizens. Although a peaceful resolution was ultimately found – the VJ halted their attempts to enter the town – the incident was indicative of the heightened tensions that existed in Montenegro.

The NATO bombing, however limited, and the continuing flow of ethnic Albanian refugees coming from Kosovo (which eventually amounted to approximately 80,000 people: over 10 per cent of Montenegro's population), put a considerable strain on Montenegro's capacity, while threatening to destabilise the republic's delicate ethnic and social balance.[28] Refugees arrived in large waves during the first week of the NATO bombing campaign – many went to northern Albania, a large number to FYR Macedonia, with large numbers also coming to Montenegro.[29] The majority of those who made the journey to Montenegro were concentrated in Plav, Gusinje and Ulcinj, all located close to the Montenegrin border with Kosovo and Albania. The residents of both towns were ill-equipped to offer anything other than the most basic of support to the refugees, but they did so nevertheless – often providing shelter to refugees in their homes.[30] The NATO campaign ended on 10 June, following the signing of a peace deal (known as the 'Military Technical Agreement') in Kumanovo, FYR Macedonia. Milosevič – who had been indicted by the International Criminal Tribunal for the former Yugoslavia (ICTY) on 27 May 1999 – did his upmost to portray the conflict with NATO as a victory, but he came under increasing pressure in the subsequent months. By then, Kosovo Albanian refugees temporarily located in Rožaje, Plav, Gusinje and Ulcinj had begun to return to Kosovo, to be replaced by Serb, Montenegrin and Roma refugees from Kosovo fleeing from reprisals by angry Albanian returnees.[31] Towns such as Andrijevica and Berane were, in particular, placed under significant pressure by the influx (though many Roma would eventually settle in the Konik and Vrela Ribnička settlements in Podgorica).

Relations between Podgorica and Belgrade had been severely damaged by the NATO bombing campaign. In its wake, the Montenegrin government sought to redefine its status vis-à-vis Serbia within the framework of the SRJ, implying that there was now a 'new minimum' which would be acceptable to Montenegro.[32] They thus drafted a plan to redefine the SRJ as a confederation of two equal states, both of which would possess separate monetary systems, separate foreign ministries, and, controversially, separate defence capabilities.[33] As expected, the proposal received a lukewarm response in Belgrade. Vojislav Šešelj immediately rejected the proposal, and Milošević thereafter despatched a representative from the SRS (Šešelj's party) to discuss the proposal. Talks, unsurprisingly, quickly broke down, and the Montenegrin government began preparing to endeavour to forge a greater level of independence – inside or outside the SRJ.[34]

Incidents involving the VJ continued to be the case of tension between Belgrade and Podgorica. These incidents were sporadic, but potentially explosive. On the evening of 8 December 1999, for example, the VJ (responding to an announcement by the Montenegrin government that Podgorica airport was 'government property') seized control of the civilian section of the airport – which had a dual civilian and military utility – and the airport's control tower for 'security reasons'.[35] Normal service soon resumed, but it was, again, demonstrative of the residual tension. And in early 2000, the VJ again provocatively deployed troops at strategic sites such as border crossings, airports and roads throughout Montenegro. Yet, despite the actions of the VJ, Milošević stated in his New Year address in January 2000 that if Montenegrins consider that life outside the SRJ would be better for them, 'then they are entitled to choose that life'.[36]

But the further actions of the VJ suggested that Milošević's conciliatory statements were somewhat disingenuous. And perhaps the most troubling development for the Montenegrin government was the emergence of the highly trained 'Seventh Battalion' of the VJ Military Police, largely comprised of Montenegrins loyal to the SNP and Milošević and estimated to number in the region of 1,000 well-trained men.[37]

Military mobilization was not the only method for coercing the Montenegrin political scene. In Montenegrin society, the *pleme* (clan or tribe) is historically fixed in the collective memory, and was channelled as a form of political divergence over the issues of state, nation and identity, adding a socio-cultural dimension to existing political dimensions. This 'exotic resurrection', argued Milan Popović, 'inserted itself in the very midst of a heavy political confrontation between Milo Djukanović's Montenegro and Slobodan Milošević's Serbia'.[38] The objective of Milošević and Bulatović was to revive traditional clan loyalties and identities as a method of mobilizing and harnessing the dissatisfaction among those Montenegrins who regarded themselves as Serbs, with the overarching aim of forging a powerful counterforce that could be used to topple the Montenegrin government.[39] They were, according to Lenard Cohen, 'a customary non-governmental association that served their political interests'.[40] Thus, in the north of Montenegro these clans were resurrected, with *plemenske skupštine* (clan assemblies) being held in the areas where the Kuči, Rovci, Vasojevići, Uskoci, Drobjanaci, Morača and Zeta clans predominated. Although the meetings seemed, at least superficially, to be spontaneous and characterized by the consumption of large amounts alcohol and listening to *guslari* (gusle player), there was a distinct political dynamic to the meetings (the vast majority of the participants were either members of or voters for the SNP).[41] But while the resurrection of the clans may have appeared like a bizarre throwback, political leaders in Montenegro recognized their potential as a destabilizing force. The NS leader, Novak Kilibarda, warned that civil war in Montenegro could begin 'with the singing of patriotic songs accompanied by playing the gusle', while Svetozar Marović acknowledged that appeals to clan support could potentially mobilize 'thousands of people'.[42] But on the pro-independence side, too, there was a mobilization of sorts. The Montenegrin Liberation Movement (*Crnogorski oslobodilački pokret* – COP), comprised of members of the Lovćen Guard that had clashed with VJ troops in May 1999, began to mobilize in Cetinje and its environs. But while the challenge from the clans would amount to little in the final analysis, the Montenegrin government were careful not to underestimate the dangers of their politicization. In a thinly veiled threat to the clan assemblies, Milo Djukanović, speaking in Berane (the home of the Vasojević clan), stated that 'Montenegro knows how to build and to defend its state'.[43]

With internal tensions simmering, the 'statehood question' remained unresolved. Following the end of the NATO bombing, the international community sent ambiguous and often contradictory signals to the Montenegrin leadership; they encouraged dissent against Milošević and offered assistance in consolidating internal security, while cautioning against explicit moves towards outright independence. The Montenegrin government did, however, endeavour to forge greater independence in the economic sphere. In order to increase levels of foreign direct investment (FDI) and attract greater numbers of tourists, the Montenegrin government dropped visa requirements. Furthermore, the Montenegrin authorities, in an attempt to minimize the influence of the Central Bank of the SRJ over its economic affairs, introduced the deutschmark (DM) as a parallel currency (Montenegro used the euro as its sole currency from 2002 onwards). Montenegro also received significant levels of aid, receiving $55 million in 1999 and twice that amount the following year.[44] By December 1999, the Montenegrin prime minister, Filip Vujanović, stated that Montenegro now possessed 'economic, customs, visa and monetary sovereignty', and this meant that 'the international community could now provide access to international organisations and business'.[45] The reaction from Belgrade was essentially to cut Montenegro off from Serbian markets (even establishing border controls between the two republics), a process which had begun in early 1999.[46]

Further asserting their independence from Belgrade, the Montenegrin government quickly established a 'foreign service', led by Branko Lukovac. Having previously been the SFRJ's ambassador to Tanzania and (later) Ethiopia, and having worked in South Africa during the transition towards democratic elections, his impressive CV made him the perfect candidate for the post of Montenegro's first effective foreign minister since 1918.[47] He chose to re-enter the realm of international relations when asked by Djukanović during the NATO bombing campaign to head a Montenegrin foreign service that would operate from Ljubljana in Slovenia. From there he established a wide range of international contacts and essentially lobbied to raise the profile of Montenegro. He became the foreign minister officially in January 2000, and in June of that year he attended a session of the UN Security Council as a guest of the Slovenian delegation. He used this platform to assert that the SRJ no longer had any right to represent Montenegro or its interests at the UN or, indeed, within other international organizations.[48] With Lukovac's determined lobbying and the establishment of 'representative missions' (which were opened in London, Rome, Ljubljana, Sarajevo and Berlin), the republic's international profile was raised, as was the dynamics of the 'Montenegrin Question'.[49]

Away from the glare of international institutions, there remained, in Montenegro, real political and social tension. A newly formed unit of Montenegrin militias, under the aegis of the Montenegrin interior ministry (*Ministarstvo unutrašnjih poslova* – MUP) and loyal to Djukanović, emerged. Known as *Specijalni* (Specials), they had undergone training with the British 'Special Air Service' (SAS) after the war in Kosovo ended.[50] Montenegro did not have an army per se, so Djukanović strengthened the Montenegrin police force to 20,000 men and comprising individuals who had previously served in the VJ, loyalists with DPS connections and others.[51] It was purged of those deemed inappropriate or potentially disloyal (member of the SNP or other pro-Serb parties), and thus many of those excluded from the police joined the Seventh Battalion of the VJ.[52] These two armed groups patrolled Montenegrin cities and towns daily and in a mutually suspicious, tense and semi-hostile mood.[53] The tension was particularly acute in Podgorica where the MUP 'Specials' loyal to Djukanović were guarding government buildings. Just across the Morača River, however, the Seventh Battalion of the VJ were located in their barracks (in nearby Preko Morače), which Djukanović labelled the 'paramilitary force' of Milošević and his supporters in Montenegro (the SNP).[54] From their respective locations in the city, the two groups eyed each other with deep and mutual suspicion – but tensions between the two groups (and between the *Specijalni* and other VJ units) were manifest far beyond Montenegro's capital.[55] Blockades of the border between Montenegro and Albania in February 2000 at Božaj (near Tuzi) raised tensions, while a grenade explosion at a police station in Bijelo Polje was suspected to be the work of two members of the Seventh Battalion, who were driving past at the time of the explosion (though they were later released after a short period in police custody).[56] On 9 March 2000, Milo Djukanović (upon his return from meetings in Sarajevo) was denied landing permission in Podgorica airport and requested, after consultations with his closest advisors, that the plane be diverted to Tivat airport instead for 'security reasons'.[57] However, tensions peaked in the summer and autumn of 2000, a dangerous period peppered with potentially explosive incidents.[58] In one such incident, a boat carrying Montenegrin police was attacked by the VJ on Lake Skadar, though the VJ later claimed that not only were they unaware that the boat belonged to the Montenegrin police and that their actions were motivated by their 'fight against smuggling' in the border area between Montenegro and Albania.[59]

In June 2000, Milo Djukanović's security advisor, Goran Žugić,[60] was assassinated by a lone gunman outside his home in Podgorica – causing, according to the Montenegrin weekly *Monitor*, 'shock, disbelief and fear' and further fuelling fears that greater political violence was inevitable.[61] In the wake of Žugić's murder, Djukanović directly implicated Milošević. Nothing, he resolved, 'will discourage and waver us in our intent to continue with the policy which will lead Montenegro as a stable, democratic and open community by the road of peace to join the company of developed European states and nations'.[62] The murder took place during the campaigning for municipal elections in both Podgorica and Herceg Novi (held in June 2000), unscheduled elections that were forced by the LSCG's abrupt withdrawal from the *Da Živimo Bolje* coalition. Their justification for this was that pre-coalition agreements had not been kept between the coalition partners. There was also wide-ranging speculation that the LSCG (which held the balance of power in both municipalities) were seeking to capitalize on what its leadership perceived as a change in the public mood vis-à-vis independence.[63] It was a risky, and ultimately unsuccessful, gambit, and one that would contribute significantly to the downfall of the LSCG. The election campaigns were also impacted by events in Serbia. On 6 June 2000, less than a week before the municipal elections, Milošević and the SRJ government adopted a series of amendments to SRJ constitution, which were designed to curtail the representation of Montenegrin interests in federal bodies. The most controversial of these revisions determined that the president of the SRJ would be directly elected rather than elected by the federal parliament, opening up the possibility of Milošević remaining in power despite any objections Montenegrin deputies in the SRJ may have. In any event, the result of the elections demonstrated in stark terms the divided nature of Montenegrin society (and the differences between specific areas). In Podgorica, the DŽB coalition won comfortably, while in Herceg Novi the *Za Yugoslaviju* (For Yugoslavia), which included the SNP and other Montenegrin Serb parties, did likewise – the victory facilitated, in part, by the votes of Bosnian and Croatian Serbs who had acquired SRJ citizenship.[64]

Following DŽB's victory in the Podgorica municipal elections, Djukanović announced that the ruling Montenegrin coalition would not participate in SRJ elections in September 2000, despite attempts by the international community to persuade him otherwise. He justified this by making reference to what he termed 'illegal' changes to the constitution and his conviction that the SRJ was a sham. Despite appeals by the Serbian opposition and the United States (Madeleine Albright flew to Rome to meet Djukanović in an attempt to persuade him, unsuccessfully, to allow his government to participate), the DPS-led coalition opted not do so. The elections, of course, went ahead regardless, and the SRJ president, Momir Bulatović, appealed to Montenegrins to ignore the boycott and vote. Even Milošević visited Montenegro on the campaign trail, briefly speaking in Berane, also telling the gathered crowd to engage in the elections and to ignore the calls for a boycott. But Bulatović's conviction that there would be large turnout in Montenegro was misplaced. Djukanović's call for Montenegrins to ignore the elections was, to a significant extent, heeded.

The 24 September 2000 elections produced what appeared a convincing victory for the Democratic Opposition of Serbia (*Demokratska opozicija Srbije* – DOS), led symbolically by Vojislav Koštunica (a former Belgrade University lecturer and constitutional lawyer), though they were aided significantly by pre-election activities of the student-led organization *Otpor* (Resistance). However, Milošević refused to accept the outcome, and though both DOS and representatives of the international community implored Milošević to step down gracefully, a stand-off ensued. Thereafter, on 5 October 2000, mass demonstrations in Belgrade forced Milošević to capitulate, albeit with the upmost reluctance. The protests (dubbed 'the October Revolution') heralded the end of Milošević's rule and a new era in Serbian politics. But it would also mark a watershed for Montenegro. With the fall of Milošević in Serbia, the policy of greater independence for Montenegro, once encouraged by Montenegro's Western allies (though, it must be said, these allies were careful never to give their formal blessing to Montenegrin independence), would now be largely discouraged by an international community keen to stabilize relations between Belgrade and Podgorica. The objective of independence (a useful lever in the struggle to undermine the Milošević regime) would, therefore, no longer be enthusiastically supported by Montenegro's powerful American and European allies.[65] Within the SRJ, the DPS boycott of the federal elections had not endeared them to DOS, many of whom, including the leader of Serbia's *Demokratska stranka* (DS), Zoran Djindjić, were opposed to Montenegrin independence (though Djindjić had sought refuge in Montenegro during the Kosovo war, knew Djukanović well and enjoyed cordial relations with him).[66] Nevertheless, while the Montenegrin government's argument that lack of democracy in Serbia and the resilience of the Milošević regime were impediments to its own democratic development, the removal of Milošević did not mean that Montenegrin aspirations for independence had ceased to exist.[67] By the time that the Milošević regime fell on 5 October 2000, Montenegro had already assumed many of the powers once possessed by the SRJ (excluding VJ and air traffic control), and Djukanović argued that Montenegro 'practically functioned as an independent state', possessing 'almost all functions of an independent state' including 'independent foreign policies, independent security policies, independent monetary policies, independent customs and foreign trade'.[68] Nevertheless, Montenegro remained de jure (if not de facto) a federal unit within the SRJ, and it was uncertain whether a majority of Montenegrins would indeed opt for independence, should they be given the option to do so.[69]

But it soon became evident that the issue of Montenegrin statehood would not disappear from the agenda, despite the obvious relief expressed in Podgorica following Milošević's fall. What became equally evident in the weeks following 5 October 2000 was that the relationship between Vojislav Koštunica and Djukanović would become little more than lukewarm. Indeed, during Koštunica's first visit to Podgorica as SRJ president on 26 October 2000, a lengthy meeting between delegations from Montenegro and Serbia proved rather uncomfortable, as it became increasingly evident that the two had divergent visions of the future structure of the SRJ and, moreover, of Montenegro's role within it.[70] Djukanović later said that his argument that the SRJ should become 'an alliance of two independent states' was not received positively by Koštunica.[71] But it was the latter that now possessed the momentum and the support of the international community in the post-Milošević SRJ, despite the fact that the political context within Montenegro (including the growing sentiment for independence) could not be easily neutralized, let alone reversed. In short, the internal dynamics of Montenegrin politics could not be changed on the basis of the democratic changes which had taken place in Serbia.[72] And while short-term objectives (the fall of the Milošević regime) had taken primacy over the medium- or long-term developments, and while the United States and its Western European allies were content to use the threat of Montenegrin secession from the SRJ to undermine Milošević, they had little appetite for a new round of Yugoslav disintegration. With no clear strategy for dealing with the residue of this policy, the United States and the EU simply hoped that the issue of Montenegrin statehood would be forced back into the margins now that Serbia had a new leadership.

Despite these external pressures, the DPS-led Montenegrin government were unwilling to give up the 'independence project'; after all, they had been instrumental in turning public opinion in favour of it.[73] Indeed, they were unlikely to surrender aspects of independence that they *had* gained since 1997; on the contrary, they harboured a desire to build an independent state, which they considered the most effective instrument for protecting the established political order in Montenegro.[74] Paradoxically, however, the government of Slobodan Milošević and the threat of a VJ attack on Montenegro had been instrumental factors in bolstering support for independence. In light of developments in Serbia, the Montenegrin government could no longer trade on the threat emanating from Belgrade, and if independence was to be achieved, it would have to be justified utilizsing different arguments and justifications. A new approach was needed, and thus a new strategy was formulated. During the DPS party congress in 2001, their party programme was modified to reflect the new reality. Indeed, where the DPS leadership once argued for the *need* for independence (due in large part to the undemocratic nature of the SRJ, Montenegro's status within it, the threat posed by Milošević), they now began to emphasize Montenegro's *right* to independence.[75] This was in spite of the January 2001 'Koštunica Proposal', which set out a new constitutional arrangement for the SRJ, which while giving Montenegro greater autonomy stopped short of creating a union of two independent states.

With negotiations stalling between Serbia and Montenegro, the DPS faced significant internal obstacles linked to the future of the SRJ. The NS decision to withdraw from the governing coalition in February 2001 (precipitated by their opposition to DPS/SDP calls for the SRJ to be reconstituted as a union of two independent states) meant that the DPS/SDP no longer possessed a parliamentary majority, and thus parliament was dissolved and fresh elections scheduled for 22 April 2001. Throughout the electoral campaign(s), the issue of Montenegro's statehood dominated, with the two largest coalitions presenting competing visions of the future of the SRJ. The DPS and their post-1997 coalition partner, the SNP, ran together as part of the pro-independence *Podjeda je Crne Gore* (Victory for Montenegro), while the NS/SNS and SNP campaigned collectively as the pro-Yugoslav *Zajedno za Jugoslaviju* (Together for Yugoslavia) coalition. The campaign was generally calm, though the campaign rhetoric was often negative, with both coalitions exchanging personal slurs and trading accusations of corruption and electoral fraud.[76]

The result was extremely tight and again demonstrated the clear division in Montenegrin society vis-à-vis the statehood issue. The DPS-led coalition won thirty-six seats in parliament, while the pro-Yugoslav coalition won thirty-three seats. The former thus required an additional coalition partner to form a government. The LSCG, which had run alone in the elections and won six seats, were the obvious candidates, but their own leaders took a tough line, seeking significant concessions from their prospective coalition partners.[77] The LSCG insisted, for example, upon being given a number of key posts in a new government – minister of police (normally a post occupied by a DPS member), minister of justice and the post of state prosecutor, among others.[78] Moreover, they insisted upon the scheduling of an independence referendum during the four-year mandate of the government. For a party that had only won six seats in the parliamentary elections, such demands seemed rather ostentatious, even given their anti-war, anti-Milošević and pro-independence credentials. It was, of course, a bold attempt to capitalize on perceived DPS weakness and place the LSCG at the centre of government, but the ambitious strategy would, ultimately, prove counterproductive. In any event, no agreement was reached and instead the LSCG committed only to 'support' for a minority government – on the basis that the DPS–SDP would schedule a referendum.[79] And statements given by the Montenegrin government implied that this would take place soon, with the Montenegrin president, Filip Vujanović, stating that the best way out of the existing constitutional crisis would be for the SRJ to agree on a consensual separation.[80]

At this juncture, the EU, sceptical about Montenegrin independence, also applied pressure on Montenegro. Their justification for so doing was underpinned by three key concerns. First, that the political and social climate in Montenegro, with an almost equally divided population, was not a terribly promising foundation for an independent state.[81] Secondly, there existed a concern that Montenegrin independence would serve to encourage others (Republika Srpska and Kosovo, for example) to seek independence. Finally, the EU was concerned about possible implications for Serbia: that the loss of Montenegro (and, potentially, Kosovo) would be a psychological blow for Serbs and dangerous for their new and unstable governing coalition. Consequently, the EU's foreign policy and security chief (and former NATO secretary general), Javier Solana, played a significant role in preventing a referendum in Montenegro; and while still relying on significant Western aid, Djukanović had only limited scope for manoeuvre.

Pressure was being brought to bear on Djukanović, and not merely in the form of EU power politics. In May 2001, the Croatian weekly *Nacional* proceeded to publish a number of articles (which were subsequently republished in the Montenegrin daily *Dan*) alleging that Djukanović had a business relationship and friendship with the notorious criminal Stanko 'Cane' Subotić, that he was directly involved in the trafficking of cigarettes (the profits from which were shared with Subotić) and of having been involved in the murder of his own security advisor, Goran Žugić, in Podgorica in June 2000.[82] The accusations were flatly denied. Soon after, however, the former Italian finance minister, Ottavio Del Turco, publicly accused Djukanović of having close links to organized crime, being the lynchpin in the illegal mechanisms that controlled the smuggling of cigarettes in the Balkans and having provided safe haven for Italian criminals in the Montenegrin town of Bar. Thereafter, the public prosecutor in the Italian port city of Bari, Guisseppe Scelsi, was initiating investigative proceedings, alleging that Djukanović (in concert with the Italian mafia and the cigarette manufacturers RJ Reynolds and Philip Morris) had been involved in smuggling untaxed cigarettes into the EU from the port of Bar – an endeavour, it was alleged, that generated significant profits for the participants, including Djukanović.[83] These profits, claimed Djukanović, were not channelled into private hands, but rather used to pay for the state's running costs during the period of UN-imposed sanctions during the 1992–95 war in Bosnia & Herzegovina. The Italians prosecutors were, however, unsympathetic to such altruistic motives and continued to pursue the case.[84]

The EU, meanwhile, was doing its upmost to discourage the Montenegrin government from scheduling a referendum, with Solana playing a key role in ensuring that an agreement could be reached between the EU, Serbia and Montenegro that would stop the latter from pursuing independence. During a visit to the SRJ in December 2001, the French president, Jacques Chirac, unambiguously stated that the EU might not recognize the independence of Montenegro even if the government held a referendum and was successful in attaining a majority in favour of it.[85] Solana's diplomacy also went into overdrive, warning the Montenegrins that independence would not be in their best interests and that the economic well-being of the republic's citizens would be threatened if its government chose this path. Eventually, after months of EU pressure, the Montenegrin delegation finally acquiesced, signing the Belgrade Agreement on 14 March 2002, much to the dismay of pro-independence Montenegrins.[86] To them not only was the formation of the state union not subject to public consultation or put to a referendum vote, but was essentially hammered out behind closed doors by political elites from Serbia, Montenegro and the EU, and thus regarded by many in Montenegro as an imposition that lacked legitimacy.[87] Arguing that this was far from the case, the Montenegrin government lauded the creation of the new state as a medium-term victory, emphasizing that Montenegro had, for the first time in almost a century, been recognized by its own state name, albeit within the new federation.[88]

Approval for the Belgrade Agreement was immediately forthcoming from supporters of the union within the Montenegrin political spectrum, with parties such as the NS and SNP heralding the creation of the state union as a consolidation of Serb–Montenegrin unity and a rejection of the DPS and SDP's 'separatist policies'.[89] But while they may have been satisfied with the signing of the Belgrade Agreement, the news, by contrast, was not well received among advocates of independence. Small protests also took place in Podgorica, with 'hundreds of citizens' gathering outside the Montenegrin Assembly on 15 March 2002 to voice their objections.⁹⁰ Additionally, those who had thrown their lot in with the DPS felt betrayed by the signing of the Belgrade Agreement. A number of ministers resigned from the Montenegrin Assembly, and leading figures within the LSCG, such as Miodrag Živković, Vesna Perović and Miodrag Vicković, raged that the actions of Djukanović represented 'one of the biggest cases of treason in European history' (the LSCG thereafter sought to inflict damage on the Montenegrin government by entering into coalitions in a number of municipalities with the pro-union SNP).⁹¹ The Montenegrin minister of foreign affairs, Branko Lukovac, who had done much to promote the cause of Montenegrin independence, resigned his post immediately, and those Montenegrin intellectuals who had tentatively backed Djukanović now turned on him (and others seen as engineering Montenegro's agreement to become part of the new state union). In an open letter to Javier Solana, one hundred of them wrote to Solana to protest at the EU's policy towards Montenegro, which they argued, deprived the republic of, 'the right of existence and self-determination that is guaranteed by the Charter of the United Nations, and by both international covenants on human rights, as well as to respect her historical rights that were confirmed by the Badinter Commission and Lord Carrington's Peace Conference in 1991'.⁹²

But reaction to the signing of the agreement was hardly one of joy in Serbia either. Rightly, some within the Serbian government questioned whether Serbia's interests were sufficiently protected by a union in which a republic with twelve times the population of Montenegro would have to endure an equal position in decision-making procedures and distribution of key posts.⁹³ Within the Serbian delegation in the negotiations which led to the signing of the Belgrade Agreement, there were suspicions that the Montenegrin leadership, while they had signed, possessed a different agenda – that they were deferring a referendum, simply playing for time. Indeed, while Djukanović had signed the EU-brokered Belgrade Agreement, he had requested inter alia a number of important concessions built into it.⁹⁴ Moreover, the structure of the state union of Serbia and Montenegro could be best described as 'minimalist'. A council of ministers comprising of only five members chaired by a president, indirectly elected, and with very few powers. Add to that a joint parliament with 126 delegates (91 from Serbia and 35 from Montenegro) who were, in fact (and largely due to Montenegrin resistance to direct state union elections), delegates from the republican parliaments of Serbia and Montenegro, respectively. The agreement bestowed some positive discrimination in favour of Montenegro in the union's institutions, which was comprised of a unicameral parliament, a council of ministers (foreign affairs, defence, international economic relations, internal economic relations, human and minority rights, and a court with little jurisdictional competence).⁹⁵

With such an inauspicious beginning the state union was unlikely to function effectively, and despite the signing of the Belgrade Agreement, March 2002 would not mark a constructive beginning of a new state, but rather a new, interim stage in the Montenegrin independence project. The 'statehood question' continued to supersede every other issue in Montenegrin politics, meaning the state union was, in essence, one with a distinct 'expiry date'.[96] The Belgrade Agreement, in fact, exacerbated the identity issue within the republic, whereby supporters of the common state increasingly identified themselves as Serbs, and the proponents of independence as Montenegrins.[97] Moreover, the newly elected president of the state union, the former speaker of the Montenegrin Assembly, Svetozar Marović, would give clear indications that the signing of the Belgrade Agreement did not exclude a future referendum on Montenegrin independence declaring that it was 'Montenegro's right to independently choose its own path'.[98]

Thus, a three-year period began in which supporters of independence and supporters of union positioned themselves, anticipating a possible referendum. The DPS-led government, too, began their preparations, while committing little to ensuring that the joint state could function effectively. Domestic battles, however, would have to be fought first. The LSCG represented an obstacle for the DPS's claim to be the genuine independence option in Montenegro, and while they were a useful ally during and after the 1997 DPS split, their refusal to support the government after the signing of the Belgrade Agreement had led to the Montenegrin prime minister, Filip Vujanović, submitting his resignation. The LSCG were now an obstacle to the DPS attaining the mantle of the party of Montenegrin independence, particularly because Slavko Perović stated unambiguously that his party would never again enter a coalition with them.[99] But given that the LSCG could never forge a governing coalition strong enough in favour of independence without the DPS, it was something of a political suicide. Moreover, by making this bold assertion Perović isolated those within the LSCG (or their supporters) who believed that a pro-independence coalition with the DPS and SDP was *only* way in which that objective could be achieved. Some within the party clung defiantly to the idea that it should continue to go it alone; others disagreed. With the LSCG facing an internal crisis vis-à-vis the future direction of party policy, the DPS leadership sought to further undermine them.

The parliamentary elections in October 2002 would be the test case for whether the LSCG's stance was strategically beneficial for the party. The DPS and SDP ran together as the 'List for a European Montenegro' (*List za evropski Crnu Goru* – LZCG), the SNP, NS and SNS as Together for Change (*Zajedno za promjene* – ZP) coalition, while the LSCG ran independently. During the pre-election campaign, the DPS focused their invective not on Montenegro's Serb parties (who were the much-needed 'bogeymen') but primarily on the LSCG. The LSCG, their leadership, their undoubted command of the moral high ground, represented a more palpable threat to the DPS, so their weakening would facilitate the manoeuvre of the DPS into the position of the sole interpreter of the independence option. The objective, then, was simple – to destroy the LSCG and adopt much of the substance of the LSCG platform. In so doing, Djukanović and the DPS could emerge from the struggle as the only true party of Montenegrin independence.[100] The attacks would come not simply from within the ranks of the DPS, but from media that had previously supported them. This process began four years before, when the editorial staff of the two independent publications *Monitor* and *Vijesti* and many previously anti-regime intellectuals shifted towards Djukanović and the DPS, as the most pragmatic approach to reaching the objective of independence. Indeed, *Monitor* (originally a staunch supporter of the anti-war policies of the LSCG) published a series of rather derogatory editorials criticising, in unambiguous language, the LSCG leadership.[101]

The elections proved disastrous for the LSCG, the party gaining only four seats (a loss of two since the last elections). Conversely, the DPS–SDP coalition, while only winning by a relative majority, could rely on the support of the *Albanci zajedno* (Albanians Together) coalition in order to form a government. With the LSCG embattled, Djukanović and the DPS (alongside their coalition partners, the SDP) were elevated to the status of those most likely capable of delivering independence. In a surprising twist, Djukanović switched from the role of president to that of prime minister, allowing Filip Vujanović to contest the December 2002 presidential elections. This switch took place in the midst of a rather bizarre scandal which broke in the media in November 2002 – one that threatened to seriously damage Djukanović and his government. The scandal surrounding a young Moldovan woman, known only as S.C., who had taken refuge in a women's safe house in Podgorica, caused a sensation. S.C. claimed that she had been trafficked to Montenegro in 1999, and while there, she had been held against her well, forced into prostitution and thereafter subjected to serious sexual and physical abuse by her 'clients' – among which, it was alleged, were several high-ranking Montenegrin government officials, judges and police and civil servants. A criminal investigation then commenced against four people, including Zoran Piperović, Montenegro's deputy state prosecutor, and three others. The case, though formally dropped by Montenegrin prosecutors in May 2003 (ostensibly for lack evidence), left numerous unanswered questions nevertheless.[102]

These toxic allegations and an unstable coalition government gave the distinct impression that the DPS were on the ropes, and the subsequent debacle of the presidential elections would further reinforce that perception. The 22 December 2002 election failed due to a low turnout (less than the required 50 per cent) and an opposition boycott; a subsequent election, held on 9 February 2003, would prove likewise.[103] Vujanović would, however, win the subsequent presidential election held on 11 May 2003, defeating the LSCG leader, Miodrag Živković, but only after the 50 per cent turnout rule was abolished.[104] It was a rather circuitous method of doing so, but the DPS, as the largest party supporting Montenegro's independence, could now consolidate and make preparations for the scheduling of an independence referendum.

8

The Road to the Referendum (2003–6)

The assassination of the Serbian prime minister, Zoran Djindjić, in Belgrade on 12 March 2003, sent the state union into something of a crisis.[1] Just one year after the signing of the Belgrade Agreement, the union seemed to be drifting. The assassination and subsequent 'Operation Sabre' in Serbia only reinforced perceptions in Montenegro that Serbia was far from ready to make the kind of democratic reforms (and cooperation with the International Criminal Tribunal for the former Yugoslavia (ICTY)) that Djindjić himself had advocated.[2] But the period during which the state union was 'functioning' was one of intense activity in Montenegro, which, despite entering into the state union agreement, seemed to be charting its own course. Advocates of independence, having recovered from Djukanović's 'betrayal' in signing the Belgrade Agreement and three subsequent presidential elections, were gaining increasing traction as it became evident that Montenegro being part of the joint state was not per se a major obstacle to the eventual scheduling of an independence referendum. The first 'litmus test' measuring the potential viability of doing so came in 2003, with the publication of the census results by the Republican Statistical Office of Montenegro (*Republički zavod za statistiku Crne Gore*, abbreviated as MONSTAT). The results of the census would, after all, be indicative of the potential support for independence. What percentage of Montenegro's population would, in national terms, define themselves Montenegrins? And would this provide an indication as to whether a sufficient number might therefore be inclined to vote for an independent Montenegrin state? The gathering of census data took place within a highly politicized context, but it would be indicative, if nothing else, of the shifts in national identification since the last Yugoslav census conducted in 1991 and the disintegration of the SFRJ. This last census had revealed that 62 per cent of Orthodox Montenegrin citizens had defined themselves as 'Montenegrins', while 9 per cent had defined themselves as 'Serbs'. For some, there was no contradiction in defining yourself as both Montenegrin *and* Serb, and defining yourself as the former was not an outright rejection of the latter. But much had happened since 1991, when the divergence between these two identities was far less politicized and thus far less pronounced.

With the publication of the 2003 census, however, it became clear that political choice and perception of national identity were closely intertwined, and that defining ethnicity/national identity was determined, in large part, by the individual's position vis-à-vis independence. A relative majority of 40.64 per cent defined themselves 'Montenegrin'; 30.01 per cent defined themselves as 'Serbs'; 9.41 per cent as 'Bosniaks'; 7.09 per cent as Albanians; 4.27 per cent as Muslims; 1.05 per cent as Croats; and 0.43 per cent as Roma ('others' represented 1.25 per cent). The census results did, therefore, demonstrate that a bifurcation of sorts had taken place.[3] There was also a distinct geographical split, with more 'Montenegrins' in central and coastal municipalities (Cetinje, Podgorica, Danilovgrad, Nikšić, Mojkovac, Kotor, Kolašin and Bar) and more 'Serbs' in northern municipalities (Andrijevica, Bijelo Polje, Berane, Pljevlja, Plužine and the coastal town of Herceg Novi). There was marginal majority of Serbs in Tivat and Žabljak, a narrow majority of Montenegrins in Budva and a near equal split in Šavnik.[4] Bosniaks and Muslims were in the majority in Rožaje and Plav, while Albanians were in the majority in Ulcinj. These figures revealed a rather complex pattern, though it perhaps signalled that if those who defined themselves as Montenegrins, Muslim/Bosniaks and Albanians voted for independence in a future referendum (a total of 62.46 per cent), then the independence project might indeed be viable. Upon publication of the results, however, Montenegrin Serbs claimed that the census figures were flawed because state employees (and by extension their families) were put under immense pressure to define themselves as 'Montenegrins'.[5] In any event, the census figures indicated that Montenegrin society was still fundamentally divided over the issue of their own national identity. In the period between 2003 and May 2006 (and beyond), it would divide families, siblings and friends.[6]

The controversy over state symbols

In the wake of the widely publicized publication of the 2003 census results, the Montenegrin government continued with the independence project. This took a number of forms, though the issue of deciding upon state symbols was one of the first crucial benchmarks. But finding symbols that would be acceptable to all Montenegro's citizens, regardless of ethnic or national identity, proved deeply problematic. The flag, the coat of arms, the national anthem and the existence or otherwise of a separate Montenegrin language all became significant foci of heated debates, and these further exposed the divergence between advocates of independence and advocates of continued union with Serbia. On 13 July 2004, the Montenegrin Assembly (which was then being boycotted by unionist parties) passed the controversial 'Law on State Symbols and Statehood Day', a concrete and legalistic step towards the crystallization of a more distinct Montenegrin state identity. State flags, emblems and symbolic days would clearly define and project what was specifically *Montenegrin*.

Montenegro had used two *zastave* (flags) up until 1876: a white cross on a red background known as *alaj-bajrak* and a later variant, the *krstaš-bajrak*.[7] The Petrović dynasty from Prince Danilo to Prince (later King) Nikola I utilized a number of flags, but by 1876 the tricoloured (red, blue and white) flag without a double-headed eagle (though a later version would include this) was in common usage. From

1918 to 1941, the Montenegrin flag was that of the KSHS and then from 1945 to 1992 the SFRJ. In 1992, the Montenegrin flag was a variant (with a lighter shade of blue) of the flag of the SRJ. This flag, though amended in 2004 to reflect a greater 'balance' within the state union, was replaced by the Montenegrin state flag – a red flag with gold borders and with a coat of arms in the centre; a new flag, yes, but one that drew heavily from colours and symbols from the Petrović dynasty from the nineteenth century onwards.[8] Similarly, the national holiday of 13 July (recognized primarily as the date of the start of the people's uprising against occupying forces in 1941) was transformed into the 'national day' in which Montenegro was recognized as the twenty-seventh independent state in the world, following the Congress of Berlin in 1878.

Perhaps more controversial, however, was the change of national anthem. During the reign of King Nikola I Petrović, the official anthem had been *Ubavoj nam Crnoj Gori* (To Our Beautiful Montenegro), though the song *Onamo', namo* (There, Over There), the words of which were written by Prince (later King) Nikola and contains references to 'Serb lands', Serbian mythology and the Battle of Kosovo in 1389, had become increasingly popular. During the existence of the SFRJ, the anthem – shared with all other Yugoslav republics – was *Hej Sloveni* (Hey Slavs), which remained the anthem of the SRJ. Now, however, it was replaced with *Oj svjetlo majska zoro* (Oh, Bright Dawn of May), which emphasizes *majka naša Crna Gora* (Our Mother Montenegro). There was a problem, however. 'Oh, Bright Dawn of May' was originally written in the late nineteenth century and was a popular folk song celebrating, broadly, Montenegrin bravery, customs and traditions, but it had been rearranged during the 1941–45 war in Yugoslavia by the Montenegrin fascist leader, Sekula Drljević, to celebrate the establishment of the Italian-backed Montenegrin puppet regime (who temporarily controlled Montenegro). Given its alleged 'fascistic' connotations, many unionists and those within Montenegro's Serb community were deeply offended and objected to its use.[9]

The language issue also became the source of fierce debate. Since the mid-1990s Montenegrin cultural organizations such as *Matica* had been lobbying for the recognition of Montenegrin as the republic's 'mother tongue'.[10] The Dukljan Academy of Sciences and Arts (*Dukljanska akedemija nauka i umjetnosti* – DANU), formed in 1998, comprised of intellectuals who opposed the 'Serbian nationalism' of the Montenegrin Academy of Sciences and Arts (CANU) and were also strong advocates of the formal recognition of Montenegrin as a separate language. Jevrem Brković, the then president of DANU, was particularly vocal in his support of the constitutional recognition of the language. In March 2004, the Montenegrin education council proposed changing the official language of the republic from *Serbian* to *Maternji jezik* (mother tongue). The proposal caused outrage among Serbs, who argued that this was an attempt by the Montenegrin government to negate their Serb roots and recast the Montenegrins as a distinct nation.

The building of new monuments celebrating (Montenegrin) national heroes also became an issue of some controversy. Most of these new monuments, like the new flag, drew heavily on symbolism from the period (1878–1918) when Montenegro was an independent state. King Nikola himself was recast as a 'true Montenegrin', belying the fact that King Nikola had defined himself as a Serb and sought to unify, at least all Serbs, with Cetinje as the Piedmont of a South Slav state. Now, however, King Nikola was celebrated as a 'real' Montenegrin who stood as a symbolic justification for the renewal of the independent Montenegrin state (though, paradoxically, the new monument to King Nikola was built on the very spot on which the building that housed the Podgorica Assembly in 1918). Additionally, many squares, streets and other public spaces which had been named after Nemajić or Karadjordjević (Serbian dynasties) were changed to reflect a distinct Montenegrin character such as Balšić, Crnojević or Petrović (Montenegrin dynasties).

Other less obviously symbolic but equally dramatic changes were under way, too. Montenegro's capital, Podgorica, underwent something of a physical reconstruction between 1997 and 2006, with many new projects beginning in the period between 2002 and 2006, which awarded the city a more modern (and hence progressive) character. Much of Podgorica had been destroyed by Allied bombing raids in 1944 (only the *Stara Varoš* and *Drač* areas remained relatively unscathed) and the reconstruction of the city continued throughout the post-war decades, creating a sometimes jarring fusion of the new and the old. By the late 1990s, Podgorica had the air of a classic, but rather grey and jaded, post-war socialist city, and many of its areas, particularly *Blok pet* and *Blok šest* (Block Five and Block Six) with its high-rise buildings, ample green space and functional facilities (sports facilities, children's parks, shops and parking facilities) were showing their age.[11] The centre, too, was in need of renewal. Much of *Trg Republike* (Square of Republic) was car parking space and was also home to something of a Podgorica institution, the *Radovče* restaurant. The impressive *Crnogorko narodno pozorište* (Montenegrin National Theatre) building, burnt down in 1989, had been reconstructed and reopened in 1997, and was among the few very modern buildings in the city. The *Rimski trg* (Roman Square) and *Vektra* buildings were also constructed in the later 1990s. By 2003, however, construction work was everywhere, and amidst the ever-increasing new glass, concrete and steel buildings the most significant symbol of 'progress' was the Millennium Bridge, an impressive structure which spanned the Morača River. Mocked by cynics as the 'Milo-ennium Bridge', it was officially opened with great pomp on 13 July 2005 (Montenegro's national day). But this was more than a physical structure that was motivated by the need for infrastructural improvement and the need to provide an additional route into Podgorica from Preko-Morače, but a powerful symbol that served a political as well as aesthetic or infrastructural purpose; it consolidated a perception of progress, the promise of a 'European future', a physical testament to Montenegro's progress since it had established a higher degree of autonomy from Serbia. Indeed, its very presence, not to mention its sleek modern design, implied confidence, progress and prosperity.

The media and the statehood/identity debates

The media, journalists and intellectuals played an equally important role in constructing a positive image of Montenegro's growing independence. By the early 2000s, Montenegrin media was far more diverse than in the early 1990s, when *Pobjeda* was the sole Montenegrin daily newspaper, so there were at least different interpretations of Montenegro's social and political reality available to the public. Print media was dominated by four daily publications (*Vijesti, Pobjeda, Republika* and *Dan*) and one weekly (*Monitor*). Of these, *Pobjeda* was the oldest publication; founded in October 1944 and state owned, it retained a pro-government orientation, rarely straying from a pro-government (and pro-independence) position. The other daily publications of significance were privately owned. But *Vijesti*, established in 1997 and partly created by journalists from the Montenegrin weekly *Monitor*, had been bought by the Germanowned *WAZ-Mediengruppe* in 2002.[12] *Vijesti* adopted a pro-independence (but not always a pro-Djukanović) stance, though they were supportive of him at pivotal moments. By contrast, *Dan* (created in December 1999) was essentially a unionist publication and read primarily by Montenegro's Serb community. In addition to their open support for the SNP, characteristic of its early content, the editorial staff of *Dan* had begun to launch personal attacks on Milo Djukanović, often writing sensationalist stories linking members of Montenegro's ruling elite with organized crime structures, republishing the controversial articles that first appeared in the Croatian weekly *Nacional* in May 2001. On 27 May 2004, the paper's editor, Duško Jovanović, was assassinated outside the editorial office in the Preko-Morače district of Podgorica, by an unknown assailant.[13] The editorial staff at *Dan* accused Milo Djukanović of bearing responsibility for his murder. Djukanović replied that the paper had been little more than a mouthpiece for the SRJ's military counterintelligence.[14] Finally, *Republika* (known until 2004 as *Publika*) was established in 2001. Owned by the 'Millennium Company', its critics alleged that the paper was owned and run by individuals close to the DPS and Montenegrin state security. It made little effort to be impartial, and often published rather suspect articles, such as one published in June 2005 which described Serbs as 'dogs' and 'very nasty people'.[15] The paper regularly published documents received from intelligence services and had, as a consequence, caused several diplomatic incidents (such as levelling accusations of 'criminal misadventure' at the then UK Ambassador to Serbia and Montenegro, Charles Crawford). *Republika* could be seen everywhere in Montenegro, despite its low circulation figures, suggesting that the operation was financed by the government.

There also existed a number of weeklies and biweeklies actively contributing to the debates over independence. The most important of these was *Monitor* – anti-war, pro-democracy, generally in support of independence but not uncritical of the DPS or its coalition partners. Other publications, with a much lower circulation, were also available. The Montenegrin Literary Paper (*Crnogorski Književni List* – CKL) was edited by the poet, and president of DANU, Jevrem Brković, and *ARS*, edited by the Montenegrin writer and independence campaigner Milorad Popović, were relatively widely available.[16] Both Brković and Popović had been forced to flee Montenegro in the early 1990s when their views on Montenegrin nationalism were deemed dangerous, but having returned from their respective periods in exile, they were fully rehabilitated. Brković, in particular, was an almost constant presence on Montenegrin television in the months and years preceding the independence referendum, regularly gracing the schedules on *Radio Televizija Crna Gora* (RTCG) and other pro-government media, enjoying a high-profile image and a permanently reserved table at the Hotel Crna Gora.[17] Both the CKL and *ARS* emphasized the uniqueness of Montenegrin national identity, but while *ARS* had the appearance of an academic journal and contained little in the way of anti-Serb content, the CKL often published more provocative material. Indeed, both the pro-independence daily *Republika* and the CKL often lapsed into making negative comments about Montenegro's Serbs and the state union.[18]

These kinds of sentiments were, thankfully, not common in mainstream newspapers (this was particularly the case during the 2006 referendum campaign, during which the media was subject to a 'Code of Conduct'). But some mainstream media were deemed too critical towards the government and too cynical about the independence project, and it was clear that if the objective of independence was going to be achieved, the media had to be brought into line as much as possible. On 19 April 2005, the unionist party NS held a press conference in Podgorica where they presented a document they claimed had emanated from within the 'Minister of Interior of the Government of Montenegro'. Clumsily titled 'An analysis of the media landscape of Montenegro in the year in which decisive steps towards state independence are to be taken', the document mapped out how to create the 'media logistics' that would facilitate a more effective dissemination of positive arguments for independence. The (anonymous) author(s) of the document noted that 'realization of the project of independence is commencing with weak media logistics', and recommended that (1) that the government's own media and information bureau be better organized; (2) that attempts should be made to influence RTCG; (3) mainstream media should be brought, if possible, closer to the government line; and (4) financial support should be provided for media in the north of Montenegro (where opposition to the government and independence was acute).[19] The leaking of the document, essentially calling for an engineered uniformity of the media, caused significant ripples, though the Montenegrin minister of foreign affairs, Miodrag Vlahović, while confirming the authenticity of the document, claimed it had not, as claimed by the NS, emanated from within the government.[20]

Pre-referendum politics and the referendum process

In November 2004, the Montenegrin government signalled that it intended to schedule a referendum by early 2006 (and, controversially, may do so unilaterally), though in late February 2005 they sent a proposal to the Serbian government that envisaged a transformation of the existing state union into a union of independent states, though the proposal was bluntly dismissed by Vojislav Koštunica.[21] As a referendum on independence became increasingly likely, the Serbs in Montenegro, working on concert with Montenegrins living in Serbia, established a movement which brought unionist forces together. The result of these endeavours was the 'Movement for the Joint European State Union of Serbia & Montenegro' (*Pokret za zajedničku evropski državu Srbiju i Crnu Goru*). Largely directed from Belgrade, the movement comprised Montenegrin Serbs, Montenegrins living in Serbia (the majority of whom supported preservation of the union), unionist political parties and their members in Montenegro, and a number of Serb–Montenegrin diaspora groups. Leading unionist politicians such as Dragan Soć and Predrag Popović of the NS, Ranko Kadić from the Democratic Serb Party (*Demokratska Srpska stranka* – DSS) and Andrija Mandić and Goran Danilović from the Serbian People's Party of Montenegro (*Srpska narondna stranka* – SNS)[22] joined but, significantly, the SNP, led by Predrag Bulatović, chose not to join the organization.[23] However, despite the non-involvement of the SNP, who sought to cast themselves as the 'moderate' Serb option, the Movement for the Joint State was not merely a collection of Serb nationalists but, rather, a diverse group of committed nationalists and moderates. Their membership reflected this. Radojka Vukčević, a professor of American literature in Podgorica, was always cautious, conveying her arguments without recourse to nationalist rhetoric and always using the language of conciliation. On the other hand, there were members, such as Andrija Mandić of the SNS, who did not shy away from fiery rhetoric.[24] These 'domestic' Montenegrins were joined by influential Montenegrins residing in Serbia: the poet Matija Bećković, the writer Ljubomir Tadić (father of the then Serbian president, Boris Tadić) and the historian, Slavenko Terzić, from SANU, Metropolitan of the SPC in Montenegro, Amfilohije Radović, were all engaged in the activities of the organization. Their objective was to make the strongest possible case for the preservation of the state union, ensure that Montenegrins living in Serbia could vote in any future independence referendum and to emphasize the brotherhood and 'unbreakable historical bonds' between Serbs and Montenegrins (though they would also not shy away from issuing stark warnings of the dangers of separation).[25]

One of the movement's core arguments was that the Montenegrin state had been 'captured' by a group of political elites, led by Djukanović, whose objective was to separate Montenegro from Serbia in order to consolidate their own political and economic power, which, it was argued, they had been amassing since the 1997 DPS split.[26] They also argued that the Montenegrin government were attempting to deny voting rights to Montenegrins residing in Serbia and, more broadly, engaged in 'whitewashing' symbols of Serbian identity from Montenegro.[27] During one of the first meetings of the organization at Maine monastery in the coastal resort of Budva in November 2004 (which the Montenegrin weekly *Monitor* described as a meeting of 'SANU, the SPC and domestic activists who are against Montenegro's independence'), their membership articulated their arguments in favour of preserving the union, and in the event of an independent Montenegro to work towards the assurance of the rights of Serbs within the Montenegrin state (i.e. if 30 per cent of Montenegrin citizens were 'Serbs', then they, by extension, should be assured that level of representation in state institutions).[28] The message that Djukanović and the political elite close to him were creating an independent state for the sole purpose of consolidating their own narrow economic interests was constant throughout their campaign. In this, they could find an ally of sorts in the de facto leader of the Group for Changes (*Grupa za promjene* – GzP), Nebojša Medojević. Though thought to be in favour of independence, he had consistently argued that the ruling Montenegrin elite had initiated the 'independence project' as a method of preserving control over both politics and business, a sentiment shared by those who felt marginalized by the DPS-led government.[29]

Similarly, the 'Movement for a Sovereign and Independent Montenegro' (*Pokret za samostalnu i nezavisnu Crnu Goru*) was formed in 2005 and was led by Branko Lukovac. Their objective was to gather together all of the pro-independence forces, make a robust case for independence and to generate support for the independence project. In so doing they were largely, if not entirely, successful. Joining the movement represented, for many within the Liberal Party (*Liberalna stranka* – LS) and many members of the then embattled LSCG, something of a pact with the devil. As a result of the DPS essentially destroying the LSCG and the political fall of Slavko Perović, Miodrag Živković (former leaders of the party) and Nikola Samardžić (the LP president of the Kotor Municipality) as a consequence of the so-called 'Trsteno Affair', relations between the LS/LSCG and the DPS were, on the whole, poor.[30] Many committed pro-independence forces in within the LS were staunchly anti-DPS and anti-Djukanović. Through gritted teeth they went along with it, on the basis that they would achieve their core objective – independence. The logic for them was simple, if risky. Gain independence first, utilizing the rather undemocratic DPS-Djukanović power structure, and then consolidate democracy in the future. But that future as an independent state was by no means guaranteed, and while they shared a common objective, it was not too difficult for Lukovac to harness these relatively disparate and diverse forces. They had one clear advantage in that they appeared less defensive than the 'Movement for Preservation'; their rhetoric had an air of renewal and positivity, and they quickly generated momentum.

At this stage, however, the independence project could have easily been derailed. It remained unclear exactly *who* would be eligible to vote in a referendum and whether Serb political parties in Montenegro would actually participate in a referendum. Threatening to boycott any unilaterally declared referendum, the leader of the SNP, Predrag Bulatović, signalled that his and other Serb parties would not participate in a referendum.[31] He later stated, however, that if the EU oversaw the referendum process, then he and his 'partners' would indeed participate.[32] Bulatović, of course, knew only too well that the EU were not enthusiastic about a referendum being scheduled (while at the same time knowing that Montenegro's right to do so was enshrined in the March 2002 Belgrade Agreement). The EU thus sought to encourage both Serbia and Montenegro to implement the agreement by encouraging the strengthening of state union institutions. To many advocates of Montenegro's independence, this was seen as a paradoxical position for the EU to take, defending, it was perceived, the continuation of the successor to Milošević's construction (the SRJ). They perceived the state union, referred to as *Solania*, as an imposition by Javier Solana, in cahoots with officials in Belgrade. This perception of cooperation between Brussels and Belgrade was further consolidated when, in June 2005, Serbian prime minister, Vojislav Koštunica, was received by EU commissioner, Oli Rehn, in Brussels. In an effort to derail a referendum, Koštunica handed Rehn a list of 264,000 voters: Montenegrins living in Serbia, who, Koštunica argued, should be permitted to vote in any upcoming referendum (the vast majority of whom would have voted to preserve the union and thus render the 'independence project' unviable). The EU gave no officially response to 'Koštunica's list'.[33]

On 10 November 2005, the European Commission (EC) sent a 'non-paper' to the Montenegrin government cautioning that failure to reach a consensus on the referendum with the opposition could have 'severely negative consequences for Montenegro's future aspirations for European integration', and that if Montenegro chose to leave the state union it would 'not inherit the right to an international legal personality' (the latter was, however, already enshrined in the Belgrade Agreement).³⁴ In the knowledge that the existing political polarization and the divided nature of Montenegrin society generally held the potential for violent conflict, the EU attempted to counter such dark scenarios by discouraging the Montenegrin government from seeking independence. But when it became evident that they would do so in any event, the EU reluctantly shifted into the role of arbiter in advance of (and throughout) the referendum process.³⁵ They subsequently endeavoured to reach agreement with Montenegrin political parties over a set of rules and conditions that would be acceptable to all, and it proved to be pivotal. Indeed, the role of the EU would be crucial in reaching a consensus on the rules of the referendum itself, something which the Montenegrin government and opposition had been unable to achieve independently.

The rather unenviable task of ensuring a smooth referendum process was awarded to young Slovakian diplomat, Miroslav Lajčak, who in late 2005 was appointed as Javier Solana's 'Special Envoy' to Montenegro.³⁶ A fellow Slovak, František Lipka, was chosen to chair the Republican Referendum Committee (RRC), the body that would arbitrate in disputes throughout the referendum process. But while both men were well versed in the idiosyncrasies of Balkan politics, spoke Serbian/Montenegrin proficiently and were diplomats who came from a Slavic country (Czechoslovakia) that had its own 'velvet divorce' – creating the independent states of the Czech Republic and Slovakia in January 1993 – reaching agreement proved problematic, impeded from the outset by fundamental disagreements about what level of majority would be required to legitimize the outcome of the referendum. Both men would, however, subsequently play a pivotal role in reaching a basic consensus between Montenegro's polarized political elites before the referendum, and continue to do so throughout the referendum process.

The EU's first intervention was to challenge Montenegro's 'Law on Referendum' (dating from February 2001), which stipulated that the referendum result would be valid if one bloc received (one vote) more than 50 per cent of the registered electorate.³⁷ To clarify the imposition of standards with regard to the referendum the Parliamentary Assembly of the Council of Europe (PACE) tasked the Venice Commission (VC) with providing expert-informed recommendations on the referendum process, which by December 2005 they had completed.³⁸ Thereafter, it was agreed (in February 2006) that for the referendum result to be deemed legitimate, 55 per cent of the valid votes must be cast in favour of either a 'yes' or 'no' option, and that at least 50 per cent (plus one) of the Montenegrin electoral body (i.e. all registered voters) must cast their votes. Thereafter, on the basis of this rather novel imposition, the Montenegrin government adopted a new 'Law on the Referendum on State Legal Status' on 1 March 2006. This would, according to the OSCE, 'regulate the establishment of the referendum administration bodies, the financing of campaign expenses, the conduct of the campaign, its coverage by the media, and the rights of observer groups'.³⁹ Furthermore, the Law on Referendum also finalized the referendum question itself: *'Do you want the Republic of Montenegro to be an independent state with full international and legal personality?'* With these parameters now established, pre-referendum campaigns now de facto commenced. In preparation for the referendum, the OSCE Office for Democratic Institutions and Human Rights (OSCE/ODHIR) established a Referendum Observation Mission

(ROM) to observe the referendum campaign and the voting process.[40] The pro-independence and unionist blocs began their respective referendum campaigns in early May, with rallies being held by either bloc in towns, cities and villages throughout Montenegro, climaxing with two large rallies in Podgorica on the eve of the 21 May 2006 referendum.

The pro-independence and unionist campaigns

The referendum environment was marked by a generally peaceful campaign. Both sides respected competing arguments and the right to convey them, and aside from a few minor incidents of negative campaigning, defacing of billboards and a few cases of inflammatory graffiti appearing, the respective pro-independence and unionist campaigns were conducted in a generally positive spirit.[41] The pro-independence campaign was excellently planned, delivered and aesthetically seductive. It did not, however, enjoy an auspicious start. While 'European standards' and 'European integration' were cornerstones of the pro-independence campaign rhetoric, the bloc ran into early problems with the EU. Comments were made by leading members of the pro-independence bloc (who travelled the world to woo the diaspora vote) that despite a 55 per cent requirement for independence, a 51 per cent vote would essentially mean independence.[42] The EU envoy, Miroslav Lajčak, berated the pro-independence bloc for their comments stating, 'There is a distinct lack of seriousness with politicians going around the world saying that as far as they are concerned fifty one per cent would be taken as a signal that the state union no longer exists'.[43] Further controversy followed in the form of the so-called 'Zeta film', which allegedly depicted DPS activists bribing voters in the Podgorica suburb of Golubovci. The film showed two DPS activists, Ivan Ivanović and Mirko Vučinić, attempting to bribe one Mašan Bošković to vote for independence by offering to pay his long-overdue electricity bill of €1,580.[44] It generated a significant scandal. Pro-independence press such as *Pobjeda* argued that the film was falsification concocted by an individual 'code-named Sparrow Hawk' (namely, Vasilije Mijović), who was reputedly acting under the instructions of Serbian intelligence services.[45] Unsurprisingly, the unionist-leaning daily *Dan* reported that the film depicted 'nothing but the truth', confirmation that the Montenegrin government was engaged in the illegal purchase of votes.[46] Naturally, the pro-independence bloc responded to the film with accusations of foul play, comparing the film to the sting on the former JNA General, Martin Špegelj, in 1991. Milo Djukanović stated that the film was an attempt to sabotage the referendum and that the whole affair 'must have its epilogue in court'.[47] Similarly, Branko Lukovac described the film as a 'method of psychological war' waged against the Montenegrin government and with the express purpose of undermining the pro-independence campaign.[48]

As their campaign continued, however, the pro-independence bloc recovered and gained momentum. Not unfamiliar with this territory – the DPS mastered the art of campaigning during the late 1990s – the pro-independence campaign proved to be rather impressive. Paradoxically, particularly given the poor relationship between the DPS and the LSCG, the imagery and symbolism were reminiscent of LSCG rallies in the early 1990s, though with a significant amount of glitz added for good measure. Indeed, even the 'L' hand signal – made with the thumb and forefinger – used by LSCG supporters in the early 1990s became the 'symbol' of the pro-independence rallies, accompanied by the chant *E viva Montenegro!* (Italian for 'Long Live Montenegro!'), also traditionally sung by LSCG supporters. The first of the pro-independence rallies was, appropriately, held in the historical capital of Cetinje. As expected, the pro-independence bloc utilized emotive rhetoric, while placing the referendum in the wider context of Montenegro's history. Contemporary Montenegrins, they argued, were presented with a unique historical mission – to correct the grievances felt by their forefathers who had to bear the loss of Montenegrin independence in 1918; in short, what their forefathers had sorrowfully lost they could thereby regain, playing their own vital role in Montenegro's destiny. On a more contemporary political level, a number of key arguments were advanced by pro-independence leaders. First, that Montenegrin interests could not be best served by playing what pro-independence leaders claimed was a subservient role within an unequal and unworkable state union. Secondly, that continued union with Serbia (a country weighed down with the baggage of, and still partly under the control of, the Milošević era) was impeding Montenegro's otherwise unhindered progress towards 'Euro-Atlantic integration'. Thirdly, they posited that an independent Montenegro would be a better foundation upon which to consolidate regional stability and build a stronger civil society. Finally, they argued, Montenegro could harness its economic potential more effectively if they were fully in control of their economic destiny. If the electorate voted for independence, stated Djukanović, the Montenegrin flag would be 'flying outside the UN building on New York's East River by September'.[49] Collectively, this emotive appeal to a 'historical mission' blended with contemporary political and economic arguments proved to be effective.

The pro-independence campaign was also notable for its inclusion of ethnic minorities as an integral part of their campaign. The DPS-led government had, since 1997, forged stronger links with Muslim/Bosniak and Albanian parties, and were almost certain that they would garner significant support from them in the independence referendum. The rhetoric of the speakers at the rally in the town of Bijelo Polje on 12 May 2006 (attended by approximately 10,000 people, many of whom had come from surrounding areas to show their support) was peppered by messages of inclusion and the rights of Montenegro's ethnic minorities.[50] Unlike the unionist bloc, who aimed their campaign almost exclusively at ethnic Serbs and Montenegrins, emphasis was placed quite significantly on the participation of Montenegro's ethnic minorities. Demonstrative of the strategy of incorporating minorities and minority concerns was the nature of the campaign literature and electronic media advertising. The pro-independence campaign literature specifically both used Albanian and Serbian (Latin *and* Cyrillic) language and conveyed a message that an independent Montenegro would be a democratic, multiethnic state. In predominantly Orthodox areas, 'Da' (Montenegrin/Serbian for 'Yes') posters were omnipotent, while in predominantly Albanian areas posters adorned with 'Po' (Albanian for 'Yes') were ever-present. It proved something of a master stroke.

There existed, however, certain key figures that were not formally part of the pro-independence campaign, though their engagement was seen as potentially pivotal.[51]

Both Mehmet Bardhi, chairman of the Democratic Union of Albanians (*Demokratska Unija Albanaca* – DUA), and Slavko Perović, the former leader of the now-defunct LSCG, were natural supporters of independence and were thus both conspicuous by their absence. The latter in particular remained a hugely influential player despite the damage incurred by the fall-out from the 'Trsteno Affair'. As the leader of the LSCG, Perović represented the voice of the anti-war generation of the early 1990s and the LSCG had been the genuine party of Montenegrin independence. Perović remained, for many, *the* legitimate leader of the movement for an 'independent, European-oriented Montenegro'. But Perović, who had devoted his entire political career for an independent Montenegro, vehemently opposed the government of Milo Djukanović and had chosen to reject engagement in the referendum campaign. Branko Lukovac, who led the Movement for an Independent European Montenegro, told the daily *Republika* that 'we still expect their [Bardhi and Perović] supporters to vote for their own state too, we would attempt to contact Mr Perović and reach a necessary level of understanding'.[52] In a context where the margins were narrow and every vote counted, Perović was regarded as crucial to attracting the votes of former LSCG supporters who were pro-independence but anti-Djukanović. Alluding to Perović's absence, Djukanović stated during the first pro-independence rally in Cetinje that it was 'not the time to be stubborn in a Montenegrin way'.[53] A man of integrity with long-held principles, Slavko Perović remained disengaged and his much-feted appearance at the pro-independence rallies did not materialize.

Several other key figures were, however, on hand to provide rhetorical support on the evening of the final pro-independence rally in Podgorica on the 18 May 2006, including the grandson of King Nikola I Petrović.[54] The rally drew around 40,000 citizens, and was impressive in both scale and aesthetic. The rally began with a rousing rendition of 'Oh, Bright Dawn of May' which produced an outpouring of emotion from many in the crowd, the majority of whom were adorned in red t-shirts emblazoned with 'Da' (Yes). The thousands of red-and-gold Montenegrin flags being waved throughout also added to what was an impressive manifestation. This style over substance set the tone for the rally. Here the rhetoric at this rally was far more emotive; real political issues were largely ignored, replaced instead by speeches from the leaders of the pro-independence bloc in which they waxed lyrical about Montenegro's glorious history, reiterating the direct link between the great Montenegrins of the past and the contemporary 'mission' to reinstate independence. But while this overtly romanticized imagery and rhetoric may have been sufficient to garner a significant number of votes, it would not in itself guarantee victory. A largely hidden and more cynical coercion behind the scenes put considerable pressure on individuals employed by state institutions, including policemen, teachers and other state employees.[55] Indeed, when questioned by journalists on alleged coercion of citizens, the DPS chief whip, Miodrag Vuković, told journalists that such pressures were normal and that state employees 'cannot work for the state and vote against it'.[56]

The unionist bloc, which brought together all of those parties who supported union (the SNP, SNS, NS and the DSS), engaged the Belgrade-based PR agency *Incognito* to direct their campaign. The commonality was their Serb identity, but in reality this was a heterogeneous and rather disorganized bloc of competing interests. In any event, much of the unionist campaign focused upon what they argued was the corrupt character of Montenegro's government, placing particular emphasis on Milo Djukanovic's links with organized crime and playing on fears that he and his DPS associates would, in the event of independence, transform Montenegro into a 'private state' within which his opponents would be economically and politically marginalized. While their rhetoric was, at times, reminiscent of the nationalist discourse of the early 1990s, the campaign was generally positive and aimed both at their traditional (older) voters and at a younger audience, the bloc's official referendum 'anthem' being a rather saccharin number entitled *Ljubav spaja* (Love Connects).[57] The cornerstone of the unionist arguments were that Serbia and Montenegro in union were a stronger economy together than the sum of their parts, that there were strong cultural bonds between the republics of Serbia and Montenegro, and that Serbs and Montenegrins possessed strong, unbreakable ethnic and historical bonds. Economic issues, too, were also at the heart of their campaign: the issues of tax, corporate registration, property ownership rights, citizenship, pensions and healthcare provision were predominant in this regard.

While the unionist bloc rightly acknowledged the importance of the youth vote, they nevertheless directed their campaign primarily at the Serb and Montenegrin communities. Typically, the unionist bloc drew most of their support from the northern Montenegrin municipalities of Šavnik, Berane, Kolašin, Pljevlja and Andrijevica, and thus their campaign was primarily aimed at the Orthodox populations of those towns. This rather narrow focus, on the whole, defined their campaign, and while they could guarantee that they would receive the votes of Montenegro's Serbs, their message held little attraction for Muslim/Bosniak or Albanian voters. And despite the attempts to cast a more positive image, some individuals within the bloc occasionally reverted to type, warning of the dangers of a 'Greater Albania', the thesis being that an independent Montenegro would be a small, weak state potentially vulnerable to incursions or insurrections by Albanians. In short, they argued that politically and economically the Montenegrin state could only survive and function properly in union with Serbia. By extension, unionist politicians emphasized what they argued was the increasing insecurity for Serbs in Montenegro.[58] In any event, unionist promotional material was only in Cyrillic script, so there was an immediate perception (by accident or design) that the campaign material was not aimed at Montenegro's minorities. The unionists did, however, endeavour to garner Muslim/Bosniak votes, by having their own 'Bosniak Bloc', a small coalition of Muslim/Bosniak non-governmental organizations, among them the influential leader of the Montenegrin SDA, Harun Hadžić.[59] But regardless of these efforts, such as they were, many Montenegrin Muslim/Bosniaks (and to a lesser extent the Albanian community) had raw memories of the early 1990s (see Chapter 4) and had expressed early on overwhelming support for the pro-independence bloc.

Predrag Bulatović made significant efforts to cast the campaign as positive and moderate, and toned down his own campaign rhetoric (he had pledged to run his campaign without using the language of 'hatred and nationalist division' to enable citizens' 'peaceful and tolerant voting for either option', though this did not seem be a vision shared by all within the bloc).[60] Since the marginalization of the outspoken Zoran Žižić from the SNP, that party had adopted a more moderate and less nationalistic rhetoric, but while Bulatović was regarded by many as a man of words, the leadership of SNS, particularly Andrija Mandić and Goran Danilović, were considered more fiery Serb nationalists.[61] Often, the more radical rhetoric would emanate not from Montenegro but from Serbia. Vojislav Koštunica added to the uncertainty felt by Montenegro's Serbs by warning that 'the creation of new borders would not cause good things to happen'.[62] Statements made by the SRS leader Tomislav Nikolić also created controversy. A statement released by the party on 12 May 2006 said that their members would support the establishment of an autonomous Serb enclave within Montenegro in the event of independence, similar to the Serbian Autonomous Area (*Srpska autonomna oblast* – SAO) established in Krajina, Croatia, in 1991 (and later in Bosnia & Herzegovina) before the outbreak of armed conflict there.[63]

To their credit, many within the unionist bloc dismissed such statements. Recognizing the dangers of such potentially poisonous association, the unionist parties in Montenegro distanced themselves from the SRS. Indeed, unlike previous election campaigns, symbols of Serbian nationalism, flags adorned with the *krst sa četeri ognjila* (the cross with the four Cyrillic Ss), posters of Ratko Mladić and Radovan Karadžić, and songs such as *Spremte se spremte Četninci* (Get Ready Chetniks) were largely absent, although a small number of individuals were photographed at the unionist rally in Herceg Novi wearing Radovan Karadžić t-shirts.[64] On the whole, however, the leaders of the unionist bloc understood that in this particular context it was not in their best interests to publicly display symbols of a tainted nationalist ideology, and its supporters largely (there were, of course, exceptions) understood the impact that negative imagery could have on the campaign. Instead, unionist politicians focused on what they argued were the benefits for retaining the union with Serbia. Economic, cultural and historical reasons were most frequently cited, and while the majority of the unionist campaigning focused substantially on these justifications, personal attacks against Milo Djukanović were commonplace throughout. Many of those gathered for the unionist rallies would chant *Milo – lopove!* (Milo is a thief!), and much of the invective was directed at the prime minister and the alleged criminal nature of his regime. The unionist message was, as expected, well received in areas that were predominantly Serb, but less well so in other areas (Predrag Bulatović was, for example, loudly heckled in Rožaje, a predominantly Muslim/Bosniak municipality). The largest of the rallies took place in Nikšić on 15 May 2006 and on *Trg Republike* (Square of the Republic) in the centre of Podgorica the following evening.

The final pro-union rally in Serbia, held in the Sava Centre in Belgrade, on 18 May 2006, was a slightly different affair. The rally was attended by some of the key players in the unionist bloc, as well as the Belgrade-based Montenegrins, Vojislav Koštunica and high-profile members of the SPC's clergy. Not subject to the OSCE's monitoring, the language was far less cautious than that utilized during the campaign in Montenegro. The attacks upon Djukanović were similar to other unionist rallies in Montenegro, but speakers in the Sava Centre went much further, arguing that the Montenegrin nation was a 'communist fiction', and that Montenegro was 'Serbian ethnic space'. These events led Žarko Korać, former deputy prime minister of Serbia, to argue that the approach taken by the unionists in Belgrade was self-defeating. 'One can', he said, 'argue in favour of the preservation of state-union, of course, but not in this way ... only after we recognize that the Montenegrin nation exists, or even more simply, the right of a large number of people to feel that way, can we talk about a joint-state'.[65]

The unionist rallies in Nikšić and Podgorica passed without trouble. The rhetoric was much the same, with the speakers focusing their invective on Djukanović, while unionist supporters chanted *Milo - lopove!* (Milo the thief) were mixed with *Milo - gotov je!* (Milo is finished). What was surprising, however, were the number of younger participants, in contrast to the stereotype of unionists being older, rural and less educated. Estimated numbers in attendance were, as one would expect, dependent upon which media one read and which politician one was inclined to listen to. The DSS leader, Ranko Kadić, claimed, for example, that 50,000 were in attendance; pro-independence media claimed 16,000 was a more realistic figure.[66] Whatever the numbers, the unionist rally in Podgorica was a pale shadow of the pro-independence rally held in the same location two days later. While major incidents were avoided, clashes between pro-independence supporters and unionist supporters and the firing of shots outside Podgorica's football stadium, *Gradski stadion*, were reported in the following day's newspapers.[67]

Immediately following the 16 May 2006 unionist rally in Podgorica, Predrag Bulatović participated in the last of the televised 'duels' between himself and Milo Djukanović. It was, of course, impossible to gauge the impact of these weekly debates, but what was evident was that those pro-independence politicians that participated in them performed far better than their opponents. The Speaker of the Montenegrin Parliament, Ranko Krivokapić, had the better of Predrag Bulatović in a debate broadcast on Radio Television Serbia (*Radio Televizija Srbije* - RTS) before Milo Djukanović was interviewed on B92 Television by Olja Bećković, presenter of the *Utisak nedelje* (Impression of the Week) programme and the daughter of the Montenegrin Serb writer, poet and participant in the pro-union campaign, Matija Bećković. Her line of questioning was direct and combative but Djukanović nevertheless remained calm and measured fielding the probing questions with efficacy. So in advance of the final debate on the evening of 16 May 2001, Djukanović entered the RTCG studio calm and assured, while Bulatović, though endeavouring to appear calm, looked far less so. The atmosphere before the debate, held in the RTCG studios in Podgorica, was tense, and neither man shook hands with the other. The exchanges were predictably antagonistic, with Bulatović accusing Djukanović of having links with organized crime groups, alleging that the 'independence project was, in fact, an attempt to create a 'private state', and implying throughout that he was 'anti-Serb'. 'A private state', said Bulatović, 'means that you control everything in it, from the police, to the courts, and most importantly, the money'.[68] Bulatović's line of questioning, however legitimate, appeared aggressive and confrontational, and Djukanović fended off the accusations, was clearly well prepared.

In addition to the televised debates, the media were a key factor in shaping public opinion. Montenegrin print and electronic media coverage was, naturally, dominated by coverage of the referendum, and were obliged to demonstrate objectivity and balance. Indeed, prior to the launch of the respective pro-independence and unionist campaigns, all media outlets of note signed a 'Code of Conduct' which committed them to act in accordance with the principles set down within it. TV coverage was, in essence, relatively balanced, but Montenegro's state-owned television RTCG, while attempting to provide a balanced overview of events, was essentially controlled by individuals close to the DPS. RTCG1 and RTCG 2, while providing coverage of both campaigns in their *Dnevnik* (News) programme, gave almost three times as much airtime to pro-independence views and arguments than they did to unionist arguments.[69] They also peppered their daily schedules with patriotic songs such as *Moja Zemlja Crna Gora* (My Country Montenegro) and documentaries that were oriented towards the Montenegrin interpretations of history.[70] Other electronic media did likewise: some (IN-TV, MBC and TV Montena) clearly gave a disproportionate amount of airtime to pro-independence views, while others (Elmag and RTS) did so in favour of unionist arguments.[71] TV Pink M, the Montenegrin sister to the Belgrade-based TV Pink, was (surprisingly) more pro-independence than expected. In short, the television coverage was not entirely representative and did not maintain the level of objectivity that the code of conduct implored them to guarantee, but it was considerably better in this regard than print media.

A more explicit level of subjectivity was evident, on a daily basis, in the print media.[72] The pro-independence dailies *Pobjeda* and *Republika* were generally biased towards pro-independence views, while the Montenegrin daily *Dan* and the Serbian dailies *Politika* and *Večernje Novosti* were likewise with regard to unionist perspectives.[73] Reflecting the worst of the unionist rhetoric, a number of Belgrade-based newspapers printed stories about Croat and Albanian plans to encourage Montenegrin independence with the intention of carving it up – though they were not, of course, limited by the parameters of the 'Code of Conduct'.[74] But as the referendum approached, these boundaries were increasingly breached. *Vijesti*, while still providing a relatively balanced coverage of the arguments of both blocs, broke from their otherwise independent line on 15 May 2006. It all appeared rather harmless, but on that day the paper gave a free baseball cap (red with the Montenegrin coat of arms) to readers – it was sold out by 7.00 am. Likewise, on the first morning of the 'referendum silence',[75] on 20 May 2006, *Vijesti* published a large front cover photograph of the previous evening's pro-independence rally.[76] The pro-union newspaper *Dan* published on both days of the media blackout stories at the centre of which were accusations of government pressure being applied on voters. On both days the paper also featured photographs of individuals wearing *Ne* (No) t-shirts.

In accordance with the 'Code of Conduct', all coverage of the referendum was suspended from the end of the 18 May 2006 pro-independence rally until after the referendum. The 'referendum silence' meant that TV and press coverage of the referendum should focus only on 'technical issues'.[77] There were, of course, still clear political messages everywhere: anyone walking through the centre of Podgorica could see Podgorica's Town Hall emblazoned the confident statement *Pobjediće Crna Gora 100%* (The Victory will be Montenegro's – 100 per cent), but with scope for influencing voters limited through constraints on the media, attention shifted towards methods of *soft* influence. And it had transpired that the politics of the referendum had already infringed upon popular culture and would do so later with regard to sporting events.

Always a hotbed of political intrigue, the 2006 Eurovision Song Contest, held in Athens, was without representation from Serbia and Montenegro – and the reasons for that absence were entirely political. In the final round of the domestic competition to decide who would represent the state union (held in the Sava Centre in Belgrade), the Montenegrin band 'No Name' won, largely because Montenegrin judges voted overwhelmingly for them. When the result was announced, the crowd was indignant and the Serbian judges openly accused their Montenegrin counterparts of voting not for the best act, but for the Montenegrin band. There were, apparently, fear that the song contest, to be broadcast the night before the referendum, could impact upon the outcome. Would the 'No Name' band make a political statement favouring a 'Yes' vote during the Eurovision final? Could such an 'intervention' change the course of the referendum result? Unlikely, of course, but given the political climate, it was subsequently decided that neither 'No Name', nor indeed their closest rivals, 'The Flamingos', should be permitted to perform in Athens.

There were, however, other opportunities to use sport and popular culture as a means to transmit political messages. With Serbia and Montenegro no longer competing in the Eurovision Song Contest, attention shifted towards the women's European Handball Federation (EHF) Cup Winners' Cup match between ŽRK Budućnost of Podgorica and Győri ETO KC of Hungary.[78] Broadcast live on the eve of the referendum, the game presented a unique opportunity to harness national pride and sentiment that sporting events invariably generate. Clearly orchestrated in advance, there were only Montenegrin flags in the Morača sports centre that evening (state union symbols were entirely absent), and many leading figures from the DPS and from the pro-independence bloc (including Milo Djukanović) were in attendance. ŽRK Budućnost won the closely contested match 51–48 and triumphantly carried off the EHF Cup Winners' Cup. As the team prepared to lift their trophy, they put on red t-shirt with 'Da!' (Yes!) written across the front. The following morning *Pobjeda* heralded the victory with the headline *Evropska budućnost* (European Future), while the paper's sport's supplement described the team as *Ponos Crne Gore* (The Pride of Montenegro).[79] Cynics were quick to express their dismay at the politicization of the event and the establishment of a direct link between the success of the handball team and the political project of independence. It was, in essence, a breach of the media code, but its overall impact on the eventual outcome was impossible to measure.

But regardless of such machinations, the Montenegrin media did not have to labour too much not to present a generally negative image of the state union of Serbia and Montenegro, and in this regard the stars aligned for the pro-independence bloc. Seemingly unrelated events, not directly connected to the independence referendum, may have had a significant impact in shaping public perceptions. First, the widely televised funeral of Slobodan Milošević demonstrated that many Serbs were still weighed down with the ideological baggage of that era, and secondly, the actions of the Serbian government, who forcibly closed down the BK television channel (owned by Boguljub Karić) in Belgrade, also gave the distinct impression that the Belgrade government remained authoritarian and far from ready for democratic reforms.[80] The EU, moreover, played into the hands of the pro-independence bloc by suspending accession (on 3 May 2006) talks with the joint state of Serbia and Montenegro over Serbia's failure to comply with the ICTY.[81]

While these events took place, thousands of Montenegrins from the diaspora began arriving by various means. Significant effort was invested by both sides to woo the diaspora vote, and, again given the narrow margins, the diaspora vote mattered.[82] Both blocs had organized events for Montenegrin diaspora in the United States, Britain and Australia. While many Montenegrins living in Serbia had no right to vote in the referendum (disqualified from so doing because they had voted in elections in Serbia), Montenegrins from all over the world returned to cast their historic vote.[83] Many came from far-flung corners of the globe, claiming that they were doing their historical duty by participating in the process which would reinstate Montenegro's right to independence. A week before the referendum, Montenegro Airlines announced it was cancelling all flights from Belgrade, the planes used instead to bring (pro-independence diaspora) back to cast their votes. This was facilitated, in part, by the opening (on 14 May 2006) by Milo Djukanović of a shiny new terminal building at Podgorica airport, which could easily deal with significant transit in a way the old, rather antiquated, airport could not.[84] The airport, according to the weekly *Monitor*, 'opened at the right time', as an estimated 15,000 diaspora with voting rights arrived in Montenegro.[85] The daily *Republika* estimated that approximately 6,000 Montenegrins came from the United States alone to cast their votes.[86] It appeared that the majority (adorned with or carrying the Montenegrin flag) were supporters of independence. Upon arrival, Blažo Sredanović, the president of the Association of Montenegrins of America (AMA), made little secret of his own preference, saying, 'For Americans it's normal to be against the government or the government or the president, but it's inconceivable to be against the state.'[87] In the predominantly Muslim/Bosniak and Albanian municipalities of Plav and Rožaje, many arrived from other parts of Europe to cast their vote. It was estimated that at least two busloads of emigrants arrived from northern Montenegrin towns in the early evening of Saturday 20 May.[88]

In Serbia, those who could vote had their travel to Montenegro organized and financed by the Serbian government, the unionists in Montenegro and the Movement for the Preservation of the State Union. Between 15 and 23 May 2006, Serbian Railways offered free return travel to eligible Montenegrin voters residing in Serbia, and, as a response to the cancellation of Montenegrin Airlines flights from Belgrade, the 'Yugoslav' state air carrier (JAT) introduced additional flights from Belgrade to Podgorica.[89] Free travel by either bus or train for Montenegrin students studying in Belgrade and other towns and cities in Serbia was also provided. As a consequence, towns in the north of Montenegro, such as Berane and Pljevlja, were positively bustling in the days approaching the referendum. In the final analysis, approximately 21,000 citizens residing abroad (not including those from Serbia) returned to Montenegro in the days immediately preceding the referendum.[90] This represented approximately 4 per cent of the total number of 484,718 eligible voters (all of whom had to be registered on the electoral roll).[91]

21 May: Referendum day

On the eve of the referendum, the leaders of both blocs both underlined the importance of the referendum being conducted in a 'European' and 'peaceful' manner, and that the result, whatever it may be, should be respected.[92] On referendum day itself, the turnout was high (estimated to be 86 per cent), and there were long queues at a number of polling stations, with some citizens waiting for hours to cast their votes. The referendum was monitored by the OSCE/ODHIR's ROM alongside observers from the OSCE Parliamentary Assembly (OSCE PA), the Parliamentary Assembly of the Council of Europe (PACE), the Congress of Local and Regional Authorities of the Council of Europe (CLRAE) and representatives from the European Parliament (EP). These bodies collectively formed the International ROM (IROM).[93] Despite a few very minor irregularities (OSCE observers reported suspicious activities which may have indicated vote-buying schemes on the part of the pro-independence bloc) and some issues with unsealed ballot boxes, the day passed without significant difficulties.[94] Pre-referendum polls predicted a close result (between 50 and 56 per cent in favour of independence), and in light of the fact many Montenegrin citizens did not trust them, some joked that the best source of an accurate prediction was the *kladionice* (bookmakers).[95] But such humour belied the stark reality that there existed a possibility that if the referendum result, whichever way it fell, was between 50 and 55 per cent, there was a probability that both sides would claim such a result as *their* victory. The so-called *siva zona* (grey zone) would, therefore, represent the worst possible outcome, meaning that there was no clear resolution to the 'statehood question'. Furthermore, there was the danger, in the event of such an outcome, that both pro-independence and unionist supporters would take to the streets claiming victory in the event of such a result, raising the possibility of violence and instability.

When polling stations closed at 9.00 pm, the air was thick with tension and anticipation. Preliminary results and a forecast of the final result were announced just thirty minutes after the polls had closed by the NGO 'CEMI'.[96] Though only preliminary results, the announcement brought pro-independence supporters on to the streets, where they let off fireworks and, on occasion, fired pistols into the air. Predrag Bulatović quickly appeared on television appealing for calm and imploring unionists and their supporters not to be intimidated by the hasty celebrations of pro-independence bloc. 'All citizens of Montenegro', he said, 'must maintain peace and demonstrate tolerance and patience', adding that 'the result of the referendum is not final until political parties on both sides accept it'.[97] Nevertheless, the celebrations continued unabated and by 11.00 pm it became evident that the pro-independence bloc had indeed triumphed, albeit by a tiny margin. But while the mood was celebratory in Podgorica, elsewhere there existed significant tensions in those areas where people were in no mood to celebrate. In Berane, where the result was closer than expected, there were a number of incidents in which shots were fired, as supporters of independence celebrated in the town's DPS offices. SNP supporters gathered outside their own offices singing nationalist songs and defacing the Montenegrin flag, and, ominously, electricity was briefly cut off in a section of the town.[98] Tensions, which peaked around 11.00 pm, had largely receded by early morning, and at 4.00 am on 22 May 2006 Milo Djukanović gave a victory speech to DPS members in the government building before stepping outside to address the crowds assembled there. There he officially declared victory and, somewhat controversially, congratulated Serbia on their own independence.[99]

On the morning of 22 May 2006, the front cover of *Pobjeda* depicted the early morning celebrations with the word *Nezavisna* (independence) in large, bold red-and-gold font[100] *Vijesti* depicted a similar scene with *Imamo državu* (we have a state).[101] Later that morning, František Lipka, the chair of the RRC, announced the first official (but preliminary) results: the total turnout was estimated at 86.3 per cent; 55.5 per cent had voted in favour of independence and 44.5 per cent in favour of the preservation of the state union. The 'grey zone' had been avoided by only 0.5 per cent.[102] As expected, the largest margins of victory for the pro-independence bloc were in the municipalities of Plav and Rožaje (91 per cent and 91.3 per cent, respectively), the predominantly Albanian municipality of Ulcinj, as well as Cetinje, Bijelo Polje, Tivat, Budva, Bar and Podgorica (though only in Bar and Cetinje were the majorities over 65 per cent)[103] Unionist support was strongest in Andrijevica, Herceg-Novi and Kolašin, while the result in Berane was a victory for the unionist but by a far smaller margin than expected.[104]

Unionists challenged the legitimacy of the result and used the figures and the geographical distribution and voting patterns to argue that most of the Orthodox population of Montenegro had voted in favour of preserving the state union, and that Montenegrin independence was essentially delivered by diaspora and Muslim/Bosniak and Albanian minorities. But with the result seemingly beyond question, celebrations were held in Cetinje on 22 May 2006. The following day *Pobjeda* trumpeted that 'the referendum result annulled the decisions of the 1918 Podgorica Assembly'.[105] But while the pro-independence bloc continued their celebrations, unionists cried foul. The four leaders of the bloc for state union requested that the preliminary results of the referendum be rechecked and that all ballot papers in all voting stations be recounted. But by 27 May, the RRC confirmed the official result as 55.5 per cent in favour of independence, and 44.5 per cent in favour of continued union with Serbia, based on the total turnout of 86.49 per cent.[106] The unionist bloc continued, however, to argue that there were irregularities with voting procedures on the day of the referendum. Leader of the NS, Predrag Popović, stated that his party and the unionist bloc collectively would not recognize the result of the referendum until its request of a recount in all polling stations was met.[107] But despite these requests, the RRC again reiterated the results for the final time on 31 May 2006, while the OSCE, upon the publication of their subsequent final referendum observation report, confirmed that the referendum was 'conducted in line with OSCE and other international standards related to democratic electoral processes'.[108]

While in Montenegro the pro-independence bloc celebrated and the unionists lamented, the reaction to the outcome of the referendum was relatively muted in Serbia. Now the president of an independent state, Boris Tadić (whose father was, of course, a key member of the Movement for the Preservation of the State Union) arrived in Podgorica on 23 May 2006, announcing that he accepted 'the majority decision by the people of Montenegro', a conciliatory message that somewhat undermined the unionist claims of irregularities and their determination to continue pursuing a recount.[109] And the reaction from the international community appeared to be one of resigned acceptance. Clearly, the EU, by imposing a 55 per cent threshold had made the pro-independence bloc's objectives more difficult to attain, had aimed to create a threshold that would prove insurmountable, but even that could not produce the desired outcome. Their primary concern was how internal politics in Serbia might be affected by the loss of Montenegro and the end of the state union in a context where Kosovo's status remained unresolved, and whether the events would lead to a radicalization of the political scene in Serbia and a possible 'domino effect' (i.e. that the 'Montenegrin model' would be copied by other potential breakaway regions in the Balkans and beyond). Thus they were quick to stress that the Montenegrin case did not set a precedent. The presence of an unofficial Basque delegation in Montenegro during the referendum was a personal matter of concern for Javier Solana, who dismissed outright that there were any similarities between Montenegro and Catalonia and the Basque Country.[110]

These events notwithstanding, the Montenegrin government declared formal independence on 3 June 2006. But while the pro-independence bloc declared the official birth of the new state and celebrated accordingly, representatives for the unionist bloc boycotted the proclamation. Notably, there was no representation from the international community or from Serbia, which officially acknowledged its own independent status on the 6 of June 2006 in a parliamentary session that was, to put it mildly, rather low-key.[111] These events, therefore, marked the end of the joint state of Serbia and Montenegro and ushered in a new era of independence for both republics. For the pro-independence bloc there was plenty to celebrate but also a realization that there were fresh challenges ahead.

9

Montenegro's Independence: The First Five Years (2006–11)

While Montenegro's status had fundamentally changed as a result of the outcome of the independence referendum, the rhetoric that had characterized the period between 1997 and 2006 (but most pronounced between 2003 and 2006) continued unabated, albeit in a new context in which the 'statehood question' had been resolved. Many of the antagonisms between the parties which comprised the competing pre-referendum blocs continued into the post-independence period. The outcome of the referendum determined that there were political casualties, blood on the carpet; winners and losers; and joy for the victors and despair for the defeated. Consequently, the country entered into this new era with a divided body politic, and a sense of embitterment among a significant minority (44.5 per cent of the population), some of whom did not recognize the legitimacy of the result. The Serbian political analyst, and erstwhile advisor to Andrija Mandić, the president of the SNS, Miša Djurković warned in 2007 that 'conflicts over the constitution, the position of the church, state symbols and the relationship between the government and the opposition represent fertile breeding grounds for new clashes'.[1] Montenegro embarked upon a new era of independence in this political and social context.

There was, however, plenty of good news for the DPS-led government to capitalize upon. Montenegro became a full member of the UN and other international institutions, consolidated its position among its neighbours, and made strides towards achieving the government's core stated objective: Euro-Atlantic integration. In June 2006, the European Union (EU) established relations with Montenegro and all EU member states recognized the country's independence. Just over a year later, in October 2007, Montenegro signed a Stability and Association Agreement (SAA). Thereafter, a formal application was submitted in December 2008 and the process of responding to the European Commission's (EC) detailed questionnaire on how the country's legislation conforms to the *acquis communautaire* (EU body of law) commenced.

Signals emanating from Brussels, with regard to Montenegro's future membership of the EU, were rather positive. Indeed, the EU often touted Montenegro as a beacon of light in a region still beset with residual problems generated by state collapse and war. While these comments were relative (and framed within the wider context of the Western Balkan accession process), Montenegro nevertheless benefited from the EU's for a positive story with regard to the Western Balkans, which was more problematic in the context of, say, Serbia, FYROM, Albania or Bosnia & Herzegovina. The Montenegrin government were quick to capitalize on this goodwill, and their endeavours were rewarded in December 2009 when its citizens were granted visa-free travel within the 'Schengen zone' (an important development because it provided tangible evidence that their government's endeavours were bearing fruit). In November 2010, the EC published its *avis* (opinion) on the country's bid to become a candidate for membership, and in December 2010, Montenegro was formally awarded candidate status by the European Commission (EC).[2] This represented a significant milestone in the wider accession process and one that represented the culmination of the significant endeavours of, among others, Montenegro's minister for European integration, Gordana Djurović.[3]

The other 'branch' of Euro-Atlantic integration was more problematic. Montenegro also made progress towards NATO membership, though there existed a lack of public consensus on the issue, not to mention significant opposition to the participation of Montenegrin troops in the International Security Assistance Force (ISAF) mission in northern Afghanistan (though these troops were not engaged in combat). The government, however, pressed on and Montenegro became a member of the Partnership for Peace (PfP) in December 2006, and engaged in 'membership dialogue' with NATO from April 2008. In December 2009, Montenegro joined the 'Membership Action Plan' (MAP), the first objective of which was to submit their first 'Annual National Programme' (ANP), which they duly did in September 2010.[4] The issue of NATO membership was, unlike that of EU membership, more problematic in that there was significant opposition to it, opposition that would become more acute as Montenegro proceeded towards full membership.

The domestic political scene after the referendum

Following the June 2006 declaration of independence, the governing DPS-led government basked in the glory of their victory. Indeed, in the weeks and months following the declaration of independence, the pages of (pro-government) press trumpeted one achievement after another: from the first recognition by an international state (Iceland being the first) to Council of Europe (COE) and UN membership. With similar news to report on a near-daily basis, the government benefited from a lengthy post-referendum honeymoon. Indeed, the strength of the ruling coalition increased, which is demonstrated by the strong showing at the post-referendum parliamentary elections in September 2006 (the DPS-SDP coalition won 48 per cent of the vote).

For those who had voted to preserve the state union, the immediate post-referendum period was one of disappointment and self-reflection. Amid the gloom, new shoots emerged, most clearly manifested by the creation of the Serb List (*Srpska lista* – SL), a coalition constructed around the SNS and led by Andrija Mandić.[5] Claiming to represent the interests of 'real' Serbs in Montenegro, their platform represented something of a departure from the approach taken by other Serb parties. They largely rejected the argument that Serbs and Montenegrins were two branches of the wider Serbian national corpus, stating that if Montenegrins were to assert an identity bereft of Serb political and cultural symbols, their primary objective should be 'the protection of the constitutionality and full affirmation of the identity and freedom of the Serb people [in Montenegro]'.[6] They had several key demands. First, that Serbs should be defined constitutionally as a distinct and equal nation (not as a 'national minority'); secondly, that Serbs should be represented on a proportional basis (in accordance with the 2003 census results – 31.99 per cent of the population) in state and local governing bodies; thirdly, that they should have the right to display Serb national symbols; and finally, that there should be a constitutional confirmation of Serbian as an official language and the Cyrillic alphabet as an official script.

The SL gathered momentum, and they became, following the September 2006 election, the strongest opposition party in Montenegro with a 15 per cent share of the vote.[7] But, of course, their success determined a split within the Serb vote. The remaining Serb parties, the SNP, the party which had, since the DPS split in 1997, been the dominant Serb party, the NS and the DSS entered into a coalition to contest the September 2006 elections. Gaining just 14 per cent of the vote, they were victims of the electoral success of the SL. The 'Serbian option' was, therefore, politically defeated and their political representatives divided. With residual bitterness still permeating after the referendum, it was essential for the Montenegrin government that they be seen to accommodate the Montenegrin Serbs. Nevertheless, the overriding perception among Serbs was that the new, independent Montenegro was not *their* state, but a 'private state' controlled by Djukanović, a small clique within the DPS and shady businessmen. As a nation, the Serbs were, it was argued, at a distinct political *and* economic disadvantage – after all, the positive effects of the economic boom that would accompany Montenegro's early months and years as an independent state were felt primarily in central and coastal municipalities (those controlled by the DPS or its coalition partners). 'Foreign direct investment' (FDI) did not find its way to the traditionally Serb northern municipalities, such as Pljevlja, Šavnik, Berane or Andrijevica.[8]

While relations between the government and Serb parties remained tense, relations between the government and the Muslim and Bosniak population remained stable. Likewise, the hitherto generally positive relations between the DPS-led government and Montenegro's Albanian community continued, though they were shaken in the wake of the arrest of several members of an alleged Albanian 'terrorist cell' located in Malesija, near Podgorica. Prior to the September 2006 parliamentary elections (during 'Operation Eagle's Flight'), Montenegrin police arrested individuals suspected of belonging to a terrorist group who, it was claimed, planned to attack key figures in the Montenegrin parliament. Criminal charges were raised against seventeen persons suspected of 'criminal acts, terrorism, and illegal possession of arms and explosive materials'; firearms, explosive devices and ammunition were confiscated.[9] Cynics, however, suggested that the affair had been instrumentalized by Montenegrin state security in order to influence the electorate prior to the elections. In any event, the subsequent fall-out damaged relations between the government and the Albanian community, though Albanian leaders, such as Ferhat Dinosha (who, it was alleged, was a target), sought to emphasize that 'Operation Eagle's Flight' was not an action aimed at Albanians.[10] Nevertheless, in the September 2006 elections, Albanian voters not only shifted away from the DPS-SDP coalition, but away from Dinosha's DUA in favour of the Albanian alternative (*Albanska alternativa* – AA) and the Democratic alliance (*Demokratski savez* – DS).

The post-referendum euphoria also quickly dissipated, even for some of those who *had* been an integral part of the pro-independence bloc. For them, it wasn't about ethnic or national distinctions. A rather heterogeneous group had forged a coalition based on the premise that they had the same objective – independence. The DPS, other pro-independence parties, nationalist (and non-nationalist) intellectuals, civil society activists and journalists and editorial staff from print media such as *Vijesti* and *Monitor* all rallied behind independence. They largely accepted the principle of 'statehood first; democracy second', expecting that a recalibration the Montenegrin political landscape would ensue in the post-referendum period. This, it was assumed, would lead to greater democratization which would, by extension, lead to the end of the dominance of the DPS and the advent of a more diffuse democratic system with greater equilibrium between political parties. As it became clear that independence may serve only to strengthen the DPS's position, however, the editorial policies of *Monitor* and *Vijesti* shifted dramatically. Djukanović and the DPS, while being necessary vehicles for attaining independence, were now cast as the main obstacle to further reform. Articles vehemently criticizing him became more frequent and bitter exchanges between editorial staff and government officials became increasingly commonplace. The war of words intensified throughout the years and months following the independence referendum and reached a zenith in September 2007 when Željko Ivanović, the editor of *Vijesti*, was assaulted by three masked men in Podgorica.[11] Almost immediately, he publicly accused Djukanović of arranging the attack upon him, stating that the assault had been a revenge for his newspaper's publication of critical articles (in particular with regard to their scathing assessment of the controversial award of an 'International League of Humanists' peace prize given to Djukanović in 2007).[12]

The tensions between *Vijesti* and the government remained high, but the former's position was weakened by the fact that many of their erstwhile supporters had embarked on a different path. Many of those who had opposed Djukanović in the past had become 'establishment' figures with newly acquired wealth or fame, rewarded for their role during the referendum process. The role of the intellectuals and journalists was, after all, to provide justifications for independence, to provide theoretical underpinnings for the government's actions, a small, but important, factor in convincing the population of the merits of independence. By so doing, many profited, in one form or another, and careers were built upon support for the government. The anti-war moral capital accumulated by some during the early 1990s was traded instead for secure positions – some in business (as directors of state companies, for example), some in government ministries, some within the university sector and others within the media. A small number of those who had played important roles (or, at least, symbolically important roles) during the referendum campaign fell from grace. Jevrem Brković, the founder of DANU and advocate of the autocephalous status of the CPC, was a case in point. Publicly rehabilitated in the early 2000s, he began to regularly appear (with increasing frequency in the run up to the referendum) on Montenegrin TV, radio and within the pages of the print media. Brković found himself at the forefront of the independence campaign. But after that objective of independence had been achieved, he was increasingly sidelined. In October 2006, Brković was assaulted, and his bodyguard (Srdjan Vojičić) killed, in Podgorica, following the release of his book *Ljubavnik Duklje* (The Lover of Duklja), which, albeit through the use of pseudonyms, alluded to the involvement of several high-ranking officials in Montenegro's criminal underworld.[13] Yet despite Brković's claims that his attack had been organized from within the government, no charges were raised against his attackers.[14]

Tensions between *Vijesti* and the DPS-led government continued to increase. The major bone of contention was the granting of a public broadcast frequency to *Vijesti TV* (formed in 2008) that would allow the station to be accessible to viewers in Podgorica. Slavoljub Sčekić, the director of *Vijesti TV*, argued that their inability to gain access to the public frequency network represented a case of 'harassment' and 'institutional violence' against the opposition press.[15] Moreover, the owners of *Vijesti* argued that the government were attempting to force them out of existence by starving the station of vital advertising revenue (that would be generated by wider access to the public) and the pursuit of excessive lawsuits against them. Matters worsened following an incident involving Miodrag Mugoša (the mayor of Podgorica and high-ranking DPS official) and two *Vijesti* journalists (Mihailo Jovović and Boris Pejović). In August 2009, the two journalists photographed Mugoša's official car illegally parked in front of an establishment known to be frequented by him. Upon seeing this, Mugoša and two of his associates arrived on the scene, a fracas ensued and, according to the two journalists, the troika assaulted them. Conversely, Mugoša claimed that it was his party who were attacked by the two journalists. Eventually, the prosecutor's office in Podgorica raised indictments against Jovović and Mugoša's son, Miljan (who was subsequently dismissed from his post in the Montenegrin diplomatic service). Editorial staff at *Vijesti* continued to claim that these indictments were raised to divert attention away from Mugoša's role in the incident, and that he himself should be subject to criminal proceedings. It demonstrated, they argued, that certain people in the DPS were 'above the law.' In April 2010, Mugoša was, albeit symbolically, fined €400 for the confrontation.

From the 2007 constitution to the recognition of Kosovo

Formally ratified and adopted on 22 October 2007, the constitution had been fiercely debated in the Montenegrin Assembly. After protracted and heated debate (lasting six months), the new constitution was eventually supported by the required two-thirds of the parliament, negating the need for a referendum on the issue. The passing of the constitution fulfilled one of the criteria required for eventual EU membership, and came just one week after the signing of the SAA. But the constitutional debates laid bare the continuing tensions between Serb parties and the DPS-led government, with the key battlegrounds being the issues of language and citizenship.[16] The new constitution recognized Montenegrin as the official language of the country, but recognized Serbian, Bosnian and Croatian as 'in official use', while Cyrillic and Latin script were recognized as equal.[17] (The recognition of Montenegrin as the country's 'official' language caused consternation among Serb parties.) The issue of dual citizenship was also highly contentious, given different approaches that Serbia and Montenegro had adopted. Serbia allows dual citizenship, and offers citizenship to Serbs wherever they live, including Montenegro. By contrast, Montenegro has feared that this might undermine its statehood, particularly if a high proportion of people in the country took dual Serbian-Montenegrin citizenship.

Amid calls from Serb parties to protest against the adoption of the 'discriminatory' constitution, Milo Djukanović, ostensibly in retirement, hailed the passing of the constitution as the completion of the restoration of Montenegrin statehood. The OSCE Mission in Montenegro also welcomed the adoption of the new constitution, noting that it was 'generally in line with recommendations from the Council of Europe (CoE) and OSCE institutions'.[18] Soon after the adoption of the constitution, a familiar figure returned to the political fold. Milo Djukanović, who had retired from the post of prime minister in 2006, returned to replace Željko Šturanović, who had stepped down owing to ill-health. Critics pointed to a conflict of interests.[19] Djukanović had, after all, spent over a year consolidating his business interests, and he owned shares in the First Bank of Montenegro (*Prva banka Crne Gore* – PBCG).[20] They also argued that he had returned to politics to invoke immunity from potential charges (for alleged involvement in cigarette smuggling) emanating from the prosecutor's office in Bari in Italy.

The issue of Kosovo, despite the 2008 declaration of independence, was not a major factor in the subsequent April 2008 presidential election campaign. Only when the Montenegrin government subsequently recognized Kosovo's independence (in October 2008) was any sense of crisis apparent in Montenegro. Hitherto, a lively presidential campaign pitted the incumbent, Filip Vujanović (DPS), against the three strongest opposition leaders – Andrija Mandić (SL), Nebojša Medojević (PzP) and Srdjan Milić (SNP), the latter reminding voters that while he represented the SNP, he was the only candidate from 'Old Montenegro'.[21] Called by the speaker of the Parliament (and president of the SDP), Ranko Krivokapić, on 17 January 2008, the presidential election was the first presidential vote to be held since the independence referendum and under the October 2007 constitution. Generally, the pre-election campaign was conducted bereft of the ethnic and national issues that dominated the constitutional debates, with all candidates focusing primarily on economic issues, European integration, development and social welfare issues.[22] Kosovo, while a significant regional issue, was rather conspicuous by its absence on the respective candidates' agendas (although both Mandić and Milić visited Kosovo during the campaign). However, it was Vujanović's well-organized and well-funded campaign that drew, ultimately, the most votes. Campaigning under the slogan of *Bez dilema* (Without Dilemma), Vujanović's 'door-to-door' campaign was more visible and effective than that of his opponents. The catchy slogan did indeed suggest that there was no dilemma among the voters, 52 per cent of whom voted for the DPS's candidate. Andrija Mandić finished runner-up with just short of 20 per cent, while Medojević and Milić won 17 per cent and 12 per cent, respectively.[23]

Throughout the campaign, the issue of Kosovo had been largely relegated to the margins. However, when the Montenegrin government eventually recognized Kosovo and signalled their intention to establish full diplomatic relations with Prishtina, it generated significant controversy. That Kosovo had been a factor in Montenegrin politics was nothing novel; it had been ever-present in Montenegrin politics (in 1989 and 1999) and was a particularly emotive issue for Montenegro's Serbs (see Chapters 2 and 7). In the wake of Kosovo's declaration of independence in February 2008, the Montenegrin government adopted a neutral position, with an emphasis being placed on the need for further dialogue.[24] But this perceived shift threatened to undermine relations between the government and the Albanian minority (5.03 per cent of the population). It would be impossible to find a satisfactory 'middle way' that would placate both Montenegro's Albanian minority *and* the, significantly larger (31.99 per cent), Serb minority.

The Serb parties opposed recognition and warned that the Montenegrin government doing so could lead to 'internal instability'.[25] In the wake of Kosovo's declaration of independence, demonstrations organized by Serb parties took place in Podgorica, with Andrija Mandić subsequently travelling to northern Mitrovica to show solidarity with the Kosovo Serbs. He implored the Montenegrin government not to recognize an independent Kosovo, adding that such recognition would represent 'an historic error.'[26] It was a clear signal Montenegro's Serbs were united over the issue, and would not be inactive in the event of recognition. Conversely, however, procrastination over recognition generated resentment among Montenegro's Albanians, who interpreted what they perceived to be an unnecessary delay in the recognition of Kosovo as 'anti-Albanian'. Relations between the government and the Albanians were, on the whole, good, and Albanians were well integrated into Montenegrin state structures. Some Albanian parties, however, had sought greater levels of autonomy in certain spheres. In terms of education, linguistic parity at all levels of education was a key issue, largely due to the fact that, in Montenegro, university education is offered only in Serbian (or Montenegrin). The second bone of contention was the status of the predominantly Albanian area of Tuzi. The third issue was the use of national symbols. Albanian leaders consistently argued that Albanian symbols should be used more liberally and expressed dismay that their flag could not be raised on the Tuzi council building. But these issues were more matters of practicality than of emotion; the issue of Kosovo was different. Though no Montenegrin Albanian leader, despite their support for an independent Kosovo, publicly called for separation or incited separatism among Montenegro's Albanians, they urged the Montenegrin government not to delay recognition.

Regional and international factors were also crucial, particularly given Montenegro's progress towards EU candidacy. The Montenegrin government were eager to avoid antagonizing their traditional ally, Serbia, with whom they enjoyed only lukewarm relations since the referendum. But they were equally eager to preserve good relations with those countries (particularly the United States and UK) that had already recognized Kosovo, and were 'encouraging' others to do likewise. Serbia's president, Boris Tadić, and foreign minister, Vuk Jeremić, appealed to the Montenegrins to support Serbia's appeal to the UN General Assembly (UNGA) to raise their case at the International Court of Justice (ICJ), warning that recognition would be seen in Serbia as a 'stab in the back'.[27] A parliamentary resolution tabled in the days prior to the UNGA meeting, however, stated that Montenegro would pursue a policy in keeping with their 'Euro-Atlantic orientation', which was a relatively unambiguous signal that they may be preparing to just that. The Montenegrin leadership delayed until the UNGA had voted on the matter, but on 9 October 2008, having voted in favour of Serbia's request to refer the case to the ICJ, they announced (in concert with FYR Macedonia) that they would formally recognize Kosovo as an independent state. Anticipating the controversy that would inevitably follow, Djukanović sought to justify the action his government had taken.[28] Presenting Kosovo's independence as a fait accompli, he argued that Montenegro could no longer deny the 'political reality' of an independent Kosovo, simultaneously appealing to citizens to recognize that it was logical to play the long game. It was implied, moreover, that recognition would bring 'benefits' (an allusion, no doubt, to an acceleration of Montenegro's EU and NATO membership). However succinct, it was not an argument accepted by Serbia, which immediately declared the Montenegrin ambassador in Belgrade, Anka Vojvodić, persona non grata.

Seeking to capitalize on the anger that was generated by recognition (and the lack of public consultation in advance of the decision), the opposition called on those who did not advocate recognition to demonstrate against what they deemed an illegal and undemocratic act. During the demonstrations, the largest of which was held in Podgorica on the evening of 13 October 2008, they set out their three key demands: that the government reverse their decision, that a referendum on recognition be held and that early parliamentary elections be scheduled by the end of the year. A series of speakers made their case in front of a responsive crowd. The atmosphere was tense but peaceful, but as the evening wore on, the atmosphere darkened. In scenes reminiscent of the attempted storming of the government building by pro-Milošević groups in January 1998 following Djukanović's victory over Momir Bulatović in the 1997 presidential elections, protestors attempted to storm Montenegro's parliament building. The police reacted, using tear gas and baton charges to disperse the crowds.[29] In the aftermath, each side sought to pin responsibility on the other, with government officials claiming that 'agitators' from Belgrade had been instrumental in orchestrating the violence. Opposition leaders argued that the violence had been orchestrated by Montenegrin state security in an attempt to discredit the demonstrators.[30]

The exchanges between the government and the opposition became increasingly adversarial and antagonistic. Acting, it was claimed, in the interests of Montenegro's citizens, the government banned further demonstrations. This was not an undemocratic act, they argued, but one which was required to avoid further violence and ensure citizens' security. In response, opposition deputies boycotted parliament and Andrija Mandić embarked upon a well-publicized hunger strike which lasted almost two weeks.[31] Both his hunger strike and his supporters' subsequent 'long march' from Berane to Podgorica received significant media coverage.[32] The Serbian Orthodox Church (SPC), too, entered the debate. Metropolitan Amfilohije Radović declared that he 'respected Andrija's sacrifice', while simultaneously warning that the actions of the Montenegrin government were helping to create the conditions for further conflict in Kosovo.[33] Yet, despite the fiery rhetoric, and the best efforts of the opposition, the momentum waned soon after Mandić ended his hunger strike.

What this course of events revealed, if nothing else, was that the opposition remained beset by deep differences (not least on the issue of Kosovo). Kosovo, a highly emotive issue for some, but less for others, served to divide rather than unite them. Conversely, recognition of Kosovo proved beneficial for the government on not one but two fronts. Domestically, they could argue that the demonstrations were evidence that the state was under threat from extremists and measures (that would increase the government's control) could justifiably be implemented to protect citizens. They appeared resolute while the opposition, having proved incapable of articulating a unified message, appeared weakened. Local elections, held in Kotor, following recognition, signalled that the DPS had indeed escaped the controversy relatively unscathed, winning twice as many votes as the runners-up (the SNP).[34]

The decision to recognize Kosovo may have ingratiated the Montenegrin government to London and Washington, but did little to stem pressure emanating from Brussels (the latter having no formal position on the issue). Despite making progress in the EU accession process, criticism over the government's lack of will in tackling the problems of corruption and organized crime, the questionable independence of the judiciary, had increased in intensity throughout 2008 and were emphasized in the 2008 EC progress report. If the Montenegrin government had assumed that the decision to recognize Kosovo would give them breathing space vis-à-vis issues of EU conditionality, they had miscalculated. Nevertheless, there was an overarching acknowledgement that the issue of Kosovo *was* a thorny one for the Montenegrin government, and they had demonstrated courage in taking the decision.[35] There may have been no tangible benefit from recognition, but it earned Montenegro credit among key states (the United States, the UK and Germany) that would now consolidate their support for Montenegro's EU accession. The Montenegrin government had, perhaps rather by luck than judgement, conspired to use Kosovo to their advantage.

Forging effective opposition

The only opposition leader to capitalize from the Kosovo recognition crisis was Srdjan Milić, the president of the SNP. The party and its leader Predrag Bulatović were demoralized and defeated after the referendum, and it was unclear whether the SNP, seemingly a spent force, could recover. The 2006 parliamentary elections appeared to confirm that the party was indeed in terminal decline; the SNP-NS-DSS coalition gathering only 14 per cent of the vote. The SNP, erstwhile associates of Slobodan Milošević and foremost articulator of the pro-union argument, would, in Milić's view, have to adapt to survive. Thus, he distanced the party from NS and DSS (its traditional ideological bedfellows) and shifted towards a social democratic position, which embraced both EU accession and NATO membership. This strategy appeared to generate little tangible success during the presidential elections, but Milić's measured comments during the Kosovo controversy indicated that the SNP had passed through a definitive transformation.

Others were also repositioning. Andrija Mandić, perhaps understanding that the SNS's current stance negated it becoming a mainstream party, signalled his intention to form a new political party, one that would draw together moderate strains within the SL. Mandić sought to forge a pro-European profile, hoping that by doing so he could broaden his party's (and his) appeal. But this, of course, meant that he had to marginalize those elements within the SL which might inhibit such a significant ideological shift. Those marginalized reacted badly to Mandić's new initiative, claiming that he had 'sold out' Serbs, accepted Montenegrin independence, and blatantly contradicted his post-referendum rhetoric. But while Mandić could survive attacks coming from the right of the SL, he needed the support of his own party (SNS). This, however, was not entirely forthcoming, and a number of prominent party members, including Novak Radulović, left the SNS, claiming that Mandić had destroyed the true spirit of the party.

Mandić's potential coalition partners, PzP, were also in some difficulty. Their own intra-party crisis reached its zenith when a number among their ranks, including the former deputy chairman, Goran Batrićević, left the party to form the Democratic Centre (*Demokratski centar* – DC). The breakaway had its roots in disagreements about both the party's orientation and Medojević's role within it. Batrićević argued that Medojević had drawn too close to the SNP and SNS, had been compromised during the Kosovo demonstrations. Moreover, it was alleged, Medojević's 'autocratic style' had alienated some within the party.[36] Batrićević's DC subsequently entered a coalition with the Liberal Party (*Liberalna stranka* – LS), both parties stressing that neither would enter any kind of pact with the DPS in the event of early elections.

In January 2009, with the opposition in disarray, the government called early elections. Having just submitted their application for EU membership, the government stated that they were going to the polls early in order to seek a further four-year mandate, time enough to complete the next stage of the EU accession process. Cynics were quick to argue that the elections were called early, not for the aforementioned reasons, but because by so doing the government could secure a new mandate before the effects of the global economic downturn became apparent. Even if such accusations were unfounded, the economy was a key, and potentially problematic, issue for the government. Having grown steadily since 2000 (when Montenegro forged an economic policy quite different from its then federal partner Serbia), the economy grew rapidly after independence. Montenegro became a member of both the International Monetary Fund (IMF) and the World Bank in January 2007, and thus had access to finance from either organization. Yet, there was little need. Between 2002 and 2008 Montenegro enjoyed the fastest gross domestic product (GDP) growth in the region. Unemployment levels dropped significantly (from 33 per cent in 2002 to 10.8 per cent in 2008), the country had a budget surplus and foreign debt was reduced from 42.6 per cent of GDP in 2005 to just 27 per cent in 2008.[37] FDI levels had also increased significantly, and by the time (in July 2007) *The Observer* had trumpeted Montenegro as 'Europe's New Golden Coast', investors from Ireland, the UK and (primarily) Russia flocked to the country.[38] High-profile concerts, held on Jaz beach, featured world-renowned bands and musicians (such as the Rolling Stones and Lenny Kravitz) further raised Montenegro's international profile.[39] As a consequence, Montenegro's development further fed the economy, the country's export market grew and further economic growth was supported by significant expansions in construction, tourism and the services sector.

The flow of FDI into Montenegro (particularly that emanating from Russia) was lightning fast.[40] This, coupled with an aggressive and rapid privatization process, created a new, and often brash, nouveau riche at the expense of many ordinary citizens. The coastal town of Budva was a case-in-point. The town and its surrounding coastline quickly became, following the referendum, the very expensive and very sought after.[41] Awash with Russian money, the area saw a number of elaborate – and at times bizarre – constructions erected, such as the so-called *Rusko selo* (Russian Village) above Sveti Stefan. This often-tasteless ostentation and the sudden appearance of shiny new glass and steel buildings (particularly in Podgorica and on the coast around Budva) masked, however, underlying problems. Indeed, the economic boom and the growing consumer and commercial confidence which existed in 2006–07 began to evaporate by 2008, as the economy began to feel the impact of the global economic downturn.[42] The property market, so buoyant in the immediate period following the referendum, slumped and businesses struggled to stay afloat as banks ceased lending. The most potent manifestation of the seriousness of the crisis, however, came in the form of the gloom that enveloped the *Kombinat Aluminijuma Podgorica* (KAP) plant. In December 2005, KAP was privatized, with 65 per cent of its shares being bought by Salomon Enterprises Limited (later renamed the Central European Aluminum Company – CEAC), owned by the Russian billionaire, Oleg Deripaska. The sale of the shares generated controversy, the final deal allegedly struck in 2005 during a private meeting between Deripaska and Djukanović. Initially, all was well – independence coincided with high aluminium prices, but the decreasing market value of aluminium and the expense of running the plant determined that KAP was losing an estimated €200,000 every day. The Montenegrin national electricity supplier (*Elektroprivreda Crne Gore* – EPCG) at one stage threatened to cease supplying electricity to the plant over unpaid bills, although it did not act upon it. The government were under pressure to act. Given that the KAP plant was one of the largest employers in Montenegro and accounted for a 15 per cent of the country's total GDP, a closure of the plant could generate significant discontent (it is estimated that 10,000 people directly or indirectly relied on KAP for their incomes). In June 2009, having had an offer of financial aid to CEAC declined, the government opted to partially renationalize, by buying back a substantial stake in the plant.[43]

The March 2009 election campaign had taken place, therefore, in a context of growing concern about the gathering economic storm and the potential implications for the Montenegrin economy.[44] At a time when the government were more sensitive to social issues, the spectre of economic crisis was still sufficiently abstract to make a tangible impact on the political scene (though its impact was beginning to become evident).[45] The DPS-led 'European Montenegro' (*Evropska Crna Gora*) coalition was returned to power in the parliamentary election. The coalition comprising of the DPS, its long-standing junior partner, the SDP and a number of minority parties garnered over 50 per cent of the vote, with the coalition winning forty-eight seats (in the eighty-one-seat) parliament, an increase compared with the forty-one that it won in the previous parliamentary election in 2006. The opposition, seeking to capitalize on the resentment generated by the Kosovo recognition, failed to make headway. They proved incapable of forging a coalition, largely due to individual parties giving primacy to their own, rather than the collective, interest. The SNP, who were the subject of speculation that they may be willing to enter a future coalition with the DPS, were particularly rigid in this regard. Having assessed that the divisions within NOVA and PzP rendered them unreliable coalition partners, they opted to run alone, with the objective of reclaiming the position it once held for a decade as Montenegro's leading opposition party. They calculated correctly, winning sixteeen seats in the parliament, an increase of five since the 2006 election.

By contrast, PzP won only five seats, less than half of those won in 2006. Early optimism that they might become a force capable of challenging the DPS's dominance remained unfulfilled. Seeking to undermine the DPS by focusing on alleged corruption and links to organized crime proved an ineffective strategy, and regardless of the increasingly difficult economic climate they could not convince voters to back them. NOVA, meanwhile, could only garner 9 per cent of the vote, giving them eight seats in parliament. Nevertheless, endeavours to forge a working opposition coalition continued unabated. Particularly active was Nebojša Medojević, who sought to bring together opposition political parties, NGOs and other non-parliamentary structures into a broad coalition front that would challenge the ruling coalition, a strategy that would, albeit slowly, bear fruit. The coalition was formed (comprising NOVA, SNP, PzP, DSS and NS) in time to contest the approaching local elections in May 2010.

The results of Montenegro's municipal elections, held on 23 May 2010, appeared to demonstrate that the country's politics continues to follow a familiar script. But while the seemingly resounding election victory of the 'Coalition for a European Montenegro' (*Koalicija za Evropsku Crnu Goru*), led by the DPS, may have, on a superficial level, seemed convincing, the result obscured the bigger picture. Increasingly nervous about the momentum of the opposition, the government called the municipal elections for 23 May against the wishes of the opposition who wanted the elections held on 6 June. The latter's objection was that the government would use the coincidence of the election campaign with the fourth anniversary of Montenegrin independence to subtly remind the electorate of the DPS's key role in delivering independence. And indeed, the leadership of the DPS-led coalition did just that, their rhetorical cornerstone being 'safety in continuity'. The inexperienced, and 'anti-Montenegrin' opposition, they argued, could not be trusted to govern at any level in these tough economic times. Nebojša Medojević, cast as an ambitious charlatan motivated by his own desire for power, was singled out as a case in point.[46] And such attacks were not merely limited to opposition politicians. On the eve of the elections, Milo Djukanović alleged that one of the Serbian President Boris Tadić's closest advisors had been tasked with providing financial and logistical assistance to the opposition, with a view, in Djukanović's words, to 'reversing Montenegro's independence'.[47]

The 'Better Montenegro' (*Bolja Crna Gora*) coalition, consisting of twelve parties, but led by the PzP, NOVA and the SNP, contested the elections following months of negotiations. The coalition, also supported by NGOs and other non-governmental structures, appeared to have little to unite them but their almost pathological hatred of the ruling elite. Nevertheless, they went to great lengths to stress their commonalities, while playing down clear differences. They attacked the government's record of managing the country's economic affairs, their alleged lack of strategy for mitigating the effects of the economic crisis and inefficiency of state institutions in the fight against organized crime. While the term 'change' was omnipresent, Medojević, adorned in his now-characteristic white shirt with rolled-up sleeves *a-la-Obama*, stuck to traditional rhetoric, speaking at length about the alleged links between Djukanović and organized crime. These public pronouncements represented a risky gambit for Medojevic, and it remains unclear whether his actions attracted or repelled voters. Yet, despite the efforts of the opposition, the DPS weathered the storm. The party claimed victory in seven of the fourteen contested municipalities, including the traditional opposition strongholds of Andrijevica, Kolašin and Žabljak, increasing their overall share of the vote. The opposition, who on the eve of the election had predicted a 'landslide' in their favour, claimed victory in Pljevlja and the SNP, who ran independently in some municipalities, did so in Plužine. The opposition drew further encouragement from the fact that the presence of a strong opposition coalition stopped the DPS from acquiring an absolute majority in Podgorica.

Milo Djukanović departs – temporarily

Milo Djukanović, undoubtedly the most charismatic, pragmatic, single-minded, (politically) intelligent and ruthless politician to emerge in Montenegro in the past few decades, had survived the cut and thrust of Montenegrin politics through the most difficult of times. His ability to adapt quickly and decisively in fluid political situations, his instinct for political survival and his ability to outwit his political opponents has been impressive. These qualities have determined his longevity as *the* dominant political figure in Montenegro. The phenomenon of Djukanović can – to some extent – be understood by how he is perceived among his countrymen. Even his most vehement critics acknowledge that he possesses qualities (bravery, strength, ruthlessness, charm, physical presence) that are highly regarded in Montenegrin society. He has become, according to the Bosnian weekly *Slobodna Bosna*, 'The New Montenegrin Vladika'.[48] And there has, since 1997 at least, little in the way of a challenge to this dominance. As the symbolic leader of the independence bloc, he generated (and had bestowed upon him) the image of 'the father of the nation', personifying the quest for independence. Retiring from politics for a short time in 2006 (to concentrate on his business interests), he returned to take the role of prime minster in 2008 – though he had remained a powerful figure operating from behind the scenes throughout.[49] (Indeed, during his brief sabbatical he retained the chairmanship of the DPS and was generally assumed to be pulling the strings from behind the scenes.[50]) And, of course, although he stepped down as prime minister, he remained the chairman of the DPS.

Djukanović, worshipped by his admirers and despised (almost pathologically) by his detractors, remained the most important figure in Montenegrin politics, though it wasn't all plain sailing. He continued to be dogged by persistent allegations of links to the Italian mafia, the Balkan underworld and alleged criminals such as Andrija

Drašković and the Swiss-based Serbian businessman, Stanko 'Cane' Subotić. This has fuelled the perception among EU officials that he may not have the will to push the reforms required to meet the EU's strict criteria.[51] Thus, Washington and Brussels had a paradoxical relationship with Djukanović: He was a man they could communicate effectively with, a man they trusted, a man who they knew possessed the clout to make things happen. Yet, his reputation was tarnished by all of the aforementioned associations.

Accusations that Djukanović had been involved in the illicit cigarette smuggling business date back to 2001, when articles appeared in the Croatian weekly *Nacional* implicating him. Almost simultaneously, the former Italian finance minister, Ottavio del Turco, publicly accused Djukanović of being closely linked to organized crime, being the lynchpin in the illegal mechanisms that controlled the smuggling of cigarettes in the Balkans, and having provided safe haven for Italian criminals in the Montenegrin town of Bar. By July 2002, the public prosecutor in the Italian port city of Bari, Guisseppe Scelsi, initiated investigative proceedings against the Montenegrin president. The accusation was that Djukanović (in concert with the Italian mafia and the cigarette manufacturers R. J. Reynolds and Philip Morris) smuggled large amounts of untaxed cigarettes into the EU from the port of Bar in Montenegro – generating significant profits for all the participants.[52] These profits, claimed Djukanović, were not channelled into private hands, but used to pay for the state's running costs during the period of UN-imposed sanctions (see Chapter 3) – a matter, not of profit, but of patriotic duty. Djukanović surprised even his critics when he travelled to Bari in March 2008, where he was questioned by Italian prosecutors.[53] The matter appeared to be at an end.

In October 2009, however, Ratko Knežević, a London-based Montenegrin businessman, one-time head of the Montenegrin trade mission in the United States and a former associate of Djukanović, gave a series of interviews to *Vijesti* and the Belgrade daily *Blic* in which he reiterated claims that the Djukanović had been a pivotal figure in a criminal organization which included the former head of the Serbian secret service, Jovica Stanišić (on trial in The Hague on war crimes charges), and Stanko 'Cane' Subotić (who was indicted for tobacco smuggling in Serbia).[54] Knežević claimed the group controlled the cigarette smuggling racket throughout the Balkans. More controversially, however, Knežević implied that this 'cartel' was responsible for ordering murders, including those of Ivo Pukanić, the owner of the Croatian weekly *Nacional*, his colleague Niko Franjić, who were killed in a car bomb in Zagreb in October 2008, and Duško Jovanović, the editor of the Montenegrin daily *Dan*, who was shot dead outside his office in Podgorica in 2004. Both Pukanić and Jovanović had investigated and written extensively about the alleged criminal activities of several high-profile Montenegrins, Djukanovic being foremost among them.[55] Eventually, Serbian prosecutors indicted Sreten Jočić (aka 'Joca' Amsterdam), along with two of his accomplices in October 2009 on charges of organizing Pukanić's murder. No link with Djukanović has ever been established.

Nebojša Medojević (PzP) also spoke publicly, and at some length, about Djukanović's alleged links with organized crime. In addition to his regular accusations that Milo Djukanović was an instrumental player in the cigarette smuggling trade in the 1990s, he also alleged that the Šarić brothers (one of whom, Darko, was wanted by Interpol and the Serbian government on drug trafficking charges) had funded the DPS's election campaign in Žabljak in August 2009.[56] Medojević also claimed that the Montenegrin businessman, Branislav Mićunović, had forged close links with Darko Šarić and had used his links with Montenegro's political elite to ensure that the latter evaded arrest in Montenegro. Highlighting organized crime and corruption cases was not without consequences; in February 2010, Medojević was attacked outside his home in Podgorica. He claimed that the assault represented a clear warning from the mafia to cease his crusade against organized crime structures in Montenegro.

While these accusations had been circulating for years, Knežević's intervention brought the uncomfortable subject to prominence once again. In a meeting between Djukanović and US deputy secretary of state, James Steinberg, in New York, the latter raised concerns that that such rumours were damaging for the Montenegrin government. Whether the continued controversy over these matters was a causal factor, on 21 December 2010, Djukanović announced that he would be stepping down as prime minster, with the mandate passing to the finance minister and deputy prime minister, Igor Lukšić. Djukanović claimed he was doing so because he had achieved many of his political ambitions, was tired of politics and wished to concentrate on his business interests.[57] However, again, as in 1989 and 1997 (two moments of cathartic political change, namely the 'anti-bureaucratic revolution' and the DPS split), change was facilitated, not through the mechanism of democratic elections, but from *within* the existing structure of power. As Lenard Cohen has pointed out, democracy in Montenegro was yet to 'be tested by the fundamental experience in succession of leadership and political parties'.[58] Indeed, by 2010 Montenegro held the unenviable record of being the only state in Southeast Europe that has been governed, uninterrupted, by the same political party (albeit with internal purges) since the first democratic elections in 1990. But rumours of a possible split within the party were the subject of intense speculation throughout 2010. In the knowledge that Djukanović would step down, two factions emerged within the party, both of which had their eyes on the succession process. Djukanović endeavoured to consolidate the position of loyalists within the DPS, investing significant energy into ensuring that primacy would be achieved by his chosen successor(s). Two became ascendants, namely Igor Lukšić and Duško Marković (the former head of the SDB). The former was, however, more 'marketable' and thus the more likely *heir apparent*, with the latter designated the role of internal party whip. Indeed, Djukanović's decision to designate Marković the post of 'minister without portfolio' was almost certainly a ploy to discipline party deputies who may be inclined to seek to acquire power. The strategy was thus: empower close allies and marginalize potential opponents, and by doing so shape the internal composition of the upper echelons of the DPS, one that would remain under his influence even in the event of his formal departure.

But not all within the DPS leadership advocated Lukšić's appointment, or the way in which the succession process was handled. Montenegro's president, Filip Vujanović, and deputy prime minister, Svetozar Marović, both resisted Djukanović's efforts to dictate terms.[59] Both endeavoured to improve their position when circumstances allowed but were ultimately unsuccessful. Having struggled to convince the key party members, they retreated in the face of determined opponents. By the time Djukanović formally retired, the succession of Lukšić was assured. Svetozar Marović stepped down on the same day, though Vujanović remained in post, albeit weakened and unlikely to possess enough support within the DPS to mount a challenge. Indeed, within days the main board of the DPS had rubber-stamped Lukšić's elevation to the role of prime minister. Igor Lukšić was perceived, at least externally, as a reformer, an individual who belongs to a new political generation, untainted by the dark days of the 1990s, and not a one-time communist youth *apparatchik*.

In his early months as prime minister, Lukšić has endeavoured to demonstrate his commitment to tackling corruption and organized crime, one of the key stipulations of the EU. In this regard, he took immediate action. He sent a very strong signal that he was serious, although these ostensibly anti-corruption measures also had a domestic political motivation. On 24 December, the mayor, Rajko Kuljača, and the deputy mayor of the coastal town of Budva were among ten arrested on charges of corruption linked to the so-called 'Zavala case', an alleged corruption affair which involved politicians, construction companies and spatial planners.[60] The deputy mayor of Budva was, significantly, Dragan Marović, the brother of Svetozar Marović, a potential political challenger within the DPS. Following the arrests, the latter said he believed that they were politically motivated, and that he urged the authorities to 'arrest me, convict me and send me to the darkest prison if that is what is good for Montenegro and in accordance with its laws'.[61] He was, however, only required to appear as a witness in the Zavala case.[62] Lukšić stated that the Budva arrests were 'not an improvisation', but part of a wider process necessary to meet conditions for EU membership.[63] These early developments gave the distinct impression that Lukšić was not simply 'Milo's man'. But his room for manoeuvre was limited. Djukanović remained the chairman of the DPS and still enjoyed strong support among the key figures within it. Djukanović has also ensured that Lukšić, his chosen successor, was flanked by his closest allies. Both Milan Roćen and Duško Marković, staunch Djukanović loyalists, were given senior roles in the government; the former retaining his post as foreign minister, the latter replacing Svetozar Marović (who was being increasingly marginalized) as deputy prime minister. Moreover, Djukanović did not rule out a return as a presidential candidate in 2013, or at some other stage.

The Montenegrin Orthodox Church in independent Montenegro

Away from the glare of day-to-day politics, the conflict between the CPC and the SPC continued unabated. In the wake of Montenegro's declaration of independence, supporters of the CPC grew in confidence; they assumed that the position of the CPC would be much stronger in an independent Montenegrin state and were determined to capitalize on the new political reality. Conversely, the SPC was uncertain of what the new political environment would mean for them and for Serbs in Montenegro. On 9 April 2007, the CPC announced of a plan to take control of all Orthodox churches in Montenegro, with or without the help of the government. The latter's reaction was that it would protect the SPC in the event of an attempt to seize control of churches, further fuelling the CPC's growing perception that the state and the SPC were engaged in a joint endeavour to deny the CPC freedom of worship.[64] It was in this context that around 300 supporters of the CPC attempted, on 18 April, to force their way into Cetinje monastery.[65] Unable to pass the police cordon surrounding the monastery, the CPC held a service outside the nearby Monastery of Saint Peter on Ćipur (where King Nikola I and Queen Milena Petrović are buried), which they were unable to enter because it had been 'occupied' by the 'Serb Orthodox Youth Brotherhood'. Three months later, in July, the CPC announced that they would hold a service outside the Church of St Archangel Michael in Nikšić, a church administered by the SPC.[66] Again, however, they were forbidden from doing so by local police. In September 2007, the SPC's Bishop Filaret of the Mileševa diocese (the centre of which is the Mileševa monastery in Prijepolje, Serbia) created controversy by camping out on the Serbian-Montenegrin border and embarking on a hunger strike, having been denied entry into Montenegro by the government on the basis that he had allegedly provided assistance to war crimes fugitives wanted by the International Criminal Tribunal for the Former Yugoslavia (ICTY).[67] His protest exacerbated tensions between the SPC and CPC and, therefore, between Serb and Montenegrin nationalists. Eventually, in an attempt to defuse tensions, the Montenegrin government agreed to allow Filaret to enter Montenegro.[68]

Two months later, however, Amfilohije's attentions were drawn back to Belgrade with the decline and death of Serbian Patriarch Pavle. In November 2007, Amfilohije was elected by the Holy Synod of the SPC to take over Pavle's duties, a role he undertook until the election of Bishop Irinej of Niš at the new Patriarch in January 2010 (the CPC making it clear that they expected little from Irinej, who is a strong proponent of the unity of the SPC). In Amfilohije's absence, the CPC intensified their activities. In January 2009, they announced that they intended to take possession of monasteries and churches built before 1920. This time, however, their actions would lead to legal proceedings being enacted against them. On 20 January, Montenegrin police placed a cordon around the Church of St John the Baptist in Bajice, near Cetinje, to deny access to priests from both the SPC and CPC, both of whom were preparing to conduct services in the church. A legal struggle over the ownership of the church began. Less than a month later, the SPC filed charges against members of the CPC for changing the lock on the church and thus violating the rights of the SPC to hold services there. The judge in Cetinje, however, dismissed the case as groundless, opting instead to open an inquiry to accusations levelled against two SPC priests, Obren Jovanović and Gojko Perović, who stood accused of illegally entering churches to hold services. Incidents continued throughout the summer of 2009, and upon Amfilohije's return, rhetorical exchanges between the SPC and the CPC intensified, this time fuelled by the SPC's construction of a new church on Sveti Stefan, a development opposed by the CPC.[69] Debate also continued to rage about the fabricated church on Mount Rumija, an issue that became a problematic one for the then Montenegrin prime minister, Igor Lukšić. His predecessor, Milo Djukanović, in the midst of his 'retirement', again implied support for the CPC, stating that although the SPC in Montenegro was autonomous (from Belgrade), it was 'still part of the Serbian Orthodox Church' and thus 'not sufficiently in line with Montenegro's national interests.'[70] He hinted also at a future unification of the churches in Montenegro, something Amfilohije rejected as impractical; indeed, a matter of days later, the SPC demonstrated it was in no mood to compromise. On 20 May 2011, the SPC filed a lawsuit against the Montenegrin state at the European Court of Human Rights (ECHR) in Strasbourg, primarily for property allegedly seized from them after the end of the Second World War. The case was eventually rejected by the court, on the grounds that 'the key provisions of the law which they had relied had been declared unconstitutional before they filed their request'.[71]

Since then, the SPC and Montenegrin government have engaged in discussion about how best to improve church–state relations. Montenegro's ruling DPS have suggested that they will strive for the creation of a single, organizationally independent Orthodox religious community in Montenegro as a way of overcoming the divisions between the SPC and CPC.[72] Milo Djukanović stated that this offered the best possible solution, while Ranko Krivokapić (an arch adversary of Amfilohije) expressed the view that such a solution represented the best way to 'correct the historical injustice' of 1920.[73] Krivokapić also suggested that the property currently under the control of the SPC (the most symbolic of which is Ostrog monastery near Nikšić) should be 'reclaimed' and handed over to the CPC. In this climate, the struggle between the SPC and the CPC continued unabated. On 21 May 2011 (the fifth anniversary of the Montenegrin independence referendum), Krivokapić stated, after laying a wreath at the tomb of Petar II Petrović 'Njegoš' on Mount Lovćen, that the Montenegrin government had the right to take back property from the SPC.[74] In the same month, Amfilohije was put on trial in Podgorica, charged with 'hate speech' – or more precisely with 'cursing all of those who wished to destroy the church on Mount Rumija'. The long, drawn-out affair led, in November 2012, to Amfilohije, who had rejected the accusations as unfounded, being cautioned.[75] The conflict between the CPC and the SPC thus remained unresolved.

10

Progress, Protests and Political Crisis (2012–16)

In January 2012, a wave of anti-government protests began. Motivated by discontent over increasing energy prices, alleged mismanagement of the privatization of public enterprises, corruption and lack of employment opportunities a diverse group comprising trade unionists, academics and members of various student organizations gathered in large numbers in Podgorica to vent their anger. While not generating a strong enough momentum to seriously challenge the government, they were demonstrative of the rising dissatisfaction among those who felt disenfranchized, and demonstrative, too, of a dissatisfaction that could be harnessed politically. Indeed, a number of either those political parties who had supported or individuals who had participated in them would subsequently establish the Democratic Front (*Demokratski front* – DF), a coalition of centre-right parties comprising NOVA, PzP and several senior SNP officials (such as the party's former leader, Predrag Bulatović) and dedicated to 'democratic change of the regime'.[1]

On 29 June 2012, Montenegro opened accession negotiations with the EU, six years after establishing formal relations with them following the 2006 referendum. The governing coalition (DPS/SDP/BS and HGI) thereafter stated that they would seek to schedule early elections (the next elections had been scheduled for the spring of 2013) in order to secure a further four-year mandate and thus a full parliamentary term to proceed with these negotiations. After a parliamentary motion in favour of elections was passed in the Montenegrin Assembly, the early elections were scheduled to be held on 14 October 2012. While confident of a victory, the continued dominance of the DPS (or DPS-led coalitions) was, to some extent, challenged by the emergence of the DF in July 2012. It seemed unlikely, after all, that the DF – particularly because of the prominence of NOVA within it – could really become a 'catch all' or 'big tent' party that could unite Montenegrins around the coalition's core objective, but under the leadership of Miodrag Lekić the DF rapidly became a powerful political factor, with Lekić reviving what had been hitherto a rather moribund opposition that had been both ineffective and hampered by internal divisions since the 2006 referendum.[2] Lekić was not charismatic per se but he possessed a serious, professorial manner that made him stand out from the other potential leaders of the DF.

The DF performed respectably in the elections, winning twenty seats in parliament, just over half that won by the DPS-led *Koalicija za Evropsku Crnu Goru* (Coalition for a European Montenegro), which won thirty-nine seats and thus required a coalition agreement with the Bosniak Party (*Bošnjačka stranka* – BS), among others, to form a government.[3] The DF's rapid ascendancy came at a time when the DPS were facing their own crisis, in the form of the 'audio recording scandal', which broke in February 2013.[4] The pro-opposition newspaper *Dan* and the NGO MANS (Network for the Affirmation of the NGO Sector) released an audio recording of a DPS meeting and a number of compromising documents. In the recording, senior DPS members discussed various ways of utilizing the state budget funds, civil service jobs and related benefits to secure more votes (methods critics of the DPS had claimed the party had used for years). A subsequent parliamentary committee to investigate the affair, led by the PzP deputy leader, Koča Pavlović, was then established but had little success in establishing the facts surrounding the allegations.[5]

The subsequent scandal caused significant embarrassment for the DPS and their partners in the governing coalition, and gave the DF a boost in advance of the 7 April 2013 presidential election, during which Miodrag Lekić (running as an independent candidate) won an impressive 48.8 per cent of the vote, losing only marginally to the DPS candidate, Filip Vujanović, who won with 51.2 per cent.[6] Both claimed victory and upon the announcement of the final results by the State Election Commission and the OSCE, the DF immediately claimed that irregularities had taken place and announced that they would commence both a parliamentary boycott and street protests.[7]

The narrow margin of the defeat had demonstrated that the DF was a credible and ascendant political force, certainly under Lekić's stewardship. Despite the DF's notable early successes, however, cracks soon began to appear. Speculation that Lekić disliked the hard-line positions that NOVA adopted vis-à-vis Serb national issues had been abundant throughout the DF's rapid ascendancy, but strains within the DF were evident by 2014. Indeed, after internal disagreements over the direction of the coalition, Lekić left in March 2015 to form his own party *Demokratski savez* (known more commonly as DEMOS) taking a number of key DF members with him, including Goran Danilović, the former vice president of NOVA. The DF, after the departure of Lekić, did not possess the level of support that its original incarnation enjoyed but his departure allowed the more radical elements within the DF to shift to reorient the coalition to a political position that would have been impossible under Lekić's leadership. So though seemingly weakened as a political force, they changed direction, opting not to challenge the DPS *within* the parliament (the DEMOS position) but to use a parliamentary boycott and a return to the 'politics of the streets' to achieve their aims.[8] Their change in strategy was underpinned by their conviction that the government were engaged in electoral fraud, that democracy in Montenegro was a sham and that the system was rigged in favour of the DPS, meaning that alternative methods of changing the government should be utilized. (Some within the DF were also firmly opposed to Montenegro joining NATO, one of the government's key strategic priorities.[9])

There were, meanwhile, other changes on Montenegro's political landscape. The United Reformist Action (URA) emerged, presenting itself as a 'citizens' movement', bringing together a wide range of politicians, independent intellectuals and NGOs. They moved seamlessly into the space created by Darko Pajović's Positive Montenegro (*Pozitivna Crna Gora* – PCG) when the latter shifted from its roots to orientate towards strong support of the DPS-led government. URA, largely untainted, claimed to offer voters a 'new form of civic engagement'. The SDP, the long-time coalition partner of the DPS, however, faced significant challenges. In July 2015, two leading figures from the SDP, Vujica Lazović and Ivan Brajović, both of whom advocated continuing support for the DPS, left the party as a consequence of differences with the SDP leader, Ranko Krivoapić, who had become far more critical of the DPS.[10] Lazović and Ivan Brajović went on to form the Social Democrats (*Socijaldemokrate Crne Gore* – SDCG), thereby weakening the SDP and splitting their support.

'Sloboda traži ljudi': The October 2015 protests

Having reached out to DEMOS, DCG and URA (who opted not to join the protests), the DF began their round-the-clock anti-government protests (which, of course, the government deemed 'unlawful') on 27 September 2015 by erecting a 'tent city' outside the parliament building, which organizers described as the 'first free territory in Montenegro'.[11] It all appeared rather chaotic at the location itself, but behind the scenes DF activists were endeavouring to give the protests a distinct 'brand'. Under the banner *Sloboda traži ljudi* (Freedom Seeks People), they launched a dedicated website (slobodatraziljudi.me), a Facebook page and a Twitter account (FreedomCalling.me), their stated aim being to 'crowd-fund the revolution' (a rather innovative initiative and certainly novel in the Montenegrin context).[12] This and other – somewhat opaque – means of funding proved successful enough for the DF, if nothing else, to purchase a large number of tents in advance of their protests. The Montenegrin government, and media close to them, claimed the DF was, in fact, funded by a network of Serb nationalists with ties to Russia.[13] Djukanović simply dismissed the protests as 'anti-Montenegrin, anti-NATO and anti-democratic'.[14] Undeterred by the government's attempts to discredit them, however, the leadership of the DF declared that the protests were not anti-NATO, that they were seeking fair elections and would continue their protests until the government resigned and a 'technical government' was installed to oversee preparations for Montenegro's 'first free and fair elections'. More specific demands included the creation of an electronic electoral roll to prevent the manipulation of voter registration, the preparation and passing into law of legislation designed to mitigate the abuse of state resources for DPS supporters.[15] Finally, they demanded the enactment of new legislation that would ensure the editorial independence of public broadcasting media, particularly RTCG.

But such ambitious demands could only be met by mobilizing sufficient numbers, and there was little evidence to suggest that they would be able to do so. (Even the weekly magazine *Monitor* – broadly supportive of the protests – speculated whether the opposition would 'destroy the DPS or themselves'.[16]) The problem was both of numbers and of image. Despite the modern, social media–savvy image that the DF attempted to project, the organizers of the protests were well-known opposition figures (such as Andrija Mandić, Slaven Radunović, Nebojsa Medojević and Predrag Bulatović, among others) with a lengthy record in opposing the DPS. Given their profile, it seemed improbable that they could appeal to an electorate beyond those who were their natural supporters, and thus equally improbable that they could meet their stated objectives.[17] Indeed, the early stages of the DF protests, in late September 2015, appeared to bear this out. Though their campaign was energetic, the relatively small numbers involved indicated that they had failed to capture the imagination of the wider public and thus present little or no threat to the government. Indeed, the DF's audacious claims that the protests were the Montenegrin equivalent of the Maidan Square protests in Kiev, Ukraine, generating mass demonstrations that would lead to the downfall of the government were not simply sounding hollow but had become the source of ridicule. The DPS dismissed the protests as those led by the 'usual suspects', and the appearance of Metropolitan Amfilohije Radović at the protests on 4 October 2016, whereupon he spoke about the importance of the historical bonds between Montenegro and Russia and dangers of joining a NATO alliance that had bombed Montenegro in 1999.[18] By mid-October the small number of tents (approximately seventy of them) located outside the parliament building gave the distinct impression that momentum had stalled. Yet the DF's leaders and the more committed protestors persisted, and for far longer than the government had envisaged. Such persistence was to pay dividends, at least in the short term.

Just as it appeared the protests had run out of steam (at 6 am on the morning of 17 October 2015, after twenty days of protest) the government took the decision to clear the 'tent city', on the pretext that it was an inconvenience to citizens.[19] During the subsequent police operation, minor stand-offs between police and demonstrators took place, though tensions quickly rose. Riot police intervened in a manner that can be best described as 'heavy handed'. Some of those that were manhandled by the police were committed DF activists, but there were ordinary citizens who were subject to the same treatment, including a number of elderly people. After these initial arrests, the clashes intensified, and in the ensuing melee, a number of DF leaders were arrested. Andrija Mandić and Nebojsa Medojević claimed to have been beaten by the police, while Milan Knežević, the leader of the Democratic People's Party (*Demokratska narodna partija Crne Gore* – DNP), was hospitalized as a consequence of injuries sustained while being arrested.[20] But the harsh nature of the police operation (they would later use stun grenades and tear gas to disperse the protestors), while facilitating the breaking of the protest and the dispersal of the protestors, played straight into the hands of the DF. It proved to be a transformative moment.

The excessive force used by the police in dismantling the 'tent city' then, later, during the subsequent protests presented the DF with the opportunity not to cast themselves as victims of 'police brutality' and 'state oppression', but to reach out to the wider citizenry. This they did with some efficacy, using social media to convey the message that this violence against citizens was the current Montenegrin government's 'Žuta Greda', where police had used violence against protestors in October 1989 a misjudgement of the public mood that heralded the demise of the then leadership of the SKCG (see Chapter 2).[21] Evidently adept at using social media, DF activists captured (largely on mobile phones) numerous images of police restraining and beating demonstrators, which were then disseminated through Facebook and Twitter. This worked to good effect. The vast majority of major international press agencies, for example, simply conveyed the DF narrative without providing much by way of context.[22] The government, conversely, appeared to have no equally effective narrative to justify the actions of the police, and thus the images of the events of that evening changed the dynamics dramatically, exceeding even the expectations of the protest's organizers. The moral victory – and the propaganda gains generated through the effective use of social media – was theirs. Even the EU Delegation to Montenegro issued a statement that acknowledged that 'while demonstrators should respect the law and refrain from violence' the 'excessive use of force by the authorities' was 'unacceptable'.[23]

The events of Saturday 17 October 2015, by accident or design, provided the DF with an opportunity to mobilize larger numbers to their cause. And, indeed, on the following evening a significantly larger crowd descended on the Square of the Republic to demonstrate against the brutality of the police and, more generally, the government. The rule of the DPS was, argued Andrija Mandić, 'nearing its end', a message warmly received by the crowd. The Montenegrin government were on the defensive; not close to collapse by any means, but seemingly rattled by the course of events. Understanding that the dynamics had shifted, and seeking to capitalize, the DF announced that they were giving the government 'six days to resign' or large demonstrations in Podgorica would go ahead the following weekend.[24] They called on citizens of Montenegro and opposition parties to join them and the momentum appeared to be increasing. Opposition parties who had not yet joined the protests stated that they might do so, while the former LSCG leader, Slavko Perović, also called on Montenegro's young to rise up and overthrow the DPS-led government (though he stopped short of endorsing the DF's protests).[25]

By early evening on Saturday (24 October 2015), it was evident that the numbers gathering in the centre of Podgorica far outstripped those of previous demonstrations. Something in the region of 5,000 people, not by any means all DF supporters but outraged nevertheless by the events of the previous weekend, began a vocal demonstration against the DPS-led government. Sensing that it was time to seize the opportunity, the DF's leaders – perhaps themselves surprised at the scale of the gathering and realizing that they may never mobilize such numbers again – sought to harness the anger and energy of the crowd by giving short but emotive speeches before appealing to the crowd to join them in marching on the Montenegrin Assembly. But though there *were* many thousand protestors present who shared feelings of discontent and a sense of injustice, what became equally evident was that a far smaller number would be willing to join the DF in their attempts to overthrow the government 'from the streets'.[26] Thus, as the rally on the square concluded, a smaller (though still significant) number of protestors walked towards the parliament, encouraged to do so by the DF's leaders. Whether they planned in advance what subsequently took place or whether they merely lost control of the crowd remains a matter of conjecture, but, in any event, the situation quickly deteriorated. As the group assembled and the DF leaders addressed next to the statue of King Nikola I (directly across from the Montenegrin Assembly), the crowd became increasingly agitated and the atmosphere, defiant though largely jovial just an hour before, turned darker. The DF leaders insisted that the speaker of the Montenegrin Assembly, Ranko Krivokapić, come to address the demonstrators and that he had ten minutes to do so. When he failed to appear, a small number of demonstrators began to throw rocks and firecrackers at the police that had encircled the assembly before surging towards the police lines. Then, having received the order from Raško Konjević, the minister of internal affairs, the Special Anti-Terrorist Unit (*Specijalni antiteroristička jedinica* – SAJ) responded with tear gas and baton charges. The centre of Podgorica descended into chaos akin to that resembling the evening of 12 January 1998, when supporters of Momir Bulatović had attempted to storm the nearby government building.

In the immediate aftermath, the government sought to retake both the initiative and the moral high ground. Having been caught off-guard by the social media activism of the DF the previous weekend, the government ensured that they prevailed in this particular information war. Viewers of RTCG1, for example, were repeatedly shown the same footage of the protestors' attempts to enter the parliament building, the overarching message being that state institutions were under attack.[27] The Montenegrin government also sought to argue that the evening's events were an attack on the state. Seeking to discredit the DF, Milo Djukanović described the protestors' actions as an attempted 'coup d'état', while stating that the DF were 'Serbian and Russian proxies seeking to reverse Montenegro's path to NATO membership and undermine the country's young statehood' (the protests, he added, 'represent an attack on Montenegro's independence').[28] Reiterating Djukanović's accusations, the pro-government daily *Pobjeda* claimed on 26 October 2015 that 'Serbian and Russian extremists' were providing logistical support to the DF[29] and that the Serbian nationalist groups *Nacionalni stroj* (National Alignment) and *Obraz* (Honor) had organized and participated in the violence.[30]

The events of 24 October 2015 proved pivotal. The gathering on the Square of the Republic demonstrated that there existed significant discontent underpinned by legitimate grievances about economic, political and social issues and with something of a civic-orientation. But in seeking to harness that anger the DF miscalculated and were, ultimately, outmanoeuvred. By issuing unrealistic ultimatums and attempting to storm the parliament building they, within one hour, transformed themselves from perceived victims into perceived aggressors, and the voices and reasoned arguments of the more civic-oriented within the DF were immediately obscured by those with a more radical orientation. If the DF was indeed capable of channelling widespread dissatisfaction and transforming the protests into a broader citizens' movement, their chance had, most likely, gone with the wind. In the wake of the violence, the DF sought to limit the damage, arguing that those responsible for the violence had been 'placed' by Montenegro's National Security Agency (*Agencija za Nacionalnu Bezbjednost* – ANB) to discredit the DF and undermine the legitimacy of the protests.

Pressure on the leaders of those opposition parties who had not supported the October demonstrations – Miodrag Lekić of DEMOS, Aleksa Bečić of Democratic Montenegro (DCG) and Žarko Rakčević of URA – had increased significantly after 17 October 2015, but the events of one week later took much of that pressure off, allowing them to capitalize from the DF protests. Seeing clearly that there was significant dissatisfaction with the DPS-led government, they set about presenting themselves as the genuine opposition, though one that would achieve the downfall of the government through democratic means and through parliamentary mechanisms. They also called on the EU to mediate between the government and opposition parties, though the EU Delegation in Montenegro made it clear that they would prefer 'internal matters' to be solved 'through dialogue not mediation' and within state institutions. The three opposition leaders appeared together on the political programme *Načisto* days after the protests to stress that they, too, supported the formation of a transitional government prior to elections and that should the government fail to respond appropriately to the demands of the opposition, they may boycott parliament, reach out to civil society, NGOs and student organizations and boycott the 2016 elections.[31] But their reluctance to boycott parliament and openly support the protests angered the DF, making the possibility of forging a broad opposition with an agreed strategy increasingly remote.

The DF continued with their protests nevertheless, and after the events of 24 October 2015 they went to great lengths to stress that any subsequent protest should be non-violent. A number of rallies through the country were followed, on the evening of 6 November 2015, by another 'manifestation' in Podgorica. A small number of DF activists held a rally outside the offices of RTCG – which the DF called the *fabrika laži* (factory of lies) – denouncing the station for peddling pro-government propaganda.[32] They also announced that they would hold another large demonstration in Podgorica on Sunday 15 November 2016. This time their strategy was to 'lay siege' to state institutions by surrounding them with a human chain; the headline for these latest demonstrations being *Opkoljeni ste!* (You're surrounded!). Protestors, again fewer in numbers, formed a human chain around government buildings. But, for all their efforts, the momentum waned. The DF's leaders also came under pressure, and with their parliamentary immunity withdrawn, both Andrija Mandić and Slaven Radunović faced being put on trial for their role in the events of 24 October 2016.[33]

Montenegro, Russia and NATO

Relations between Podgorica and Moscow had been relatively positive until it became evident that Montenegro would indeed join NATO (and that it would do so without recourse to a referendum); the once-cosy relations began to cool.[34] Following Montenegro's independence, Russian investment had been significant, particularly in the tourism and real estate sectors. In November 2008, Montenegro and Russia signed a visa-free regime for their citizens, facilitating easier travel and trade between the two countries and the Montenegrin coast (particularly the area around Budva) became a very popular destination for Russian tourists. Relations, however, gradually soured, driven both by Montenegro's seemingly inexorable trajectory towards NATO membership and the government's support of EU sanctions against Russia in July 2014. This not only generated sharp criticism from the Russian ambassador in Montenegro, Andrei Nesterenko, but from his counterpart in Serbia, Alexander Cepurin, who commented that the Montenegrin government's attempts to join NATO were akin to 'monkeys chasing a banana'.³⁵ Thereafter, a number of anti-Russian billboards appeared in Podgorica emblazoned with messages such as 'Better a banana in the hand than a Russian boot in the neck' and (drawing on a quote from the Montenegrin communist, writer and dissident, Milovan Djilas) 'Russians have never been friends to Montenegrins; we have always been bargaining chips to them'.³⁶ Then, on 27 March 2015, a football match held at the *Gradski stadion* in Podgorica (the home of FK Budućnost) between Montenegro and Russia was abandoned after missiles were thrown by home fans at Russian players, injuring their goalkeeper, Igor Akinfeev.³⁷

Thereafter, Montenegrin government claims that Russia had been behind the October 2015 protests fuelled a further deterioration of bilateral relations.³⁸ Indeed, following these accusations, the Russian Ministry of Foreign Affairs (MFA) announced that they were 'perplexed' by the accusations but they expressed concern about the alleged excessive use of force by the police. The Montenegrin government responded by saying that the statement from Moscow neglected to mention that the protestors had been throwing Molotov cocktails at the police and that this 'only confirms Prime Minister Milo Djukanović's claims about Russia's involvement in anti-NATO protests in Montenegro'.³⁹ Yet while little concrete evidence has been provided to prove that Russia has anything other than rhetorically supporting the DF (and anti-NATO) protests, the Montenegrin government has not deviated from the narrative linking the two. Djukanović argued that Russia continued to interfere in the political life of Montenegro, though stating that Montenegro's damaged relations with Moscow was primarily a 'collateral effect' caused by current geopolitics and a reflection more of Russia's own deteriorating relationship with NATO. He added, however, that 'Russia has great bilateral relations with many countries that are NATO members today… I really don't think Montenegrin membership in NATO means an automatic worsening of relations with Russia'.⁴⁰

Montenegro's formal invitation to join the NATO alliance, received on 2 December 2015, to become NATO's twenty-ninth member, saw a shift in the DF's strategy – with more focus being placed on a 'No to NATO' campaign (though they continued to focus on their efforts to create the conditions for a transitional government). While not strictly organized by the DF (this gathering was organized by NOVA), an anti-NATO protest went ahead in Podgorica on 12 December 2015. The focus was entirely on the issue of Montenegro's accession to the military alliance. Speakers expressed outrage that Montenegrin troops may be deployed in neighbouring Kosovo as part of NATO-KFOR (Kosovo Protection Force) and were joined on stage by a 'special guest', the former Montenegrin president and SRJ prime minister Momir Bulatović, who opined that the government were forcing the country into NATO 'to avoid being held responsible for their criminal activities'.⁴¹ Subsequent speakers warned of the possibility of an armed uprising against the government if the decision to join NATO was taken without a referendum on the issue.⁴² The mood was defiant but the rally was peaceful, though the pro-government daily *Pobjeda* was quick to allege that chants of 'Putin!, Putin!' and 'Russia!, Russia!' could be heard emanating from the crowd.⁴³ Other opposition parties were more measured in their approach towards Montenegro's membership of NATO. URA's Dritan Abazović argued that membership of the alliance, paradoxically, would damage the DPS in the longer term, as becoming a member of the alliance would hasten the process of democratization. Miodrag Lekić of DEMOS said he would support NATO membership, but only if there was a referendum on the issue.[44] Vesko Garčević (Montenegro's Coordinator for NATO) stated that he expected the invitation from NATO to increase public support for membership, despite the tensions generated by it.[45] A few days after the protests, however, Dmitry Rogozin, the Russian deputy prime minister (and close ally of Vladimir Putin), stated that he would 'regret' Montenegro joining NATO and that it was equally regrettable that Montenegrins would be given the right to decide in a referendum. He added that he believed Montenegrins would, nevertheless, 'have their say about this'.[46]

Political crisis and the 'interim' government

In the midst of ongoing DF and anti-NATO protests and demands from other opposition parties to create a 'transitional government', the DPS-led administration, while hardly on the verge of collapse, came under significant pressure from within their own governing coalition. The DPS's junior coalition partner, the SDP, had become increasingly critical of the government's efforts to reform the judiciary and over the freedom of the media. The growing distance between the long-time coalition partners had been evident for some time, but the fallout from the October 2015 protests further exposed the growing rift. The SDP's leader, Ranko Krivokapić, had adopted a somewhat softer line towards the protests, in stark contrast to the DPS line, signalling that relations between the DPS and SDP were strained to the point of being irreparable. Under growing pressure from within and without, Djukanović (on 27 December 2015) called for a vote of confidence in the government to be held 'in the shortest possible period'.[47] The DF dismissed the exercise as a stunt, but it stymied any possibility of the opposition still in the parliament from joining the DFs boycott, at least until after the vote of no-confidence. In the interim, the DF continued their protests, the largest of which took place in the centre of Podgorica on 13 January 2016. Those assembled could, while enjoying the festivities, also sign a petition against Montenegro's NATO membership. Perhaps the most surprising development of the evening was, however, the appearance of NOVA's 'party police', dressed in quasi-police outfits and there to provide security at the event, which the pro-government daily *Dnevne novine* were drawn from the ranks of the former 'Seventh Battalion' of the VJ (see Chapter 7).[48]

In January 2016, the 'working group for parliamentary dialogue', involving those opposition parties which had not boycotted the parliament and the government began in earnest, while speculation on the outcome of the vote of confidence motion intensified. The SDP made no clear commitment that they would support the DPS, only that they would be unified in any decision.[49] The Montenegrin president, Filip Vujanović (DPS), made it clear that the motion would make it 'clear whether the SDP were in the ruling coalition or the government'.[50] The debates prior to the vote began on 23 and concluded on 25 January 2016, and during these protracted sessions the DF continued their protests outside the assembly building, stating that if the DPS-led government were to fall they would suspend their protests, declare victory and call on all opposition parties to meet to discuss the formation of an interim government. In a symbolic act, each of the DF protestors raised red cards to Milo Djukanović.[51] Inside the assembly, MPs traded barbs over a number of issues: who had (and who had not) supported Montenegro's independence; who had close relations with Slobodan Milošević in the 1990s; who bore responsibility for the sale of the country's coastline to Russians and for the numerous privatizations that had turned sour. The tension between the DPS and SDP was particularly evident. On the opening day of negotiations, the SDP stated that they would not support the government. Ranko Krivokapić also stated that he would not resign from his post as speaker of the assembly if the government survived the vote. In response, Djukanović stated that he would, in such an event, initiate the procedure to impeach Krivokapić.[52]

As the relationship between the DPS and SDP was dissolving, the relationship between the DPS and PCG (which had supported a number of government initiatives in previous months and whose support proved pivotal) was cementing. In exchange for their support the DPS agreed to give five seats in the cabinet to the opposition (interior minister, finance minister, agricultural minister, minister of labour and one of the deputy prime minister posts), more than PCG had originally requested and more than the opposition had expected (perhaps catching them off guard). Nevertheless, URA, DCG and DEMOS rejected the offer, and with the outcome becoming evident URA's Dritan Abazović stated that the DPS and PCG were engaged 'in an act of political corruption and villainy', making it possible for the government to survive.[53] Indeed, with PCG's support, the government survived the vote of no-confidence by a narrow margin. Forty-two of 81 MPs voted against the motion. From outside the assembly, the leaders of the DF demonstrated their dissatisfaction; Andrija Mandić claiming that 'political robbery' had taken place.[54] The opposition parties which had voted against the government now retired to consider their options.

Although the DPS-led government won their vote of confidence, the crisis had not passed. An irreparable split has taken place between the DPS and SDP and URA, and DCG and DEMOS had rejected the DPS offer of five posts in the cabinet. Nevertheless, all agreed to enter into dialogue to find a mutually acceptable solution. The alterative was unviable. Boycotting parliament or joining the DF protests would have required a level of compromise between opposition parties that had proved elusive in the past. The DF, having sustained their protests since September 2015, considered themselves as the rightful leaders of any subsequent protests. In any event, Miodrag Lekić (DEMOS) implied that his party had little intention of joining the DF protests and stated Djukanović should be prepared for the 'continuation of parliamentary dialogue' including further discussions on monitoring and controlling of the election process and the creation of an interim government.[55] Talks began on 2 February 2016, though nothing definitive was agreed. The gap between the DPS and the opposition appeared, however, to be closing, and in the subsequent days the leaders of URA and DEMOS met to forge a united front in their negotiations with the government. They sought, they said, not simply cabinet posts, as had been offered by Djukanović, but oversight of the work of State Election Commission, the Montenegrin Intelligence Agency (ANB) and the public broadcaster, RTCG, which would allow them to 'build u a democratic infrastructure to control abuses'.[56]

At the same time, in a rather surprising development, the DF's Andrija Mandić, Milan Knežević and the former SNP leader Predrag Bulatović were in Moscow meeting with a high-level Russian delegation, including the president of the Duma, Sergey Narishkin. There they conveyed the DF's desire to maintain good relations with Moscow and pledged that if they attained power they would reverse the Montenegrin government's decision to support EU sanctions on Russia.[57] They also discussed Montenegro's invitation to NATO, expressing the hope that their proposal of a 'the Swiss model' (whereby Montenegro would not join the NATO alliance but instead declare neutrality) would gain traction. The meeting, while undoubtedly welcomed by many within the grass roots of the DF, served to bolster Djukanović's claim that the DF were Moscow's proxies.

By April 2016, a 'power-sharing' agreement was reached between the opposition and the government, one that would give five ministries to the opposition and thus foster greater confidence in election processes. During the process of appointing these ministers to the interim government, there were some lively exchanges in the Montenegrin Assembly. On 13 May 2016, DF parliamentarians, who had been boycotting the assembly since September 2015, took their seats (albeit fleetingly) before rising to their feet as Djukanović was addressing the assembly to propose new ministers, shouting *Milo, lopove!* (Milo is a thief!) The prime minister responded by calling them *idioti* (idiots) before a minor scuffle broke out between DF and DPS parliamentarians. Following the incident, Djukanović refused to attend the subsequent parliamentary meeting, though first of the new ministers was appointed soon thereafter.[58] But just a few days later, despite the protests of the DF and their calls to hold a referendum to decide upon NATO membership, Montenegro signed the 'accession protocol' with the alliance, the final stage in advance of full membership.

As the interim government prepared for Montenegro's 'free and fair elections', scheduled to take place in October 2016, the country celebrated the ten-year anniversary of the restoration of its independence. A distraction from the ongoing political crisis, it was a more muted affair than might have been expected. The Montenegrin flag was everywhere, and the advertising billboards emblazoned with *Da je vječna Crna Gora* (Eternal be our Montenegro) – the final line of the Montenegrin anthem *Oj, svijetla majska zoro* (Oh, Bright Dawn of May) – were equally omnipresent. The celebrations in Podgorica were, however, highly stage-managed and strictly by invitation. As a consequence, it was all formality: sharp suits, expensive Italian dresses, bodyguards and chauffeur-driven black Audis, delegations from the EU, numerous ambassadors from EU and non-EU countries, Montenegro's most esteemed artists and entertainers, as well as the cream of Montenegro's political elite on hand to lend the event the gravitas it deserved. What was missing, however, was ordinary Montenegrins, who were rather conspicuous by their absence. The need for a heightened level of security was, seemingly, underpinned by fears that the opposition (or, more precisely, the DF) would attempt to disrupt the events. On that evening, however, the opposition stayed away.

While the events in Podgorica were mundane, there was a bigger and far less formal manifestation in Montenegro's historical capital Cetinje, where the Montenegrin singer Željko Šamardžić and the renowned Sarajevo-based Bosnian singer, Dino

Merlin, topped the bill in a concert to celebrate the anniversary. Here the atmosphere was different, with a youthful audience enjoying what was a high-spirited and well-organized public event. But one wondered whether the large crowds gathered in Cetinje were motivated by the occasion to celebrate ten years of Montenegro's independence or merely to enjoy the music. Indeed, one only had to read the Montenegrin press throughout the celebrations to see the differing perceptions of the first decade of independence. To commemorate events, *Pobjeda* published a glossy special magazine entitled *Mi, sami* (We, Alone)[59] that celebrated the achievements of the Montenegrin government, while *Monitor*, for example, ran with a lead piece asking, 'Where is independence?'[60]

The October 2016 parliamentary elections and the 'State Coup'

The tone and content of the pre-election campaigns was as expected. The DPS claimed that a vote for them would be a *sigurnim korakom* (safe step): a vote for stability, economic growth, increased investment in the country's infrastructure and an affirmation of Montenegro's independence and future integration into NATO and the EU. But even the upper echelons of the party, experienced in election campaigns, seemed acutely aware of the potential for an uncertain outcome. In mitigation, they launched an energetic campaign, during which Djukanović warned that the stakes were high and that the DPS were faced with an opposition that was unpatriotic, irresponsible, treacherous and willing to 'jeopardise public peace and order, violating laws and undermining state institutions' to gain power, though he stated that he saw no justification for anyone in Montenegro giving their vote to those who were trying to 'stop Montenegro dead in its tracks'.[61] In this regard, the DPS leadership singled out the DF as those most likely to cause trouble during elections and, equally, those most likely to be a disaster in government. Indeed, Djukanović pulled no punches in his assessment of the DF. They were, he alleged, a dangerous and untrustworthy group who were not only attempting to undermine Montenegro's sovereignty, but were accepting money from Russia to finance their 'anti-Montenegrin' and 'anti-NATO' campaign.

Aware of growing discontent, opposition parties attempted to capitalize by emphasizing the need for a change of government after twenty-seven years of DPS rule, growing unemployment and high-level corruption. They also claimed throughout their campaign that the DPS had used state resources to provide various 'incentives' such as the writing-off of utility bills and purchasing identity cards to buy votes. The DF's campaign was well organized and relatively glossy; it gained momentum as the election approached.[62] Their rhetoric was, at times, lively. In a DF rally in Bar, Slaven Radunović described Milo Djukanović as 'a cancer eating Montenegro', while Milan Knežević trumpeted that the DF was entering the final stages of the 'encirclement of the DPS and Milo'.[63] The *Ključ* (Key) coalition – comprising the Democratic Alliance (DEMOS), the Socialist People's Party (SNP) and United Reform Action (URA) – claimed, for example, that the DPS had plundered Montenegro's wealth and had been an abject failure in government. During a pre-election rally in Podgorica, Miodrag

Lekić, the de facto leader of Key, said the coalition wanted to 'put Montenegro back on the right path'. Aleksa Bečić's Democratic Montenegro (DCG) ran independently but also ran an energetic campaign during which his party expressed their willingness to work for a grand alliance of anti-DPS opposition parties after the election. On the face of it, the opposition appeared in a strong position to challenge the DPS, certainly since the 2006 referendum. If united, they *could* be stronger than the ruling party, but the opposition again failed to do so when it mattered. The DF, Key and the DCG implied that a post-election coalition was possible and that a 'good basis for a ruling coalition involving opposition parties' existed (though previous attempts had demonstrated that this was an optimistic assessment).[64]

Allegations of irregularities in the electoral process were commonplace. The DPS were accused by anti-government media of mobilizing the diaspora and paying €250 for one vote.[65] Goran Danilović of the SNP (and the minister of interior) refused to endorse the electoral roll, believing it to be inaccurate (the DPS-led government arranged for it to be signed in his stead), and, in addition, the non-governmental organization MANS claimed that the elections would be, as elections have in the past, characterized by irregularities. They also claimed that the DPS's election campaign had drawn significantly from state funds, and that €18.5 million had been spent on 'employment, subsidies, loans and debt write-offs'.[66] As a result of this, they argued, the DPS had a significant advantage.

As the election drew closer, the exchange of accusations intensified. The DPS alleged that the DF may, in the event of a DPS victory in the election, attempt to destabilize Montenegro. Djukanović warned that the government would respond firmly to 'any attempts at jeopardising public peace and order, violating law and undermining state institutions'.[67] Thereafter, the director of the Montenegrin Police, Slavko Stojanović (who the opposition claim explicitly aligned with the DPS), announced prior to the election that not only were the police prepared for riots during election day and after, but that his organization possessed 'operational information' that suggested that certain (opposition) elements may attempt to instigate unrest and that the police were 'prepared for such incidents'.[68] In a surprising twist, Montenegrin police began to reveal details of what they argued was an attempted 'state coup'. Just two days before the election, a former policeman, Mirko Velimirović, entered a police station in Podgorica and revealed of a plot to disrupt the elections and to install a 'pro-Russian' government. On the basis of the information provided by Velimirović, Montenegrin police (on 15 October 2016) arrested Bratislav Dikić, a former member of the Serbian Gendarmerie, who, they alleged, was part of an armed criminal organization that aimed to subvert the election process and to attack citizens and police officers near government buildings in Podgorica. It was further alleged that a key to a warehouse where weapons were stored was found in his car.[69] Dikić immediately denied involvement claiming that he had been 'framed' during a short visit to Montenegro, where he had come to visit Ostrog monastery near Nikšić on account of his ill-health.[70] Nineteen others (all Serbian citizens) were also arrested in what the government claimed was an attempt to stage a coup d'état during which Djukanović would be the target of an assassination attempt. The DF immediately dismissed his arrest as a stunt to discredit the opposition and intimidate voters.

On polling day, turnout was relatively high (compared to elections in 2009 and 2012), and by 8 pm, when polling stations closed, 73.2 per cent of those eligible to vote had done so. The day was tense and not without incident, with party activists involved in scuffles outside polling stations, the most serious of them in the northern town of Rožaje. To add to the sense of crisis, Montenegro's Agency for Electronic Communications (*Agencija za elektronske komunikacije* – AEK) ordered all of the country's three mobile operators to bar the use of the Viber and WhatsApp messaging services (used quite effectively by opposition parties, particularly the DF), on the pretext that a significant volume of 'spam' was being sent via mobile networks. The AEK's justification was rubbished by the opposition, who argued that they had been blocked to stop citizens reporting electoral irregularities. As early results came in, it was evident that while the DPS vote did not collapse, they had only achieved a relative majority, failing to garner enough votes to secure a parliamentary majority (41.4 per cent of the vote and 36 seats in parliament). The opposition, particularly DF, performed well with 20.3 per cent of the vote and eighteen seats, opening the possibility of a governing coalition should the DPS fail to secure enough support from potential coalition partners. The key coalition secured only 11 per cent of the vote and nine seats; the DCG gained eight seats, while SDCG won two seats. Predictably, the Montenegrin media had very different views on the outcome. *Pobjeda* called the result, 'a great victory of the pro-Western option'; the headline on the front page of *Vijesti* stated that with only thirty-six seats won by the DPS 'the opposition could have 40 or 41 [depending on the decision of minority parties]'; *Dan* stated that the DPS has 'less seats' than in previous elections and would thus have to make more significant concessions to build a governing coalition.[71]

Nevertheless, as the party with the largest share of the vote, it was incumbent on the DPS to attempt to form a governing coalition, one that would possess at least forty-one of the eighty-one seats in the Montenegrin Assembly. However, Milo Djukanović, addressing supporters in Podgorica in the early morning, seemed confident that the DPS would be successful in creating a coalition. The new government, which included many new faces, was eventually formed on 28 November 2016. The horse-trading thus began, but it was not the formation of the government that became the Montenegrin government's primary problem. There were claims and counter-claims over the existence of the so-called 'state coup', with the Montenegrin government providing what they claimed was evidence of an organized coup attempt. On 17 October 2016, the Montenegrin state prosecutor, Ivica Stanković, announced that the government had 'reasonable suspicion' that an 'organised criminal group' comprising twenty Serbian citizens and led by Bratislav Dikić had plotted to launch a coup d'état on the night of the election.[72] Thereafter, the government released what they claimed were transcripts of a conversation between Dikić and one Aleksander Sindjelić – a Serbian citizen who allegedly fought for the *Novorossiya* (New Russia) forces in Eastern Ukraine – who was accused of being one of Dikić's co-conspirators.[73] Montenegro's minister of interior, Goran Danilović, was quick to suggest that the transcripts were a fabrication and a deliberate hoax to divert the investigation.[74] Three days later, Montenegro's special prosecutor for organized crime, Milivoje Katnić, appeared on the television programme *Načisto* to tell the host, Petar Komnenić, that the government had evidence that 'terrorists' had, on the evening of 16 October 2016, planned to embed themselves within a group of protestors assembled outside parliament before entering the building dressed as police officers to take over the Montenegrin Assembly by force of arms and announce that the 'party of their choice' had won the election. Only quick action on behalf of Montenegro's security services, he said, had prevented Montenegro 'from being shrouded in black'. Asked by Komnenić how the government had acquired advance information about these plans, Katnić replied 'with the help of God'.[75] The reaction to Katnić's interview was, predictably, mixed: the DF, for example, argued that there were many unanswered questions and that Katnić's appearance on the show was 'scandalous'.[76] However, on 24 October 2016, the Serbian prime minister, Aleksander Vučić, announced that arrests had been made in Serbia connected to the coup attempt, a development that appeared to lend credence to the government's claims, though he added that those arrested in Serbia (including three Russian citizens) appeared to be unconnected to those arrested in Montenegro.[77]

The growing controversy was interrupted briefly with the news that Milo Djukanović would step down as prime minister. During the election campaign, there was no evidence that Djukanović had tired of front-line politics, but having already heavily implied that he considered Duško Marković to be the man to form a new government, Djukanović formally announced on 28 October 2016 that he would be retiring (amid denials that that he was under pressure from the United States to do so) and that Duško Marković, the former head of Montenegro's state security, had been nominated by the main board of the DPS to succeed him.[78] Dubbed by the opposition as the *crna kutija* (black box) of Montenegrin politics (or even as 'Putin from Mojkovac'), Marković's past, as the head of state security, meant that he was both respected and feared. No one, perhaps, has his finger so firmly on the pulse of social and political developments in Montenegro, and while he is not a slick as Djukanović, he is, undoubtedly a shrewd and highly capable operator and one that can enforce discipline within the DPS. Montenegro's fragmented opposition were united in their assessment of Marković as a quintessential 'DPS man' who has sought to preserve party interests over the national interest, while never undermining 'his own people'. They also claimed, however, that he was not the right person to fight corruption, organized crime or create conditions that would allow for much-needed political reconciliation, though some opposition figures acknowledged that a government led by Marković was preferable to one led by Djukanović.

So Djukanović's departure did not herald fundamental political change, merely a change of stewardship. This was, after all, his third departure from the role of prime minister in a decade, having stepped down from the role twice before. On both occasions, he not only chose who would succeed him, but remained a powerful and influential figure within the party, albeit operating from behind the scenes. So at only fifty-four, he remains the chairman of the DPS, giving him oversight of party developments and considerable influence over party matters, and has stated that he will be 'helping' Marković to govern Montenegro when his experience is called upon. Much like his departure from formal political roles in the past, therefore, it is unlikely that Djukanović will retreat into quiet retirement. Moreover, if recent history is anything to go by, one cannot exclude Djukanović's return to a senior political role in future, perhaps even as the successor to Filip Vujanović, when the current Montenegrin president's mandate expires in 2017.

While Marković proceeded with the creation of a DPS-led governing coalition, the 'state coup' controversy took numerous twists and turns. On the day he announced that he intended to step down, Djukanović stated that the DF was 'most probably' connected to the alleged Serbian terrorists, and while there was no concrete evidence of a link, it did 'not mean that an investigation wouldn't prove such involvement'.[79] On 27 October 2016, Aleksander Vučić revealed that Serbian Security Information Agency (*Bezbednosno-informativna agencija* – BIA) had proof that 'certain groups' were closely monitoring Djukanović's movments, while also revealing that €125,000 and a number of stolen Montenegrin police uniforms had been seized (these were, it was alleged, to be worn by the three core members of the terrorist group during the attack).[80] Two Russian citizens (named as Eduard Vladimirovich Shirokov and Vladimir Nikolaevich Popov) who were alleged to have been members of Russian Military Intelligence and had been held in Serbia were permitted to return to Moscow after a visit to Belgrade by Nikolai Patrushev, a senior Russian security official.[81] However, on 1 November 2016, Aleksander Sindjelic turned himself over to Montenegrin authorities, having been visited by them in Belgrade during the previous week.[82] While in custody, he negotiated a plea bargain that would mean a more lenient prison sentence, if he agreed to provide prosecutors with specific details about the planning of the attack. Apparently on the basis of this information, the Montenegrin prosecutor, Milivoje Katnić, declared thereafter that a plan resembling a 'Ukrainian scenario', whereby the attacks on the Montenegrin Assembly and the arrest of Milo Djukanović would be used to cause panic, unrest and a destabilization of Montenegro – all with the aim of halting the country's accession to NATO.[83] The DF's response to this was simply that the state prosecutors were siding with the DPS, which had, according to Andrija Mandić, 'fabricated the entire case'.[84]

In the meantime, on 7 November 2016, the new Montenegrin government was formally constituted at a ceremony in Cetinje, after tough negotiations between the DPS and BS. Neither the DF nor the Key members of the assembly were in attendance and the DCG and SDP members were similarly conspicuous by their absence. All stated that they did not recognize the result of the election and that they would not return to parliament until the 'state coup' was investigated by an independent commission.[85] Further developments in the investigation of the state coup hardened their resolve to continue with their boycott. On 24 November 2016, Aleksander Sindjelić, hitherto the main suspect in the 'state coup' case, was released from Spuž prison near Podgorica, having been given the status of a 'protected witness' by the Montenegrin High Court. He was permitted to return to Belgrade on the basis that he would continue to assist prosecutors. Thereafter, Montenegrin prosecutors applied pressure on the leaders of the DF, questioning Andrija Mandić and stating their intention to interview other from within the coalition's leadership. Mandić remained defiant after his interview, stating that the DF 'would not allow the case of the alleged coup to be covered up', while simultaneously declaring that he had absolutely no trust in Milivoje Katnić in being capable of investigating it properly.[86] Nevertheless, the implication that DF had been involved in the alleged coup continued.[87]

The ongoing political crisis showed little sign of abating by the end of 2016. The DF were emboldened by the election of Donald Trump, and though the US president is unlikely to take much interest in the Western Balkans, he may also be less inclined to put pressure on Russia if the latter continues to attempt to seek to influence political events in the region. The 2016 European Commission (EC) Progress Report, published on 9 November 2016, noted that the Montenegrin political scene remained 'fragmented', while acknowledging that Montenegro had made 'moderate' progress in key areas.[88] Nevertheless, Montenegro's EU accession continues, albeit at a slow pace and determined not only by internal factors but by the EU's ongoing troubles elsewhere. NATO membership is secured (despite Donald Trump's pre-election insinuation that he regarded NATO as outdated and obsolete - a position that has since softened) and Montenegro became a formal member of the alliance in June 2017. Eleven years after the independence referendum, the Montenegrin government will have achieved one of their key strategic objectives, despite the fact that it is an objective that has never enjoyed overwhelming public support.

Conclusion

More than a decade has now passed since the re-establishment of Montenegro's independence in 2006. The country has been on a subsequent trajectory that, while uneven, has been largely positive. In the immediate period following the independence referendum the country experienced something of a post-referendum economic boom and appeared to be stabilizing politically (given that the 'statehood question' had been largely resolved). That extended honeymoon has long since passed and Montenegro is, at the time of writing, going through its most acute political crisis since the 2006 referendum. The political landscape is deeply fragmented, with the opposition, full of resentment for the ruling DPS, maintaining a boycott of parliament. Exchanges of accusations over the alleged 'state coup' in October 2016 have further poisoned the political landscape and fuelled a combative and, at times, dangerous internal political struggle. This internal political crisis is being played out in a wider international context where the EU is in crisis and geopolitical dynamics are shifting and in a regional context in which democracy is increasingly under threat across the Balkans.

However, to understand and assess Montenegro's progress as an independent state and to better understand its current political situation, one has to first frame these events within a wider historical context. As we have seen, Montenegro has experienced trauma and political and social flux throughout the twentieth century that far outstrips anything the country is experiencing today. Montenegro's experience is such that a Montenegrin who was born in, say, Cetinje in 1912 and who lived there throughout their life would have been born a citizen of Montenegro but thereafter a citizen of the Kingdom of Serbs, Croats and Slovenes (later the Kingdom of Yugoslavia), the Socialist Federal Republic of Yugoslavia, the Federal Republic of Yugoslavia, the joint state of Serbia and Montenegro, before becoming the citizen of an independent Montenegro again at the ripe age of ninety-four. They would also have lived through years of war and occupation. This hypothetical example alone is, therefore, illustrative of the flux that Montenegro's has experienced in its modern history. The internal political crisis of the early twentieth century, the First World War, the flight into exile of the Petrović dynasty, the Austro-Hungarian occupation, the loss of statehood following the Podgorica Assembly in 1918 and the *Zelenaši-Bjelaši* conflict that followed – all this took place within just over a decade. Thereafter, economic marginalization and internal political conflicts were then followed by occupation and a bitter civil war between 1941 and 1945, during which Partisan, Chetnik and *Zelenaši* fought each other and the occupying forces; conflicts that wrought destruction on many Montenegrin towns and villages and during which thousands of both combatants and civilians were killed. And only three years after the end of the war, Montenegro was again the centre of a bitter political conflict, fuelled by the 1948 Tito–Stalin split; before, as a republic within the SFRJ, Montenegro enjoyed decades-long period of stability and economic and infrastructural development that ended only with the economic crisis of the 1980s.

By the time of Slobodan Milošević's rise to power in Serbia in 1987, the economic crisis that crippled the SFRJ, during which the economic well-being of many Montenegrins was significantly affected, brought significant social and political consequences that would determine the subsequent trajectory of Montenegrin politics and that of the wider Yugoslav federation. The pre-existing economic crisis (and resulting social dislocation caused by it) dovetailed with the issue of the rights of Serbs and Montenegrins in Kosovo, creating a toxic political environment in Montenegro. This charged social and political atmosphere was exploited by Slobodan Milošević and his allies in Montenegro and channelled through the so-called 'anti-bureaucratic revolution'. Presented as a democratic 'happening of the people' in which the people's demands must be met, it was, in fact, little more than a coup *within* the SKCG using the 'will of the people' as a populist mobilizing slogan. As a consequence of the anti-bureaucratic revolution, the ageing leadership of the SKCG was replaced by a young leadership which not only had few solutions to the overarching social and economic problems facing Montenegro, but owed their political careers, or at least their sharp career trajectories, to Milošević. As a consequence, they would remain, on the whole, loyal and pliable through the war in Croatia (during which they would lead Montenegrins into a war in Croatia and the regrettable and politically damaging attack on Dubrovnik and its environs in late 1991) and in Bosnia & Herzegovina. The very same political elite essentially oversaw Montenegro's entry into the SRJ through a highly controlled and legally questionable referendum process.

Though Montenegro largely escaped the violence that accompanied the disintegration of the SFRJ, the impact of the wars in neighbouring Croatia and Bosnia & Herzegovina generated significant social and political discord. Montenegro, while not formally engaged in the war in Bosnia & Herzegovina, was significantly impacted by the instability wrought by it. Subject to United Nations sanctions, imposed in May 1992, Montenegro was essentially isolated, an international pariah alongside Serbia, their partner in the asymmetric federation that was the SRJ. Internal politics during this period were dominated by the war in Bosnia & Herzegovina and the economic ravages of the sanctions (though the government proved adept at circumventing them). Despite the efforts of opposition parties such as the LSCG, Montenegro remained firmly under the control of the DPS throughout the war in neighbouring Bosnia & Herzegovina, though the LSCG's anti-war activities and the party's commitment to independence, democratic values demonstrated hope in an otherwise challenging and bleak political environment. Though the party would later dissolve, supporters of the LSCG, and particularly their leader, Slavko Perović (though by no means him alone), took significant personal risks in their commitment to an anti-war stance and had to function in what was undoubtedly a harsh political climate. The most significant impact during this period, however, was on Montenegro's ethnic minorities, particularly its Muslim and Bosniak populations. The violent events in places like Pljevlja and Bukovica, the expulsion of Bosnian Muslim refugees, and the trials of SDA activists in Bijelo Polje, demonstrated that interethnic relations were seriously challenged. Subsequent political events would, however, transform the Montenegrin political landscape and provide opportunities for ethnic minority parties to emerge from the margins into the mainstream.

The year 1997 proved pivotal for Montenegro. Initiated by Milo Djukanović and his allies within the DPS, the cathartic split within the hitherto monolithic party led, ultimately, to a subsequent division of the body politic into two distinct blocs. Though the initial division was based along pro- and anti-Milošević lines – characterized, even personified, by the political struggle between Milo Djukanović and Momir Bulatović – it soon evolved into a political battle between pro- and anti-independence forces (the DPS and SNP), which was often fought by proxy (though the conflict between the CPC and the SPC, for example). In the immediate years following the DPS split, and as the Montenegrin government distanced itself from Belgrade, there were a number of occasions where political and social tensions could have led to violence (particularly following the October 1997 presidential elections and the 1999 NATO bombing of the SRJ), though such dark scenarios were, ultimately, avoided. The fall of the Milošević regime in October 2000 did not, however, result in the diluting of aspirations for independence, and though signing the Belgrade Agreement in March 2002 (during which the Montenegrin government gained the concession that they could schedule an independence referendum after three years), preparations for the independence referendum proceeded nevertheless.

The referendum, held on 21 May 2006, paved the way for the country becoming an independent state once again. Though the margin of victory for the 'Yes' campaign (55.5 per cent in favour of independence, 44.5 per cent in favour of state union) was very narrow, it delivered the independence that the DPS-led coalition had sought. It bequeathed, however, a divided body politic and a divided society, jaded by almost a decade in which politics was dominated by the statehood question. But for all of Montenegro's internal problems, the country made significant progress in the immediate period following the referendum. Montenegro is a formal EU candidate making slow but steady process towards full membership. At the time of writing, twenty-six negotiating 'chapters', including the 'Rule of Law' and 'Judiciary and Fundamental Rights) (chapter 23) and 'Justice, Freedom and Security' (chapter 24) have been opened. Two chapters ('Science and Research' – chapter 25; and 'Education and Culture' – chapter 26) have been provisionally closed. Opening benchmarks have been set for eleven chapters. Montenegro's EU accession will, however, be determined as much by the political landscape within the EU as it will be determined by the speed and trajectory of political reform in Montenegro). While there is consensus on this, the issue of Montenegro's NATO membership remained a genuine problem.

Beyond further (and deeper) Euro-Atlantic integration, economic issues will certainly remain a key factor in Montenegro's continued success. Presently, the country's small economy faces significant challenges; the post-referendum boom was essentially reversed by the onset of the global economic downturn, and the economy contracted sharply in 2009. The Montenegrin economy relies heavily on income generated from tourism, and while the trends are positive any instability in the wider region would have significant implications for Montenegro's tourist-driven economy. Montenegro's industrial base, once employing significant numbers, is severely diminished. The additional (and major) problem is that Montenegrin society has become one in which the gap between the wealthy and the poor has increased significantly; this is particularly visible in such a small country. These growing levels of economic disparity, between the north of the country and the central and southern areas, has been one of the most striking characteristics of independent Montenegro and will need to be addressed if social and political stability is to be preserved in the longer term.

Likewise, the political scene since the referendum has been marked by both continuity and change. The DPS remain in government, as they have done since Montenegro's first multiparty elections in 1990, and in spite of the party's split in 1997. There has been no change of government through the mechanism of democratic elections; the only change that has emanated is from *within* the system (i.e. within the DPS). Their position as the 'party of power' has not been seriously challenged, however, and the reasons for this are determined not by how well they govern, but how effective they are at undermining any emergent opposition and their ability to evolve, to be ideologically flexible and to operate within a political system that is engineered to allow for their continued dominance. The problem, ultimately, remains that the lines between the DPS, the government they lead and state institutions are blurred. To some extent, the party *is* the state, and the DPS's well-established control over the instruments of it awards them a significant advantage over the opposition. Their budget for election campaigns alone significantly outstrips their closest competitors, and in elections voters continue to support the DPS because they are the likely victors and because they understand that to function outside the system of patronage may not be in their interests. The patronage of those in power is crucial to employment (particularly those who work in the public sector) and social advancement. This presents something of a problem for the DPS in that Montenegro's independence is increasingly regarded, even by many who voted for it, as a DPS-led project that had benefited, in the main, senior party members and their families, and, albeit to a lesser extent, the party rank and file.

By contrast, the opposition has been unable to find sufficient common ground to unite, even if their primary goal (to unseat the DPS) is essentially the same. Splits, realignments and the emergence of new parties and coalitions have meant that the opposition, with the exception of the pre-split DF coalition that contested the 2012 parliamentary elections, have largely failed to pose too much of a threat to the DPS's hold on power. Moreover, no opposition politician has yet emerged that has been charismatic enough to challenge Milo Djukanović. The greatest challenge came in the form of the DF coalition, led by Miodrag Lekić, in 2012, but this coalition did not, ultimately, prove durable. Lekić's departure (to create his own party, DEMOS), along with others close to him, left the DF as a smaller coalition and one that has opted for more radical methods to undermine the DPS, thereby paving the way for the bitter political conflicts so evident today. The opposition, meanwhile, remains relatively fragmented, and although they share similar aims, are in disagreement over strategy. The radical approach taken by the DF since 2015 has also determined that the forging of an effective opposition, for now, seems remote. So in the meantime, the DPS remain dominant, albeit within a coalition government and despite a rather unconvincing performance in the 2016 parliamentary elections. With Djukanović's departure from the formal political scene, Duško Marković, a staunch Djukanović ally, became

Montenegro's new prime minster in October 2016. Milo Djukanović remains, however, the chairman of the DPS, a role that means he continued to assert significant influence over party matters. He has also not ruled out a return to the political front lines – possibly to replace Filip Vujanović (who cannot run for a third term) as president.

Despite the often-combative political environment and the lack of executive rotation, however, Montenegro's achievements have to be acknowledged. Broadly, the country *has* made significant progress an independent state, perhaps exceeding the expectations of its supporters and surprising those detractors who questioned the viability of such a small state in the Balkans. The tensions surrounding the referendum were tangible and conflict, even if only of a low intensity, was a genuine possibility. In the wake of such a divisive referendum campaign, the country faced significant challenges in the first years of its independence, challenges that could have proved insurmountable. Yet Montenegro has consolidated and its government continuing in its stated strategic goal of assuring Montenegro's Euro-Atlantic integration, despite the fact that NATO membership did not (and does not) enjoy the level of public support that the government laboured so hard to generate.

While there is sufficient scope for optimism, there is, conversely, no room for complacency. Myriad challenges lie ahead and Montenegro's domestic political scene is more febrile than at any time since the 2006 referendum; moreover, Montenegro risks becoming the centre of a tug-of-war between Russian and the West. Though Montenegro's limited military capacity is of little concern to Russia, Moscow will not wish to see NATO expand further in the Balkans – and this is particularly acute with regard to Serbia (where the prospect of NATO membership is even less popular than in Montenegro). In the meantime, Montenegro, whose NATO membership commenced in June 2017, may have laid the foundations for its Euro-Atlantic future, but it did so in a context where the international political climate has significantly altered. The certainties of the past and the seeming inevitability of eventual EU membership can no longer be taken for granted. Indeed, the speed or even realization of this will depend more upon developments within the EU (including the Brexit negotiations, ongoing security issues, the Euro crisis and related economic difficulties in some member-states) than Montenegro's own success at meeting key benchmarks. Yet, while there is much yet to be done before Montenegro's political problems are resolved, particularly within the domestic political sphere, it's important to see these current issues in the wider context. Montenegro and its citizens have faced greater challenges in the past and have prevailed. Doubtless they will do so again, despite the inevitable challenges the country will face in the coming years.

Notes

Chapter 1

1. For a detailed description of the composition of the Montenegrin *pleme* (clans), see Christopher Boehm, *Montenegrin Social Organization and Values: Political Ethnography of a Refuge Area Tribal Adaptation*, New York: AMS Press, 1983, pp. 53–64.
2. According to Ivo Banac, 'By 1878, when the powers at the Congress of Berlin finally recognized Montenegro as an independent state, it bulged into Old Herzegovina to embrace the tribes of Banjani, Nikšički, Šaranci, Drobnjaci, Pivljani, and a large number of Rudinjani. In the east and south it expanded into the lands of the Vasojevići, the most numerous highland tribe, and then along both shores of Lake Skadar, gaining, too, the coveted exit to the Adriatic on the littoral from Bar to the south of Ulcinj.' See Ivo Banac, *The National Question in Yugoslavia*, Ithaca, NY and London: Cornell University Press, 1984, p. 275.
3. For a detailed analysis of these negotiations, see Novak Ražnatović, *Crna Gora i Berlinske kongres*, Titograd: Istroijski institut CP Crne Gore, 1979.
4. See Marko Špadijer & Stanko Roganović, *Diplomatska poslanstva u Kraljevini Crnoj Gori*, Cetinje: Matica Crnogorska, 2004.
5. Nikola, in fact, built two palaces in Cetinje, and one in Bar, Podgorica and Nikšić. For the construction of building in Cetinje throughout the nineteenth century, see Dušan Martinović, *Cetinje: buntovno i revolucionarno*, Cetinje: Obod, 2003, pp. 9–10.
6. Banac, *The National Question in Yugoslavia*, p. 276.
7. Ibid., p. 277.
8. This 'Club of Montenegrin University Youth in Belgrade', led by Marko Daković and Jovan Djonović, were active in agitating against Prince Nikola and promoting the cause of Serbian-Montenegrin unification. See Banac, *The National Question in Yugoslavia*, p. 278.
9. See Srdja Pavlović, *Balkan Anschluss: The Annexation of Montenegro and the Creation of the Common South Slavic State*, West Lafayette, IN: Purdue University Press, 2007, p. 87, and Nikola Škerović, *Crna Gora na osvitku XX vijeka*, Beograd: Naučno delo, 1964, pp. 486–487.
10. Among those sentenced (albeit in absentia) were Marko Daković and Jovan Djonović of the 'Club of Montenegrin University Youth in Belgrade'. See Jagoš Jovanović, *Istorija Crne Gore*, Podgorica: CID, 2001, pp. 293–296, and Banac, *The National Question in Yugoslavia*, p. 278.
11. John Treadway, *The Falcon and the Eagle: Montenegro and Austria-Hungary, 1908–1914*, West Lafayette, IN: Purdue University Press, 1983, p. 29. See also Dimitrije Vujović, *Crnogorski federelalisti 1919–1929*, Kniga 2, Titograd: CANU, 1981.
12. According to Dedijer, a group of Belgrade-based Montenegrin youths organized a secret society with the express aim of assassinating those in Montenegro who were working against the goals of the NS. Only Montenegrins resident in Belgrade could

become members, and their commitment and radicalism can be demonstrated by their formation of a suicide pact which stated that members (if apprehended) had to commit suicide in order to maintain the integrity and the secrecy of the wider group. See Vladimir Dedijer, *The Road to Sarajevo*, London: MacGibbon and Kee, 1967, pp. 291–292. See also Škerović, *Crna Gora na osvitku XX vijeka*, pp. 486–487.

13 For an in-depth analysis of the events surrounding the Kolašin Conspiracy (in English), see Treadway, *The Falcon and the Eagle*, pp. 51–55.

14 Šerbo Rastoder, 'A Short Review of the History of Montenegro', in Florian Bieber (ed.), *Montenegro in Transition: Problems of Identity and Statehood*, Baden-Baden: Nomos Verlagsgesellschaft, 2003, p. 126.

15 Banac, *The National Question in Yugoslavia*, p. 275.

16 For a detailed account of these events, see Andrej Mitrović, *Serbia's Great War 1914–1918*, London: Hurst & Co., 2007.

17 Gavro Perazić, *Nestanak crnogorske države u Prvom svetskom ratu*, Belgrade: Vojnoistorijski Institut, 1988, p. 43. See also Novica Rakočević, *Crna Gora u Prvom svetskon ratu 1914–1918*, Titograd: Istorijski institut u Titogradu, 1969, p. 127.

18 Rakočević, *Crna Gora u Prvom svetskom ratu 1914–1918*, pp. 162–164.

19 Pavlović, *Balkan Anschluss*, p. 87.

20 Srdja Pavlović, 'The Podgorica Assembly in 1918: Notes on the Yugoslav Historiography (1919–1970) about the Unification of Serbia and Montenegro', *Canadian Slavonic Papers*, Vol. XLI, No. 2, June 1999, p. 160.

21 Perazić, *Nestanak crnogorske drzave u prvom svetskom ratu*, p. 158.

22 Jozo Tomasevich, *Peasants, Politics and Economic Change in Yugoslavia*, California: Stanford University Press, 1955, p. 228. See also Jovanović *Istorija Crne Gore*, pp. 340–343.

23 Šerbo Rastoder & Živko Andrijašević, *The History of Montenegro*, Podgorica: CICG, 2006, p. 150.

24 For a more detailed analysis of the Montenegrin *komiti*, see Mile Kordić & Mihajlo Ašanin, *Komitski pokret u Crnoj Gori 1916–1918*, Belgrade: Nova kniga, 1985.

25 For analyses of the Podgorica Assembly, see Pavlović, *Balkan Anschluss*; Dimitrije Vujović, *Ujedinjenje Crne Gore i Srbije*, Titograd: Istorijski institut Narodne Republike Crne Gore, 1962; Dragoljub Živojinović, *Crna Gora u borbi za opstanak, 1914–1922*, Belgrade: Vojna knjiga, 1996, and Šerbo Rastoder, *Skrivana strana istorije: Crnogorska buna i odmetnićki pokret 1918–1929*, Cetinje: Obod, 2005.

26 Facsimile of the 'Resolution of the Serb People of Montenegro passed at the Sitting in Podgorica, November 26 1918', in Andrija Radović et al., *The Question of Montenegro*, Paris: Graphique, 1919, p. 41.

27 Mitrović, *Serbia's Great War 1914–1918*, p. 324.

28 For the sake of brevity, wider political events within the Yugoslav state in the interwar period will be dealt with here rather superficially. However, there are a number of outstanding books that students and scholars interested in this period should consult. For the unification of Serbia and Montenegro, see Vujović, *Ujedinjenje Crne Gore i Srbije*; for the immediate period following the creation of the KSCS, see Banac, *The National Question in Yugoslavia*; for a succinct analysis of the 'invalid question' and the legacy of the First World War, see John Paul Newman, 'Forging a United Kingdom of Serbs, Croats and Slovenes', in Dejan Djokić & James Ker-Lindsay (eds.), *New Perspectives on Yugoslavia: Key Issues and Controversies*, London & New York: Routledge, 2011, pp. 46–61; for the period between 1918 and 1939, see Dejan Djokić, *Elusive Compromise: A History of Interwar Yugoslavia*, London: Hurst & Co., 2007

and Jacob Hoptner, *Yugoslavia in Crisis 1934-1941*, New York and London: Columbia University Press, 1962.

29 Krsto Popović left Montenegro for Argentina in 1922 (where there was a small Montenegrin diaspora), though he returned to Europe in 1929 and settled in Belgium. From there he wrote to King Aleksander Karadjordjević appealing that he be pardoned for his role in the Christmas Uprising. He was subsequently pardoned and returned to Montenegro, living in retirement until the war broke out in Yugoslavia in April 1941. For an account of the life of Krsto Popović, see Veljko Sjekloća, *Krsto Popović u istorijskoj gradji i literature*, Cetinje: Obod, 2001. For more on the Montenegrin diaspora in Argentina, see Katalina Milović, *La Montenegrina*, Cetinje: Matica, 2004.

30 According to Ivo Banac, the *Zelenaši* splintered between those who were in favour of a militant approach and those who were not. This fundamental division damaged the effectiveness of their uprising. See Banac, *The National Question in Yugoslavia*, pp. 286-287.

31 For a detailed description of these events, see Mustafa Memić, *Pojave prozilitizma u plavsko-gusinje kraju 1913 i 1919. godine*, Sarajevo: OKO, 2004.

32 Ibid., p. 298.

33 Mehmedalija Bojić, *Historija Bosne i Bošnjaka (VII-XX vijek)*, Sarajevo: TKD Šahinpašić, 2001, p. 503.

34 For a very detailed account of the work of the Montenegrin government-in-exile, see Šerbo Rastoder, *Crna Gora u egzilu (knjiga 1)*, Podgorica: Istorijski institut Crne Gore, 2004, and Šerbo Rastoder, *Crna Gora u egzilu (knjiga 2)*, Podgorica: Istorijski institut Crne Gore, 2004. For Montenegro at the Paris Peace Conference, see Warren Whitney, *Montenegro: The Crime of the Paris Peace Conference*, New York: Brentano's, 1922.

35 A fascinating character with a background in social work and education, Alexander Devine was an energetic campaigner for Montenegro. He had been the chairman of the British Relief Committee to Montenegro during the First World War and had lobbied for Montenegro's independence after the Assembly of Podgorica. He consistently argued that Montenegro's annexation was 'an outrage against international law'. See, for example, Alexander Devine, *The Martyred Nation: A Plea for Montenegro*, London, 1924, p. 25. For an excellent account of Devine's engagement with the Montenegrin cause, see John D. Treadway, 'Engleski Crnogorac Aleksandar Divajn', *Alexandria*, Belgrade, Vol. 1, No. 7, 1988, pp. 14-20.

36 For the role of France, see Šerbo Rastoder, *Uloga Francuske u nasilnoj aneksiji Crne Gore*, Bar: Conteco, 2000. For the Anglo-American position, see John D. Treadway, 'Anglo-American Diplomacy and the Montenegrin Question', *Occasional Papers*, Woodrow Wilson Centre, European Institute, East European Program, No. 26, April 1991, pp. 1-20.

37 The remains of King Nikola I Petrović and his family were reinterned in Montenegro in September 1989 during a ceremony in Cetinje. His remains, and those of Queen Milena, were reburied in the Ćipur chapel in Cetinje, close to Nikola's former palace. See Svetislav Vujović, *Prenos i sahrana posmrtnih ostataka Nikole I Petrovića Njegoša*, Cetinje: Obod, 1994.

38 Banac, *The National Question in Yugoslavia*, pp. 270-271.

39 Vujović, *Crnogorski federalisti 1919-1929*, p. 55. See also, Šerbo Rastoder, *Politički stranke u Crnoj Gori 1918-1929*, Bar: Conteco, 2000, and Čedomir Pejović, *KPJ u Crnoj Gori 1919-1941*, Podgorica: CID, 1999.

40 Rastoder, *Politički stranke u Crnoj Gori 1918–1929*, p. 533.
41 Banac, *The National Question in Yugoslavia*, p. 290.
42 Pejović, *KPJ u Crnoj Gori 1919–1941*, p. 111.
43 Puniša Račić had been accused and sentenced to death *in absentia* in 1909 by the Montenegrin courts for his role in the attempt to assassinate King Nikola I Petrović in Kolašin in 1907. See Banac, *The National Question in Yugoslavia*, p. 279.
44 The introduction of the banovina regions was controversial, but the objective was to detract from the mentality of narrow nationalism and encourage individuals to identify with a centralized Yugoslav state and to identify as Yugoslavs.
45 For a detailed analysis of this period, see Djokić, *Elusive Compromise*.
46 For more detail on the events in Belveder, see Martinović, *Cetinje: buntovno i revolucionarno*, pp. 44–48.
47 Andrijašević & Rastoder, *The History of Montenegro*, p. 207.
48 Enver Redžić, *Bosnia and Herzegovina in the Second World War*, London & New York: Frank Cass, 2005, p. 5.
49 Milan Deroc, *British Special Operations Explored: Yugoslavia in Turmoil 1941–1943 and the British Response*, East European Monographs, Boulder, CO: Columbia Press, 1988, p. 2.
50 Ibid., p. 2.
51 For the demonstrations in Cetinje, see Martinović, *Cetinje: buntovno i revolucionarno*, pp. 57–58.
52 For an exceptionally detailed analysis of the events that led to the dismemberment and occupation of Yugoslavia, see Velimir Terzić, *Slom Kraljevine Jugoslavije 1941*, Belgrade: Narodna knjiga, 1983.
53 Yugoslavia was partitioned thus: Germany occupied northern Slovenia. Italy occupied the majority of Montenegro, much of the Croatian coastline and islands and some of the Croatian hinterland (central Dalmatia, Konavle). The Italian-sponsored 'Greater Albania' acquired the majority of Kosovo, Plav, Gusinje, Ulcinj and Rožaje in Montenegro, a portion of the Sandžak region and much of western Macedonia. Hungary was 'awarded' areas in Serbia (Vojvodina, Baranja and Bačka). The Bulgarians acquired most of Macedonia, Pirot (Serbia) and a small portion of Kosovo.
54 For the Italian occupation of the Balkans, see Davide Rogondo, 'Italian Soldiers in the Balkans: The Experience of Occupation (1941–1943)', *Journal of Southeast Europe and the Balkans*, Vol. 6, No. 2, August 2014, pp. 125–144.
55 Jozo Tomasevich, *War and Revolution in Yugoslavia 1941–1945*, Stanford University Press, 2001, pp. 138–139.
56 The original Italian plan had been to reconstitute an independent Montenegro with Prince Mihailo Petrović, the grandson of the late King Nikola, on the throne. However, he refused the offer of the throne, throwing the Italian plan into chaos.
57 For the Italian plans for their 'independent' Montenegro, see Elizabeth Roberts, *The Realm of the Black Mountain*, London: Hurst & Co., 2007, pp. 334–347.
58 For a description of the KPJ's formation and activities in Montenegro during the existence of the KSHS, see Rastoder, *Politički stranke u Crnoj Gori 1918–1929*, pp. 415–434. For the 'Bijelo Polje group', see Pejović, *KPJ u Crnoj Gori 1919–1941*, pp. 407–408.
59 Burdžović was recognized as a national hero after the war. Numerous streets, schools and institutes carry (or carried) his name, including student halls in Titograd/Podgorica. See Mustafa Memić, *Poznati Bošnjaci Sandžaka i Crne Gore*, Sarajevo: Matica, 1998, p. 120.

60 Milovan Djilas, *Memoir of a Revolutionary*, New York: Harcourt Brace Jovanovich, 1973, pp. 75–76.
61 Milovan Djilas, *Wartime*, London: Martin Secker and Warburg, 1977, pp. 18–19.
62 British Special Operations Executive (SOE), 'Some Notes on the Yugoslav Revolt', 22 June 1942, HS5/938. See also Zoran Lakić, *Partizanska autonomija Sandžaka, 1934–1945*, Belgrade: Stručna knjiga, 1992, pp. 369–370.
63 See, for example, Jozo Tomasevich, *The Chetniks*, Stanford University Press, 2001; and Lucien Karchmar, *Draža Mihailović and the Rise of the Chetnik Movement, 1941–1942, Vol. 2*, London: Garland Publishing, 1987.
64 For an extensive biography of Pavle Djurišić, see Radoje Pajović, *Pavle Djurišić*, Podgorica: Grafo, 2005, p. 103.
65 Andrijašević & Rastoder, *The History of Montenegro*, p. 215.
66 Tomasevich, *War and Revolution in Yugoslavia 1941–1945*, p. 143. See also Radoje Pajović, *Kontrarevolucija u Crnoj Gori: četnicki i federalisticki pokret*, Cetinje: CANU, 1977, p. 34.
67 Pajović, *Pavle Djurišić*, pp. 58–59. It was alleged in the post-war trial of Draža Mihailović that Djurišić's Chetniks killed as many as 1,400 Muslims in the Bijelo Polje district in January 1943 alone. See *The Trial of Dragoljub-Draža Mihailović: Stenographic Records and Documents from the Trial of Dragoljub-Draža Mihailović*, Belgrade, 1946, p. 521.
68 Jozo Tomasevich, *The Chetniks*, p. 232.
69 Ibid., pp. 250–252.
70 Heather Williams, *Parachutes, Patriots and Partisans*, London: Hurst & Co., 2003, p. 243.
71 Deroc, *British Special Operations Explored*, p. 2.
72 At the time, the British mission did not have a clear grasp of *who* the resistance groups were. During their stay they sent a telegram sent to London recommending that the British government offer assistance to what he described rather ambiguously as 'Montenegrin National Freedom troops'. See Mark Wheeler, *Britain and the War for Yugoslavia 1940–1943*, East European Monographs, New York: Columbia University Press, 1980, pp. 70–71.
73 Williams, *Parachutes, Patriots and Partisans*, p. 245.
74 F.W.D. Deakin, *The Embattled Mountain*, Oxford: Oxford University Press, 1971, p. 180.
75 The other members of 'Operation Typical' were Corporal Walter Wroughton, Sergeant John Campbell and Sergeant 'Rose', a Palestinian Jew called Peterz Rosenberg. See Roberts, *Tito, Mihailović and the Allies 1941–1945*, Durham: Duke University Press, 1967, p. 117, and Williams, *Parachutes, Patriots and Partisans*, p. 139.
76 Djilas, *Wartime*, p. 253.
77 Deakin, *The Embattled Mountain*, pp. 13–14.
78 Djilas, *Wartime*, p. 259.
79 British War Cabinet Document W.P. (44) 234, 'Yugoslavia: Memorandum by the Secretary of State for Foreign Affairs', May 1944, Cab/66/49/34.
80 Andrijašević & Rastoder, *The History of Montenegro*, p. 223.
81 ZANVOCG transformed into the Montenegrin Anti-Fascist Assembly (*Crnogorska antifašistička skupština* – CASNO) in July 1944 a body tasked with re-establishing Montenegro's sovereignty within the nascent socialist Yugoslavia. See Zoran Lakić, *Narodna vlast u Crnoj Gori 1941–1945*, Cetinje: Obod, 1981, p. 128.

82 Andrijašević & Rastoder, *The History of Montenegro*, p. 225.
83 Fitzroy MacLean, *Eastern Approaches*, London: Jonathan Cape, 1949, p. 460.
84 Headquarters of the Balkan Air Force, 'A History of the Balkan Air Force', July 1945, AIR 23/882, p. 4.
85 Balkan Air Force (BAF), 'Report on the Situation in 2nd Corps Areas', 17 July 1944. WO 202/152: AIR 23/882, p. 79.
86 Headquarters of the Balkan Air Force (BAF), 'Report on the First Year of the RAF Liaison with Partisans', 12 December 1944. AIR 20/9035, p. 5.
87 According to F.W.D. Deakin, the Partisans had developed, despite the difficulties it would cause, a 'cult of the care of the wounded'. This caused significant logistical difficulties, however. 'The conduct of Partisan warfare', he said, 'was dependent on mobility and concealment, and this in turn created the shape and nature of the medical organisation of the movement. There was no static front and no rear area where base hospitals could be set up. Temporary "free territories" were held and organised, but the military need for sudden moves, and the often long marches, imposed a correspondingly special and novel medical structure to succour and protect the wounded'. See Deakin, *The Embattled Mountain*, p. 38.
88 Headquarters of the Balkan Air Force (BAF), 'A History of the Balkan Air Force', July 1945, AIR 23/882, p. 97. See also British War Office Records, 'Report on the evacuation of 900 wounded from Brezna by Flt Lt. T.R. Mathias', 16 August 1944. WO 202/512, p. 4.
89 Some estimates place the number of evacuated at over 1000. See for example, George Saunders & Dennis Richards, *The Royal Air Force 1939-1945, Vols. I-III*, London: Her Majesty's Stationery Office, 1954. They place the number at 1,078 individuals: comprising 1,059 Partisans, 16 Allied pilots and 3 members of the SOE mission.
90 For more on these BAF bombing raids, see Peter J. Hatcher, *Partisan Wings: The Biferno Journal*, Miami, FL: Trente Nova Publishing, 1994.
91 Rastoder, 'A Short Review of the History of Montenegro', p. 136.
92 Tomasevich, *The Chetniks*, p. 453. See also Pajović, *Pavle Djurišić*, p. 103.
93 Tomasevich, *The Chetniks*, p. 448.
94 Union of the Journalist's Associations of the Federative People's Republic of Yugoslavia, *The Trial of Dragoljub-Draža Mihailović: Stenographic records and documents from the trial of Dragoljub-Draža Mihailović*, pp. 529-531.
95 Radoje Pajović, *Crna Gora kroz istoriju*, Cetinje: Obod, 2005, p. 36.
96 Andrijašević & Rastoder, *The History of Montenegro*, p. 225.
97 Milan Brajović et al., *Titograd u slobodi 1944-1974*, Titograd: Titogradska tribina/Pobjeda, 1974, p. 66.
98 Djilas, *Wartime*, p. 445.
99 The Yugoslav state was known as the 'Federal People's Republic of Yugoslavia' until 1963. It was known thereafter as the 'Socialist Federal Republic of Yugoslavia' until its demise in 1992.
100 Montenegrins were well represented within the Central Committee of the KPJ, even after the 1948 Cominform crisis. Veljko Vlahović, Svetozar Tempo-Vukmanović, Milovan Djilas, Veljko Zeković, Blažo Jovanović, Nikola Kovačević, Andrina Mugoša Krsto Popivoda and Vlado Popović were all members of the Central Committee of the KPJ. Mitar Bakić, Spaso Drakić, Radovan Zogović, Savo Joksimović, Veljko Mičnuvić, Savo Brković and Jovo Kapičić were also influential members of the KPJ.
101 Rastoder, 'A Short Review of the History of Montenegro', p. 136.

102 See Brajović et al., *Titograd u slobodi 1944-1974*, p. 38.
103 Paul Shoup, *Communism and the Yugoslav National Question*, New York: Columbia University Press, 1968, p. 180.
104 Edvard Kardelj, *Reminiscences: The Struggle for Recognition and Independence – The New Yugoslavia, 1944-1957*, London: Summerfield Press, 1982, p. 184.
105 Roberts, *The Realm of the Black Mountain*, p. 403.
106 For Yugoslav ambitions with regard to Albania, see Jeronim Perović, 'The Tito-Stalin Split: A Reassessment in Light of New Evidence', *Journal of Cold War Studies*, Vol. 9, No. 2, Spring 2007, pp. 42-48.
107 Richard J. Crampton, *The Balkans since the Second World War*, London: Longman Press, 2002, p. 30.
108 See Milovan Djilas, *Conversations with Stalin*, London: Rupert Hart Davies, 1962, and Kardelj, *Reminiscences*.
109 The CONINFORM crisis and the internal struggle within Yugoslavia have been the subject of numerous films, such as Stole Popov's film *Sreća nova '49* (Happy New '49), Emir Kusturica's *Otac na službednom putu* (When Father Was Away on Business), Krsto Papić's *Život sa stricem* (My Uncle's Legacy) and Dušan Kovačević's comedy *Balkanski špijun* (Balkan Spy).
110 Rastoder, 'A Short Review of the History of Montenegro', p. 137. See also, Shoup, *Communism and the Yugoslav National Question*, p. 138.
111 Ivo Banac, *With Stalin against Tito*, Ithaca, NY and London: Cornell University Press, 1988, p. 151.
112 Banac, *With Stalin against Tito*, p. 164.
113 According to Paul Shoup, 'In Montenegro, the ratio of Party members to expulsions was six to one, while in Bosnia and Herzegovina it was twenty-three to one; in Croatia, twenty to one; and in Macedonia, thirty-one to one'. See Shoup, *Communism and the Yugoslav National Question*, p. 138.
114 See Živko Andrijašević, 'Crnogorska 1948', *Matica*, broj 59, jesen 2014, p. 120.
115 See ibid., p. 138. See also, Aleksandar Rankovic, *Izabrani govori i članci*, Belgrade: Kultura, 1951, pp. 8-9.
116 Shoup, *Communism and the Yugoslav National Question*, p. 164.
117 Andrijašević & Rastoder, *The History of Montenegro*, p. 237.
118 There existed a saying in Yugoslavia that referred to the omnipotence of the Yugoslav Secret Services: *Ozna sve Dozna* (OZNA knows everything).
119 Banac, *With Stalin against Tito*, p. 112. For more on Vlado Dapčević's activities, see Rifat Rastoder & Branislav Kovačević, *Crvena mrlja*, Titograd: Pobjeda, 1990, pp. 48-56. For the killing of Arso Jovanović, see Milovan Djilas, *Rise and Fall*, San Diego, CA: Harcourt Brace Jovanovich, 1985, pp. 231-215.
120 Banac, *With Stalin against Tito*, p. 237.
121 Andrijašević & Rastoder, *The History of Montenegro*, p. 237.
122 Rastoder, 'A Short Review of the History of Montenegro', p. 137.
123 For more on the economic development of Montenegro during the socialist period, see Radovan Radonjić, *Socializam u Crnoj Gori*, Podgorica: Matica Crnogorska, 2013, pp. 446-449. For Titograd specifically, see Brajović et al., *Titograd u slobodi 1944-1974*.
124 The Montenegrin coast became increasingly popular holiday destination for Western tourists in the 1970s. Numerous celebrities such as Richard Burton, Elizabeth Taylor, Sophia Loren, Kirk Douglas and other stayed at the exclusive Sveti Stefan resort, and the naturist resorts at *Velika plaža* near Ulcinj became increasingly popular throughout the 1970s and 1980s.

125 Ibid., p. 137. According to Elizabeth Roberts, the population of Nikšić rose from only 5,000 in 1945 to 50,000 by the 1980s, while the pre-war population of Podgorica (Titograd) multiplied five times. See Roberts, *Realm of the Black Mountain*, p. 421.
126 Roberts, *Realm of the Black Mountain*, p. 417.
127 Much of Djilas's work while in prison was published by Harcourt Brace Jovanovich (or Harcourt Brace and World). William Jovanovich, himself of Montenegrin descent (his father, Ilija, was born in Montenegro but had emigrated to the United States in 1907), was director of Harcourt Brace and World before the company changed its name to Harcourt Brace Jovanovich in 1970. He visited Djilas in Belgrade on several occasions and facilitated the publishing of many of Djilas's works (which were forbidden in Yugoslavia) in the United States. See William Jovanovich, *The Temper of the West: A Memoir*, Columbia: University of South Carolina Press, 2003.
128 Dennis Russinow, 'Nationalities Policy and the "National Question"', in Pedro Ramet (ed.), *Yugoslavia in the 1980's*, Boulder, CO: Westview Press, p. 131.
129 According to Srdja Pavlović, 'In Montenegro, Serb nationalist forces gained prominence for a short period (1970–73) by publicly denouncing communist ideology and advocating the ideas of the *Četnik* movement'. Among these were several journalists from the daily *Pobjeda*. See Srdja Pavlović, 'Literature, Social Poetics and Identity Construction in Montenegro', *International Journal of Politics, Culture and Society*, Vol. 17, No. 1, Fall 2003, p. 140 and p. 161, fn.38.
130 Roberts, *Realm of the Black Mountain*, p. 423. See also Shoup, *Communism and the Yugoslav National Question*, p. 269.
131 Pavlović, 'Literature, Social Poetics and Identity Construction in Montenegro', p. 139.
132 Andrijašević & Rastoder, *The History of Montenegro*, p. 254.
133 John Allcock, 'Montenegro', in Bogdan Szajkowski (ed.), *Political Parties of Eastern Europe, Russia and the Successor States*, London: Longman, 1994, p. 184
134 For an assessment of how the 1974 Constitution was interpreted by Serb nationalists, see Helsinki odbor za ljudska prava u Srbiji, *Kovanje antijugoslovenske zavere*, Belgrade: Biblioteka Svedočanstva (Br.26), 2006, pp. 15–20.
135 Veljko Vlahović was a high-raking, celebrated KPJ official from Montenegro who had fought as a volunteer for the 'International Brigades' during the Spanish Civil War before becoming one of the key members of the Partisan leadership. During the 1941–45 war, he was the director of *Radio slobodna Jugoslavija* (Free Yugoslavia Radio), which operated from Moscow, and later became the editor of the Belgrade daily newspaper *Borba*. Vlahović died in 1975, and the university was renamed in his honour.
136 CANU was regarded by Montenegrin nationalists as 'pro-Serb', and a parallel academy called the Doclean Academy of Arts and Sciences (*Dukljanska akademija nauka i umjetnosti* – DANU) was formed in 1998. The two academies merged in April 2015.
137 According to Nebojša Čagorović, Montenegrins had always been comfortable in Tito's Yugoslavia primarily because they could rely on federal funds; after all, he claims, 'laziness and the right to someone else's support have always been considered natural rights in Montenegro'. See Nebojša Čagorović, 'Montenegrin Identity: Past Present and Future', *The Journal of Area Studies*, No. 3, 1993, p. 133.
138 See United Nations Education, Scientific and Cultural Association (UNESCO), *Montenegro Earthquake: The Conservation the Historic Monuments and Art Treasures*, Paris: UNESCO, 1984.

139 Perhaps the only obvious successor was the Slovene theoretician, Edvard Kardelj. Although his political orientation was almost identical to Tito's, his long, complex and practically incomprehensible speeches on Communist Party dialectics made him appear colourless in comparison. But Kardelj died one year before Tito in February 1979, leaving no obvious successor.
140 Andrijašević & Rastoder, *The History of Montenegro*, p. 245.
141 See Miloš Bešić, 'Nationalism versus Civic Option in Montenegro', in Dragica Vujadonović et al. (eds.), *Between Authoritarianism and Democracy: Serbia, Montenegro, Croatia – Vol. II: Civil Society and Political Culture*, Belgrade: CEDET, 2005, p. 219.
142 For an excellent analysis of the debates surrounding Montenegrin identity (both historical and contemporary), see Jelena Džankić, 'Reconstructing the Meaning of Being Montenegrin', *Slavic Review*, Vol. 73, No. 2, Summer 2014, pp. 347–372.
143 Roberts, *Realm of the Black Mountain*, p. 37.
144 Banac, *The National Question in Yugoslavia*, p. 274.
145 Ibid.
146 Allcock, 'Montenegro', p. 188.
147 Milovan Djilas, 'O Crnogorskom nationalnom pitanju', *Članci 1941–1946*, Kultura, Beograd, 1947, p. 3.
148 Ibid., p. 4.
149 Andrijašević & Rastoder, *The History of Montenegro*, p. 259.
150 For these debates, see Špiro Kulišić, *O etnogenezi Crnogoraca*, Titograd: Pobjeda, 1980. See also Radonjić, *Socijalizam u Crnoj Gori*.
151 Pavlović, 'Literature, Social Poetics and Identity Construction in Montenegro', p. 141.
152 The controversy surrounding the building of the mausoleum took place during a period where there was a growing nationalism in Montenegro – both Serbian and Montenegrin. In 1972, the so-called *Bijela knjiga* (white book) was 'published' by the SKCG which included a series of directives required because of 'the manifestation of nationalist and other ideologically unacceptable attitudes'. Seventeen intellectuals – such as the Montenegrin writer Radovan Zogović and the linguists Vojislav Nikčević and Pavle Ilić – were diametrically opposed in their views of the Montenegrin language. The 'white paper' instructed Montenegrin communists working in the press and publishing houses to maintain 'a high level of ideological alertness' when making decisions to publish authors' works. See Veseljko Koprivica, *Naj Crna Gora: monografski leksikon*, Podgorica: Dan Press, 2002, p. 181.
153 For detailed analysis of the dynamics of the debates focusing on Montenegrin identity, see Milorad Popović, *Crnogorske pitanje*, Cetinje: Dignitas, 1999; Milan Popović, *Montenegrin Mirror: Polity in Turmoil (1999–2001)*, Podgorica: Nansen Dialogue Centre, 2002; Milan Popović, *Crnogorska alternativa: Neizvesnost promene*, Podgorica: Vijesti, 2000. Some aspects of the identity debate can also be found in Marko Špadijer, *Crnogorska raskršća*, Podgorica: Matica Crnogorska, 2007.
154 Tanjug Domestic Service (Belgrade), 26 February 1988, FBIS, *Daily Report* (Eastern Europe), FBIS-EEU-88-040. In an article entitled *The Ethnic Structure of the Population of Montenegro*, Vujadin Rudić argued that 'there are differences between the Serbs in Montenegro and those in Serbia, but they are insufficient to determine them as separate peoples. The Montenegrins are the mainstay of the Serbian ethnic being and Montenegro as a state has been its guardian throughout the centuries'. See Vujadin Rudić The Ethnic Structure of the Population of Montenegro, in Hadži-Jovacić, Dušanka (ed.), *The Serbian Question in the Balkans*, Belgrade: Faculty of Geography, University of Belgrade, 1995, p. 245.

Chapter 2

1. As early as 1984, the SKCG leadership recognized the dangers. Vidoje Žarković, the then secretary of the Central Committee of the SKCG, cautioned that *bratstvo i jedinstvo* (brotherhood and unity) in Montenegro, and throughout the SFRJ, must be vigorously defended against what he described as 'retrograde nationalist forces' *Tanjug Domestic Service (Belgrade)*, 5 August 1984, FBIS, *Daily Report (*Eastern Europe), FBIS-EEU-84-152.
2. Central Intelligence Agency (CIA) Directorate of Intelligence, 'Yugoslavia: Key Questions and Answers on the Debt Crisis', EUR-84-100011, January 1984, p. 9.
3. Dennison Rusinow, *Yugoslavia: Oblique Insights and Observations*, Pittsburgh: Pittsburgh University Press, 2008, p. 319. Šerbo Rastoder noted that Montenegro's economic development (and the greatest increase in economic efficiency) was recorded between 1961 and 1970, thanks mainly to a more developed communications and economic infrastructure (such as the Bar-Belgrade railway line which was completed in 1976). See Rastoder, 'A Short Review of the History of Montenegro', p. 137.
4. Milica Uvalic, *Serbia's Transition: Towards a Better Future*, London: Palgrave Macmillan, 2010, p. 24.
5. Branka Magaš, *The Destruction of Yugoslavia: Tracking the Break-Up, 1980–1992*, London: Verso Press, 1993, p. 170.
6. *RFE/RL Report on Eastern Europe*, 21 December 1990, p. 29.
7. *Borba* (Belgrade), 7 August 1987, p. 3.
8. Magaš, *Destruction of Yugoslavia*, p. 170.
9. Ibid.
10. *Borba*, Belgrade, 3 August 1987, p. 1.
11. A report in the Belgrade daily *Borba* noted that bread prices in Montenegro equated with those in other Yugoslav republics. However, it was further noted that in Montenegro, 'personal incomes are far below that of the Yugoslav average ... it is [therefore] easy to assume that any price increase has a major effect and causes a fall in the standard of living'. See *Borba*, Belgrade, 5 August 1987, p. 1.
12. *Tanjug Domestic Service (Belgrade)*, FBIS, *Daily Report* (Eastern Europe), FBIS-EEU-14-152, 14 August 1987.
13. *RFE/RL Report on Eastern Europe*, 22 November 1991, p. 12.
14. Branka Magaš estimated that by 1988, 4,000 workers were living and supporting their families on the minimum wage of 230,000 dinars (£25) per month and that since 1986 6,000 workers had lost their jobs and thousands were desperately seeking 'non-existent work'. See Magaš, *Destruction of Yugoslavia*, p. 170.
15. Introducing his report Radović warned of the social and political consequences that could emerge from further economic hardship in an already-'overheated social atmosphere'. He also warned of the dangers of creeping nationalism imploring his colleagues to 'fight a resolute battle with the proponents of all nationalist phenomena'. See *Tanjug Domestic Service (Belgrade)*, FBIS, *Daily Report* (Eastern Europe), FBIS-EEU-88-101, 25 May 1987.
16. *Borba* (Belgrade), 15 January 1988, p. 1.
17. For an in-depth analysis of Slobodan Milošević's rise to power, see Vidosav Stevanović, *Milošević: The People's Tyrant*, London: IB Tauris, 2004, pp. 23–33.
18. Roberts, *Realm of the Black Mountain*, p. 432.

19 Andrijašević & Rastoder, *History of Montenegro*, p. 261.
20 See Veseljko Koprovica & Branko Vojičić, *Prevrat '89*, Podgorica: Liberalni Savez Crne Gore, 1994.
21 Radonjić, *Socijalizam u Crnoj Gori*, p. 575.
22 *Tanjug Domestic Service (Belgrade)*, 26 February 1988, FBIS, *Daily Report* (Eastern Europe), FBIS-EEU-88-040. In an article entitled *The Ethnic Structure of the Population of Montenegro*, Vujadin Rudić argued that 'there are differences between the Serbs in Montenegro and those in Serbia, but they are insufficient to determine them as separate peoples. The Montenegrins are the mainstay of the Serbian ethnic being and Montenegro as a state has been its guardian throughout the centuries'. See Rudić, *The Ethnic Structure of the Population of Montenegro*, p. 245.
23 *Tanjug Domestic Service (Belgrade)*, 5 August 1984, FBIS, *Daily Report* (Eastern Europe), FBIS-EEU-84-152.
24 A study conducted in 1985–1986 by the Serbian Academy of Sciences and Arts (SANU) entitled 'The Migration of Serbs and Montenegrins from Kosovo and Metohija' emphasized their plight. Since 1948, Montenegrins had never represented more than 4 per cent of the province's population (it was 3.9 per cent in 1948, but had dropped to 1.7 per cent in 1981). Montenegrins primarily settled in the region of Peć (Albanian: Peja) and the statistics almost certainly included those who left seeking better economic opportunities elsewhere in Yugoslavia. However, the authors argued that Serbs and Montenegrins were victims of an ethnic-Albanian policy of forced migration. While ostensibly an objective, detached demographic analysis, the language utilized by the authors lends it a highly emotive character. The study contains extensive interview data with those who had departed the province, including an interview with a 'Montenegrin mother of four', who said, 'I had hoped [our problems] would be resolved, that the Yugoslav authorities would do something ... The years went by, and nothing .... I lived, worked, loved, hoped for better days for my children ... [but eventually] I left behind a house and land for their safety. See Ruža Petrović & Marina Blagojević, *Seobe Srba i Crnogoraca sa Kosova i iz Metohije*, Srpska Akademija Nauka i Umetnosti (SANU), Beograd: Demografski Zbornik, 1988, p. 75.
25 *Tanjug Domestic Service (Belgrade)*, FBIS, *Daily Report* (Eastern Europe), FBIS-EEU-88-144, 27 July 1988.
26 *Politika*, Belgrade, 21 August 1988, p. 1.
27 For a critical analysis of the role of Šolević during the protests in Montenegro in 1988/89, see *Monitor*, Titograd, 19 October 1990, pp. 7–10.
28 Jovanović was born in Montenegro in 1922 and was one of a group of Montenegrin intellectuals who supported the view that Montenegrins were essentially Serbs. He is best known for his book on history of the 13 July Uprisings in Montenegro in 1941 (*Trinaesto julski ustanak*, Beograd: NIRO, 1984). His book focusing on Kosovo is entitled *Kosovo, inflacija, socijalne razlike*, Beograd: Partizanska knjiga, 1985; and two books within which he essentially negates the existence of distinct Montenegrin nation (though the latter is far more pronounced in that regard) are: *Crnogorci o sebi*, Beograd: Narodna knjiga, 1986, and *Rasrbljivanje crnogoraca – duhovni genocid*, Beograd: Srpska školska knjiga, 2003.
29 The terrace of the Hotel Crna Gora (which was built in 1953 and designed by the architect Vujadin Popović) was a short walk from the Montenegrin Assembly. It was (and remained until it was sold to the Hilton Hotels Group in 2012 and rebuilt) frequented by SKCG members and was a well-known location for political elites to

meet and discuss political matters. By the early 2000s, the terrace of the Hotel Crna Gora was no longer *the* place for political elites to gather, with cafés such as the 'Grand' and 'Maša' on Bulevar Svetog Petra becoming the new locations of choice.
30 *Politika*, Belgrade, 21 August 1988, p. 1. For Jovanović's views on the situation in Kosovo (forged, in part, by his engagement with the issue during his time as a member of the SFRJ parliament), see Batrić Jovanović, *Kosovo, inflacija, socijalne razlike*, Beograd: Partizanska knjiga, 1985.
31 See Koprovica & Vojičić, *Prevrat '89*, p. 59.
32 *Oslobodjenje*, Sarajevo, 20 September 1988, p. 2. The protestors also received support from a number of Serb-oriented Montenegrins, such as the poet and writer Matija Bećković. Born into a family of Montenegrins who resettled in Vojvodina, he was one of Montenegro's most famous post-war writers (alongside Montenegrin-born writers such as Miodrag Bulatović, Mirko Kovač, Borislav Pekić and Mihailo Lalić). In an interview with the Belgrade weekly *NIN* in June 1989, he stated that the protests and the solidarity with wider Serb cause represented a 'rehabilitation of Montenegro ... and a return to its authentic roots and origins'. See *NIN*, Belgrade, 9 July 1989, p. 3.
33 *Borba*, Belgrade, 26 September 1988, p. 3.
34 Parts of the SDB documentation pertaining to these operations can be found in Vladimir Keković, *25 godina poslije*, Podgorica: Crnogorska izdanja, 2014, pp. 55–107.
35 According to Nebojša Vladisavljević, the workers at Radoje Dakić had scheduled their own protests to begin on 12 October but, animated by the protests in Novi Sad, decided to bring the date forward to 7 October. See Nebojša Vladisavljević, *Serbia's Antibureaucratic Revolution: Milošević, the Fall of Communism and Nationalist Mobilization*, New York: Palgrave MacMillan, 2008, p. 160.
36 *Informator* (Radoje Dakić newspaper), October 1988, Titograd, No. 239, p. 1.
37 For a personal account of the events of October 1988 to January 1989, see Marko Orlandić, *U vrtlogu*, Podgorica: Montenegropublic, 1997, and Marko Orlandić, *O jednom vremenu i njegovim ljudima*, Podgorica: Montcarton, 2007.
38 For the thirteen key demands, see Koprovica & Vojičić, *Prevrat '89*, pp. 73–74.
39 According to Branka Magaš, nationalist slogans were commonplace at the 7 October protests. There were, she said, slogans such as: 'We want to work and earn our living!', 'We demand bread!'; 'We have had enough of waiting!'; 'Long live the LCY (League of Communists, Yugoslavia)'. By the evening, however, nationalist slogans became more frequent, which included: 'Long live the Serbian leadership!'; 'You have betrayed Slobodan Milošević – you have betrayed Serbdom!'; 'Who says Serbia is small', 'Slobodan, we are your soldiers – we shall kill or we shall die!' and 'Slobodan, you Serb son, when will you come to Cetinje?!' See Magaš, *Destruction of Yugoslavia*, p. 170.
40 Vladisavljević, *Serbia's Antibureaucratic Revolution*, p. 161.
41 Koprovica & Vojičić, *Prevrat '89*, p. 200.
42 This event was mythologized through both the Serbian media and the use of the *gusle*, the traditional musical instrument played by the Serbs (although its usage is not limited to Serbs). The Montenegrin gusle player, Vojo Radusinović, and the poet Žarko Šobić composed a piece called *Sumrak bogova kod Žute grede* (Twilight of the Gods at Žuta Greda). According to Žanić, 'the pro-Milošević media assigned the event almost mythic dimensions, turning it into a propaganda core for the preparation of a new, violent attempt to take power in Podgorica, which succeeded in January 1989'. See Ivo Žanić, *Flag on the Mountain: A Political Anthropology of War in Bosnia and Croatia*, London: Saqi Books, 2007, pp. 93–94.

43 Vladisavljević, *Serbia's Antibureaucratic Revolution*, p. 161.
44 Žanić, *Flag on the Mountain*, p. 101.
45 Andrijašević & Rastoder, *History of Montenegro*, p. 261.
46 Koprovica & Vojičić, *Prevrat '89*, p. 200. In an interview for the Belgrade daily *Borba* in November 1988, Dr Miljan Radović, the president of the SKCG Central Committee Presidium, acknowledged mistakes made at both Titograd and Žuta Greda. 'We all regret it now', he said, 'With the benefit of hindsight, many things could have been corrected and done better ... let us not forget that such measures were introduced in our country for the first time. I do not ask for an absolution of sins but for an understanding of the situation and the conduct in that situation.' See *Borba*, Belgrade, 19 November 1988, p. 5.
47 *Tanjug Domestic Service (Belgrade)*, FBIS, *Daily Report* (Eastern Europe), FBIS-EEU-88-196, 8 October 1988.
48 Vladisavljević, *Serbia's Antibureaucratic Revolution*, p. 162.
49 Koprovica & Vojičić, *Prevrat '89*, p. 162. See also *Tanjug Domestic Service (Belgrade)*, FBIS, *Daily Report* (Eastern Europe), FBIS-EEU-88-199, 13 October 1988.
50 *Tanjug Domestic Service (Belgrade)*, FBIS, *Daily Report* (Eastern Europe), FBIS-EEU-88-200, 14 October 1988.
51 *Tanjug Domestic Service (Belgrade)*, FBIS, *Daily Report* (Eastern Europe), FBIS-EEU-88-208, 27 October 1988.
52 *Pobjeda* (Titograd), 8 November 1988, p. 1.
53 Vladisavljević, *Serbia's Antibureaucratic Revolution*, p. 163.
54 *Pobjeda* (Titograd), 25 December 1988, p. 1.
55 *Pobjeda* (Titograd), 10 January 1989, pp. 1–3.
56 The Belgrade daily *Politika* provided a rather detailed report on these slogans. They included messages such as 'We shall persevere to the end!'; 'Bureaucrats: act according to the will of the people!'; 'Žuta Greda: Montenegro's Sorrow'; 'Think of the children and their future!'; 'We want the courageous and decisive!'; 'Had you listened to the people you would not have disgraced yourself!'; 'Long live Slobodan [Milošević], Freedom, Montenegro, Serbia and Yugoslavia!'; 'Resignations, that is the least we are demanding!'. The report also noted that 'Well known songs and those dedicated to Slobodan Milošević were also sung'. See *Politika*, Belgrade, 12 January 1989, p. 5.
57 See Koprovica & Vojičić, *Prevrat '89*, p. 258.
58 For more detail on the resignations and the post-resignation statements of, for example, Božina Ivanović and Veselin Djuranović, see *Borba*, Belgrade, 14 January 1989, p. 11. A special edition of the Montenegrin daily *Pobjeda*, published in the late afternoon of 11 January 1989, described the 'resignations in front of one hundred thousand people' as a triumph for the working classes and for reformist forces. See *Pobjeda* (Titograd), 11 January 1989, p. 1.
59 There were also sweeping changes within the upper echelons of the SDB. The Montenegrin SDB chief, Vladimir Keković, was forced out of the organization and replaced by Lazar Boričić.
60 Koprovica & Vojičić, *Prevrat '89*, p. 257. For Momir Bulatović's account of the 'January Coup' see Momir Bulatović, *Manje od igre – više od života*, Novi Sad: Književna zajednica novog sada, 1991, pp. 38–49.
61 Srdjan Darmanović, 'The Peculiarities of Transition in Serbia and Montenegro', in Dragica Vujadinovic et al. (eds.), *Between Authoritarianism and Democracy: Serbia, Montenegro, Croatia (Vol.1: Institutional Framework)*, Belgrade: CEDET, 2003, p. 153. Nebojša Vladisavljević also noted that there was a generational dynamic to the

political conflict within the SKCG. 'Many opponents of Montenegro's leaders were', he said, 'youthful, well-educated and spotless officials and the confrontation, inevitably, though perhaps unfairly, came to be seen as unfolding between the old guard, that is, an old-fashioned, clannish and ineffective party leadership, with little authority over the population, and those who represented the future of Montenegro'. See Vladisavljević, *Serbia's Antibureaucratic Revolution*, p. 164.

62 Darmanović, 'The Peculiarities of Transition in Serbia and Montenegro', p. 153.
63 Nebojša Čagorović, 'Montenegrin Identity: Past Present and Future', *Journal of Area Studies*, Vol. 1, No. 3 (1993), pp. 129–136. Others went further. In an interview for AS in September 1989, the Montenegrin writer Jevrem Brković questioned who was supporting the new leaders and singled out the Montenegrin academic Boško Gluščević, who, he implies, had close links to the Serbian intelligence services (though he refers to them as 'an invisible nucleus'). See Jevrem Brković, 'Crnogorci nijesu Srbi', AS, Titograd, September 1989 in Koprovica & Vojičić, *Prevrat '89*, pp. 338–339. See also
64 Andrijašević & Raštoder, *The History of Montenegro*, p. 261.
65 See Vladisavljević, *Serbia's Antibureaucratic Revolution*, pp. 165–166.
66 According to Veselin Pavičević, the new leadership of the SKCG were under pressure to formally open the process of political pluralism. Domestic and international factors – such as the activities of the Democratic Forum in Montenegro, the collapse of the Yugoslav League of Communists (SKJ) in January 1990 and (later) the 'domino effect of the fall of the Berlin wall' – determined that they must follow that path. See Veselin Pavičević, 'The Electoral System in Montenegro', in Dragica Vujadinovic et al. (eds.), *Between Authoritarianism and Democracy: Serbia, Montenegro, Croatia (Vol. 1: Institutional Framework)*, Belgrade: CEDET, 2003, p. 225.
67 Koprovica & Vojičić, *Prevrat '89*, p. 341. See also Darmanović, 'The Peculiarities of Transition in Serbia and Montenegro', p. 156.
68 Televizija Titograd merged with Radio Titograd to become *Radio televizija Crne Gore* (RTCG) in 1990. For a brief discussion on the merger, see Rajko Cerović, 'Televizija kao inspirator i izlog nacionalne kulture', *Matica*, Cetinje/Podgorica, Godina VI, broj 22/23, 2005, p. 14.
69 In June 1989, for example, the price of basic commodities rose again, with the price of bread increasing by another 50 per cent. See *Tanjug Domestic Service (Belgrade)*, FBIS, *Daily Report* (Eastern Europe), FBIS-EEU-89-108, 7 June 1989. In August 1989, the Presidium of the Montenegrin Trade Union Association made a public statement urging the new authorities to introduce price freezes on basic goods, lest there be 'social unrest of wider proportions that could have unforeseen consequences'. See *Borba*, Belgrade, 9 August 1989, p. 1.
70 Darmanović, 'The Peculiarities of Transition in Serbia and Montenegro', p. 155.
71 *Borba*, Belgrade, 21 August 1989, p. 3.
72 According to Stefano Bianchini, relations between Slovenia and Serbia had been steadily worsening for a long period prior to the January 1990 KPJ Congress. In essence, he said, 'The Slovenian elite increasingly blamed the redistribution of resources (jointly decided in Belgrade) for the underdeveloped regions and republics, by ambiguously identifying the Serbian and federal governments as the culprits'. Conversely, he noted, 'The intellectuals of the Serbian academy [SANU] vehemently criticised a supposed economic and cultural discrimination of the Serbs outside Serbia, while Milošević began to mobilise the Serbs against the leaderships of Kosovo, Vojvodina and Slovenia' [the author does not mention Montenegro].

See Stefano Bianchini, 'The Resurgence of Nationalism in Times of Crisis', in Srdja Pavlović & Marko Živković (eds.), *Transcending Fratricide: Political Mythologies, Reconciliations and the Uncertain Future in the Former Yugoslavia*, Baden-Baden: Nomos Verlagsgesellschaft, 2013, pp. 55–56.

73 *RFE/RL Report on Eastern Europe*, 22 November 1991, 27. In the same report, Milan Andrejevich notes that the change of leadership was perceived in some circles to represent a revival of the Montenegrin national movement of the late 1960s.

74 Roberts, *Realm of the Black Mountain*, p. 435.

75 Stanković resigned from the SKCG in February 1990, following the SKCG Titograd Communal Committee meeting, citing 'Intolerance and lack of readiness to discuss any different views or the possibility of transforming the SKCG'. He added, 'Almost the only reply to all views expressed so far has been to tell those people who disagree with the present situation that they should leave the SKCG. I am doing exactly that now.' See *Pobjeda*, Titograd, 6 February 1990, p. 3.
Darmanović left the SKCG in March 1990, stating that he was 'not prepared to agree to an alliance with what are obviously conservative political forces and groupings within the party and outside it'. See *Borba*, Belgrade, 23 March 1990, p. 4.

76 Pavičević, 'The Electoral System in Montenegro', p. 225.

77 The SKCG were accused by the parties that would emerge as their opponents as undermining their activities, including using the police to disrupt their rallies and tapping the phones of political rivals. See *Borba*, Belgrade, 5 December 1990, p. 3.

78 According to Veselin Pavičević, 'Broadly interpreting Paragraph 2 of Article 359 of the Socialist Republic of Montenegro's Constitution, the Assembly of the Republic, at a session held on July 11 1990, adopted the Law on Association of Citizens. This law legalized the already existing political parties and associations. The constitutional framework for the adopted legal provisions was supplied later on by constitutional amendments, which introduced radical changes into the existing authorized electoral system and the structure of the assemblies of the socio-political communities and the Presidency of the Republic'. 'This had to be done', he said, 'so that democratic, competitive elections could be held within a suitable structure of the legal political order. Thus the Basic Legal Act enabled the implementation of the multi-party elections for the one-house assembly with 125 members of parliament (MPs), who were elected by direct vote and by secret ballot in a multi-party system.' See Pavičević, 'The Electoral System in Montenegro', pp. 225–226.

79 *RFE/RL Report on Eastern Europe*, 22 November 1991, 27. See also *Monitor* (Titograd), 19 October 1990, p. 6.

80 Vladimir Goati, *The Party Systems of Serbia and Montenegro*, Belgrade: CEDET, 2000, p. 169.

81 According to Borisav Jović, the then Serbian representative in the Yugoslav Presidency and a close confidant of Milošević, in Montenegro he was 'relying on Kilibarda's People's Party', but was 'also counting on the communists [SKCG]'. He added that 'All are consulting him [Milošević] regarding their activities.' See Borisav Jović, *Poslednji dani SFRJ*, Beograd: Politika, 1995, p. 108.

82 A split within the ranks of the NS, however, led to the formation of the People's Democratic Party (*Narodna demokratska stranka* – NDS), a small party formed by more radical elements of the NS.

83 The Bosnian SDA was established in Sarajevo (the party's launch took place in the city's iconic Holiday Inn hotel) in March 1990. There were sister parties subsequently established in both Serbia and Montenegro (in the Sandžak region) led by Sulejman

Ugljanin and Harun Hadžić, respectively. See Kenneth Morrison & Elizabeth Roberts, *The Sandžak: A History*, London: Hurst & Co., 2013, pp. 134–139 and Milovan Djilas & Nadežda Gace, *The Bosniak*, London: Hurst & Co., 1998, pp. 135–145.
84 Questioned about the financing of the SKCG election campaign, Momir Bulatović brushed off accusations about the use of state funds for the SKCG campaign. Instead, he claimed, 'We established an enterprise and managed to earn the necessary funds on the market. We engaged several young and bright people'. He went on to say, 'In the present economic conditions, as we all know, trade and various specialist services produce results very quickly and pay off'. Bulatović did not provide further clarification on these creative means of funding. See *Borba*, Belgrade, 5 December 1990, p. 3.
85 *Borba*, Belgrade, 22 October 1990, p. 3.
86 A fascinating narrative (and equally fascinating photographs of the pre-election campaign) can be found in Bulatović, *Manje od igre – više od života*, 1991.
87 *Borba*, Belgrade, 5 December 1990, p. 3.
88 See *Monitor*, Titograd, 19 October 1990, pp. 10–11.
89 Vladimir Goati, *Elections in the FRY from 1990 to 1998: Will of the People or Electoral Manipulation?*, Belgrade: CESID, 2001, p. 204.
90 Ibid., p. 206.
91 *Pobjeda*, Titograd, 14 January 1991, p. 4.
92 *Pobjeda* Titograd, 17 January 1991, p. 1.
93 Veselin Vukotić, 'The Economic Situation and Economic Reforms in Montenegro', in Nicholas Whyte (ed.), *The Future of Montenegro: Proceedings of an Expert Meeting, 26 February 2001*, Brussels: CEPS Paperbacks, 2001, p. 45.
94 Popović, *Crnogorska alternativa*, pp. 12–13. Popović describes the period between 1989 and 1997 the 'first phase' of Montenegro's post-communist transition, which ended with the DPS split in 1997. See ibid and Milan Popović, *Montenegrin Mirror: Polity in Turmoil (1991–2001)*, Podgorica: Nansen Dilague Centre, 2002, pp. 11–12.
95 For an extensive (if rather dry) discussion of the future of the SFRJ and Montenegro's place within it, see Crnogorska akademija nauka i umjetnosti (CANU), *Novi ustav i preobražaji Jugoslovenskog društva: Radovi sa naučnoj skupa*, Titograd: CANU, 1991.

Chapter 3

1 *Borba* (Belgrade), 25 April 1990, p. 3.
2 *Tanjug Domestic Service* (Belgrade), 21 December 1990, FBIS, *Daily Report* (Eastern Europe), FBIS-EEU-90-250. The rebellion was staged by the Croatian branch of the Serbian Democratic Party (*Srpska demokratska stanka* – SDS), whose support was among rural Serbs, not among the majority of Serbs in Croatia that inhabited Croatian cities.
3 *Tanjug Domestic Service* (Belgrade), FBIS, *Daily Report* (Eastern Europe), FBIS-EEU-91-068, 8 April 1991.
4 A stone was, however, later thrown at Tudjman's car as he left Cetinje by a thirty-year-old Montenegrin citizen, Vasilije Djurišić, who was subsequently arrested by Montenegrin police. See *Tanjug Domestic Service* (Belgrade), FBIS *Daily Report* (Eastern Europe) FBIS-EEU-91-086, 3 May 1991.
5 *Tanjug Domestic Service* (Belgrade), FBIS, *Daily Report* (Eastern Europe), FBIS-EEU-91-089, 7 May 1991.

6   In this short chapter it is not possible to provide more of an analysis of the ill-considered Dubrovnik campaign beyond discussing the basic events/parameters. However, for a detailed analysis of the course of events that led to the Montenegrin/JNA attack on Dubrovnik, see Srdja Pavlović, 'Reckoning: The Siege of Dubrovnik and the Consequences of the "War for Peace"', *Spaces of Identity*, Vol. 5, No. 1, 2005, pp. 55–88. See also 'Final Report of the United Nations Commission of Experts Established Pursuant to Security Council Resolution 780: Annex XI.A – The Battle of Dubrovnik and the Law of Armed Conflict', S/1994/674/Add. 2 (Vol. V), 28 December 1994.
7   See Pavlović, 'Reckoning', p. 60.
8   According to Robin Harris, in his extensive history of Dubrovnik, Serbian intellectuals sought to make the case that Dubrovnik and that 'a cultural programme which stressed the "Serbian-ness" (*srpstvo*) of Dubrovnik was sponsored from Belgrade'. The fact that, he said, 'this ideological programme was espoused by some of the finest historians of Dubrovnik, such as Jorjo Tadić and Miroslav Pantić ... endowed it with an intellectual respectability which would otherwise have been lacking'. See Robin Harris, *Dubrovnik: A History*, London: SAQI Press, 2006, p. 421.
9   James Gow, *The Serbian Project and Its Adversaries*, London: Hurst & Co., 2003, p. 64.
10 Susan Woodward, *Balkan Tragedy: Chaos and Dissolution after the Cold War*, Washington DC: Brookings Institution, 1995, p. 269. See also Mile Bjelajac and Ozren Žunec, 'The War in Croatia, 1991–1995', in Charles Ingrao and Thomas A. Emmert (eds.), *Confronting the Yugoslav Controversies: A Scholars' Initiative*, West Lafayette, IN: Purdue University Press, 2009, pp. 231–270.
11 *Pobjeda* (Titograd), 5 September 1991, p. 1.
12 Pavlović, 'Reckoning'. See also Tanjug Domestic Service, 2 October 1991, FBIS, *Daily Report* (Eastern Europe), FBIS-EEU-91-192.
13 For excellent analyses of the role played by Pobjeda and RTCG respectively, see Živko Andrijašević, *Nacrt za ideologiju jedne vlasti*, Bar: Conteco, 1999 and Snežana Rakonjac, 'Mediji u službi rata – zaostavština TVCG', *Matica*, Podgorica, broj. 50, ljeto 2012, pp. 137–152.
14 Pobjeda and RTCG, the long-time political partners of the political establishment, became, even in the changed social circumstances – the so-called transition – an extended arm of the regime. Unaccustomed to free, critical opinion, public debate and truth, they were to become perfect instruments of political will in the critical period of Yugoslav disintegration. For an excellent analysis of the character of regional media in the early 1990s, see Mark Thompson, *Forging War: The Media in Serbia, Croatia and Bosnia-Hercegovina*, London: Article 19, 1994.
15 Andrijašević, *Nacrt za ideologiju jedne vlasti*, p. 95.
16 'We believed', said Marović, 'that history would never repeat itself, but life and historic tragedy are repeated. It is impossible to secure peace in any other way but with force.... it is sometimes necessary to control evil through greater force'. See *Pobjeda*, Titograd, 18 September 1991, p. 1.
17 Pavlović, 'Reckoning', p. 61.
18 According to Dragan Djurić, many of these recruits came from the lower social strata. They were, he said, 'impoverished, under-educated labour, without sufficient urban experience and civil tradition' and 'an ideal basis for manipulation'. See Dragan Djurić, *The Economic Development of Montenegro*, p. 139.
19 According to Pavlović, 'Mobilization was not proceeding smoothly in spite of the brave face the authorities were trying to put on. Frequent criticism of deserters and

pacifists in the media indicate that a considerable number of Montenegrins were reluctant to don a uniform and fight for an imaginary category such as the undying spirit of Serbdom.' See Pavlović, 'Reckoning', p. 62.

20 Interview with Milo Djukanović in Pobjeda (Titograd), 18 September 1991, quoted in Srdja Pavlović, in *Rat za mir* (Podgorica: Obala Production Company, 2004).

21 In the prevailing political climate it became extremely dangerous to be openly anti-war. According to Pavlović and Dragojević, 'Anti-war activities in Montenegro in the early 1990s were few and far between. Activists had limited resources and insufficient organisational capabilities. The relentless pressure exerted by the government and security services upon those who voiced their disapproval of official policies was the greatest obstacle anti-war activists had to overcome'. As a consequence, they noted, different anti-war groups 'never cooperated in organising even one major anti-war protest. See Srdja Pavlović & Milica Dragojević, 'Peaceniks and Warmongers: Anti-War Activism in Montenegro, 1989–1995', in Bojan Bilić and Vesna Janković (eds.), *Resisting the Evil: Post-Yugoslav Anti-War Contention*, Baden-Baden: Nomos Verlagagesellschaft, 2012, p. 146.

22 According to Frantisek Šištek and Bodhana Dimitrivova, the Croatian leadership in Zagreb showed little interest in the issue of Croats in Montenegro. There was, they said, 'little interest in Croatia in the position of Montenegro's Croats' and that 'even during the nationalist rule of President Franjo Tudjman, there were no attempts politically to instrumentalise the issue of Croats in the Boka, let alone to raise territorial demands'. See Frantisek Šištek and Bodhana Dimitrivova, 'National Minorities in Montenegro after the Break-Up of Yugoslavia', in Florian Bieber (ed.), *Montenegro in Transition: Problems of Identity and Statehood*, Baden-Baden: Nomos Verlagsgesellschaft, 2003, p. 174.

23 The term *crnolatinaši* was also used as a derogatory slur to describe members of the LSCG and pro-independence Montenegrins such as the writer, Jevrerm Brković. They were denounced as 'Red Croats', who supported the thesis of Savić Marković Štedimlija that posited that Montenegrins were in fact Croats and once of the Catholic faith.

24 See Andrijašević, *Nacrt za ideologiju jedne vlasti*, pp. 197–198.

25 See Janusz Bugajski, *Ethnic Politics in Eastern Europe*, London: M.E. Sharpe, 1995, p. 189. The Boka Mariners Association had, according to Ivo Žanić, 'no military dimension whatsoever' and its origins lay 'in the maritime fraternities that existed in medieval times throughout Europe in cities with developed maritime commerce, such as Kotor, Tivat, Perast and other towns in the Boka'. See Žanić, *Flag on the Mountain*, pp. 474–475.

26 Bugajski, *Ethnic Politics in Eastern Europe*, p. 175.

27 Skupština Republike Crne Gore: Služba za informativno-dokumentalističke poslove (YU:ISSN 0544–9111), Stenografske bilješke (8. Sjednica skupštine Republike Crne Gore, 20 September 1991) in Helsinki odbor za ljudska prava u Srbiju, *Rat za mir*, Belgrade: Biblioteka svedočanstva, 2006, p. 253.

28 Ibid., p. 251.

29 Snežana Rakonjac, 'Mediji u službi rata – zaostavština TVCG', *Matica*, Podgorica, broj 50, ljeto 2012, p. 141.

30 *Pobjeda* (Titograd), 1 October 1991, p. 1.

31 Gow, *The Serbian Project and Its Adversaries*, p. 53.

32 'Final Report of the United Nations Commission of Experts Established Pursuant to Security Council Resolution 780: Annex XI.A – The Battle of Dubrovnik and the

Law of Armed Conflict', S/1994/674/Add. 2 (Vol. V), 28 December 1994, p. 11. The mayor of Trebinje (and close associate of Radovan Karadžić), Božidar Vučirević, the man who would (in 1992) initiate the expulsion of Muslims from the town and the destruction of Islamic heritage in it, had something of an aversion to Dubrovnik. See Žanić, *Flag on the Mountain,* pp. 254–255.

33 Neum, Bosnia & Herzegovina's only coastal town, was tense during the bombing of Dubrovnik. Many of the hotels and private houses in the town received refugees from Trebinje and Dubrovnik.

34 UN ICTY, 'The Prosecutor v Pavle Strugar, Miodrag Jokić and Vladimir Kovačević (Amended indictment)', Case No. IT-01-42, 31 March 2003, p. 4.

35 *Pobjeda* (Titograd), 2 October, 1991, p. 2. See also Helsinki odbor za ljudska prava u Srbiju, *Rat za mir* (Belgrade: Biblioteka svedočanstva, 2006), p. 628.

36 'Final Report of the United Nations Commission of Experts Established Pursuant to Security Council Resolution 780: Annex XI.A – The Battle of Dubrovnik and the Law of Armed Conflict', S/1994/674/Add. 2 (Vol. V), 28 December 1994, p. 12.

37 *Pobjeda* (Titograd), 9 October 1991, p. 1. For these claims and other interviews with Montenegrin volunteers on the Dubrovnik front see the documentary film 'Rat za Mir', Director: Koča Pavlović, Podgorica: Obala Productions, 2004.

38 Srdja Pavlović, 'Morinj Camp and the Art of Reconciliation in Montenegro', in Srdja Pavlović & Marko Živković (eds.), *Transcending Fratricide: Political Mythologies, Reconciliations and the Uncertain Future in the Former Yugoslavia,* Baden-Baden: Nomos Verlagsgesellschaft, 2013, p. 216. For filmed excerpts of interviews with some of those interned, see 'Rat za Mir', Director: Koča Pavlović, Podgorica: Obala Productions, 2004.

39 *Pobjeda* (Titograd), 3 October 1991, p. 1.

40 Skupština Republike Crne Gore: Služba za informativno-dokumentalističke poslove (YU:ISSN 0544–9111), Stenografske bilješke (8. Sjednica skupštine Republike Crne Gore, 20 September 1991) in Helsinki odbor za ljudska prava u Srbiju, *Rat za mir,* Belgrade: Biblioteka svedočanstva, 2006, p. 267.

41 Ibid., pp. 277–281.

42 *Pobjeda* (Titograd), 21 October 1991, p. 1.

43 Florian Bieber, 'Montenegrin Politics Since the Disintegration of Yugoslavia', in Florian Bieber (ed.), *Montenegro in Transition: Problems of Identity and Statehood,* Baden-Baden: Nomos Verlagsgesellschaft, 2003, p. 18.

44 In addition to being the base for many international journalists, the Hotel Argentina was also home to the European Community Monitoring Mission (ECMM) delegation.

45 See, for example, Tim Judah, *The Serbs: History, Myth and the Destruction of Yugoslavia,* New York: Yale NB, 2000, and Alec Russell, *Prejudice and Plum Brandy,* London: Michael Joseph, 1993.

46 Indeed, Slavko Perović rejected the use of violence, regardless of the cause. According to Nebojša Čagorović, 'At anti-war rallies where supporters were chanting their readiness to become martyrs for their cause, the leader of the Liberal Alliance, Slavko Perović, implored them to reject these notions. He told them that the new times required Montenegrins to embrace European values and not their ancient war-like traditions' See Nebojša Čagorović, 'Anti-Fascism and Montenegrin Identity Since 1990', *History,* 2012, pp. 578–590.

47 There were, despite the dangerous environment in which they were operating, groups vocally against the war. Aside from the anti-war parties (of which the LSCG was

foremost), these tended to be small groups with little organizational capacity – many of them comprising academics and students. For an excellent analysis of the activities and roles of these groups, see Pavlović & Dragojević, 'Peaceniks and Warmongers'.
48 See 'Final Report of the United Nations Commission of Experts Established Pursuant to Security Council Resolution 780: Annex XI.A – The Battle of Dubrovnik and the Law of Armed Conflict,' S/1994/674/Add.2 (Vol. V), 28 December 1994, pp. 142–144.
49 The former SFRJ president (and Milošević ally) Borisav Jović was asked by the acting US secretary of state Laurence Eagleburger about the shelling of Dubrovnik; he replied: 'I said that Dubrovnik had not been shelled and this was a case of completely unfounded propaganda, except in the case where two shells were fired by mistake. L. Eagleburger agreed that there had been strong propaganda, pointing out that the mayor of Dubrovnik [Petar Polanjić] visited Washington and showed pictures depicting the damage to the city. I repeated [that] the Old City had not been damaged and that it was untrue that Dubrovnik had been attacked. Everything that happened in connection with that has been pure propaganda.' See Jović, *Poslednji dani SFRJ*, p. 246.
50 *Večernje Novosti* (Belgrade), 21 October 1991, p. 3.
51 *Pobjeda* (Podgorica), 16 December 1992, p. 4.
52 Bugajski, *Ethnic Politics in Eastern Europe*, p. 175.
53 *Borba*, Belgrade, 9 December 1991, p. 11.
54 Interview with Momir Bulatović, 7 October 1994, 'Death of Yugoslavia Archive', Roll 75E, No. 124, p. 9.
55 Speech by Milo Djukanović in 'Rat za mir', Obala Productions (Dir: Koča Pavlović), Podgorica, 2004.
56 Interview with Lord Carrington, 4 January 1995, 'Death of Yugoslavia Archive', Roll 73E, U-BIT, No. 121.
57 Interview with Gianni De-Michelis, 17 June 1994, 'The Death of Yugoslavia Archive', Roll 71E, U-BIT No. 34, p. 7.
58 Bulatović recalled that the night before he had flow to The Hague, the meetings in the Montenegrin Assembly were long and did not produce a clear outcome. 'In the Montenegrin parliament', he said, 'the president sits very near the floor and can see you every moment, even shade of feeling on the faces of the people who were criticizing or praising you. I knew that I had to fly to The Hague at 6.00 am in the morning, the session was continuing well into the night and I was wondering why I had to listen to all of these arguments, because I had spent hours considering every possible element of that plan, and then you must sit and hear people accuse you of being a traitor, of being an amateur diplomat, but that's what you had to do. You had to listen to all [of] these speeches and I think that the best way was to take all the responsibility on myself and to say what Montenegro really wanted.' See interview with Momir Bulatović, 7 October 1994, 'Death of Yugoslavia Archive', Roll 75E, No. 124, p. 9.
59 Slobodan Vučetić, 'Serbia and Montenegro: From Federation to Confederation', in D. Vujadinović et al. (eds.), *Between Authoritarianism and Democracy: Serbia, Montenegro and Croatia, Vol.1 Institutional Framework*, Beograd: CEDET, 2003, p. 73. Bulatović's decision didn't come as complete surprise to the Serbian leadership. Borisav Jović was informed on 18 October 1992, the day before The Hague Conference, by Branko Kostić. See Jović, *Poslednji dani SFRJ*, p. 229.
60 *Tanjug Domestic Service (Belgrade)*, FBIS, *Daily Report* (Eastern Europe), FBIS-EEU-14-152, 21 October 1991. For his own overview of events in Montenegro

throughout the 1990s (including the controversy generated by Bulatović's acceptance of the Carrington Plan) see Gavro Perazić, *Kuda ide Crna Gora*, Beograd: Versal Press, 1999.

61 In his memoirs, Borisav Jović noted that Montenegro's position was made clear to him on 18 October, one day prior to The Hague Conference. 'In Branko Kostić's office, before he left for Titograd to attend the session of the Montenegrin Assembly to take up the same question, suddenly and without hesitation tells me that, "Montenegro will support Lord Carrington's proposal!." I look at him in disbelief, as if he is fooling around. I tell him to stop joking. Very seriously, he repeats what he has just said. I told him that that would be a highly treacherous knife in the back of Serbia and its leadership.' See Jović, *Poslednji dani SFRJ*, p. 229.

62 Bulatović acknowledged how tough it was to sell The Hague proposals to DPS members in Ivangrad (Berane), a town he described as one 'with a very powerful political tradition' with 'close links to Serbia and Serbdom'. See Momir Bulatović, *Pravila ćutanja*, Belgrade: Alfa Press, 2005, pp. 82, 83.

63 Ibid., p. 83.

64 Ibid., p. 82.

65 Interview with Momir Bulatović, 7 October 1994, 'Death of Yugoslavia Archive,' Roll 75E, U-BIT, No.124.

66 Ibid., p. 9.

67 Jović, *Poslednji dani SFRJ*, p. 233.

68 Bulatović, *Pravila Ćutanja*, p. 83.

69 Final Report of the United Nations Commission of Experts Established Pursuant to Security Council Resolution 780: Annex XI.A – The Battle of Dubrovnik and the Law of Armed Conflict', S/1994/674/Add. 2 (Vol. V), 28 December 1994, pp. 14–15.

70 For the events of 5 and 6 April 1992 in Sarajevo, see Kenneth Morrison, *Sarajevo's Holiday Inn on the Frontline of Politics and War*, London: Palgrave MacMillan, 2016, pp.103–115.

71 Vučetić, 'Serbia and Montenegro: From Federation to Confederation', p. 73.

72 Lenard Cohen, *Serpent in the Bosom: The Rise and Fall of Slobodan Milošević*, Boulder, CO: Westview Press, 2001, p. 163.

73 The content of the Montenegrin leadership's initial proposal in January 1992 was remodelled following a meeting between the Serbian delegation (Slobodan Milošević, Borisav Jović, Radoman Božović and Aleksandar Bakočević) and its Montenegrin counterpart (Branko Kostić, Momir Bulatović and Milo Djukanović) held in Podgorica on 5 February 1992. See Bulatović, *Pravila ćutanja*, pp. 92–93.

74 Robert Thomas, *Serbia under Milošević: Politics in the 1990s*, London: Hurst & Co., 1999, p. 120.

75 A number of Montenegrin writers went into exile in the early 1990s. Jevrem Brković was forced to leave Montenegro in 1991. An early supporter of Slobodan Milošević and a personal acquaintance of the leader of the Serbian Democratic Party (*Srpska demokratska stranka* – SDS) in Bosnia & Herzegovina, Radovan Karadžić, and the Montenegrin Serb poet, Matija Bećković, he later 'converted' to become one of the leading advocates of Montenegro's independence. Dubbed an *Ustaša* by Serb-oriented Montenegrins, his life threatened as a consequence, he fled to Zagreb. Milorad Popović, the Montenegrin writer and anti-war campaigner, was also forced to leave, while Mirko Kovač, the Belgrade-based poet and essayist, who had consistently been critical of the policies of the Milošević government gradually became persona non grata and chose to leave his home in Belgrade in 1992 for a life in exile in Rovinj,

Croatia (he later became a Croatian citizen). For Kovač's views on both, see *Monitor* (Titograd), 19 October 1990, pp. 18–21. For Brković's views on Montenegrin politics seen from the perspective of exile see *Monitor* (Podgorica), 23 December 1994, pp. 20–23.

76 *Monitor* (Titograd), 7 February 1992, p. 9. For a personal (and insider) account of the LSCG's operations throughout this period, see Ranko Djonović, *Ne pristajem! Vrijeme časti i beščašća u Crnoj Gori (1989–2013)*, Podgorica: Art Gloria, 2013.
77 Banners carried at the rally included one declaring *Crnogorci ne jedu svoje korijenje!* (Montenegrins do not eat their roots!) – a play on Branko Kostić's statement that 'Montenegrins would rather eat roots' than bow to foreign pressure. See ibid., p. 9.
78 *Politika* (Belgrade), 3 February 1992, p. 6.
79 *Monitor* (Titograd), 7 February 1992, 7.
80 *Liberal* was first published in 1990 and initially as either a monthly or fortnightly magazine. It later became (from 1994) a weekly magazine. Many of the journalists who wrote for *Monitor* also contributed to *Liberal*.
81 Koprivica was one of the key organizers (and funders) of the removal and internment of King Nikola I Petrović's remains in Cetinje in September 1989 (see Chapter 1).
82 Pavlović & Dragojević, 'Peaceniks and Warmongers', p. 155
83 *Monitor* (Titograd), 14 February 1992, p. 7.
84 *Monitor* (Titograd), 14 February, p. 7.
85 Vučetić, 'Serbia and Montenegro: From Federation to Confederation', p. 74.
86 *Politika* (Belgrade), 15 February 1992, p. 7.
87 Geert-Hinrich Ahrens, *Diplomacy on the Edge: Containment of Ethnic Conflict and the Minorities Working Group of the Conferences on Yugoslavia*, Baltimore, MD: The John Hopkins University Press, 2007, p. 212.
88 *Monitor* (Titograd), 14 February 1992, p. 6.
89 *Pobjeda* (Titograd), 12 March 1992, p. 5.
90 *Pobjeda* (Titograd), 3 February 1992, p. 3.
91 *Pobjeda* (Podgorica), 12 March 1992, p. 5.
92 *Borba* (Belgrade), 31 March 1992, p. 5. There were other changes unrelated to the Žabljak Constitution. On 1 April 1992, the Montenegrin Assembly voted to change the name of the Montenegrin capital Titograd (which had been formally named thus on 13 July 1946 in honour of Josip Broz Tito) back to its original name, 'Podgorica'. A week later the northern Montenegrin town of Ivangrad reverted to its original name, 'Berane', after a vote by the town's municipal assembly.
93 Of course, Montenegrin nationalists, who advocated an independent Montenegrin state, did not simply disappear. Many channelled their energies not through political parties but through cultural organizations such as the Montenegrin PEN Centre, formed in 1991, by Montenegrin writers who wished to challenge the dominant Serb nationalist discourse in Montenegro. In 1993, *Crnogorska Matica* (Montenegrin Matica) was formed. Members of the latter were 'committed to preserving the cultural and historical identity of Montenegro' and, equally, committed to the re-establishment of Montenegrin state (and autocephalous church) and the recognition of the Montenegrin language as separate from Serbian. See Montenegrin Matica, 'The Program of Montenegrin Matica', Cetinje, 1999 and Matica Crnogorska, 'Crnogorski kao maternji jezik', *Godišnjak 1999–2003*, MCG: Cetinje.
94 UN ICTY Press Release, 'Dubrovnik Indictment', The Hague, 2 October 2002, Doc. No. S.P/P.I.S/625. See also UN ICTY, 'The Prosecutor v Pavle Strugar, Miodrag Jokić and Vladimir Kovačević (Amended indictment)', Case No. IT-01-42, 31 March 2003.

Chapter 4

1. The data from the 1991 census has to be treated with some scepticism. According to Frantisek Šištek & Bodhana Dimitrova, 'The 1991 census, carried out in atmosphere of nationalist tensions, did not precisely reflect the real situation and somewhat under-represented the number of minorities.' See Šištek & Dimitrivova, 'National Minorities in Montenegro after the Break-Up of Yugoslavia', p. 159, fn.3.
2. Montenegro's Muslims (and Slavic Muslims throughout Yugoslav territory were identified as 'Muslim' until 1993. In a meeting at Sarajevo's (besieged) Holiday Inn hotel – the *Drugi Bošnjački sabor* (The Second Bosniak Congress), Muslim intellectuals and representatives from Muslim organizations agreed that the term *Bošnjaci* (Bosniak) was the most appropriate replacement for the term *Muslimani* (Muslims). However, the debates over which name to use were more pronounced in Montenegro than in other former Yugoslav republics. Thus, the author uses the term 'Muslim' until September 1993 and then 'Muslim/Bosniak' thereafter. For the dynamics of the debate, see Šerbo Rastoder, 'Muslimani/Bošnjački, kako vam ime?', *Almanah*, broj 23–24, 2003. (The entire edition is dedicated to these debates.) See also Bodhana Dimitrovova, 'Bosniak or Muslim? Dilemma of One Nation with Two Names', *Southeast European Politics*, Vol. II, No. 2, October 2001, pp. 94–108.
3. In 1991, there were five municipalities in the Montenegrin portion of the Sandžak (Berane, Bijelo Polje, Plav, Pljevlja and Rožaje) and six in the Serbian part of the Sandžak (Nova Varoš, Novi Pazar, Priboj, Prijepolje, Sjenica and Tutin). Plav and Gusinje were not part of the 'Sandžak of Novi Pazar' but the *Sandžak of Scutari*. Pljevlja was part of the Sandžak of Novi Pazar until 1880, when it became part of the *Pljevlski Sandžak* (Sandžak of Pljevlja). For a broad historical overview of the history of the area, see Morrison & Roberts, *The Sandžak,* and Harun Crnovršanin & Nuro Sadiković, *Sandžak: Porobljena zemlja: Bosna, Sandžak i Kosovo kroz historiju*, Frankfurt: Sandžačka riječ, 2002.
4. See, for example, Aleksandar Zeković, 'Primjeri diskriminacije Bošnjaka/Muslimana u Crnoj Gori', *Almanah*, broj 29–30, Podgorica, 2005, p. 271.
5. Banac, *The National Question in Yugoslavia*, p. 277.
6. Mehmedalija Bojić, *Historija Bosne i Bošnjaka*, pp. 502–503.
7. Milovan Djilas, *Land without Justice*, New York: Harcourt, Brace & Co., 1958, p. 207.
8. For a reassessment of these events, see Redžep Škrijelj, 'Osam i po decenija od zločina u Šahoviću i Vranešu', *Bošnjačka riječ,* Novi Pazar, 2009, godine IV, broj 13–16, January 2009, pp. 130–145.
9. See, for example, Redžep Škrijelj, 'Sandžački Bošnjacu u Makedoniji', in Internacionalni univerzitet u Novom Pazaru, *Sandžak juče, danas i sutra*, Novi Pazar, 2005, pp. 245–282. For the events in Šahovići in 1924, see Šerbo Rastoder, *Šahovići 1924: Kad su vakat kaljani insani*, Podgorica: Almanah, 2011; and Djilas, *Land without Justice*, pp. 204–213.
10. For historical 'justifications' for Sandžak's incorporation into the NDH and any subsequent Croatian state, see Miljenko Dabo-Peranić, *Hrvatsko Sandžaka*, Madrid: Drina, 1966.
11. For an intimate account of the Battle of Pljevlja in November (and the subsequent 'mistakes of the left'), see Djilas, *Wartime.*
12. For a detailed analysis of the structure of ZAVNOS, their creation and their dissolution, see Lakić, *Partizanska autonomija Sandžaka, 1934–1945*. For a personal account, see Mirko Ćuković, *Sandžak u narodnooslobodilačkoj borbi*, Belgrade, 1964.

13 Plav, Gusinje and Berane were not part of ZAVNOS's nominal territory – they fell under the territory of the Land Assembly for the National Liberation of Montenegro and Boka (*Zemaljsko antifašističko vijeće narodnog oslobodjenja Crne Gore i Boke* – ZANVOCGB), established in the Montenegrin town of Kolašin in November 1943. Its name was later changed, in June 1944, to the Montenegrin Anti-Fascist Assembly of National Liberation (*Crnogorska antifašistička skupština narodnog oslobodjenja* – CASNO).
14 For a detailed study on the religiosity of Yugoslavia's Muslims during the existence of the SFRJ, see Tone Bringa, *Being Muslim the Bosnian Way*, Upper Saddle River, NJ: Princeton University Press, 1995.
15 For Muslim identity in the context of the SFRJ, see Lily Hamourziadou, 'The Bosniaks: From Nation to Threat', *Journal of Southern Europe and the Balkans*, Vol. 4, No. 2, November 2002, pp. 141–156.
16 For a broad history of the Plav-Gusinje region, see Mustafa Memić, *Gusinjsko-Plavska krajina u vrtlogu historije*, Sarajevo: University of Sarajevo, 2008.
17 Sandžački odbor za zaštitu ljudskih prava i sloboda, *Prava manjina u multietničkim sredinama u Sandžaku*, Novi Pazar, 2006, p. 9. See also, Murat Kahrović, *Bošnjaci Sandžaka u odbrani Bosne: 1992–1995*, Sarajevo: Udruženje gradjana porijeklom iz Sandžaka u FBiH, 2006, p. 176. See also Andrijašević, *Nacrt za ideologiju jedne vlasti*, and, for an excellent analysis of the nationalist rhetoric within the print media in the SFRJ, see Thompson, *Forging War*.
18 Sandžački odbor za zaštitu ljudskih prava i sloboda, *Prava manjina u multietničkim sredinama u Sandžaku*, p. 9.
19 *Pobjeda* (Titograd), 15 January 1989, p. 3.
20 *Pobjeda* (Titograd), 26 January 1989, p. 3.
21 *Pobjeda* (Titograd), 27 January 1989, p. 7.
22 *Pobjeda* (Titograd), 29 January 1998, p. 11.
23 For the key demands of the MNVS, see Muslimansko nacionalno vijeće Sandžaka (MNVS), 'Sanjak and Sanjak Muslims', Novi Pazar, December. 1991. See also Muslimansko nacionalno vijeće Sandžaka (MNVS), 'Resolution: 28 April 1992, Novi Pazar, Doc. No. 54/92.
24 The president of the MNVS was Sulejman Ugljanin; the vice president was Harun Hadžić.
25 For more detail on the referendum, see Morrison & Roberts, *The Sandžak*, pp. 139–144; for a detailed analysis of the arguments of those advocating autonomy for the Sandžak, see Aleksander Zdravkovski, *Politics, Religion and the Autonomy Movement in Sandžak*, NTNU Doctoral Thesis, February 2017.
26 For an Albanian perspective on the arguments over Plav and Gusinje, see Idriz Lamaj, *Diplomatic Reports Relating to Albanian-Montenegrin Conflict over Plava and Gucia*, New York (Self Published), 1999.
27 *Politika* (Belgrade), 3 February 1992, p. 7. Montenegrin politicians also entered the fray. According to Radončić, Novak Kilibarda, the leader of NS, was one of those Montenegrin intellectuals whose task was 'to spread and foster hatred of Muslims and Croats in Montenegro'. See Šeki Radončić, *A Fatal Freedom*, Belgrade: Humanitarian Law Center, 2006, p. 9.
28 *Monitor* (Podgorica), 15 February 1992, p. 5. The NS allegedly had its own paramilitary units with 'several hundred men under arms'. See Bugajski, *Ethnic Politics in Eastern Europe*, p. 183.
29 Dimitrovova, 'Bosniak or Muslim? Dilemma of One Nation with Two Names', p. 98.

30 For a detailed analysis of the ethnic cleansing in the Drina River valley, see Edina Bećirević, *Genocide on the Drina River*, New Haven, CT and London: Yale University Press, 2014, pp. 83–143.
31 See *Tanjug Domestic Service (Belgrade)*, FBIS, *Daily Report* (Eastern Europe), FBIS-EEU-92-111, 5 June 1992. See also Safet Bandžović, *Otmice u Sandžaku (1992–1993)*, Novi Pazar: Sandžački odbor za zaštitu ljudskih prava i sloboda, 1996, pp. 13–14.
32 Milan Andrijevich, 'Sandžak: A Perspective on Serb–Muslim Relations', in Hugh Poulton and Suha Taji-Farouki (eds.), *Muslim Identity and the Balkan State*, London: Hurst & Co., 1997, p. 187.
33 See, for example, Miodrag Todorov Bojović, 'Pljevaljski musmimani/bošnjaci izemđu stvarnosti i iluzije', *Almanah*, broj 27–28, Podgorica, 2004, p. 254.
34 Although many of the worst acts of intimidation were carried out by Serbian and Montenegrin paramilitary groups, most specifically the elite unit *Beli orlovi* (White Eagles), there were also Muslim *Zelene beretke* (Green Berets) operating in the town.
35 The SRS were a constant thorn in the side of the Montenegrin authorities. According to Bugajski, the SRS 'established as "Serbian Council of Zeta" in an area of Montenegro where the twelfth-century state had been forged by tribal leaders; it proposed the creation of autonomous Serbian regions in Boka, Pljevlja and Zeta; it engaged in anti-Muslim attacks in the Sandžak area and it attempted to stimulate conflicts with the Muslim and Albanian minorities by depicting these groups as anti-Montenegrin separatists'. The SRS, he goes on, 'were also intent on capitalizing on social disquiet against deteriorating economic conditions; there were indications that its leaders were in favour of a second "anti-bureaucratic revolution" to unseat the Bulatović administration'. See Bugajski, *Ethnic Politics in Eastern Europe*, pp. 184–185.
36 Bojović, 'Pljevaljski musmimani/bošnjaci izemđu stvarnosti i iluzije', p. 254.
37 Vreme News Digest Agency, No. 48, August 1992.
38 Bukovica encompasses a number of mountain villages including Kovačevići, Borošići, Planjska, Bunguri, Ravni, Klakorina, Stražice, Cejrence and Rosulje among other smaller settlements. It accounts for almost a third of the population of the Pljevlja municipality. See Humanitarian Law Center, *Spotlight on Human Rights Violations in Times of Armed Conflict*, Belgrade: Humanitarian Law Center, 1995, p. 22.
39 Helsinki Committee for Human Rights, *Montenegro: Human Rights Practices 1993*, Belgrade, 1993, p. 10.
40 Andrijevich, 'Sandžak: A Perspective on Serb–Muslim Relations', p. 188. See also *Vreme*, Belgrade, 7 June 1993, p. 29.
41 See Bulatović, *Pravila Ćutanja*, p. 89.
42 Andrijevich, 'Sandžak: A Perspective on Serb–Muslim Relations', p. 188.
43 *Pobjeda* (Podgorica), 2 August 1992, p. 3.
44 Tanjug, Belgrade, 27 July 1992, in 'Daily Report: Eastern Europe', FBIS-EEU-92-145.
45 For a snapshot of life in Pljevlja during the summer of 1992, see *Monitor* (Podgorica), 7 August 1992, pp. 6–7. In the same edition of the magazine, the journalist Rajko Cerović wrote an open letter to the mayor of Pljevljia, Momčilo Bojović, in which he appealed to him to take action (while criticizing him for inaction) to stop Muslims, a community that were an integral part of the fabric of the town, leaving Pljevlja. See ibid., p. 9.
46 Nazim Ličina, 'Sjećaš li se Bukovice?', *Bošnjačka riječ*, Novi Pazar, godine II, broj 8, Oktobar–decembar 2007, pp. 19–20.
47 *Vreme*, Belgrade, 17 May 1993, p. 35. For a detailed account of events in Štrpci see, Ramiz Crnišanin, *Sandžak izmedju Srbije i Crne Gore*, pp. 219–222; Bandžović,

Otmice u Sandžku (1992–1993), pp. 15–63; and Humanitarian Law Center, *Otmica u Štrpcima: analiza, sudjena za ratni zločin – Činjenice, pravna pitanja i političke implikacije*, Belgrade: Humanitarian Law Center, February 2003.
48   See UN-ICTY Case No. IT-98-32/1-T, 'The Prosecutor v. Milan Lukić and Sredoje Lukić' (Prosecution final trial brief), 12 May 2009. See also YIHR, *War Crimes in Serbia: Sandžak Case*, February 2010, p. 4.
49   See Humanitarian Law Center, *Nestanci: Otmice Muslimana iz Srbije i Crne Gore u vreme oružanuh sukoba BH*, Izveštaj , broj 22, May 1996, pp. 9–11. See also *Monitor* (Podgorica), 9 August 1996, pp. 8–11.
50   Interview with Nikola Pejaković broadcast on Radio Televizja Crne Gore (RTCG), FBIS Daily Report Eastern Europe, FBIS-EEU-92-155, 11 August 1992.
51   *Monitor* (Podgorica), 25 September 1992, p. 11.
52   UN Economic and Social Council, 'Report on the situation of human rights in the territory of the Federal Republic of Yugoslavia: Submitted by Mr. Tadeusz Mazowiecki, Special Rapporteur of the Commission on Human Rights', E/CN.4/1993/50, 10 February 1993, p. 39. See also *Monitor* (Podgorica), 11 June 1993, p. 16.
53   Vojvoda means 'military commander' in Serbian tradition. It has also been used to denote a governor of a province.
54   Šeki Radončić, 'Iza maske: tajna ratovi u tajnoj policiji', Montenegrina: digitalna biblioteka crnogorske culture, http://montenegrina.net/pages/pages1/istorija/cg_od_1990/tajni_ratovi_u_tajnoj_policiji.htm [last accessed 27 June 2016].
55   *Vreme* (Belgrade), 7 June 1993, p. 29. For a description of the experience of Muslims living in Nikšić during this period see *Monitor* (Podgorica), 7 May 1993, p. 23.
56   Šeki Radončić, 'Iza maske: tajna ratovi u tajnoj policiji', Montenegrina: digitalna biblioteka crnogorske culture, http://montenegrina.net/pages/pages1/istorija/cg_od_1990/tajni_ratovi_u_tajnoj_policiji.htm [last accessed 27 June 2016].
57   See *Monitor* (Podgorica), 12 August 1992, pp. 10–11.
58   For a detailed account of these arrests and deportations, see Radončić, *A Fatal Freedom*. See also Alen Drljević's documentary film *Karneval* (Carnival) based on Šeki Radončić's book *Kobna Sloboda* (A Fatal Freedom), Sarajevo: Mediacentar, 2006. Srdja Pavlović points out that while the book and documentary present 'valuable narratives of pain and suffering', the author 'absolves the war-time Prime Minister, Milo Djukanović, of any criminal or political responsibility'. Radončić, claims Pavlović, thus 'tried his best to locate the culprit for the crime of deportation outside the war-time structures of power'. See Srdja Pavlović, 'Morinj Camp and the Art of Reconciliation in Montenegro', p. 224, fn32.
59   Pavle Bulatović entered politics in 1988 at the time of the 'anti-bureaucratic revolution' in Montenegro. He had worked as an assistant lecturer in the Faculty of Economics at the University of Montenegro in Titograd (Podgorica), but had become involved in the anti-government protests in October 1988. In the wake of the 'January Coup' in 1989, Bulatović was given the post of interior minister, and during his first months in the job he embarked upon a purge of the police and the SDB. He made little secret of the fact that he supported the objectives of the Serbs in Croatia, Kosovo and Bosnia & Herzegovina. See *Bosnia Report*, No.15/16, London, March–June 2000.
60   For a detailed biography of Radovan Karadžić in the English language, see Robert Donia, *Radovan Karadžić: Architect of the Bosnian Genocide*, Cambridge: Cambridge University Press, 2015.

61 A number of Montenegrin citizens did, however, participate in the war in Bosnia & Herzegovina, particularly in the areas close to the Montenegrin border. According to a detailed UN report, 'The Montenegro Guard' were active the attack, alongside Serb paramilitaries on the attack on Foča in May 1992, while what the report describes as 'Special Forces from Nikšić' allegedly participated in attacks on the non-Serb population of Gacko in June and July 1992. See UN Security Council, 'Final Report of the United Nations Commission of Experts: Annex III – The Military Structure, Strategy and the Tactics of the Warring Factions', S/1994/674/Add.2 (Vol. I), 28 December 1994, pp. 107–109.

62 Radončić, *A Fatal Freedom*, p. 145.

63 See *Vreme* (Belgrade), 10 May 1993, pp. 27–29. According to the same report, Hasan Klapuh had been a warden in Foča prison when Janko Janjić (a well-known criminal from Foča) had been serving one of a number of sentences there. The murder may, therefore, have been motivated by revenge or a petty grievance stemming from Janjić's time in prison. Janjić, apparently feared even by his close associates, is alleged to have been heavily involved in numerous rapes and murders in Foča. Janjić committed suicide by detonating a hand grenade while being arrested by German troops from a NATO-led peacekeeping force in Foča (at that time called 'Srbinje') in October 2000. See UN-ICTY, 'The Prosecutor Vs. Kunarac et al: Indictment', Case No. IT-96-23-I, and Julian Borger, *The Butcher's Trail*, New York: Other Press, 2016, pp. 208–209.

64 *Vreme* (Belgrade), 10 May 1993, p. 28.

65 The ECMM staff that patrolled the border area was located in the Hotel Onogošt in Nikšić. The hotel, which had been designed by Ivan Štraus (who also designed the famous Holiday Inn in Sarajevo), had fallen on harder times and was, according to Ian Oliver, a British member of the ECMM delegation in Montenegro, 'a desperate place to live' and was dubbed by ECMM staff as 'The Hotel Holocaust'. See Ian Oliver, *War & Peace in the Balkans: The Diplomacy of Conflict in the Former Yugoslavia*, London: IB Tauris, 2005, p. 28.

66 See Morrison & Elizabeth Roberts, *The Sandžak: A History*, pp. 158–159.

67 For a detailed account of the arrests and the subsequent trials, see Šeki Radončić, *Crna kutija (2)*, Podgorica: Vijesti, 2003, pp. 47–72.

68 Fabian Schmidt, 'The Sandžak: Muslims between Serbia and Montenegro,' RFE/RL Research Report, Vol. 3, No. 6, 11 February 1994, p. 33. See also UN General Assembly (Security Council), 'Human Rights Questions: Human Rights Situations and Reports of the Special Rapporteurs and Representatives: Situation of Human Rights in the Former Yugoslavia (Note by the Secretary General), A/49/641/S/1994/1252, 4 November 1994, p. 45.

69 *Monitor* (Podgorica), 11 November 1994, p. 11. See also AIM Press, 9 July 1994. For an insider's (SDA) perspective see Ibrahim Ćikić, *Gdje sunce ne grije*, Podgorica: Dokumenti, 2008.

70 Such conditions effectively negated the possibility of a fair judicial process. According to a 1994 report by the Humanitarian Law Center, 'Most of the accused in this case have already referred to more than once on Serbian and Montenegrin state television as "separatists caught with weapons intended for a violent assault on the territory of the FR Yugoslavia". These reports have made public many of the details from police and court investigation files. According to a number of independent sources, however, the police found no weapons in the homes of some of the accused.' See Humanitarian Law Center, *Spotlight on Human Rights Violations in Times of Armed Conflict*, pp. 112–113.

71 AIM Press (Zurich), 15 January 1995. See also *Monitor*, Podgorica, 23 December 1994, pp. 27–28.
72 *Monitor* (Podgorica), 6 July 1994, p. 6.
73 *Monitor* (Podgorica), 11 March 1994, p. 8.
74 *Monitor* (Podgorica), 11 November 1994, pp. 11–12.
75 František Šistek & Bodhana Dmitrovová, 'National Minorities in Montenegro after the Break-Up of Yugoslavia', p. 164.
76 See, for example, Aleksandar Zeković, 'Primjeri diskriminacije Bošnjaka/Muslimana u Crnoj Gori', pp. 271–300.
77 Plav and Gusinje possess some of the most beautiful and ornate *džjamije* (mosques) in the Balkans. Both the Emperor's mosque in Plav and the Vizier's mosque in Gusinje are striking examples of mosques with wooden minarets. The backdrop of the *Prokletije* mountain range only serves to enhance their beauty.
78 FK Komovi's ground *Stadion Prljanje* has a capacity of only 300, and thus it is likely that their normal Andrijevica-based support was supplemented by hooligans and Serb nationalist extremists from nearby Berane (whose *Gradski stadion* holds approximately 11,000 and whose matches are far better attended).
79 See Šeki Radončić, *Crna kutija (2)*, p. 47.
80 On retirement from active police service, Damjan Turković established an 'independent' television station in Berane. He would also build a hotel in his hometown of Plav called *Kula Damjanova* (Damjan's Tower), though he died, under mysterious circumstances, before its completion in 2007.
81 For interviews with a number of those who claimed to have been subject to maltreatment in the wake of the match, see *Monitor* (Podgorica), 7 June 1996, pp. 11–13.
82 Rakočević claimed that he had been approached by the administration of FK Komovi, who, he claimed, offered him a bribe in foreign currency to fix the game. He was also presented with a detailed scenario of what was going to happen during and after the game. 'They threatened they would get me dismissed from my job with the help of their connections and the Democratic Party of Socialists (DPS). They said that it was all directed by Montenegrin State Security (SDB) and Mr Turković and that I had no choice.' See *Monitor* (Podgorica), 16 November 1996, p. 12.
83 UN Economic and Social Council, 'Report on the situation of human rights in the Federal Republic of Yugoslavia', E/CN.4/1998/15, 31 October 1997, p. 21.
84 Radenko Škekić, 'Politička previranja u Crnoj Gori 1996–1998. godine', *Matica*, Podgorica, broj 49, proljeće 2012, p. 139.
85 Indeed, according to Geert-Hinrich Ahrens, the DPS split (and the sharpening of divisions into pro- and anti-Milošević factions thereafter) 'transformed the Muslim and Albanian minorities, who together accounted for almost one-quarter of the population, into an interesting political partner [for the DPS], useful for securing majorities. As they loathed Milošević, whom they held responsible for what happened in BiH (Muslims) and Kosovo (Albanians). Djukanović could count on their vote. Furthermore, Djukanović needed Western support, which was easier to get if he observed acceptable standards of human and minority rights. Consequently, he made certain concessions to these minorities, whose situation improved'. See Geert-Hinrich Ahrens, *Diplomacy on the Edge: Containment of Ethnic Conflict and the Minorities Working Group of the Conferences on Yugoslavia*, p. 273.
86 Ibid., p. 264.

87 Sistek & Dimitrivova, 'National Minorities in Montenegro after the Break-Up of Yugoslavia', p. 169.
88 Hugh Poulton, *The Balkans: Minorities and States in Conflict*, London: Minority Rights Publications, 1994, p. 75.
89 Ibid., p. 75.
90 Vladimir Goati, *Elections in the FRY from 1990 to 1998*, Belgrade: CESID, 2001, p. 67.
91 A film made in 1988 and entitled *Bruklin i Gusinje* (Brooklyn and Gusinje), directed by Želimir Žilnik (one of the major figures of the so-called *Crni talas* (Black Wave) of Yugoslav cinema), provides some interesting insights into life in Gusinje in the 1980s. The film depicts the experiences of a young woman who leaves her job as a seamstress in a small factory Novi Pazar to work in a restaurant in Gusinje. There she befriends another young woman, the head waitress in the restaurant, and two brothers, American Albanians originally from Gusinje. The narrative is essentially constructed around the developing romance between two women and the US-based brothers, so while not a film about the migration of Montenegrin Albanians to the United States per se, it nevertheless provides a fascinating filmic account of their perceptions of life in the Gusinje/Plav region in the 1980s and the relations between Serbs/Montenegrins and Albanians.
92 Geert Hinrich-Ahrens, *Diplomacy on the Edge: Containment of Ethnic Conflict and the Minorities Working Group of the Conferences on Yugoslavia*, p. 268.
93 Goati, *Elections in the FRY from 1990 to 1998*, p. 170.
94 In March 1991, an estimated 1,600 Serbs and Montenegrins who lived in Albania fled the country and established makeshift camps in Bijelo Polje, Zeta and Danilovgrad. See *Tanjug Domestic Service (Belgrade), 7 March* 1991, FBIS, *Daily Report* (Eastern Europe), FBIS-EEU-91-046.
95 *Borba* (Belgrade), 18 March 1992, p. 4.
96 Ibid., p. 4.
97 According to an article in the Belgrade daily *Politika,* Bhardi made clear that while his party favoured a Yugoslav state that 'consists of equal members', they opposed a 'Yugoslavia comprised only of Serbia and Montenegro'. See *Politika* (Belgrade), 25 March 1992, p. 6.
98 Jovan Nikolaidis, 'Multiculturalism in Montenegro and the City of Ulcinj', in Nenad Dimitrijević (ed.), *Managing Multiethnic Local Communities in the Countries of the Former Yugoslavia*, Budapest: OSI, 2001, p. 453.
99 *Politika* (Belgrade), 25 March 1992, p. 6.
100 Jovan Nikolaidis, 'Multiculturalism in Montenegro and the City of Ulcinj', p. 454.
101 AIM Press, 27 September 1994.
102 *Politika* (Belgrade), 18 September 1992, p. 14.
103 Tirana TVSH Television Network, translated and published in FBIS–EEU–96–025, 6 February 1996, p. 67.
104 According to Frantisek Šištek & Bodhana Dimitrova, 'Before the early parliamentary elections of 1998, a new law codified the creation of a special single electoral district composed of the most compact, predominantly ethnic Albanian areas (the municipality of Ulcinj and the Albanian-inhabited parts of the Podgorica and Bar municipalities). The law guaranteed that five of the total number of 78 deputies in the Montenegrin parliament would be elected from this Albanian electoral district.' See Šištek & Dimitrova, 'National Minorities in Montenegro after the Break-Up of Yugoslavia', p. 170.

Chapter 5

1. Vučetić, 'Serbia and Montenegro: From Federation to Confederation', p. 78.
2. See *Vreme* (Belgrade), 27 April 1997, pp. 12–13.
3. *Vreme* (Belgrade), 14 June 1993, p. 17.
4. At a news conference called upon their return, Milenko Gazdić, the vice chairman of the Serbian Radical Party (*Srpska radikalna stranka* – SRS) accused Djukanović and Marović of preparing the secession of Montenegro, adding that his party had material evidence (in the form of reports that, they claimed, were already in their possession). See *Naša Borba* (Belgrade), 9 November 1995, p. 4.
5. *Monitor* (Podgorica), 10 May 1996, p. 19. According to an article (written by Veljko Lalić and Veljko Miladinović) published in the Serbian weekly *Nedeljnik* in May 2016, the Montenegrin independence project began with a meeting held at the Hotel Jugoslavia in New Belgrade between Milo Djukanović, Vukašin Maraš (head of the Montenegrin state security) and a British MI6 agent, Joseph 'Joe' Busby. Drawing upon what they claimed were files from the Serbian state security archive, the article also claims that Serbian state security was monitoring (and recorded) the meeting. See *Nedeljnik* (Belgrade), 19 May 2016, p. 23.
6. *Pobjeda* (Podgorica), 13 July 1996, p. 2.
7. See Morrison & Roberts, *The Sandžak: A History*, pp. 169–171.
8. The US ambassador to the FRY, Robert Gelbard, noted later that, 'We began to try to work to test the Serbian opposition and to see what kind of people they really were. At the same time, of course, on a slightly different track, but related, we wanted also to begin to talk with Djukanović, who was on the verge of becoming President of Montenegro and at that time was still the Prime Minister.' See Interview with Robert Gelbard, in 'The Fall of Milošević' archive, Cat no. 5/5, p. 1. See also Madelaine Albright, *Madam Secretary: A Memoir*, New York: MacMillan Press, 2003, p. 380.
9. Interview with Milo Djukanovic, in 'The Fall of Milošević' archive, No. 1/12b, Roll 155, p. 1.
10. Interview with Zoran Lilić, in 'The Fall of Milošević' archive, No. 1/24b, Roll 149. See also *Vreme* (Belgrade), 18 May 1996, p. 6.
11. For a daily account of the events that led to the DPS split, see Ljubiša Mitrović & Aleksander Eraković (eds.), *Sto dana koji su promijenili Crnu Goru*, Vijesti, Podgorica: Daily Press, 1997.
12. An ongoing feud, played out through the media, had strained relations between the Milošević's and the Montenegrin prime minister. Mira Marković had alleged that Djukanović was enriching himself and his associates by indulging in shadowy economic activities during UN-imposed sanctions. See Cohen, *Serpent in the Bosom*, p. 330.
13. *AIM Press* (Zurich), 4 October, 1995, http://www.aimpress.ch/dyn/trae/archive/data/199510/51004-004-trae-pod.htm [last accessed 4 June 2011].
14. Bulatović, *Pravila Ćutanja*, p. 247.
15. *Vreme* (Belgrade), 22 February 1997, pp. 6–9. Extensive analysis and comment about Djukanović's interview can be found in *Pobjeda* (Podgorica), pp. 4–5. Reactions to the controversial interview can be found in *Vreme* (Belgrade), 1 March 1997, pp. 6–8.
16. *Monitor* (Podgorica), 28 February 1997, p. 9.
17. *AIM Press* (Zurich), 5 March 1997, http://www.aimpress.ch/dyn/trae/archive/data/199703/70305-001-trae-pod.htm [last accessed 21 June 2011].

18 For the official (and rather superficial) post-split DPS version of events, see Demokratske partije socijalista Crne Gore, 'Izvještaj o radu DPS Crne Gore između dva kongresa', 31 October 1998, pp. 15–18.
19 The Main Board of the DPS consists of 99 members. See Mitrović & Eraković (eds.), *Sto dana koji su promijenili Crnu Goru*, pp. 21–22.
20 Mitrović & Eraković (eds.), *Sto Dana koji su Promijenili Crnu Goru*, pp. 21–22.
21 *Monitor* (Podgorica) 16 May 1997, p. 8.
22 Ibid.
23 Later Milo Djukanović would claim that, 'Mr Bulatović chaired it [the session] in a completely biased way. He often retorted and cut off those who thought differently than he did. I remember that he did not allow Mr Marović, Vice President of DPS, to speak. However the final farce of the session was the voting because Mr Bulatović manipulated the situation in such a way that he turned this voting into not voting between his conception and my conception, but into voting for or against Yugoslavia'. See Interview with Milo Djukanović, in 'The Fall of Milošević' archive, No. 1/12b, p. 2.
24 AIM Press (Zurich), 17 March 1997, http://www.aimpress.ch/dyn/trae/archive/data/199703/70330-002-trae-pod.htm [last accessed 21 June 2001].
25 For an analysis (or 'who's who') of the DPS Main Board and who voted which way, see *Monitor* (Podgorica), 4 April 1997, p. 9.
26 Maraš's support for Djukanović was particularly significant. Head of the SDB, he was a powerful figure and one known to have poor relations with Momir Bulatović (the two men appeared to have very different visions of Montenegro's future within the SRJ and regarding relations with Slobodan Milošević). See *Vreme* (Belgrade), 19 April 1997, pp. 16–17, *Pobjeda* (Podgorica), 24 April, p. 2, and *Monitor* (Podgorica), 27 June 1997, pp. 14–15.
27 The seven who supported Djukanovic were Filip Vujanović, Svetozar Marović, Duško Marković, Milutin Lalić, Vojin Đukanović and Blagoje Cerović.
28 *Monitor* (Podgorica) 16 May 1997, pp. 10–11. According to the European Stability Initiative (ESI), Djukanović's core supporters were well rewarded for their loyalty, with many of them being given key position in government and business. See European Stability Initiative (ESI), 'Autonomy, Dependency, Security: The Montenegrin Dilemma', ESI Report, Podgorica & Berlin, 4 August 2000, p. 4.
29 The proposal for constitutional change was controversial – it essentially revoked the ability of the Federal Assembly to decide upon whom would be federal president. The federal president was to be elected by the people in direct elections.
30 For the struggle to wrest control of RTCG, see *Monitor* (Podgorica), 2 May 1997, pp. 12–13.
31 *AIM Press* (Zurich), 30 March 1997, http://www.aimpress.ch/dyn/trae/archive/data/199703/70330-002-trae-pod.htm [last accessed 21 June 2011].
32 *Monitor* (Podgorica), 8 August 1997, p. 10.
33 Getting to a position where two DPS candidates would be permitted to stand was complex and convoluted. According to the OSCE's final report on the elections, 'Following the split in the Democratic Party of Socialists (DPS) and submission of nomination papers from the incumbent President, Momir Bulatović, and the Prime Minister, Milo Djukanović, in August, the REC [Republican Electoral Commission] justified that both Mr. Bulatović and Mr. Djukanović were considered as candidates of two different political parties. This was because Mr. Bulatović was considered a member of a DPS registered at federal level and Mr. Djukanović was a member of

a DPS registered and only operating in Montenegro. On the basis of a complaint with reference to Article 5 in the Electoral Law from one faction of the DPS, the Montenegrin Constitutional Court cancelled and overruled the decision made by the REC. The Montenegrin Constitutional Court based its decision on the fact that only political parties registered in Montenegro can nominate candidates. On 18 August, Mr. Bulatović lodged a complaint to the Federal Constitutional Court on the basis that his constitutional right to stand as a candidate was being violated. On 10 September 1997 the Federal Constitutional Court declined the complaint and decided to abolish Article 5 of the Electoral Law. And the REC accepted two candidates from DPS in the election.' See OSCE/ODHIR: 'Republic of Montenegro: Presidential Election 5th and 18th October 1997, Final Report', 1997, p. 17.
34 Kilibarda's willingness to join Djukanović's coalition was eventually the cause of a schism within the NS, and as a consequence a breakaway faction within the party, led by Božidar Bojović, refused to co-operate on the basis of what Bojović described as Djukanović's 'separatist tendencies'.
35 Darmanović, 'Peculiarities of Transition in Serbia and Montenegro', p. 161.
36 Some analysis of intra-LSCG debates can be found in Djonović, *Ne pristajem*, 2013.
37 OSCE/ODHIR: 'Republic of Montenegro: Presidential Election 5th and 18th October 1997, Final Report', 1997, p. 19.
38 *Monitor* (Podgorica), 8 August 1997, pp. 10–11.
39 Bieber, 'Montenegrin Politics since the Disintegration of Yugoslavia', p. 31.
40 There were, in fact, eight candidates for the presidency during the first round (Momir Bulatović Milo Djukanović, Novica Stanić, Acim Višnjić, Dragan Hajduković, Novica Vojnović, Milan Radulović and Slobodan Vujačić), though the contest was essentially a two-horse race from the outset.
41 Thomas, *Serbia under Milosević: Politics in the 1990s*, p. 379.
42 Ibid., p. 379.
43 Goati, *The Party Systems of Serbia and Montenegro*, p. 175.
44 Following the DPS split, there were officially a higher number of satellite dishes in northern Montenegro (and in pro-Serbian areas generally) because the Serbs in the north perceived RTCG (*Radio Televizija Crne Gore*) as being an organ of Djukanović's DPS; thus, many installed satellite dishes that facilitate the viewing of Serbian television.
45 Bulatović, *Pravila Ćutanja*, p. 82.
46 The Montenegrin print media reflected this split. In 1997, the Montenegrin press flourished. In September of that year, the daily newspaper *Vijesti* was established. The paper was independent though it was, at least initially, favourable towards Djukanović, whose party the DPS already controlled Montenegro's state daily *Pobjeda*. Pro-Serb Montenegrins responded by establishing the newspaper *Dan* which became something of a mouthpiece of the SNP and, to an extent, Milosevic's policy in Montenegro.
47 A further, though relatively small, group of Bosnian Serb refugees settled in Podgorica after the outbreak of war in Bosnia in April 1992. Many Serbs fleeing the war in Bosnia & Herzegovina (largely from areas such as Trebinje, Nevesinje and Gacko in Herzegovina) also settled in the coastal municipality of Herceg Novi between 1992 and 1995.
48 International Crisis Group, 'Montenegro's Socialist People's Party: A Loyal Opposition?', ICG Balkans Report No. 93, Podgorica/Washington/Brussels, 28 April 2000, p. 3. See also Goati, *Elections in the FRY*, p. 214.

49 See Radenko Šćekić, 'Politička previranja u Crnoj Gori 1996–1998 godine', Matica, broj 49, proljeće 2012, pp. 148–149.
50 See Goati, *Elections in the FRY*, p. 216.
51 *AIM Press* (Zurich), 23 October 1997, http://www.aimpress.ch/dyn/trae/archive/data/199710/71023-037-trae-pod.htm [last accessed 23 June 2011].
52 OSCE/ODHIR: 'Republic of Montenegro: Presidential Election 5th and 18th October 1997, Final Report', 1997, p. 5.
53 *Monitor* (Podgorica), 24 October 1997, p. 8.
54 Bulatović claimed that the United States had helped to engineer the vote and that US Secretary of State, Madeleine Albright had already known the result before the electoral commission had declared it. He claimed: 'The chairman of the electoral commission, the Judge Marko Dakić (who in my mind was a fair person and an excellent lawyer) asked me to see him amongst the audience. He was on the verge of physical and mental breakdown and visibly under huge pressure as a consequence of continuous lack of sleep. He explained in a rather confused manner what was happening ... that they were under intolerable pressure to announce the result. He was mentioning threats that had been directed at him and that he had a fear both for his family and himself. All in all, it was clear that he had to announce that Milo [Djukanović] was the victor.' See Bulatović, *Pravila Ćutanja*, p. 271.
55 *Vreme* (Belgrade), 25 October 1997, p. 8.
56 *Monitor* (Podgorica), 24 October 1997, p. 12.
57 AIM Press, 18 December, 1997. Accusations that Milo Djukanović was involved in a number of criminal enterprises became a central part of Bulatović's attempts to undermine the Montenegrin president. He writes extensively about these accusations in his memoirs, *Pravila Ćutanja*. And he would continue to do so for many years after he had formally ceased to be engaged in Montenegrin politics.
58 *Pobjeda* (Podgorica), 11 October 1997, p. 7.
59 *Monitor* (Podgorica), 16 January 1998, p. 6. See also *Vreme* (Belgrade), 27 December 1997, p. 14.
60 *Monitor* (Podgorica), 23 January 1998, p. 9.
61 Thomas, *Serbia under Milosevic: Politics in the 1990s*, p. 385.
62 Darmanović, 'Peculiarities of Transition in Serbia and Montenegro', p. 161.
63 *Monitor* (Podgorica), 23 January 1998, p. 9.
64 The crowds gathered outside the RTCG building sang a number of Serbians songs and chanted *Srušićemo Rožaje!* (We're going to destroy Rožaje!): a direct threat to Montenegro's Muslim/Bosniak community, the majority of whom had voted for Djukanović during the presidential elections.
65 The government building in Podgorica remains one of the most striking pieces of modernist architecture in the city. It was designed by Radosav Zeković and completed in 1965, and looks akin to two huge slabs (coffins) on concrete plinths. The building was the constructed to house the Central Committee of the SKCG.
66 According to a report in *Monitor*, the protestors were armed with seventy-nine pistols (one of which was unlicensed), two cases of dynamite, and a number of other explosive devices. See *Monitor* (Podgorica), 23 January 1998, pp. 10–11.
67 As Djukanović later noted, the atmosphere inside the government building grew increasingly tense, with those ensconced inside fearing the worst. 'These peaceful demonstrations' he said, 'grew into what we had expected – a brutal act of violence, with the intention of storming into the government building, and considering that most of the demonstrators were armed, I am absolutely sure that this would have been

a bloody showdown where most of us within the building would have been killed.' See Interview with Milo Djukanović, in 'The Fall of Milošević' archive, No. 1/12b, p4.
68 Bulatović, *Pravila Ćutanja*, p. 277.
69 The VJ chief of staff at that time was General Momčilo Perišić. He was known to have opposed Milošević's increasingly aggressive posture on Kosovo, and it was rumoured that he enjoyed good relations with Djukanović. According to James Gow, additional rumours included a claim that Perišić 'might be helping to engineer a coup d'état in Belgrade to install Djukanović in Milošević's place'. See Gow, *The Serbian Project and Its Adversaries*, p. 73.
70 BBC News, 'US Blames Serb Leader for Montenegrin Riots', 15 January 1998, http://news.bbc.co.uk/1/ hi/47554.stm [last accessed 24 March 2010]
71 See Radenko Šćekić, 'Politička previranja u Crnoj Gori 1996–1998 godine', p. 163.
72 *AIM Press* (Zurich), 15 February 1998, http://www.aimpress.ch/dyn/trae/archive/data/199802/80220-021-trae-pod.htm [last accessed 25 June 2011].
73 International Crisis Group (ICG), 'Montenegro's Socialist People's Party: A Loyal Opposition?' p. 3. For the formation of the party see Bulatović, *Pravila Ćutanja*, pp. 283–284.
74 Bulatović, *Pravila Ćutanja*, p. 285.
75 OSCE/ODHIR, 'Republic of Montenegro (Federal Republic of Yugoslavia): Parliamentary Elections 31 May 1998', Warsaw, 5 July 1998, p. 13.
76 See *Vreme* (Belgrade), 18 April 1998, pp. 12–13, and Thomas, *Serbia under Milosevic: Politics in the 1990s*, p. 380.
77 The LSCG was disunited in advance of the May 1998 parliamentary elections. Some within the party were openly critical of Perović's policy of not cooperating with the DPS. In the wake of these intra-party arguments, graffiti appeared in Podgorica that summed up the sentiments of Perović's critics. The message read: *Slavko, ivinite, ali posao je posao* (Slavko, apologies, but business is business).
78 The DŽB ran as a coalition of DPS–SDP–NS throughout Montenegro's twenty-one municipalities with two exceptions. In Rožaje, the SDP and DPS ran separate campaigns, and in Plav the SDP ran separately from the DŽB coalition.
79 In the wake of Djukanović becoming president, foreign aid started to flow into Montenegro, meaning that an economic recovery (and the onset of economic restructuring) began to take place. See Djurić, *The Economic Development of Montenegro*, p. 152.
80 OSCE/ODHIR, 'Republic of Montenegro (Federal Republic of Yugoslavia): Parliamentary Elections 31 May 1998', Warsaw, 5 July 1998, p. 13.
81 Goati, *Elections in the FRY 1990–2000*, p. 303.
82 *AIM Press* (Zurich), 8 June 1998, http://www.aimpress.ch/dyn/trae/archive/data/199806/80608-019-trae-pod.htm [last accessed 26 June 2011].
83 The transformation of the party's agenda is demonstrated in their party statute on October 1998. See Demokratske partije socijalista Crne Gore, 'Statut: DPS Crne Gore', Podgorica: 31 October 1998; and Demokratske partije socijalista Crne Gore, 'Izvještaj o radu DPS Crne Gore između dva kongresa', 31 October 1998.
84 Bulatović, *Pravila Ćutanja*, p. 285.
85 Roberts, *The Realm of the Black Mountain*, 2006, p. 23.
86 *AIM Press* (Zurich), 4 March 1998, http://www.aimpress.ch/dyn/trae/archive/data/199803/80305-028-trae-pod.htm [last accessed 3 July 2011].
87 Djurić, *The Economic Development of Montenegro*, 2003, p. 152.
88 Ibid., p. 152.

Chapter 6

1. *NIN* (Belgrade), 20 August 1993, p. 22.
2. Michael Radu, 'The Burden of Eastern Orthodoxy', *Orbis*, Vol. 42, No. 2, Spring 1998, p. 283.
3. See, for example, Mirko Djordjević, 'The Balkan God Mars – The Religious Factor in the [Yugoslav] Wars 1991–1999', in D. Vujadinović et al. (eds.), *Between Authoritarianism and Democracy: Serbia, Montenegro, Croatia, Vol. II, Civil Society and Political Culture*, Belgrade: CEDET, 2005, pp. 133–143.
4. For a succinct account of the role of the SPC in modern Serbian society and political life (since 1989), see Radmila Radić & Milan Vukmanović, 'Religion and Democracy in Serbia since 1989: The Case of the Serbian Orthodox Church', in Sabrina P. Ramet (ed.), *Religion and Politics in Post-Socialist Central and Southeastern Europe: Challenges since 1989*, London: Palgrave MacMillan, 2014, pp. 180–211.
5. These were: the autocephalous Serb Orthodox Church with five episcopates; the autocephalous Orthodox Church in Vojvodina (the Metropolitanate of Karlovac) with seven episcopates; the autocephalous Montenegrin Orthodox Church with three episcopates; and the autonomous church in Bosnia & Herzegovina (under the formal jurisdiction of the patriarchy of Constantinople with four episcopates).
6. See, for example, Vladimir D. Jovanović, *Crna Gora: Kapija pravoslavja*, Podgorica: OKTOIH, 1994.
7. *Novi list* (Rijeka), 4 December 1993, p. 8.
8. Pljevlja was located within the Sandžak of Novi Pazar until 1880 (the year of Dožić's birth). In that year it became part of the Pljevaljski Sandžak (*Sanjak of Taşlıca*). Pljevlja was incorporated into Montenegrin territory during the First Balkan War in 1912.
9. For a detailed account of Gavrilo V's incarceration in Dachau, see Predrag Ilić, *Srpska pravoslavna crkva i tajna Dahaua: mit i istina o zatočeništvu patrijarha Gavrila i episkopa Nikolaja u koncentracionom logou Dahauu*, Beograd, 2006.
10. Sabrina Ramet, *Balkan Babel*, Boulder, CO: Westview Press, 1999, p. 109.
11. *Monitor* (Podgorica), 3 December 1993, p. 9.
12. Ramet, *Balkan Babel*, p. 109.
13. Images of the destruction of the chapel still carried some weight (and were thus subject to political manipulation) in the 1990s. The Pro-Serbian 'People's Party' (*Narodna stranka* – NS), led by Novak Kilibarda, released a promotional party broadcast in 1992 in which grainy black-and-white images of the chapel being destroyed in 1972. There was no narrative, simply images followed by a voice stating the party name.
14. Petar II Petrović 'Njegoš was *Vladika* (Prince-Bishop) until his death, from tuberculosis, at the age of 37 in 1851. As Vladika he played a pivotal role in uniting Montenegro's *pleme* (clans) and as a politician he was a proponent uniting the Serbian nation (as well as an early proponent of Yugoslavism). As a poet he was best known for *Gorski vijenac* (The Mountain Wreath), which is considered to be one of the most important pieces of South Slav literature. For a detailed account of the life of Petar II Petrović 'Njegoš in the English language, see Milovan Djilas, *Njegoš*, New York: Harcourt, Brace and World, 1966.
15. The existing monument on Lovćen was built to house the bones of Njegoš, which were moved there from nearby Cetinje in 1925. The event was attended by King Aleksander Karadjordjević and numerous members of the SPC hierarchy. See Andrew

Baruch Wachtel, *Making a Nation, Breaking a Nation: Literature and Cultural Politics in Yugoslavia*, Stanford, CA: Stanford University Press, 1998, p. 105.

16 Vjekoslav Perica, *Balkan Idols*, Oxford: Oxford University Press, 2002, pp. 49–50. For a detailed analysis of the politics behind the building on the mausoleum, see František Šistek, 'Njegoševa grobnica na Lovćenu', *Matica*, broj 51, jesen/zima 2012, pp. 105–140.

17 In December 1990, Pavle was elected patriarch of the SPC despite the fact that his predecessor, Patriarch German II, was still alive. At the same congress, Amfilohije Radović was elected Metropolitan of Montenegro and the Littoral and Irinej Bulović was elected the Episcope of Bačka. Six months later, in May 1991, Bishop Artemije was elected Episcope of Raška and Prizren, and Atanasije Jeftić was elected the Episcope of Banat.

18 One such event was in May 1996, when the bones of Saint Vasilije Ostroški were paraded through the Montenegrin town of Nikšić. According to Ivan Čolović,

> In the eyes of the church, the earthly remains of saints, martyrs or prominent priests and reliquaries (the boxes in which their remains are kept) like their graves and parts of their clothing, have supernatural, miraculous power. They heal sickness of the body and spirit. This is the power, for instance, of the *sanctorum reliquiae* of Saint Vasilije Ostroški. When his relics were carried recently in a religious procession through Nikšić, it was conceived and carried out as a kind of collective therapy. The organizers explained that through the miraculous power of the holy relics they wished to influence the spiritual state of the inhabitants of that Montenegrin town, where over the last few years there had been an exceptionally large number of murders and suicides.

See Ivan Čolović, *The Politics of Symbol in Serbia*, London: Hurst & Co., 2001, p. 166.

19 *Vijesti* (Podgorica), 16 September 2002, p. 6.

20 See Šerbo Rastoder, 'Religion and Politics – The Montenegrin Perspective', in D. Vujadinović et al. (eds.), *Between Authoritarianism and Democracy: Serbia, Montenegro, Croatia, Vol. II, Civil Society and Political Culture*, Belgrade: CEDET, 2005, p. 117.

21 For Amfilohije's views on some of the key elements of Montenegrin history, see Mitropolit Amfilohije et al., *Duhovno i političko biće Crne Gore*, Nikšić: ETNOS, 2002. (This edited volume also contains a number of articles by, among other the Montenegrin Serb writer and poet, Matija Bećković.)

22 See Olga Popović-Obradović, 'The Church, the Nation and the State – The Serbian Orthodox Church and Transition in Serbia', in D. Vujadinović et al. (eds.), *Between Authoritarianism and Democracy: Serbia, Montenegro, Croatia, Vol. III, Civil Society and Political Culture*, Belgrade: CEDET, 2005, p. 158.

23 See *NIN* (Belgrade), 20 August 1993, p. 24. Among supporters of the CPC there were certainly those who were more committed to using the church as effectively a political tool. For an assessment of the tensions within the 'Board for an Autocephalous CPC', see *Monitor* (Podgorica), 12 August 1994, pp. 18–19.

24 The gusle is a traditional single-stringed instrument associated with the Serbs (though Herzegovinian Croats have also been known to play the instrument). The instrument has traditionally been used to accompany the recitation of epic poems, many of which are associated with cathartic events in Serbian history. The instrument

became something of a symbol for nationalist Serbs and enjoyed a revival in the late 1980s and was often played to 'motivate' the troops before battle. For an assessment of the use of the gusle in the political context of the 1990s, see Žanić, *Flag on the Mountain*, 2007.
25 Vešeljko Koprivica, *Amfilohijeva sabrana nedjela*, Podgorica: Vijesti, 1999, p. 25.
26 Rastoder, 'Religion and Politics – The Montenegrin Perspective', p. 124.
27 See *NIN* (Belgrade), 12 August 1994, p. 17.
28 Rastoder, 'Religion and Politics – The Montenegrin Perspective', p. 124.
29 *Monitor* (Podgorica), 3 December 1993, p. 9.
30 See Danilo Radojević, 'Autokefalna Crnogorska pravoslavna crkva', *Elementa Montenegrina hrestomatija (Crnogorska narod i srpska politika genocida nad njim)*, Zagreb, Vol. 1, 1990. See also *Liberal* (Cetinje), January 1991, Godina II, broj 12, pp. 26-29.
31 Such an argument can be found in Živko Andrijašević, 'Cetinjski mitropoliti prema pećkim patrijarsima', Matica, Cetinje/Podgorica, Godina VI, broj 22/23, 2005, pp. 183-212. See also See Novak Adžić, *Kratka istorija Crnogorske pravoslavne crkve (od sredine XV vijeka do 1920.godine)*, Dignitas: Cetinje, 2000. A counterargument vis-à-vis the CPC's autocephalous status can be found in Ljubomir Durković Jakšić, *Mitropolija Crnogorska nikad nije bila autokefalna*, Beograd: Cetinje, 1991.
32 For detailed analyses of the CPC, see Sreten Zekovic (ed.), *Elementa Montenegrina hrestomatija (Crnogorska pravoslavna crkva)*, Zagreb: 1991; Danilo Radojevic, *Iz povijesti hriscanskih crkava u Crnoj Gori*, CDNK: Cetinje, 2000; Branko Nikac, *Crnogorska pravoslavna crkva: clanci – rasprave – studije*, Cetinje: 2000; Koprivica, *Amfilohijeva sabrana nedjela*, Podgorica: Monitor, 1999; Adzic, *Kratka istorija Crnogorske pravoslavne crkve (od sredine XV vijeka do 1920.godine)*.
33 Perica, *Balkan Idols*, p. 49.
34 *Liberal* (Cetinje), January 1991, Godina II, broj 12, p. 13.
35 See *NIN* (Belgrade), 20 August 1993, p. 22. The demonization of Amfilohije became something of a cottage industry in the 1990s, with a number of publication appearing that were hugely critical of him. See, for example, Koprivica, *Amfilohijeva sabrana nedjela,* and Milorad Tomanić, *Srpska crkva u ratu*, Belgrade: Medijska knjižara krug, 2001.
36 *Borba* (Belgrade), 28 December 1990, p. 15.
37 *NIN* (Belgrade), 20 August 1993, pp. 22-24. The LSCG president, Slavko Perović, denied that his party were *instrumental* in the re-establishment of the church, stating that, the LSCG had little to do with the project 'except on the basis that the LSCG supports human rights'. See *Novi List* (Rijeka), 4 December 1993, p. 9.
38 Interviewed in the Montenegrin weekly *Monitor*, Vojislav Šešelj, the leader of the Serbian Radical Party (*Srpska radikalna stranka* – SRS), rejected the widely held perception that Cetinje was a stronghold for Montenegrin secessionists, claiming that 'there are 20,000 people there, and only 2000 are Liberals and Greens [Zelenaši] in Cetinje, but the liberals are aggressive, so the impression [is created] that the town favours sovereignty'. He also claimed that 'the SRS has plenty of members in Cetinje, who are too afraid of the Liberals to form an SRS communal committee'. See *Monitor* (Podgorica), 24 September 1993, pp. 20-21.
39 A number of banners appeared in Podgorica, including a large one making reference to dissatisfaction with Amfilohije Radović being anointed as the Metropolitan of Montenegro and the Littoral. One read 'The Montenegrin Vladika is elected by the Montenegrins and no other. We won't allow usurpers and occupiers on the throne

of Saint Peter'. See Sreten Zeković, *Nauk(a) o samobitnosti Crnogoraca V: Crnogorski autokefalni pokret*, Cetinje: Crnogorska prijestonica, 2003, p. 233.

40 *NIN* (Belgrade), 20 August 1993, p. 20. This meeting brought together some of those who were leading pro-independence figures in Montenegro, among them Slavko Perović, Sreten Žeković and the poet and writer Jevrem Brković. See Zeković, *Nauk(a) o samobitnosti Crnogoraca V: Crnogorski autokefalni pokret*, p. 210.

41 *NIN* (Belgrade), 20 August 1993, p. 21. See also *Liberal* (Cetinje), August 1990, Godina I, broj 5, pp. 21–22.

42 Orlovi krš (Eagle's rock) is the hill behind the Cetinje monastery where the grave of Bishop Danilo I is located. See *Liberal* (Cetinje), July–August, Godina II, broj 16–17, p. 2.

43 *Liberal* (Cetinje), July-August 1993, Godina II, broj 16–17, p. 2.

44 *Liberal* (Cetinje), January 1993, Godina IV, broj 9, p. 19.

45 Writing about the event in *The European*, the veteran Balkan correspondent Duško Doder noted, 'There are distinct rumblings of discontent in Montenegro ... when the Serb patriarch arrived here to consecrate a new church last week, he was greeted with whistles and boos of demonstrators shouting "This is not Serbia. We want a separate church". See *The European* (London), 19–22 August 1993, p. 7.

46 Vladimir Keković, *25 godina poslije*, p. 129. For an interview with Božidar Bogdanović in the wake of the events in Cetinje in September 1993, see *Monitor* (Podgorica), 29 October 1993, pp. 22–23.

47 UN Economic and Social Council, 'Situation of Human Rights on the Territory of the Former Yugoslavia: Fifth periodic report on the situation of human rights in the territory of the Former Yugoslavia (submitted by Mr. Tadeusz Mazowiecki, Special Rapporteur to the Commission on Human Rights), E/CN.4/1994/47, 17 November 1993, p. 32. For details on the ensuing court case against those arrested in Cetinje, see *Monitor* (Podgorica), 23 December 1994, pp. 18–19.

48 In a letter to Bartholomew I, Archbishop of Constantinople, Istanbul, from Archbishop Theodosius, Archbishop of Washington, Metropolitan of All America and Canada, the latter claimed, 'On 28 October 1993, His Holiness Patriarch Pavle informed us that a retired cleric (Archimandrite Anthony Abramovich) was falsely representing himself as an auxiliary bishop of Edmonton (Canada) of the Orthodox Church in America. He has (as we have officially informed) become involved in and supporting the uncanonical and un-Christian act of causing schism and division in the Holy Serbian Orthodox Church. On 29 October 1993, we faxed a response in which we affirmed that Anthony Abramovich was never consecrated by us or, to my knowledge, by any other canonical Orthodox church.' See Letter to Bartholomew I, Archbishop of Constantinople, Istanbul, from Archbishop Theodosius, Archbishop of Washington, Metropolitan of All America and Canada, in Budimir Alekšić & Slavko Krstajić, *Trgovci dušama*, Nova Varoš: Bonart, 2003, p. 36.

49 *Monitor* (Podgorica), 3 November 1993, p. 6. Jevrem Brković, the Montenegrin writer living in exile in Croatia, immediately contacted his Montenegrin associates throughout Croatia to 'congratulate them' on the formal re-formation of the CPC. 'What happened today in Cetinje was', he said, 'very important for Montenegro'. For more on Brković's assessment of these events, see Jevrem Brković, *Dnevnici (Vol. 2)*, Podgorica: CANU, 2001, p. 810. Letters sending congratulations to Abramović from Montenegrins living in exile in Croatia (Jevrem Brković, Veljko Bulajić and Mirko Kovač) were published in *Liberal* (which was then edited by Jevrem Brković's son Balša). See *Liberal* (Cetinje), November 1993, Godina IV, broj 1, p. 5.

50 For an early interview with Antonije Abramović after his consecration, see *Monitor* (Podgorica), 3 December 1993, pp. 8–9.
51 *Liberal* (Cetinje), November 1993, Godina IV, broj 1, pp. 6–7.
52 Letter to Bartholomew I, Archbishop of Constantinople, Istanbul, from Archbishop Theodosius, Archbishop of Washington, Metropolitan of All America and Canada, in Alekšić & Krstajić, *Trgovci dušama*, p. 36.
53 Despite this being 'common knowledge' within the SPC, there is no substantial proof that Abramović was a homosexual.
54 The CPC also reached out to the Montenegrin diaspora, creating, for example, the *Sveti Luka* (Saint Luka) church in Roscoe Street, London.
55 See, for example, interview with 'Vladika Antonije' in *Monitor* (Podgorica), 30 December 1994, pp. 22–23.
56 Letter from Antonije Abramović (CPC) to Milo Djukanović (Prime Minster of Montenegro), CPC Doc. No. 34, 21 June 1996 in Zeković, *Nauk(a) o samobitnosti Crnogoraca V: Crnogorski autokefalni pokret*, pp. 276–277.
57 *Monitor* (Podgorica), 19 November 1999, p. 9.
58 See Adžić, *Kratka istorija Crnogorske pravoslavne crkve (od sredine XV vijeka do 1920. godine)*, p. 64.
59 *Monitor* (Podgorica), 3 December 1993, p. 10.
60 Zeković, *Nauk(a) o samobitnosti Crnogoraca V: Crnogorski autokefalni pokret*, p. 163.
61 See *Srpska Pravoslavna Crkva i novi srpski identitet*, Belgrade: Helsinski odbor za ljudska prava u Srbiji, 2006, pp. 5–11 at http://www.helsinki.org.rs/serbian/doc/Studija-Kupres.pdf
62 For Momir Bulatović's assessment of Amfilohije's support for Djukanović during this period, see Momir Bulatović, *Pravila Ćutanja*, p. 267.
63 *Monitor* (Podgorica), 8 January 1999, p. 11.
64 *Monitor* (Podgorica), 12 March 1999, p. 30.
65 The Vlaška church in Cetinje is famous for its perimeter fence made from approximately 1500 barrels of Turkish guns captured by Montenegrins during the late nineteenth century. The CPC and SPC both claimed ownership of it.
66 The SPC stated that Nikčević was 'risking his life' to defend the church because the Montenegrin government could not be trusted to enforce law and order. The statement also read: 'We are expressing our sincere hope that Montenegro will choose the right path founded and embedded in its ages long experience and proven values, and eventually free itself from the new Docleo-pagan mytho-mania, obviously an offspring of a Bolshevik-Titoist ideology.' See Public Statement of the Orthodox Metropolitanate of Montenegro and the Littoral, December 2000, http://www.mitropolija.me/stari/aktuelno/saopstenja/e001216.html [last accessed 23 June 2013].
67 AIM Press (Zurich), 6 January 2001, http://www.aimpress.ch/dyn/trae/archive/data/200101/10106-002-trae-pod.html. [last accessed 12 January 2008].
68 The president of the Federal Republic of Yugoslavia, Vojislav Koštunica, also added fuel to the fire by publicly stating during a visit to Montenegro (whereupon he met with Amfilohije) that he 'did not recognise' the CPC, a statement that unleashed 'a wave of disapproval among its adherents and followers'. See ibid.
69 See for example Matica Crnogorska, 'Kontinuitet provokacija Srpske Pravoslavne Crkve', *Matica Crnogorska Godišnjak 1999/2000*, Cetinje, pp. 132–133.
70 Aleksić & Krstajić, *Trgovci dušama*, p. 73.
71 Rastoder, 'Religion and Politics – The Montenegrin Perspective', p. 120.
72 Perica, *Balkan Idols*, p. 175.

73 As a result, he faced protests by the SPC and the 'Orthodox Youth', the latter of which tried to organize a Montenegrin version of the Serbian youth organization *Otpor* (resistance) in an effort to forge a critical mass that could oust Djukanović, as Milošević had been on 5 October 2000. For the registration of the CPC see *Monitor* (Podgorica), 31 March 2000, p. 11.
74 *Monitor* (Podgorica), 5 May 2000, pp. 11-12.
75 The SPC had, for a long time, been critical of the Montenegrin government. In one withering statement published on the website of the Metropolitanate of Montenegro and the Littoral it was posited that 'instead of trying to heal the old wounds that divide the population, current regime seems to be doing just the opposite by generating hatred and trying to translate the conflict into the Church's sphere'. The Montenegrin government, it went on, 'instead of trying to tackle these real issues that are seriously threatening the souls of young Montenegrins and the dignity of their country this regime is likely to be remembered for managing to fabricate fictitious 'Academies of Arts', 'academics', false 'churches' and false 'priests' and readily label as traitors all those who happen to think and act in a different manner. See Public Statement of the Orthodox Metropolitanate of Montenegro and the Littoral, December 2000, http://www.mitropolija.me/stari/aktuelno/saopstenja/e001216.html [last accessed 23 June 2013].
76 See Svetigora Press: 'Official announcement regarding [the] attack on Radio Station Svetigora', 5 October 2004, http://www.mitropolija.me/stari/aktuelno/saopstenja/e041004.html [last accessed 23 June 2013].
77 *Monitor* (Podgorica), 29 July 2005, p. 11.
78 See *Monitor* (Podgorica), 12 August 2005, p. 14.

Chapter 7

1 Facsimile of speech by Milo Djukanović, The Mayflower Hotel, Washington DC, United States, 21 April 1998 (private collection).
2 These allegations were detailed by the VJ and presented in a secret report prepared for the SRJ Federal Ministry of Foreign Affairs and signed by the VJ chief of general staff, Momčilo Perišić. See Federal Republic of Yugoslavia: Chief of General Staff of the Yugoslav Army/ STR. Conf. 615-10, 16 July 1998, p. 3. These allegations were not without substance. According to James Pettifer and Miranda Vickers, Montenegro (particularly the area around Plav and Gusinje) was both important to the KLA 'as a relatively safe operating area for running the war around the strategically important town of Peje (Peć)' and 'as a very valuable conduit for people and supplies to Kosova' (which was used as a supply route by the KLA). See James Pettifer and Miranda Vickers, *The Albanian Question: Reshaping the Balkans*, London: IB Tauris, 2009, p. 193 and pp. 239-240.
3 According to Elizabeth Roberts, 'Djukanović went as far as to impose his veto in the Supreme Defence Council, a step that was in principle constitutionally binding, but which Milošević simply ignored'. See Roberts, *Realm of the Black Mountain*, p. 455.
4 Interview with Milo Djukanović, in 'The Fall of Milosević' archive, No. 1/12b, Roll 155, p. 13.
5 See Ivo Daadler and Michael O'Hanlon, *Winning Ugly: NATO's War to Save Kosovo*, New York: Brookings Institution, 2001, p. 128.
6 *Pobjeda* (Podgorica), 25 March 1999, p. 3.

7   Srdjan Darmanović, 'Montenegro Survives the War', *The East European Constitutional Review*, Vol. 8, No. 3, 1999. For the bombing of Podgorica airport and the reactions of citizens who lived close to it, see *Pobjeda* (Podgorica), 29 March 1999, p. 1.
8   *Pobjeda* (Podgorica), 25 March 1999, p. 3.
9   *Pobjeda* (Podgorica), 27 March 1999, p. 3. The following day, Djukanović stated that the maintenance of peace was the 'obligation' of every Montenegrin citizen, regardless of their political persuasion. See *Pobjeda* (Podgorica), 28 March 1999, p. 3.
10 *Pobjeda* (Podgorica), 2 April 1999, p. 3.
11 *Vijesti* (Podgorica), 2 April 1999, p. 2.
12 Djukanović's situation was made even more precarious by his refusal to sit on the Supreme Military Council of the SRJ during the Kosovo conflict, negating any engagement with the SRJ's federal president, Momir Bulatović.
13 Interview with George Robertson in 'The Fall of Milošević' archive, No. 4/11, Roll 855, p. 17. See also the interview with Robertson in *Monitor* (Podgorica), 22 September 2000, pp. 14–15.
14 Interview with Milo Djukanović in 'The Fall of Milošević' archive, 12b, Roll 156, p. 24.
15 Wesley Clark, *Waging Modern War: Bosnia, Kosovo and the Future of Combat*, New York, NY: Public Affairs, 2001, p. 255.
16 Interview with Javier Solana in 'The Fall of Milošević' archive, Roll 842, p. 11.
17 Interview with Jacques Chirac in 'The Fall of Milošević' archive, Roll 828–829, p. 12.
18 A rather protracted 'exchange' took place between Chirac and Clinton regarding the NATO actions in Montenegro. Chirac claimed that when he raised the issue with Bill Clinton, the US president had claimed that Djukanović had agreed to the bombing. Skeptical of this, Chirac telephoned Djukanović to confirm Clinton's claim. According to Chirac, 'What I got from this conversation was that he was entirely against any kind of bombing of Montenegro and he confirmed that bombing Montenegro would be playing into Milošević's hands. I then reported back to Bill Clinton and the matter was left at that.' See interview with Jacques Chirac in 'The Fall of Milošević' archive, Roll 828–829, p. 12, and interview with Bill Clinton in 'The Fall of Milošević' archive, Roll 443, p. 5.
19 The damage incurred by the NATO bombing was documented and presented in a booklet entitled 'NATO Aggression on Civilian Population and Facilities in Yugoslavia'. See Vojska Jugoslavije, *NATO Aggression on Civilian Population and Facilities in Yugoslavia – Trace of Inhumanity: Yugoslavia, wartime spring of 1999*, Belgrade, 'Vojska', 1999.
20 *Vijesti* (Podgorica), 17 April 1999, p. 3. According to Tim Judah, 'Throughout the 78-day bombing campaign the government of Montenegro ... constantly raised the alarm, saying that Milošević was attempting to mount a "creeping coup" in the republic by using the army [VJ].' See Tim Judah, *Kosovo: War and Revenge*, New Haven, CT and London: Yale NB, 2002, pp. 255–256.
21 IWPR Balkans Crisis Report (London), No. 88, 29 October 1999.
22 *Vijesti* (Podgorica), 17 April 1999, p. 2.
23 NATO Press and Media, 'Statement by the Secretary General following the meeting of the North Atlantic Council', 12 April 1999, Press communique PR (1999) 058, p. 2.
24 Interview with Milo Djukanović, in 'The Fall of Milošević' archive, No. 1/12b, p. 19.
25 European Stability Initiative (ESI), 'Autonomy, Dependency, Security: The Montenegrin Dilemma', ESI Report, Podgorica & Berlin, 4 August 2000, p. 22.
26 *AIM Press* (Zurich), 29 May 1999, http://www.aimpress.ch/dyn/trae/archive/data/199905/90529-002-trae-pod.htm [last accessed 26 June 2013].

27 *Monitor* (Podgorica), 4 June 1999, p. 11.
28 Florian Bieber, *Montenegrin Politics since the Disintegration of Yugoslavia*, p. 33. The United Nations High Commissioner for Refugees (UNHCR) estimated that there were already 73,000 refugees in Montenegro by 19 April 1999. See *Monitor* (Podgorica), 3 July 1999, p. 2.
29 *Pobjeda* (Podgorica), 29 March 1999, p. 3.
30 *Monitor – Specijalni dodatak: Izbeglice u Crnoj Gori* (Podgorica), 18 June, pp. 2–3 and *Monitor – Specijalni dodatak: Izbeglice u Crnoj Gori* (Podgorica), 30 July 1999, pp. 2–5.
31 *Pobjeda* (Podgorica), 29 October 1999, p. 3. It was estimated by Srdjan Vukadinović that there were (according to the 1991 census figures) only 3,282 Roma in Montenegro. However, approximately 43,000 Roma arrived in Montenegro during and after the war in Kosovo. While many left the country soon after, legally or otherwise, around 10,000 remained in Montenegro. See Srdjan Vukadinović, 'The Status of Gypsies in Montenegro', *Philosophy and Sociology*, Vol. 2, No. 8, 2001, p. 520.
32 *Monitor* (Podgorica), 9 July 1999, p. 9.
33 Ramet, *Balkan Babel*, p. 348.
34 Vucetić, *Serbia and Montenegro: From Federation to Confederation*, p. 80.
35 *Monitor* (Podgorica), 17 December 1999, p. 10.
36 *AIM Press* (Zurich), 25 January 2000, http://www.aimpress.ch/dyn/trae/archive/data/200001/00125-001-trae-pod.htm [last accessed 28 June 2013].
37 *Monitor* (Podgorica), 3 March 2000, p. 11.
38 Milan Popović noted the essential political character of these clan assemblies. 'One of the most telling characteristics of their second arrival in Montenegro is their one-party membership. Namely, they are almost exclusively consisting of members of the SNP, which is the main pro-Milošević party in Montenegro.' He goes on to say that as a member of the Kuči clan he, as someone who supported Montenegro's independence, had 'never been invited and allowed to participate into the gatherings of this newly-established SNP-Kuči community'. See Popović, *Montenegrin Mirror*, p. 21.
39 *Monitor* (Podgorica), 24 September 1999, p. 12.
40 Lenard Cohen, *Serpent in the Bosom*, p. 337.
41 *Monitor* (Podgorica), 18 June 2000, p. 6.
42 *Monitor* (Podgorica), 3 September 1999, p. 13.
43 Ibid., p. 14.
44 Djurić, 'The Economic Development of Montenegro', p. 155.
45 *The Guardian* (London), 9 December 1999, p. 18.
46 The Montenegrin weekly *Monitor* described the economic war between Serbia and Montenegro as *Bratska ljubav – kroz žicu* (Brotherly love – through the wire [fence]). See *Monitor* (Podgorica), 19 February 1999, p. 8.
47 Though the position of Montenegrin foreign minister had existed since the inception of the SRJ in May 1992 (it had been held initially by Miodrag Lekić), it, in effect, had little significance. Any authority once enjoyed by the Montenegrin foreign minister had been incrementally eroded by 1999.
48 European Stability Initiative (ESI), 'Autonomy, Dependency, Security: The Montenegrin Dilemma', p. 20. See also *Vijesti* (Podgorica), 24 June 2000, p. 2.
49 For Lukovac's activities while with the Slovenian delegation to the UN, see *Monitor* (Podgorica), 21 July 2000, pp. 14–16.
50 *The Independent* (London), 29 July 2000, p. 18.

51 Interviewed for a BBC documentary in 2000, the SNP leader Predrag Bulatović argued that 'Djukanović's specials' were 'not a classic police force' and that 'aside from ordinary guns they have heavy weapons and armored personnel carriers'. As a result, he continued, 'many people are starting to believe that they must arm themselves in order to protect their families'. Transcript of interview with Predrag Bulatović in 'The Final Battle of Yugoslavia', 'Correspondent', Dir. Phil Rees, BBC, Broadcast 5 August 2000.
52 There were also smaller quasi-military structures operating throughout Montenegro and loyal to the government, such as the 'Lovćen Guard', an armed group based in Cetinje and self-proclaimed 'defenders of Montenegrin statehood'.
53 Popović, *Montenegrin Mirror*, p. 11.
54 *Monitor* (Podgorica), 25 February 2000, p. 25.
55 NATO was also monitoring the situation in Montenegro closely. In a press communique from December 1999, NATO ministers statement read 'We remain concerned about continued tensions between Belgrade and the democratically-elected government of Montenegro. We are therefore playing very close attention to developments there. We call on both sides to resolve their differences in a peaceful and pragmatic way and refrain from any destabilising measures'. See NATO Press and Media Service: Ministerial Meeting of the North Atlantic Council held at NATO Headquarters, Brussels, on 15 December 1999, Press Communique M-NAC-2 (99) 166, p. 5.
56 European Stability Initiative (ESI), 'Autonomy, Dependency, Security: The Montenegrin Dilemma', p. 22.
57 *Monitor* (Podgorica), 10 March 2000, p. 11.
58 *Monitor* (Podgorica), 3 March 2000, p. 11. Monitor described the activities of the VJ in Montenegro as a 'silent occupation'. See *Monitor* (Podgorica), 11 August 2000, pp. 10–12.
59 International Crisis Group (ICG), 'The Current Legal Status of the FRY, and of Serbia and Montenegro', Balkans Report No. 101, 19 September 2000, p. 32.
60 Though the son of Montenegrin parents, Goran Žugić had only been resident in Montenegro since 1992. Having been born and raised in Tuzla, he later embarked upon a law degree at the University of Sarajevo. He had been the head of the Security Centre in his hometown when the war broke out in Bosnia & Herzegovina in 1992, but had left the city to become head of the Security Centre in Herceg Novi. He remained in that post until 1995 whereupon he became the head of the Podgorica Security Centre and was, in 1998, appointed to the role of Milo Djukanović's security advisor. Žugić and Djukanović had a close personal relationship, and the latter had been *kum* (best man) at Žugić's wedding. See *Monitor* (Podgorica), 9 June 2000, p. 16.
61 Žugić's assassination was one of a number of (ostensibly political) assassinations that took place in Podgorica in early to mid-2000. Misha Glenny, however, argues that these assassinations were linked to a gang war (known as *the Bloody Spring*) fought over the cigarette smuggling business in both Serbia and Montenegro. See Misha Glenny, *McMafia: Crime without Frontiers*, London: The Bodley Head, 2008, p. 35.
62 *AIM Press* (Zurich), 5 June 2000, http://www.aimpress.ch/dyn/trae/archive/data/200006/00605-007-trae-pod.htm [last accessed 21 February 2014].
63 International Crisis Group (ICG), 'Montenegro's Local Elections: Testing the National Temperature', ICG Background Briefing, 26 May 2000, p. 1.
64 Florian Bieber, *Montenegrin Politics since the Disintegration of Yugoslavia*, p. 34.
65 In a visit to Podgorica on 14 October 2000 (prior to the first meeting between Djukanović and Koštunica), the US president's advisor on the Balkans, James O'Brian, told Djukanović bluntly that following the fall of Milošević the United States no

longer supported Montenegro's endeavours for attaining greater independence. He advised the Montenegrin president to instead reach an agreement with the new Serbian government on the continuation of the SRJ. See Roberts, *Realm of the Black Mountain*, p. 458, fn.70.
66 Bieber, 'Montenegrin Politics since the Disintegration of Yugoslavia', p. 35. Djindjić had been given protection in Montenegro following the murder of Slavko Ćuruvija. While in Montenegro he was based in the coastal town of Herceg Novi, but continued to have control over the DS.
67 Beáta Huszka, 'The Dispute over Montenegrin Independence', in Florian Bieber (ed.), *Montenegro in Transition: Problems of Identity and Statehood*, Baden-Baden: Nomos Verlagsgesellschaft, 2003, p. 43.
68 Interview with Milo Djukanović, in 'The Fall of Milošević' archive, No. 1/12b, Roll No. 159, p. 39.
69 According to the International Crisis Group's analysis of the legal status of Montenegro, published in September 2000, 'Montenegro cannot be said to possess complete sovereignty as it has not declared independence, been recognised by any states, nor established accredited diplomatic missions in other states. The ability of Montenegro to possess sovereignty is further limited by the continued presence of the Yugoslav Army on its territory. The internal political situation within Montenegro also leaves it uncertain as to whether a significant majority of the population would support a declaration of independence.' See International Crisis Group (ICG), 'The Current Legal Status of the FRY, and of Serbia and Montenegro', Balkans Report No. 101, 19 September 2000, p. 35.
70 See *Monitor* (Podgorica), 17 November 2000, pp. 8–9.
71 'It seemed to me', said Djukanović, 'that it was best that instead of one non-functional country, under which two totally old Balkans states functioned separately – Serbia and Montenegro – to establish an alliance of two independent and internationally recognized states, where each one would work on organizing its own "interior", but through an alliance, it would more rationally carry out certain joint business and synchronize its path to European integration. That is how my position became clearly defined as well as the position of my associates, in regard to the relations of Serbia and Montenegro. I explained this ... [and] I must say that Mr Koštunica took this with great reservation.' See Interview with Milo Djukanović, in 'The Fall of Milošević' archive, No. 1/12b, p. 39.
72 Huszka, 'The Dispute over Montenegrin Independence', p. 14.
73 CEDEM polls conducted in the immediate period following Milošević's fall suggested a slim majority of the population supported Montenegrin independence. See CEDEM Newsletter, January 2001, No. 1. For an analysis of the growing public support for independence, see *Monitor* (Podgorica), pp. 14–16.
74 Reneo Lukić, 'From Yugoslavia to the Union of Serbia and Montenegro', in Sabrina Ramet and Vjeran Pavlaković (eds.), *Serbia since 1989*, University of Washington Press, p. 88.
75 See Nina Caspersen, 'Elite Interests and the Serbian-Montenegrin Conflict', *Southeast European Politics*, Vol. IV, No. 2-3, November 2003, pp. 104–121.
76 In their post-election assessment of the April 2001 parliamentary elections, the OSCE noted that there existed a 'blurring of government and political activities' and that there were numerous allegations that the government had applied pressure on government workers to 'secure their allegiance to the governing party', though they added that 'these allegations are difficult to prove'. They did, however, stress that 'this

kind of influence has no place in a democratic society'. See OSCE/ODHIR, 'Republic of Montenegro (Federal Republic of Yugoslavia): Parliamentary Election', 22 April 2001, Warsaw, 12 June 2001, p. 13.

77 For a detailed discussion of the dynamics of the post-election 'discussion with agreement' between the DPS and LSCG, see Marko Orlandić, *Crnogorsko posrtanje*, Podgorica: Montcarton, 2005, pp. 233–248.
78 *Monitor* (Podgorica), 18 May 2001, p. 8.
79 The LSCG would later withdraw their support on the basis that the government had failed to schedule an independence referendum within the agreed timescale.
80 Lukić, 'From Yugoslavia to the Union of Serbia and Montenegro', p. 80.
81 Judy Batt, *The Question of Serbia*, Chaillot Paper No. 81, Brussels, August 2005.
82 *AIM Press* (Zurich), 31 May 2001, http://www.aimpress.ch/dyn/trae/archive/data/200106/10613-001-trae-pod.htm [last accessed 20 June 2014].
83 According to Misha Glenny, 'Two Montenegrin companies, both controlled by Djukanović and the secret service, levied £20 on each case transited through the country', making it at highly profitable venture. See Glenny, *McMafia*, p. 36.
84 A Montenegrin parliamentary commission was later established to investigate but whilst their findings acknowledged the existence of organized crime structures in Montenegro, it rejected claims that Djukanović himself was involved.
85 Lukić, 'From Yugoslavia to the Union of Serbia and Montenegro', p. 81.
86 See *Vijesti* (Podgorica), 15 March 2002, p. 3. For a withering critique of the events that led to the establishment of the joint state of Serbia and Montenegro, see Čedomir Lješević, *Solanijada ili: još jedan genocide nad Crnom Gorom*, Podgorica: Pobjeda, 2005.
87 Živko Andrijašević & Šerbo Rastoder, *Istorija Crne Gore*, Podgorica: CICG, 2006, p. 271.
88 *Vijesti* (Podgorica), 17 March 2002, p. 2.
89 See *Vijesti* (Podgorica), 15 March 2002, p. 4.
90 *Vijesti* (Podgorica), 16 March 2002, p. 4.
91 *Vijesti* (Podgorica), 15 March 2002, p. 4. See also *Dan* (Podgorica), 15 March 2002, p. 3.
92 'Letter of Protest Addressed to Western Democracies by Montenegrin Intellectuals', http://www.montenet.org/2003/repotpis.html [last accessed 21 May 2014].
93 Batt, *The Question of Serbia*, Chaillot Paper No. 81, August 2005.
94 See *Monitor* (Podgorica), 22 March 2002, pp. 10–11.
95 *Vijesti* (Podgorica), 7 March 2002, p. 2.
96 Andrijašević & Raštoder, *Istorija Crne Gore*, p. 271.
97 CEDEM, *Montenegrin Public Opinion in 2002*, CEDEM, Podgorica 2002, pp. 9–10.
98 Institute for War and Peace Reporting (IWPR). *Serbia and Montenegro: An Unhappy Marriage*, Institute for War and Peace Reporting, Balkan Report No. 493, 22 April 2004.
99 *Monitor* (Podgorica), 25 May 2001, p. 25.
100 Koča Pavlović, *Montenegrin Independence: Media Discourse*, Podgorica, 2005, p. 15.
101 In the 25 May 1998 edition of *Monitor*, for example, Miodrag Perović published an editorial entitled *Pad* (Fall), attacking the leadership of the LSCG for their role in breaking any possibility of a DPS-SDP-LSCG coalition. See *Monitor* (Podgorica), 25 May 2001, p. 5.
102 S.C. was sentenced in 2014 *in absentia* by the Montenegrin courts for allegedly fabricating the entire story. The sentencing drew significant condemnation from international human rights groups. See, for example, Amnesty International: 'Public

Statement – Montenegro: Trafficked Woman Sentenced while Perpetrators Stay Free', Amnesty International Press Office, London, 21 November 2014, AI Index: EUR 66/006/2014.
103 See OSCE/ODHIR Election Observation Mission Report, 'Republic of Montenegro (Serbia and Montenegro): Presidential Elections, 22 December 2002 and 9 February 2003', Warsaw, 3 April 2003.
104 *Pobjeda* (Podgorica), 12 May 2003, p. 1. The May 2003 presidential elections were the last that the LSCG contested.

Chapter 8

1 For a detailed account of the events that led to the assassination of Djindjić, see Miloš Vasić, *Atentat na Zorana*, Belgrade: Narodna kniga, 2005.
2 Lack of cooperation with the ICTY (and the EU's threat to suspend accession negotiations with the state union in 2005) was oft-used by pro-independence campaigners as a justification for why Montenegro needed to become independent. Just two weeks before Djindić's assassination (late February 2003), the ICTY's chief prosecutor, Carla Del Ponte, visited Podgorica whereupon she met with Milo Djukanović, who proceeded to complain to her that [Vojislav] Koštunica and the army were 'thwarting reforms and blocking Serbia and Montenegro's cooperation with The Hague'. According to Del Ponte, Djukanović lamented that 'Montenegro will suffer the consequences of Serbia's failure to cooperate with the tribunal'. 'Montenegro' he said, 'does not want to be a hostage to Serbia any longer'. Del Ponte added that Djukanović was also reluctant to be a witness at the Milošević trial and that doing so would 'damage him politically in Montenegro'. See Carla Del Ponte (with Chuck Sudetic), *Madame Prosecutor: Confrontations with Humanity's Worst Criminals and the Culture of Impunity*, New York: Other Press, 2009, p. 171.
3 According to Judy Batt, the deepening of this division could be seen 'in the way that the previously overlapping Serbian/Montenegrin identities' had disaggregated into 'clearly polarized political alternatives'. 'Those in favour of independence', she continued, 'are now redefining Montenegrin identity as a separate national identity, while Montenegrin supporters of the federation with Serbia increasingly insist on their Serbian identity. The preliminary results of the 2003 census ominously confirmed this'. See Judy Batt, *The Question of Serbia*, p. 24.
4 For a detailed breakdown of the 2003 census results, see MONSTAT (Republički zavod za statistiku), 'Popis stanovništva, domaćinstava i stanova 2003: Prva rezultati po opštinima, naseljima i mjesim zajednicama', MONSTAT: Podgorica, December 2003. See also *Monitor* (Podgorica), 19 December 2003, p. 9.
5 See *Dan* (Podgorica), 26 March 2006, p. 3.
6 In December 2005, six months before the independence referendum, Aleksander Apostoloviski, a journalist from the Serbian daily *Politika*, visited the town of Mojkavac, where in the 2003 census 54.77 per cent had declared themselves 'Montenegrins' and 40.88 per cent had defined themselves 'Serbs'. In the town, he claimed, the divisions even manifested themselves in the town's café's, many of which were divided into pro-independence and unionist. See *Politika* (Belgrade), 21 December 2005, p. 10.

7 For a very detailed account of Montenegro's historical state symbols (including flags), see Milan Jovićević, *Montenegrin State and Dynastic Symbols*, Cetinje: National Museum of Montenegro, 2001.
8 The debates over the symbols of the state union, in particular the flag, rolled on for months after the signing of the Belgrade Agreement in March 2002. The Serbian proposal for the state union flag was a darker blue than the Montenegrin, so a compromise was eventually reached. The shade of blue known as 'C300' was eventually accepted by both Serbia and Montenegro.
9 According to Miša Djurković, Serbs saw 'Sekula Drljević as a fascist war criminal and close ally of the [Croatian] Ustasha regime in World War II. [So] Understandably, members of the Serbian and pro-Serb parties in Montenegro reject such symbols'. See Miša Djurković, *Montenegro: Headed For New Divisions*, Conflict Studies Research Centre, Balkans Series, 07/11, March 2007, p. 6.
10 See, Matica Crnogorska, 'Crnogorski kao maternji jezik', *Godišnjak 1999–2003*, Podgorica: Matica, 2003, pp. 134–136.
11 Of course, Podgorica had more than its share of impressive modern architecture. The 'Hotel Podgorica' on the banks of the Morača River, built in 1967 and designed by Svetlana Radević, was not simply a standard socialist-era structure. Radević incorporated pebbles and stones from the banks of the river into the façade of the building to create a sense of continuity with the hotel's natural environment. The nearby Morača Sports Centre, built in 1978, is also a rather impressive structure. See Vladimir Kulić et al., *Modernism In-Between: The Mediatory Architectures of Socialist Yugoslavia*, Berlin: Jovis, 2012, p. 84.
12 WAZ held a 50 per cent stake in *Vijesti*'s publishing company 'Daily Press' until 2007, whereupon those shares were sold to the US-based 'Media Development Investment Fund' (25 per cent) and the Austrian-based 'Styria Medien MG' (25 per cent).
13 Jovanović's murder has, to date, never been solved. The only conviction in the case was against Damir Mandić, who was jailed in 2009 for a period of eighteen years as an accomplice to the killing. His case was reopened in February 2014 but no conviction has been forthcoming.
14 *Vijesti* (Podgorica), 17 June 2004, p. 2.
15 See *Republika* (Podgorica), 20 June 2005, p. 6.
16 The CKL was first published in 2001 and, with the objective of Montenegro's independence attained, ceased publication immediately after the May 2006 independence referendum.
17 See Srdja Pavlović, *Civil Society Building or Autocracy in the Making*, 2005, p. 10.
18 In a June 2005 edition of the paper, CKL claimed that Serbs had an obsession with weapons and war, stating that, 'Serbia has two souls – both in uniform: the army and the gendarmerie'. In the same edition, one author, Mirko Zečević, argued, 'The current common state of Serbia and Montenegro is the worst possible choice in which we are not living a better, more dignified and safer life' that the 'common state benefits the unhindered process of assimilation, where the will of the Montenegrin people to decide about their own future is being raped'. See *Crnogorski književni list* (Podgorica), 15 June 2005, p. 4.
19 Facsimile of document entitled, 'Analysis of the Media Landscape of Montenegro in the year in which decisive steps towards state independence are to be taken', Podgorica, April 2005.
20 SEEMO, 'Southeast European Media Handbook 2005/06', Vienna: SEEMO – IPI, 2006, p. 498.

21 International Crisis Group (ICG), 'Montenegro's Independence Drive', Crisis Group Report No. 169, Brussels, 7 December 2005, p. 8.
22 The SNS had originally been formed in 1997 as an offshoot of the NS led by Božidar Bojović (who opposed the NS leader Novak Kilibarda's decision to form a collation with the DPS in 1997). The SNS split in 2002, with a group led by Božidar Bojović and Ranko Kadić leaving the party to form the NSS. Andrija Mandić thereafter led the SNS.
23 The leader of the SNP, Predrag Bulatović, recognized that the party's interests could be damaged by close association with more nationalistic parties whom, he argued, exploited the SNP. The party leadership split, with the more nationalistic Zoran Žižić (who had briefly been the prime minister of the SRJ after Milošević's fall) leaving the party. Žižić would, however, continue to play a leading role in the Movement for the Joint European State Union of Serbia and Montenegro.
24 Despite being perhaps the most radical of the unionist politicians, Andrija Mandić remained a popular figure among supporters of the state union, and, according to locally conducted polls remained consistently the most trusted politician among Montenegro's Serbs. See CEDEM Public Opinion Poll, CEDEM Newsletter, No. 16 January–April 2006.
25 See *Monitor* (Podgorica), 18 February 2005, pp. 10–11.
26 According to an International Crisis Group (ICG) report from 2005, preservation of the state union was not the sole motivating factor for members of the movement. Djukanović's eight years in power had left many of them out in the cold and a number were 'anxious to have a chance to come to power and share in the distribution of wealth that is taking place under the current privatization drive'. See International Crisis Group (ICG), 'Montenegro's Independence Drive', p. 11.
27 Ibid., p. 11.
28 *Monitor* (Podgorica) 12 November 2004, p. 3.
29 The GzP was founded by Svetozar Jovićević and Nebojša Medojević in 2003. Originally, a 'group of experts' similar to GI7 Plus in Serbia, they became a serious political force. The leadership of the GZP split in 2006 when Jovićević and a number of other members left the organization after the leadership failed to agree on whether or not to call their supporters to vote for independence. The GzP became a political party called 'Movement for Changes' (*Pokret za promjeme* – PzP) following the referendum in 2006.
30 The 'Trsteno Affair' was essentially a corrupt land deal involving a number of members of the so-called *mali kabinet* – a small 'inner circle' within the leadership of the LSCG. The scandal generated by the affair led to the downfall of Miodrag Živković (who had a bitter personal and political split with Slavko Perović) and though he was replaced as party leader in October 2004 by Vesna Perović, the party would eventually (in March 2005) disband. Živković would, in the same month as he was expelled from the LSCG to form Liberal Party who, alongside the DPS, SDP and ethnic minority parties, supported the independence campaign. Slavko Perović refused to do so, choosing instead to freeze the activities of the LSCG. Detailed documentation pertaining to the Trsteno Affair can be found at: http://www.lscg.org/content/bivsi-lider-miodrag-zivkovic-DOKUMENTACIJA-afere-helkom-investment-grbalj-trsteno.html [last accessed 2 March 2015].
31 International Crisis Group (ICG), 'Montenegro's Referendum', Crisis Group Europe Briefing No. 42, 30 May 2006.
32 *Vijesti* (Podgorica), 1 December 2005, p. 2.

33 The right to vote in the Montenegrin referendum subsequently given to those who 'normally enjoy suffrage for presidential and parliamentary elections in Montenegro: an eligible voter was one aged over 18 years, who held Montenegrin citizenship and who had been permanently resident in Montenegro for a period of at least 24 months. By law, these qualifications meant that an eligible voter also included any Serbian citizen with a permanent residence in Montenegro for the same period, as well as a Montenegrin citizen who was temporarily resident in Serbia or abroad but who had retained a registered permanent residence at an address in Montenegro'. This, of course, excluded those Montenegrins who were registered as permanently resident in Serbia. See OSCE/ODHIR, 'Republic of Montenegro: Referendum on State-Status 21 May 2006 – OSCE/ODHIR Referendum Observation Mission Final Report, Warsaw, 4 August 2006, p. 8.

34 EC Troika 'non-paper' of 10 November 2005, quoted in International Crisis Group (ICG), 'Montenegro's Independence Drive', p. 10.

35 The United States adopted a more hands-off approach to the issue of Montenegro's independence. According to the International Crisis Group (ICG), the US ambassador made it clear that his country would not take a position on Montenegro's independence and that the United States considered it to be an internal (state union) issue. See ibid., p. 12.

36 Miroslav Lajčak would, in 2007, take over from Stephan Schwarz-Schilling as the international community's high representative (HR) for Bosnia & Herzegovina in early 2007.

37 See OSCE, 'Assessment of the Referendum Law: Republic of Montenegro, Federal Republic of Yugoslavia', Warsaw, 6 July 2001.

38 The Venice Commission is the commonly used name for the European Commission for Democracy Through Law (ECDTL), the constitutional arm of the Council of Europe.

39 OSCE/ODIHR, 'Referendum Observation Mission 2006, Republic of Montenegro (Serbia and Montenegro), Interim Report 1', Podgorica, 28 March–20 April 2006.

40 There existed two administrations working alongside the RRC. There were 21 municipal referendum commissions (MRCs) and 1,118 polling boards (PBs). Membership of each body was distributed equally between pro-independence and unionist political actors. Two commissions were also established (again, with a balanced membership) to monitor the media and campaign financing.

41 See OSCE/ODHIR, 'Republic of Montenegro: Referendum on State-Status 21 May 2006 – OSCE/ODHIR Referendum Observation Mission Final Report', Warsaw, 4 August 2006, p. 9.

42 The campaigns to agitate for or against independence had been operational since the signing of the Belgrade Agreement in 2002. Much was invested by either side to woo the diaspora vote in the United States, Australia and throughout Europe.

43 Mina News Agency, Podgorica, 23 March 2006.

44 *Vijesti* (Podgorica), 24 March 2006, p. 3. See also *Vreme* (Belgrade), 30 March 2006, pp. 18–19.

45 *Pobjeda* (Podgorica), 24 March 2006, p. 6.

46 *Dan* (Podgorica), 24 March 2006, p. 1.

47 Interview with Milo Djukanović on RTGG, broadcast on 26 March 2006.

48 *Republika* (Podgorica), 27 March 2006, p. 2. See also *Monitor* (Podgorica), 31 March 2006, p. 17.

49 See *Vijesti* (Podgorica), 12 May 2006, p. 3, and *Pobjeda* (Podgorica), 12 May 2006, p. 2.

50 *Vijesti* (Podgorica), 13 May 2006, p. 3.
51 Besides politicians, significant effort was invested into attracting Montenegro's most high-profile sportsmen and entertainers to support independence. Among the sportsmen who supported the pro-independence campaign publicly were the former FK Red Star Belgrade, AC Milan and Rapid Vienna player, Dejan Savićević (known to AC Milan fans as – *Il Genio* – *The Genius*), who was the sitting president of the Montenegrin Football Association, and former Fiorentina and Real Madrid striker, Predrag Mijatović.
52 *Republika* (Podgorica), 27 March 2006, p. 2.
53 *Vijesti* (Podgorica), 29 April 2006, p. 3.
54 *Vijesti* (Podgorica), 15 May 2006, p. 7.
55 Foreign journalists covering events commented to the author prior to the referendum that given the omnipotent Montenegrin flag, the outcome was somewhat inevitable. However, significant funds were provided by the Montenegrin government to manufacture flags that would then be given to DPS activists in Podgorica (and other Montenegrin towns). The prevalence of the Montenegrin flag was merely a testament to the organizational efforts of the pro-independence bloc, rather than a demonstration of predominantly pro-independence sentiment in Podgorica.
56 *Dan* (Podgorica), 17 May 2006, p. 2.
57 Traditionally, in Montenegro younger voters tended to be attracted to pro-independence parties. However, the campaign was aimed at those youth who were to an extent disenfranchized from economic opportunities because they were sons or daughters of unionist families.
58 A catalogue of alleged attacks and threats against unionist supporters were reported in pro-union daily *Dan* in the weeks preceding the referendum. See *Dan* (Podgorica), 13–19 May 2006.
59 The appearance of Harun Hadžić at unionist rallies clearly came as quite a surprise. Hadžić had been jailed in 1994 by members of the same political option to whom he now gave his support. He and others within the leadership of the Montenegrin branch of the SDA were accused of plotting against the state by preparing an insurrection in Montenegro with the objective of creating an independent Sandžak (see Chapter 4). He was later pardoned by the then Montenegrin president, Momir Bulatović.
60 See *Dan* (Podgorica), 28 April 2006, p. 3. When being booed by a crowd of pro-independence supporters in Rožaje, Bulatović responded by blowing kisses and smiling at them. 'With smiles and kisses' he later said, 'Montenegro should go forward'. See *Vijesti* (Podgorica), 13 May 2006, p. 6.
61 The SNS were the most nationalist Serb party and are perceived to be ideologically close to the Serbian Radical Party (SRS). Often their rhetoric was abundant with accusations of prejudice against Serbs in Montenegro and the mortal dangers that would be faced by them in the event of independence.
62 *Dan* (Podgorica), 12 May 2006.
63 Statement by the Serbian Radical Party (SRS), Radio B92, Belgrade, 12 May 2006.
64 The Four Ss (Cs in Cyrillic) stand for *Samo sloga Srbina spasava* (Only Unity Saves the Serbs). For more on the Herceg Novi rally, see *Vijesti* (Podgorica), 15 May 2006, p. 3.
65 *Nezavisne Novine* (Banja Luka), 16 May 2006, p. 5.
66 *Vijesti* (Podgorica), 17 May 2006, p. 2.
67 Ibid., p. 2.
68 Djukanović v. Bulatović debate on RTCG 1, broadcast on the 16 May 2006. See also *Vijesti* (Podgorica), 17 May 2006, p. 3.

69 OSCE/ODHIR, 'International Referendum Observation Mission: Referendum on State Status, Republic of Montenegro (Serbia and Montenegro)', Podgorica 22 May 2006, p. 6.
70 The content of RTCG's programming may well have been inconsequential to many unionist supporters anyway. In the predominantly Serb areas in the north of Montenegro, there is a much higher ratio of satellite dishes enabling access to Serbian television.
71 IN TV was known to be owned by Milo Djukanović's brother, Aleksander 'Aco' Djukanović.
72 The OSCE/ODHIR noted that while 'generally, television news coverage had provided a balance' the printed press was 'not balanced, with some newspapers being inflammatory at times'. See OSCE/ODHIR, 'Referendum Observation Mission 2006: Republic of Montenegro – Interim Report, 21 April–5 May 2006.
73 Weeklies such as *Monitor* were not subject to the OSCE/ODHIR's monitoring of the media. See OSCE/ODHIR, 'International Referendum Observation Mission: Referendum on State Status, Republic of Montenegro (Serbia and Montenegro)', Podgorica, 22 May 2006, p. 6.
74 International Crisis Group (ICG), 'Montenegro's Referendum', p. 4.
75 In all elections in Montenegro, and in much of continental Europe, there is a ban on canvassing twenty-four hours – or even forty-eight hours – prior to the opening of polling stations, remaining in place until voting ends.
76 See *Vijesti* (Podgorica), 20 May 2006, p. 1.
77 *Vijesti* (Podgorica), 19 May 2006, p. 3.
78 In the leaked analysis of the Montenegrin media scene, the authors had asserted that, 'It seems that none, very few or almost nobody in the administration or in media comprehends that successes in sports and culture are the best way to affirm a state.' See Montenegrin Ministry of Foreign Affairs, 'An Analysis of the Media Scene in Montenegro in the year when Decisive Steps Toward State Independence are to be Made', Podgorica 15 February 2005, p. 6.
79 *Pobjeda* (Podgorica), 21 May 2006, p. 1. See also *Pobjeda: Sport plus* (Podgorica), 21 May 2016, p. 1. The 21 May 2006 cover of *Vijesti* also depicted the victorious handball team holding aloft the trophy. See *Vijesti* (Podgorica), 21 May 2006, p. 1.
80 Although the owner of BK television, Bogoljub Karić, was a close associate of Milošević and widely perceived as corrupt, Montenegrin television frequently reported this case framed as an authoritarian action by the Serbian government. Furthermore, it was not uncommon to hear ordinary Montenegrins say that Serbia (and in particular the Mladić issue) was an impediment to Montenegro's accession to the EU. See International Crisis Group (ICG), 'Montenegro's Referendum', p. 6.
81 See *Vijesti* (Podgorica), 4 May 2006, p. 3.
82 See Milan Vukčević, *Crnogorska Dijaspora*, Podgorica: Centar za iseljenike Crne Gore, Grafotisak, 2006.
83 It was deemed that those Montenegrins residing in Serbia who had previously voted in elections there could not do so in both republics.
84 *Vijesti* (Podgorica), 15 May 2006, p. 8. See also *Pobjeda* (Podgorica), 15 May 2006, p. 3.
85 *Monitor* (Podgorica), 18 May 2006, p. 24.
86 See *Republika* (Podgorica), 22 May 2006, p. 2.
87 *Monitor* (Podgorica), 18 May 2006, p. 25.
88 See *Vijesti* (Podgorica), 23 May 2006, p. 1, and *Monitor* (Podgorica), 26 May 2006, p. 4.

89 See the International Crisis Group (ICG), 'Montenegro's Referendum', p. 3. See also *Vijesti* (Podgorica), 10 May 2006, p. 4.
90 *Vijesti* (Podgorica), 20 May 2006, p. 1.
91 The Republican Referendum Commission (RRC) confirmed that this figure was the exact amount of eligible voters. Mina News Agency (Podgorica), 12 May 2006.
92 *Vijesti* (Podgorica), 18 May 2006, p. 2.
93 OSCE/ODHIR, 'International Referendum Observation Mission: Referendum on State Status, Republic of Montenegro (Serbia and Montenegro)', Podgorica, 22 May 2006.
94 The OSCE/ODHIR report does, however, note, 'There were two instances – in Plevjla and Berane – where international observers reported suspicious activities that may indicate vote-buying schemes on behalf of the pro-independence bloc. A number of instances were also observed of voters taking photographs of their marked ballot papers.' See ibid., p. 8.
95 The bookmakers in Montenegro did not take bets on the independence referendum but bookmakers in Serbia did so.
96 CEMI used initial reports from polling stations throughout Montenegro which were carefully selected to represent the overall electorate as closely as possible. The Montenegrin NGO CDT (Centre for Democratic Transition), perhaps having seen the chaos caused by the preliminary results given by CEMI, chose a more cautious approach. Their spokesperson, Milica Kovačević, stated, 'We are of the opinion that the referendum commission should be allowed to complete its work and count all ballot papers. The projections show a very tight result. The CDT does not want to contribute to confusion.' Statement by CDT, broadcast on Radio Televizija Crne Gore (RTCG) 21 May 2006.
97 Statement by Predrag Bulatović on RTCG 1, broadcast on Radio Televizija Crne Gore (RTCG), 21 May 2006.
98 MINA News Agency (Podgorica), 21 May 2006.
99 Speech by Milo Djukanović on RTCG1, broadcast on Radio Televizija Crne Gore (RTCG), 22 May 2006. See also *Vijesti* (Podgorica), 22 May 2006, p. 3.
100 *Pobjeda* (Podgorica), 22 May 2006, p. 1.
101 *Vijesti* (Podgorica), 22 May 2006, p. 1.
102 Statement by František Lipka (Chairman of the RRC), broadcast on Radio Televizija Crne Gore (RTCG), 22 May 2006.
103 See *Vijesti* (Podgorica), 25 May 2006, p. 5.
104 Ibid., p. 5.
105 *Pobjeda* (Podgorica), 23 May 2006, p. 3.
106 International Crisis Group (ICG), 'Montenegro's Referendum', p. 12.
107 Mina News Agency (Podgorica), 23 May 2006.
108 OSCE/ODHIR, 'Republic of Montenegro: Referendum on State-Status 21 May 2006 – OSCE/ODHIR Referendum Observation Mission Final Report, Warsaw, 4 August 2006, p. 1.
109 Beta News Agency (Belgrade), 23 May 2006. In the months following the referendum, the pro-union parties NS, DSS and SNP produced a *Bijela knjiga* (White Book) which, they claimed, documented instances of electoral fraud throughout the referendum process. The extensive 1,290-page book includes hundreds of letters sent by the prop-union bloc to the RRC (and the responses by the latter) regarding voters' lists and other alleged irregularities. The vast majority of the documentation was generated and sent to the RRC after the referendum and this

collection of documents thus demonstrates not only the volume of material sent, but the efforts to persuade the RRC of electoral fraud. See NS/DSS/SNP, *Bijela knjiga: Referendum u Crnoj Gori 2006 – Zbornik dokumenata*, Belgrade/Niš: Narodna misao, 2006.
110 International Crisis Group (ICG), 'Montenegro's Referendum', p. 2, fn. 3.
111 In the Serbian parliamentary session in which independence was declared, neither Boris Tadić (the president of Serbia) nor Vojislav Koštunica (the prime minister of Serbia) were present.

Chapter 9

1 Miša Djurković, 'Montenegro: Headed for New Divisions?' Conflict Studies Research Centre, UK Defence Academy, Balkans Series, 07/11, p. 11.
2 See European Commission (EC), 'Commission Opinion on Montenegro's application for membership of the European Union' (COMMUNICATION FROM THE COMMISSION TO THE EUROPEAN PARLIAMENT AND THE COUNCIL, Brussels, 9.11. 2010 COM (2010) 670, {SEC (2010) 1334}.
3 Djurović was, rather unceremoniously, sidelined when the responsibilities of the Ministry for European Integration were merged with the Ministry of Foreign Affairs under the new name of the 'Ministry of Foreign Affairs and European Integration'. This change was confirmed when the new government was formed in December 2010. Milan Roćen retained the post of foreign minister and will head the new ministry.
4 See Government of Montenegro, 'Annual National Programme', Podgorica, 16 September 2010. According to a CEDEM poll conducted in Montenegro in July 2010, 40 per cent said they would vote against NATO membership, 32 per cent would support it, while 28 per cent said they 'did not know'. See CEDEM Newsletter 30, Podgorica, May–September 2010, p. 12.
5 For a brief overview of Mandić's own view of the Montenegrin political scene after the referendum, see Andrija Mandić, 'Šta posle referendum?', in Želidrag Nikčević (ed.), *Prava Srba u Crnoj Gori*, Belgrade: Focus, 2006, pp. 53–55. For an outline of the Serbian List's pre-2006 election platform, see Miša Djurković, 'Izborni program', ibid., pp. 67–71.
6 Party Program of The People's Party of Montenegro (SNS), December 2006, p. 3.
7 Republika izborna komisija Crne Gore, 'Izborni rezultati: 2006'.
8 The United Nations Development Programme (UNDP) research confirms this pattern. See UNDP, National Human Development Report: 'Montenegro – Society for All', UNDP/ISSP, Podgorica, 2009, pp. 78–81.
9 Mina News Agency, Podgorica, 11 September 2006.
10 *Republika* (Podgorica), 12 September 2006, p. 24.
11 Assaults on journalists became, if not commonplace, more frequent. In March 2012, *Vijesti* journalist Oliviera Lakić (who had written several articles about what she alleged were illegal activities on the part of the Montenegro Tobacco Company) was assaulted outside her apartment. In August 2013, an explosive device was detonated outside the Berane house of the *Vijesti* journalist Tufik Softić (who had been the victim of an assault in the same town in November 2007), and in December 2013, a similar device was detonated outside the Podgorica offices of *Vijesti*, one of a series of attacks on the newspaper's property.

12 In a ceremony in Budva on 28 May 2007, the Sarajevo-based International League of Humanists awarded both Milo Djukanović and Svetozar Marović peace prizes for the positive role they played during the 2006 referendum. *Vijesti*, however, were very critical, noting that both men were key in organizing the 1991 attack on Dubrovnik. The editorial on the day after the award ceremony (written by the director of *Monitor*, Miodrag Perović) stated unambiguously that 'neither Djukanović nor Marović have anything to do with humanism and have, moreover, never expressed any regret over the things they did during the early 1990s'. See *Vijesti*, 29 May 2007, pp. 1–2. For the exchanges between Ivanović and Djukanović after the incident, see *Vijesti* (Podgorica), 3 September 2007, pp. 2–3.
13 *Dan* (Podgorica), 25 October 2007, p. 9.
14 In a column written for the daily *Vijesti*, Jevrem Brković's son, Balša, suggested that the order for the attack came from within 'court circles'. See *Vijesti* (Podgorica), 28 October 2006.
15 *Vijesti* (Podgorica), 20 August 2009, pp. 1–2.
16 For an excellent analysis of the evolution of citizenship policy in Montenegro, see Jelena Džankić, 'Transformations of Citizenship in Montenegro: A context-generated evolution of citizenship policies', CITSEE Working Papers Series, March 2009.
17 The Constitution of Montenegro and the Constitutional Law for the Implementation of the Constitution of Montenegro (Article 13), 19 October 2007, p. 2.
18 OSCE Mission to Montenegro: OSCE Mission congratulates Montenegro on adoption and proclamation of new constitution, Podgorica, 22 October 2007, www.osce.org/montenegro/49069
19 *Monitor* (Podgorica), 29 February 2008, p. 9. See also *Vijesti* (Podgorica), 4 March 2008.
20 For an in-depth analysis of the controversies surrounding the bank, see Institut Alternativa, 'The Case of the First Bank: Experiences for Supervisors and Other Decision Makers', Podgorica, June 2009.
21 *Vijesti* (Podgorica), 26 February 2008, p. 3.
22 OSCE/ODIHR, Republic of Montenegro: Presidential Election, 6 April 2008, OSCE/ODIHR Election Observation Mission Final Report, Warsaw, 1 September 2008, p. 3.
23 Ibid., p. 18.
24 For the debates in the wake of Kosovo's declaration of independence, see *Monitor* (Podgorica), 22 February 2008, pp. 8–12.
25 *Vijesti* (Podgorica), 22 June 2008, p. 6.
26 *Dan* (Podgorica), 28 June 2008, p. 3.
27 *Vijesti* (Podgorica), 17 September 2008, p. 4.
28 Montenegrin journalist, Esad Kočan, sardonically noted, 'The authorities in Pristina should erect, at Gazimestan, a monument of gratitude to the people who have done the most for Kosovo's independence today – Slobodan Milošević, and his Montenegrin followers. Djukanović deserves to get two busts: one for being in Milošević's ranks when the routes to Kosovo's independence were being traced, and the other because he has accepted the consequences of his pioneering policy with the recognition of the state of Kosovo.' *Monitor* (Podgorica), 17 October 2008, p. 11.
29 *Vijesti* (Podgorica), 15 October 2008, p. 2.
30 *Dnevnik* (Novi Sad), 14 October 2008, p. 4,. See also *Vijesti* (Podgorica), 15 October 2008, p. 3.
31 *Dan* (Podgorica), 20 October 2008, p. 1.
32 *Večernje Novosti* (Belgrade), 20 October 2008, p. 4.

33 *Dan* (Podgorica), 27 October 2008, p. 1.
34 The DPS won fifteen out of thirty-three seats, four more than they had won in the previous Kotor elections in 2004, and were (by a margin of nine votes) by far the strongest party in the municipal assembly. What is unclear, however, is whether voters were declaring their satisfaction with the DPS or were expressing their dismay with the opposition's ineffective response to the Kosovo recognition controversy (PzP, for example, received only 533 votes). See *Monitor* (Podgorica), 14 November 2008, p. 9.
35 In January 2011, there were calls by some opposition MP's to reconsider Montenegro's recognition of Kosovo in the light of the EC's adoption of Dick Marty's controversial report on Kosovo. However, Lukšić stated that the adoption of the report should not be linked to the stance towards the foreign policy of the [Montenegrin] government. *Vijesti* (Podgorica), 27 January, 2011, p. 3.
36 *Vijesti* (Podgorica), 29 December 2008, pp. 1–2.
37 Veselin Vukotić, 'Lessons for Small Economies: The Case of Montenegro', in Will Bartlett & Vassilis Monastiriots (ed.), *South Eastern Europe after the Crisis: A New Dawn or Back to Business as Usual*, London: LSEE – Research on South Eastern Europe, European Institute, LSE, 2010, p. 97.
38 *The Observer* (London), 15 July 2007, p. 33.
39 *Monitor* (Podgorica), 22 February 2008, pp. 22–23.
40 For an analysis of the flow of Russian money into Montenegro, see European Parliament (Directorate General External Policies of the Union), 'The Russian Economic Penetration in Montenegro', Briefing Paper, December 2007.
41 See *Monitor* (Podgorica), 21 July 2006, pp. 10–12.
42 Veselin Vukotić, 'Lessons for Small Economies: The Case of Montenegro', p. 97.
43 The government was forced to provide loan guarantees of €49 million in November 2009 to cover KAP's debt to commercial banks and finance the cost of redundancies. CEAC agreed to hand over half its holdings to the government and withdraw claims for €300 million in damages over allegations that the government falsely evaluated the assets of the company before the 2005 takeover. The global market value of aluminium increased throughout 2010, mitigating further problems. But the issue of KAP continues to hang in limbo, lurching from one crisis to another.
44 The Montenegrin government developed an innovative, if controversial, idea to attract more foreign investment. In August 2009, they unveiled their proposals for an 'economic citizenship plan' that would grant citizenship for those willing to invest at least 500,000 Euros in Montenegro. Critics argued that this mechanism would attract criminals seeking to circumvent legal processes in their own countries and, moreover, that it would only consolidate Montenegro's pre-existing reputation as a haven for criminals. The proposals followed the equally controversial announcement that the Montenegrin government had given citizenship to the former Thai prime minister, Thaksin Shiniwatra (who, having been overthrown in a military coup in 2006, was wanted for myriad criminal offences in Thailand), on the basis that he would invest in Montenegro's tourist industry. Following sharp criticism from the EU, the Montenegrin government shelved the plan.
45 See Nikola Fabris, 'Impact of the Global Financial Crisis on the Labour Market and Citizens Social Status in Montenegro', in Will Bartlett & Milica Uvalić (eds.), *The Social Consequences of the Global Economic Crisis in Southeast Europe*, London: LSEE, 2012, pp. 131–42.
46 *Pobjeda* (Podgorica), 17 May 2010, p. 4.

47 *Dan* (Podgorica), 18 May, p. 4. See also *VIP News Daily Report* (Belgrade), 24 May 2010, p. 4.
48 *Slobodna Bosna* (Sarajevo), 11 December 2008, p. 21. From the sixteenth century, Montenegro was ruled by *Vladike* – Orthodox bishops (and later prince-bishops). They were drawn from families of exemplary note and from many different Montenegrin tribes (until 1697 – thereafter they were drawn solely from the Petrović family). They represented the main (and highest) source of authority and sought to unite Montenegro's tribes in the face of Turkish aggression, often with some difficulty. See Kenneth Morrison, *Montenegro: A Modern History*, pp. 17–19.
49 Some opposition politicians were sceptical about Djukanović's return. Ranko Kadić, the president of the DSS claimed that the purpose was to 'implement accession to NATO and to recognise the false state of Kosovo'. See *Bezbjednosti* (Podgorica), October 2008, p. 17.
50 *Monitor* (Podgorica), 29 February 2008, pp. 8–10.
51 For a more detailed account of the relationship, both business and personal, between Djukanović, Subotić and Drašković, see *Monitor* (Podgorica), 8 June 2007, pp. 8–10, and *Vreme* (Belgrade), 22 March 2007, pp. 16–21.
52 Misha Glenny, *McMafia: Crime without Frontiers*, p. 36. See also *Monitor* (Podgorica), 30 November 2007, pp. 12–14.
53 In his controversial book 'Mafia Export', the former Italian MP, Francesco Forgione, who led the Italian parliament's anti-mafia commission between 2006 and 2008, claimed that Djukanović as one of the key players in the cigarette smuggling trade in the Balkans. He also claimed that Djukanović had invoked the immunity granted to him by his position of prime minister.
54 See *Vijesti* (Podgorica), pp. 1–3. For a counterargument in defence of Milo Djukanović and a rejection of Knežević's accusations, see *Pobjeda* (Podgorica), 29 October 2009, pp. 1–2.
55 For an analysis of the Pukanić affair, see *Monitor* (Podgorica), 31 October 2008, pp. 12–14.
56 *Vijesti* (Podgorica), 17 February 2010, p. 2.
57 Exactly how wealthy Djukanović has become as a result of his business interests is a matter of some conjecture. In May 2010, the British daily *The Independent* claimed that he was one of the twenty richest political leaders in the world, in a list that included the King of Thailand, the Sultan of Brunei, King Abdullah of Saudi Arabia and Silvio Berlusconi. See *The Independent* (London), 19 May 2010, p. 24.
58 Lenard Cohen, 'Detours on the Balkan Road to EU Integration', *Current History*, March 2009, p. 128.
59 Svetozar Marović began his political career in 1989, one of the dubiously titled 'young, handsome and intelligent' troika comprising Momir Bulatović, Milo Djukanović and Marović himself. He later became president of the joint state of Serbia and Montenegro and a key member of the pro-independence bloc, but is perhaps best known as the architect of the *Rat za mir* (War for Peace). He provided ideological justifications for Montenegro's attack on Konavle and Dubrovnik in 1991 in his column in the daily *Pobjeda*, then Montenegro's only newspaper. See Helsinki odbor za ljudski prava u Srbiji, *Dubrovnik: Rat za mir*
60 See MANS, 'European Commission censures Montenegro for corruption in the urban development sector', 13 November 2010, www.mans.co.me/en/arhiva/2010/11/european-commission-censures-montenegro-for-corruption-in-the-urban-development-sector/ [last accessed 12 June 2015].

61 Some of the government's most vocal critics were also cynical about the motivations for the arrests. The renowned Montenegrin scholar, Milan Popović, stated, 'Had people in camouflage knocked at dawn on Djukanovic's door as well as Svetozar Marovic, we might think the rule of law had finally arrived.' See Milka Tadić-Mijović, 'Budva Dragnet Raises Hackles in Montenegro, Balkan Insight', 10 January, 2010 [last accessed 20 June 2015].

62 The Montenegrin NGO, MANS has argued that the decision not to prosecute Svetozar Marović confirms their suspicions that the Zavala investigations 'were not aimed at genuinely getting to the bottom of this case or bringing to account its key players,' MANS Press Release, 29 December 2010. www.mans.co.me/en/arhiva/2010/12/failure-to-pursue-svetozar-marovic-in-zavala-affair-is-scandalous-mans/. To compound these suspicions, the former spatial planning minister, Branimir Gvozdenović, was appointed general secretary of the DPS in January 2011.

63 *Vijesti* (Podgorica), 30 December 2010, p. 1.

64 *Dan* (Podgorica), 11 April 2007, p. 1.

65 *Vijesti* (Podgorica), 19 April 2007, p. 1.

66 While the CPC railed against the government for providing support to the SPC, the government showed that they were willing to adopt a combative stance with both churches. In early August 2007, the SPC's controversial Bishop Filaret was asked to leave Montenegro on the basis that he had entered the county illegally. As justification for the actions, the then Montenegrin prime minister, Željko Sturanović, stated that the bishop had been asked to leave Montenegro because he was on an ICTY list of persons suspected to be aiding indicted fugitive war criminals. See *Dan* (Podgorica), 3 August 2007, p. 1.

67 See *Evropa* (Belgrade), pp. 12–13.

68 *Monitor* (Podgorica), 14 September 2007, p. 26.

69 *Pobjeda* (Podgorica), 25 April 2011, p. 3.

70 *Balkan Insight* (Belgrade), 'Djukanović Supports Independent Church in Montenegro', www.balkaninsight.com/en/article/ djukanovic-supports-independent – church-in-montenegro [last accessed 23 June 2015].

71 European Court of Human Rights, 'Decision in the Case of Eparhija Budimljansko-Nikšića and Others V. Montenegro' (application no. 26501/05), Press Release, ECHR 387 (2012), 19 October 2012, http://hudoc.echr.coe.int/sites /eng/pages/search. aspx?i=003-4125009-4857539 [last accessed 13 October 2013].

72 In response to the DPS 'initiative', Amfilohije said, 'It is astonishing that questions of church unity should be made part of the program of a secular party. It is not clear, either, how it is possible in a country where state and church are separate under the law that politicians should make statements of this kind that constitute interference in the internal affairs and organization of the church. The Metropolitanate of Montenegro and the Littoral has existed for eight centuries. It is only in our times that some politicians in Montenegro, for the sake of their own ideological and partisan ends, are trying to violate the law and constitution to deny the legal identity and continuity of the Metropolitanate. I am sure these are just the growing pains of Montenegrin society and that it will grow out of them.' See *Večernje novosti* (Belgrade), 19 May 2011, p. 6.

73 *Vijesti* (Podgorica), 17 May 2011, pp. 2–3.

74 *Pobjeda* (Podgorica), 23 May 2011, p. 10.

75 *Dan* (Podgorica), 20 November 2012, p. 3. In May 20102, Amfilohije submitted a request for retirement, though a spokesperson for the SPC stated that he would continue to conduct religious services. VIP Daily News Report (Belgrade), 10 May 2012, p. 4.

Chapter 10

1. The SNP, led by Srdjan Milić, did not join the DF but members of his party (particularly those within the 'main board' allied to the SNP's former leader, Predrag Bulatović) chose to leave the SNP and join the DF in August 2012.
2. Lekić's served as the ambassador of the SRJ in Italy (and Malta) for two terms in the 1990s and early 2000s, having previously served as SFRJ Ambassador in Mozambique and Lesotho. His opponents (and pro-government media) would often try to undermine him by referring to him as 'Slobodan Milošević's ambassador in Italy' and someone who worked against Montenegro's independence.
3. During the October 2012 elections, the BS secured three parliamentary seats, and in December 2012, the BS leader, Rafet Husović, was named as one of four deputy prime ministers. The Croatian Civic Initiative (*Hrvatska građanska inicijativa* – HGI), led by Marja Vučinović (who became a 'Minister without Portfolio), and the ethnic-Albanian party FORCA, led by Nazif Cungu, also joined the DPS-led governing coalition.
4. In its 2016 annual report, the European Commission (EC) noted that while 'there were some developments in judicial follow-up of the alleged misuse of public funds for party political purposes (the "audio recordings affair"), it has not been completed'. The report added that 'To date, there has been no political follow-up'. See European Commission, 'Montenegro 2016 Report', Brussels, 9 November 2016, SWD (2016) 360 Final, p. 7.
5. Pavlović claimed that the cross-party committee, which was given only forty-five days to conclude its work, was impeded by DPS and SDP members and that the EU Delegation in Podgorica also met with constant obstruction.
6. Only two candidates ran in the presidential elections. Those parties that did not put forward a candidate openly supported one of the two existing candidates. Vujanović was supported by LS, the Albanian Coalition, BS and HGI; Lekić's campaign was supported by SNP, PCG and the DSS. See OSCE/ODHIR, 'Montenegro: Presidential Election' 7 April 2013 – Limited Election Observation Mission Final Report', Warsaw, 25 June 2013.
7. For an interesting 'parallel interview' with both Vujanović and Lekić (and their competing arguments over the outcome), see *NIN* (Belgrade), 25 April 2013, pp. 28–31.
8. In advance of the DF protests, efforts to convince other opposition parties to join them had met with little success, leading Nebojsa Medojević, president of PzP and member of the presidency of the DF stated (via his Twitter account) that he believed DEMOS, PCG, URA and DCG to be 'systematically obedient agents' working in the service of the DPS.
9. Problematically, there has never existed a consensus among Montenegro's citizens regarding NATO membership and opinion is sharply divided. The majority of the country's Serb population still have raw memories of the seventy-eight-day NATO bombing campaign of the SRJ in 1999. But there was not absolute unity over the issue even within the DF. Some within the PzP, for example, did not take such a hard line on NATO accession but believed nevertheless that the question of whether Montenegro joined should be decided by referendum not merely by a parliamentary vote.
10. For an analysis of Ivan Brajović's political career before he left the SDP, see *Monitor* (Podgorica), 3 October 2014, pp. 18–19.

11 *Vijesti* (Podgorica), 4 October 2015, p. 3.
12 For information on 'crowd funding', see the 'Sloboda traži ljudi' website: http://slobodatraziljude.me/doniraj/ [last accessed 13 January 2016].
13 See, for example, *Pobjeda* (Podgorica), 26 October 2015, p. 2.
14 *Vijesti* (Podgorica), 7 October 2015, p. 3.
15 *Vijesti* (Podgorica), 8 October 2015, p. 2.
16 See *Monitor* (Podgorica), 2 October 2015, p. 8.
17 The Montenegrin writer Andrei Nikolaidis stated that the protests represent an attempt to stage a 'Chetnik revolution in Podgorica'. See *Globus* (Zagreb), 2 October 2016, p. 24.
18 *Vijesti* (Podgorica), 5 October 2015, p. 3.
19 *Pobjeda* (Podgorica), 18 October 2015, p. 2. *Pobjeda* consistently referred to the DF demonstrations as 'anti-NATO demonstrations' and, equally consistently made the case that Russia were behind them. See, for example *Pobjeda* (Podgorica), 19 October 2015, p. 3.
20 Among those arrested were the MP's Slaven Radunović and Vladislav Bojović, both leading figures in the DF. Also arrested were Dražen Živković, a journalist for the anti-government daily newspaper *Dan*, and Gojko Raičević, the editor of the anti-government web portal 'IN4S'. In the days after the events, IN4S posted (on YouTube) a video entitled 'The War in Montenegro Has Begun', which detailed the treatment of a number of leading DF figures at the hands of the Montenegrin police. See IN4S, 'The War in Montenegro Has Begun', https://www.youtube.com/watch?v=JGFZaaOT1IE [last accessed 6 January 2016].
21 For a withering critique of the DF's protests and the methods they utilized, see *Slobodna Bosna* (Sarajevo), 22 October 2015, pp. 38–39.
22 Others entered the 'debate' following the breaking of the protests. On 17 October 2015, Doris Pack, the EU's former head of the European Parliament delegation for Southeast Europe, wrote on her Twitter account that in Montenegro the 'autocratic Prime Minister has set himself above the law, arresting peaceful protestors'. One week later, on 24 October, she tweeted that the protests were 'Not against NATO but against Djukanović'. See *Vijesti* (Podgorica), 25 October, http://www.vijesti.me/vijesti/doris-pak-ostavka-dukanovica-i-izbori-po-novim-pravilima-857377 [last accessed 10 January 2016].
23 European Union Delegation to Montenegro (EUDM), 'Statement of the Delegation of the European Union to Montenegro Regarding the Recent Events in Podgorica', EUDM Press Release, Podgorica, 19 October 2015. The 2016 European Commission (EC) Progress Report for Montenegro further noted that by late 2016 'Results of investigations of all incidents of violence and allegations excessive use of force by the police during the October 2015 protests are still pending'. See European Commission (EC), 'Montenegro 2016 Report', Brussels, 9 November 2016, SWD (2016) 360 Final, p. 7.
24 *Vijesti* (Podgorica), 19 October 2015, p. 4.
25 *Vijesti* (Podgorica), 23 October 2015, p. 3.
26 Despite the large number present at the 24 October demonstrations, a CEDEM poll conducted in November 2015 showed that support for the DF among citizens most likely to vote for the opposition, while having risen by almost 3 per cent since June peaked at 8.7 per cent in November 2015. DEMOS, URA and DCG, by contrast, stood at 21.1 per cent. See CEDEM, 'Političko javno mjenje Crne Gore', Podgorica, November 2015, p. 8.

27 Parts of the live feed from RTCG was filmed from either close to police lines or, indeed, behind them. This showed events from the perspective of the police and proved effective in shaping the events as an attack upon law and order and state institutions.
28 *Pobjeda* (Podgorica), 31 October 2015, p. 2. Djukanović has, however, emphasized on numerous occasions that he believes the government in Serbia have had absolutely no role in supporting the DF protests. See, for example, Radio Slobodna Evropa, 'Djukanović: Russia is Meddling in Montenegro, 18 December 2015, http://www.slobodnaevropa.org/content/djukanovic-russia-is-meddling-in-montenegro/27435598.html [last accessed 14 January 2016].
29 See *Pobjeda* (Podgorica), 26 October 2015, p. 1.
30 *Pobjeda* (Podgorica), 28 October 2015, p. 2. In an interview for the Bosnian weekly *Dani*, Žarko Korać (a professor in the Faculty of Philosophy and Belgrade and an independent MP in the Serbian parliament), argued that both the October 2015 protests in Montenegro and the September referendum on 'statehood day' in Republika Srpska were evidence of a new and more robust Russian engagement in the Balkans. See *Dani* (Sarajevo), 23 September 2016, pp. 10–13.
31 *Načisto*, TV Vijesti, Broadcast on 29 October 2015. The full interview can be seen at https://www.youtube.com/watch?v=6s8tkCSz1Tc [last accessed 17 November 2015].
32 *Vijesti* (Podgorica), 7 November 2015, p. 3.
33 See *Pobjeda* (Podgorica), 30 October 2015, pp. 2–3. For an analysis of Montenegro's relations with Russia, in a historical context, see Marko Kusovac, 'Odnos Crne Gore i Rusije', *Matica*, zima 2013/proljeće 2014, pp. 53–72.
34 See *Monitor* (Podgorica), 25 April 2014, p. 4.
35 *Vijesti* (Podgorica), 9 May 2014, p. 4.
36 See Petar Komnenić, 'Russia Protests over Anti-Russian Billboards in Montenegro', Reuters, 28 November 2014, http://uk.reuters.com/article/uk-montenegro-russia-billboards-idUKKCN0JC13920141128 [last accessed 13 January 2016].
37 *Vijesti* (Podgorica), 28 March 2015, p. 2.
38 See *Vijesti* (Podgorica), 23 October 2015, p. 3.
39 Public Relations Service of the Government of Montenegro, 'Statement by the Russian Foreign Ministry confirms PM Djukanović's claims about Russia's involvement in anti-NATO protests'. 27 October 2016, www.gov.me/en/News/ 153783/Statement-by-Russian-Foreign-Ministry.html [last accessed 14 January 2016].
40 See Radio Slobodna Evropa, 'Djukanović: Russia Is Meddling in Montenegro', 18 December 2015, http://www.slobodnaevropa.org/content/djukanovic-russia-is-meddling-in-montenegro/27435598.html [last accessed 14 January 2016].
41 *Dan* (Podgorica), 13 December 2015, p. 1.
42 *Vijesti* (Podgorica), 13 December 2015, pp. 2–3.
43 *Pobjeda* (Podgorica), 13 December 2015, p. 2. As one might expect, Podjeda published a number of scathing articles about the protests that were deeply critical of those involved. See, for example, *Pobjeda* (Podgorica), 16 December 2015, pp. 2–3.
44 *Pobjeda* (Podgorica), 16 January 2016, p. 2.
45 A poll conducted by the Damar Agency in January 2016 indicated that 47.3 per cent of Montenegro's citizens supported NATO membership, 37.1 per cent opposed it and the rest (15.6 per cent) were undecided. The poll was conducted in ten Montenegrin municipalities and based on a sample of 1,100 people. The Montenegrins NGO, 'The Movement for Neutrality' stated that the poll could not be trusted. See *Dnevne* novine (Podgorica), 2 February 2015, p. 3.

46　Rogozin, who was invited to visit Montenegro by the DF leadership in January 2016, was informed by the Montenegrin government that he would be unable to do so because his name was on a list of fifty Russian officials banned from the country as a consequence of EU sanctions. See *Pobjeda* (Podgorica), 11 January 2016, pp. 2–3.
47　*Pobjeda* (Podgorica), 28 December 2015, p. 2.
48　*Dnevne novine* (Podgorica), 23 January 2015, p. 2. Footage of the 'NOVA party police' can be found at: http://www.cdm.me/ drustvo/crna-gora/foto-ovo-je-policija-demokratskog-fronta [last accessed 3 February 2016].
49　*Dnevne novine* (Podgorica), 5 January 2016, p. 2.
50　*Vijesti* (Podgorica), 4 January 2016, p. 2. Similarly, Miodrag Vuković, a DPS MP, stated that the relationship between the DPS and SDP was becoming unbearable. He assessed, however, that the SDP would not formally leave the government and would support the DPS in the vote of confidence motion. See *Pobjeda* (Podgorica), 8 January 2016, p. 3.
51　*Dan* (Podgorica), 25 January 2016, p. 2.
52　*Vijesti* (Podgorica), 27 January 2016, p. 4.
53　*Dan* (Podgorica), 27 January 2016, p. 2.
54　*Vijesti* (Podgorica), 28 January 2016, p. 3.
55　*Vijesti* (Podgorica), 29 January 2016, p. 2.
56　*Pobjeda* (Podgorica), 5 January 2016, p. 2.
57　*Dan* (Podgorica), 2 February 2016, p. 2.
58　*Dan* (Podgorica), 20 June 2016, p. 3.
59　*Pobjeda* (Podgorica), 'Deset godina od Crnogorske nezavisnosti: Mi, sami' (special edition), May 2016.
60　*Monitor* (Podgorica), 21 May 2016, pp. 7–10.
61　*Dnevne novine* (Podgorica), 14 October 2016, p. 2.
62　According to an OSCE/ODHIR report, interlocutors with their own election monitors alleged that 'the high quality and quantity of DF campaign materials' was due to the coalition 'receiving foreign funding'. The report, however, provides no concrete evidence of this. See OSCE/ODHIR International Election Observation Mission, 'Montenegro – Parliamentary Elections, 16 October 2016, Statement of Preliminary Findings and Conclusions', Podgorica, 17 October 2016, p. 7.
63　*Pobjeda* (Podgorica), 11 October 2016, p. 3.
64　For other opposition parties, prospects were mixed: The SDP and PCG were in a fight for their very survival. Conversely, they could be kingmakers, deciding whether to enter a coalition with the DPS or unite with in a grand coalition. However, the DCG's Aleksa Bečić cautioned against considering a post-election coalition with the DPS, stating that any party that did so would be 'the biggest traitors in Montenegrin history'.
65　See *Vijesti* (Podgorica), 11 October 2016, p. 2 and *Dan* (Podgorica), 11 October 2016, p. 3.
66　*Vijesti* (Podgorica), 14 October 2016, p. 11.
67　*Dnevne novine* (Podgorica), 14 October 2016, p. 3.
68　*Dnevne novine* (Podgorica), 14 October 2016, p. 6.
69　According to the Montenegrin daily *Vijesti*, five of the detained arrived in Montenegro on a train, after being invited by Dragan Maksić to a celebration organized by the Ravna Gora Chetnik movement. See *Vijesti* (Podgorica), 19 October 2016, p. 15.

70 Ostrog monastery, set in the large rock of Ostroška Greda, is a place of pilgrimage for many Orthodox Christians (and of other faiths). It is known for being the location of the bones of *Sveti* (Saint) Basil of Ostrog, and pilgrims who are suffering ill-health believe they can be cured or their pain eased by praying next to his body. In an interview for *Dan*, Dragan Dikić (Bratislav Dikić's brother) claimed that his brother had gone to Ostrog for this reason and that he was not only 'gravely ill' having undergone an operation due to a form of cancer, but had, since the operation, difficulty speaking. See *Dan* (Podgorica), 20 October 2016, p. 3.

71 See *Pobjeda* (Podgorica), 17 October 2016, p. 1; *Vijesti* (Podgorica), 17 October 2016, p. 1, and *Dan* (Podgorica), 17 October 2016, p. 1.

72 *Pobjeda* (Podgorica), 18 October 2016, pp. 8–9.

73 According to a report in *Pobjeda*, Sindjelić had fought with pro-Russian rebels in Eastern Ukraine in 2014 and 2015. Citing a Ukrainian web portal *Teror* they claimed that Sindjelić was proclaimed a terrorist by the Ukrainian president Petro Poroshenko's cabinet. See *Pobjeda* (Podgorica), 4 November 2016, p. 11.

74 *Vijesti* (Podgorica), 20 October 2016, p. 12.

75 *Načisto*, TV Vijesti (Podgorica), broadcast on 20 October 2015. The full interview with Milivoje Katnić can be found at: https://www.youtube.com/watch?v=QnuNtGgePn0 [last accessed 21 December 2016].

76 *Dan* (Podgorica), 22 October 2016, p. 3.

77 *Vijesti* (Podgorica), 25 October 2016, p. 11. See also *Pobjeda* (Podgorica), 25 October 2016, p. 4.

78 *Pobjeda* (Podgorica), 26 October 2016, p. 2.

79 *Vijesti* (Podgorica), 26 October 2016, p. 2.

80 *Dan* (Podgorica), 28 October 2016, p. 4.

81 *The Economist* (London), 4 November 2016, http://www.economist.com/node/21709635/ [last accessed 9 December 2016].

82 *Vijesti* (Podgorica), 3 November 2014, p. 14. However, the waters were muddied even further regarding Sindjelić's role in the 'state coup'. The leader of Serbia's Ravna Gora Movement, Bratislav Živković, claimed that Sindjelić had been offering money to members of the group to go to Podgorica, but that many refused because it was widely suspected that he was cooperating with both Serbian and Montenegrin intelligence services. See *Dan* (Podgorica), 6 November 2016, p. 2. For the role of Živković and other Serbian volunteers in Eastern Ukraine, see *Slobodna Bosna* (Sarajevo), 2 April 2015, pp. 36–40.

83 *Pobjeda* (Podgorica), 8 November 2016, p. 2.

84 *Vijesti* (Podgorica), 8 November 2016, p. 2.

85 *Dan* (Podgorica), 8 November 2016, p. 2.

86 *Vijesti* (Podgorica), 20 December 2016, pp. 14–15.

87 The daily *Dan* claimed in an article published on 26 December 2016 that there existed 'reasonable doubt' that part of the evidence in the state coup case had been falsified by prosecutors. The newspaper stated that documentation in which two of the alleged conspirators (Aleksander Sindjelić and Mirko Velimirović) are listed on the document as having used the same phone number when discussing their plans, which was, the author argued, 'technically impossible'. See *Dan* (Podgorica), 26 December 2016, p. 10.

88 European Commission (EC), 'Montenegro 2016 Report', Brussels, 9 November 2016, SWD (2016) 360 Final, p. 7.

Bibliography

Abdagić, Muhamed, 'Rifat Burdžović Tršo', *Bošnjačka riječ*, godina. 5, broj 19–20, Jul – decembar 2010, pp. 73–78.
Adžić, Novak, *Kratka istorija Crnogorske pravoslavne crkve (od sredine XV vijeka do 1920. godine)*, Cetinje: Dignitas, 2000.
Ahrens, Geert-Hinrich, *Diplomacy on the Edge: Containment of Ethnic Conflict and the Minorities Working Group of the Conferences on Yugoslavia*, Baltimore, MD: John Hopkins University Press, 2007.
Albright, Madeleine, *Madam Secretary*, London: MacMillan Press, 2003.
Alekšić, Budimir, & Krstajić, Slavko, *Trgovci dušama*, Nova Varoš: Bonart, 2003.
Alexander, Stella, *Church and State in Yugoslavia since 1945*, Cambridge: Cambridge University Press, 1979.
Allcock, John, *Explaining Yugoslavia*, London: Hurst & Co., 2000.
Amnesty International, 'The Federal Republic of Yugoslavia: Torture and Unfair Trail of Muslims in the Sandžak Region', AI Index EUR 17/70/95, November 1995.
Amnesty International, 'Public Statement – Montenegro: Trafficked Woman Sentenced while Perpetrators Stay Free', Amnesty International Press Office, AI Index: EUR 66/006/2014, London, 21 November 2014.
Andrejevich, Milan, 'Montenegro to introduce Multi-Party Elections', RFE Report on Eastern Europe, 23 February 1990.
Andrejevich, Milan, 'The Elections in Montenegro', RFE Report on Eastern Europe, 21 December 1990.
Andrejevich, Milan, 'Montenegro Follows Its own Course', RFE Report on Eastern Europe, 22 November 1991.
Andrejevich, Milan, & Bardos, Gordon, 'Serbia and Montenegro', in RFE Special Report, 'The Media in Regions of Conflict', RFE/RL Research Report, Vol. 1, No. 39, 2 October 1992.
Andrijašević, Živko, *Nacrt za ideologiju jedne vlasti*, Bar: Conteco, 1999.
Andrijašević, Živko, *Nacija s greškom*, Cetinje: Djurdje Crnojević, 2004.
Andrijašević, Živko, 'Cetinjski mitropoliti prema pećkim patrijarsima', *Matica*, Number 22/23, Year 6, Summer 2005.
Andrijašević, Živko, 'Cetinjski mitropoliti prema pećkim patrijarsima', *Matica*, Cetinje/Podgorica, broj 22/23, godina VI, 2005, pp. 183–212.
Andrijašević, Živko, & Rastoder, Šerbo, *The History of Montenegro*, Podgorica: CICG, 2006.
Andrijašević, Živko, 'Crnogorska 1948', *Matica*, broj 59, jesen 2014.
Andrijašević, Živko, & Zoran, Stanojević, *Pokrštavanje Muslimana 1913*, Podgorica: Almanah, 2003.
Andrijevich, Milan, 'The Sandžak: The Next Balkan Theater of War?' RFE/RL Research Report, Vol. 1, No. 47, 27 November 1992.
Andrijevich, Milan, 'Sandžak: A Perspective on Serb – Muslim Relations', in H. Poulton, & S. Taji-Farouki (eds.), *Muslim Identity and the Balkan State*, London: Hurst & Co., 1997.

Auty, Phyllis, *Tito: A Biography*, London: Penguin Books, 1980.
Avakumović, Ivan, *History of the Communist Party of Yugoslavia*, Vol. 1, Aberdeen: Aberdeen University Press, 1964.
Avdić, Hakija, *Položaj Muslimana u Sandžaku 1912–1941*, Sarajevo: Biblioteka ključanin, 1991.
Avdić, Hakija, *Rifat Burdžović Tršo – život i djelo*, Novi Pazar: Matica Bošnjaka Sandžaka, 2003.
Balkan Air Force Report on the Situation in 2nd Corps Areas, 17 July 1944. WO 202/152.
Banac, Ivo, *The National Question in Yugoslavia; Origins, History, Politics*, Ithaca, NY and London: Cornell University Press, 1984.
Banac, Ivo, *With Stalin against Tito*, Ithaca, NY and London: Cornell University Press, 1988.
Banac, Ivo, 'Historiography of the Countries of Eastern Europe: Yugoslavia', *The American Historical Review*, Vol. 97, No. 4, October 1992.
Bandžović, Safet, & Kačar, Semiha, *Sandžak: historija i činjenice*, Novi Pazar: Sandžak Committee for Protection of Human Rights and Freedoms, 1994.
Bandžović, Safet, *Otmice u Sandžaku (1992–1993)*, Novi Pazar: Sandžački odbor za zaštitu ljudskih prava i sloboda, 1996, pp. 13–14.
Bartlett, Will, & Monastiriotis, Vasillis (eds.), 'South Eastern Europe after the Crisis', London: LSEE Research on Southeast Europe, European Institute, London School of Economics, November 2010.
Basić, Goran, *Položaj u Bošnjaka u Sandžaku*, Belgrade: Centar za antiratnu akciju, 2002.
Batt, Judy, *The Question of Serbia*, Chaillot Paper No. 81, Brussels, August 2005.
Beloff, Nora, *Tito's Flawed Legacy*, London: Victor Gollancz, 1984.
Benz, Ernst, *The Eastern Orthodox Church*, New York: Anchor Books, 1963.
Bideleux, Robert, & Ian Jeffries, *A History of Eastern Europe: Crisis and Change*, London and New York: Routledge, 1998.
Bieber, Florian (ed.), *Montenegro in Transition: Problems of Identity and Statehood*, Baden-Baden: Nomos Verlagsgesellschaft, 2003.
Bilić, Bojan, & Vesna, Janković (eds.), *Resisting the Evil: Post-Yugoslav Anti-War Contention*, Baden-Baden: Nomos Verlagagesellschaft, 2012.
Biševac, Safeta, 'Bosniaks in Sandžak and Inter-Ethnic Tolerance in Novi Pazar', in N. Dimitrijević (ed.), *Managing Multi-Ethnic Communities in the Countries of the Former Yugoslavia*, Budapest: LGI/OSI, 2000.
Boehm, Christopher, *Montenegrin Social Organization and Values: Political Ethnography of a Refugee Area Tribal Adaptation*, New York: AMS Press, 1983.
Boehm, Christopher, *Blood Revenge: The Enactment and Management of Conflict in Montenegro and Other Tribal Societies*, Pennsylvania: Pennsylvania University Press, 1986.
Bojić, Mehmedalija, *Historija Bosne i Bošnjaka (VII–XX vijek)*, Sarajevo: TKD Šahinpašić, 2001.
Bojović, Miodrag Todorov, 'Pljevaljski musmimani/bošnjaci izemđu stvarnosti i iluzije', *Almanah*, broj 27–28, Podgorica, 2004.
Borger, Julian, *The Butcher's Trail*, New York: Other Press, 2016.
Bose, Sumantra, *Bosnia after Dayton: Nationalist Partition and International Intervention*, London: Hurst & Co., 2002.
Bougarel, Xavier, 'Bosnian Muslims and the Yugoslav Idea', in Dejan Djokić (ed.), *Yugoslavism: Histories of a Failed Idea*, London: Hurst & Co., 2003.

Brajović, Milan et al., *Titograd u slobodi 1944–1974*, Titograd: Titogradska tribina/Pobjeda, 1974.
Bringa, Tone, *Being Muslim the Bosnian Way*, Princeton, NJ: Princeton University Press, 1995.
British Cabinet Papers, 'Memorandum by the Secretary of State for Foreign Affairs: Central and South-Eastern Europe', (de-classified document), CP 257 (38).
British Special Operations Executive (SOE), 'A Note on the Morale of German Forces in Question,' Draft, Appx 'J', 20 March 1944, HS5/922.
British SOE, 'Report Drawn up by Lieutenant Glenn on His Relations with Yugoslavs', 17 November 1941, HS5/938.
British SOE, 'Some Notes on the Yugoslav revolt', 22 June 1942, HS5/938.
British War Cabinet, Weekly Resume of the Naval, Military and Air Situation from 07.00 16th November to 07.00 23rd Novmber, 1944, No. 273, WP (44) 683.
British War Office (BWO), Report on the Political Situation in Montenegro by Captain R.H. Brodie to the Director of Military Intelligence, British War Office, 25 February 1919, Charles Furlong Collection, Hoover Institute, Stanford, CWF/Box No.3.
British War Office (BWO), Director of Military Intelligence, M.I. 3b, 27 April 1943 (Most Secret), 'A Short History of the Revolt in Yugoslavia'; PRO Archives, document FO 371/33469.
Brkljačić, Maja, *Popular Culture and Communist Ideology: Folk Epics in Tito's Yugoslavia*, Budapest: Central European University, 2000.
Brković, Jevrem, 'Crnogorci nijesu Srbi', *AS*, Titograd, September 1989, p. 4.
Brković, Jevrem, *Dnevnici (Vol. 2)*, Podgorica: CANU, 2001.
Brown, J.F., *Nationalism, Democracy and Security in the Balkans*, Dartmouth: RAND Research, 1991.
Bugajski, Janusz, *Ethnic Politics in Eastern Europe*, London: M.E. Sharpe, 1995.
Bulatović, Momir, *Manje od igre – više od života*, Novi Sad: Književna zajednica novog sada, 1991.
Bulatović, Momir, *Pravila ćutanja*, Belgrade: Alfa Kniga, 2005.
Burg, Stephen L., & Shoup, Paul, *The War in Bosnia-Herzegovina: Ethnic Conflict and International Intervention*, New York and London: M.E. Sharpe, 2000.
Čagarović, Nebojša, 'Montenegrin Identity: Past Present and Future', *The Journal of Area Studies*, Vol. 1, No. 3, 1993, pp. 129–136.
Čagarović, Nebojša, 'Anti-Fascism and Montenegrin Identity since 1990', *History*, Vol. 3, 2012, pp. 578–590.
Calović, Vanja, & Deletić, Milena. *Pravo da znam*, Podgorica: MANS, 2006.
Carnegie Endowment for International Peace, *Report of the International Commission to Inquire into the Causes and Conduct of the Balkan Wars*, publication no. 4, published by the Endowment, Washington, DC, 1914.
Carter, F.W., *Dubrovnik (Ragusa); A Classic City State*, London and New York: Gemini Press, 1972.
Caspersen, Nina, 'Elite Interests and the Serbian-Montenegrin Conflict', *Southeast European Politics*, Vol. IV, No. 2–3, November 2003, pp. 104–21.
CEDEM, 'Javno mnjenje Crne Gore', CEDEM, Podgorica, January 2000.
CEDEM, 'Montenegrin Public Opinion in 2002', CEDEM, Podgorica, April 2002.
CEDEM, *Tranzicija u Crnoj Gori: Legislativa, mediji, privatizacija*, broj 19 (Jul – Septembar 2003).
CEDEM, 'Local Community and Uniform Police: An Analysis of Public Survey Results', Podgorica, December 2004.

CEDEM, 'Javno mnjenje Crne Gore, Godišnjak br.2', CEDEM, Podgorica, Maj 2005 – April 2006.
CEDEM, Public Opinion Poll, CEDEM Newsletter, No.16 January – April 2006.
CEDEM, 'Političko javno mjenje Crne Gore', Podgorica, November 2015.
Ćemović, Momčilo, *Djilasi odgovori*, Belgrade: Svetlostkomerc, 1997.
Centar za iseljenike Crne Gore, *Crnogorska dijaspora: Zbornik asocijacija crnogorskih isljenika*, Podgorica: Grafotisak, 2006.
Central Intelligence Agency (CIA) Directorate of Intelligence, 'Yugoslavia: Key Questions and Answers on the Debt Crisis', EUR-84-100011, January 1984.
Cerović, Rajko, 'Televizija kao inspirator i izlog nacionalne kulture', *Matica*, Cetinje/Podgorica, Godina VI, broj 22/23, 2005.
Ćikić, Ibrahim, *Gdje sunce ne grije*, Podgorica: Dokumenti, 2008.
Ćirković, Sima M., *The Serbs*, Oxford: Blackwell Publishing, 2004.
Clapham, Christopher (ed.), *Private Patronage and Public Power: Political Clientelism in the Modern State*, London: Frances Pinter, 1982.
Clark, Wesley, *Waging Modern War: Bosnia, Kosovo and the Future of Combat*, New York: Public Affairs, 2001.
CMI Report, 'Corruption in Montenegro 2007: Overview of Main Problems and Status of Reforms', CHR Michelsen Institute, September 2007.
Cohen, Lenard J., *The Socialist Pyramid: Elites and Power in Yugoslavia*, London: Tri-Service Press, 1989.
Cohen, Lenard J., *Serpent in the Bosom: The Rise and Fall of Slobodan Milošević*, Boulder, CO: Westview Press, 2001.
Cohen, Lenard J., 'Detours on the Balkan Road to EU Integration', *Current History*, March 2009.
Cohen, Lenard J., & Dragović-Soso, Jasna (eds.), *State Collapse in South-Eastern Europe: New Perspectives on Yugoslavia's Disintegration*, Indiana: Purdue University Press, 2006.
Cohen, Lenard J., & Lampe, John R., *Embracing Democracy in the Western Balkans: From Postconflict Struggles toward European Integration*, Washington, DC and Baltimore, MD: Woodrow Wilson Center Press and John Hopkins University Press, 2011.
Čolović, Ivan, *The Politics of Symbol in Serbia*, London: Hurst & Co., 2001.
Ćosić, Dobrica, 'Uspostavljanje istorskog uma', *Književne novine*, No. 779-780, 1–15 July 1989.
Crampton, Richard J., *The Balkans since the Second World War*, London: Longman Press, 2002.
Cross, Sharyl, & Komnenich, Pauline, 'Ethnonational Identity, Security and the Implosion of Yugoslavia: The Case of Montenegro and the Relationship with Serbia', *Nationalities Papers*, Vol. 33, No. 1, March 2005.
Crnišanin, Ramiz, 'Autonomija Sandžaka i Sreten Vukosavljević', *Zbornik Sjenice*, Br.15-16, 2004.
Crnogorska akademija nauka i umjetnosti (CANU), *Novi ustav i preobražaji Jugoslovenskog društva: Radovi sa naučnoj skupa*, Titograd: CANU, 1991.
Crnovršanin, Harun, & Sadiković, Nuro, *Sandžak: Porobljena zemlja*, Frankfurt: Sandžačka riječ, 2001.
Conference for Security and Cooperation in Europe (CSCE), 'Declaration on the Yugoslav Crisis, Adopted by the CSCE Summit, Helsinki, 10 July 1992 (Article 4)', UN Doc.S/24308, Annex.
CSCE, 'Summary of Conclusions: Decision on Peaceful Settlement of Disputes', Stockholm, December 1992.

CSCE, 'Sandžak and the CSCE: A Report Prepared by the Staff of the Commission on the Security and Cooperation in Europe', Washington, April 1993.

CSCE, 'Conference on Security and Cooperation Missions in Kosovo, Sandžak and Vojvodina', Decision of 9 August 1993: Resolution 855 (1993), August 1993.

Ćuković, Mirko, *Sandžak u narodnooslobodilačkoj borbi*, Belgrade: Nolit, 1964.

Daadler, Ivo, & O'Hanlon, Michael, *Winning Ugly: NATO's War to Save Kosovo*, New York: Brookings Institution, 2001.

Dabo-Peranić, Miljenko., *Hrvatsko Sandžaka*, Madrid: Drina, 1966.

Darby, H.C., 'Montenegro', in Stephen Clissold (ed.), *A Short History of Yugoslavia*, Cambridge: Cambridge University Press, 1968.

Darmanović, Srdjan, 'Montenegro: Destiny of a Satellite State', *East European Reporter*, No. 27, March–April 1992.

Darmanović, Srdjan, 'Montenegro Survives the War', *East European Constitutional Review*, Vol. 8, No. 3, 1999, pp. 145–153.

Darmanović, Srdjan, 'Montenegro: Dilemmas of a Small Republic', *Journal of Democracy*, Vol . 14, No. 1, January 2003.

Deakin, F.W., *The Embattled Mountain*, Oxford: Oxford University Press, 1971.

Dedijer, Vladimir, *Tito Speaks*, London: Weidenfield and Nicholson, 1953.

Dedijer, Vladimir, *The Beloved Land*, London: MacGibbon & Kee, 1961.

Dedijer, Vladimir, *The War Diaries of Vladimir Dedijer, Volume 2 (November 28 1942 to September 10 1943)*, Ann Arbor: University of Michigan Press, 1990.

Del Ponte, Carla (with Chuck Sudetic), *Madame Prosecutor: Confrontations with Humanity's Worst Criminals and the Culture of Impunity*, New York: Other Press, 2009.

Deroc, Milan, *British Special Operations Explored: Yugoslavia in Turmoil 1941–1943 and the British Response*, Boulder/New York: Columbia Press (East European Monographs), 1988.

Destani, Beitullah, *Montenegro: Political and Ethic Boundaries, 1840–1920*, 2 vols, Chippenham, Wilts: Archive Editions, 2001.

Dević, Ana, 'Anti-War Initiatives and the Un-making of Civic Identities in the Former Yugoslav Republics', *Journal of Historical Sociology*, Vol. 10, No. 2, June 1997.

Devine, Alexander, *Montenegro in History, Politics and War*, New York: Frederick Stokes, 1918.

Devine, Alexander, *The Martyred Nation: A Plea for Montenegro*, London, 1924.

Dimitrovova, Bodhana, 'Bosniak or Muslim? Dilemma of One Nation with Two Names', *Southeast European Politics*, Vol. II, No. 2, October 2001.

Dizdarević, Raif, *Od smrti Tita do smrti Jugoslavije*, Sarajevo: OKO, 1999.

Djilas, Aleksa, *The Contested Country: Yugoslav Unity and Communist Revolution 1919–1953*, New York: Harvard University Press, 1991.

Djilas, Aleksa, *Najteže pitanje*, Belgrade: Arthouse, 2005.

Djilas, Milovan, 'O Crnogorskom nationalnom pitanju', *Članci 1941–1946*, Kultura, Belgrade, 1947.

Djilas, Milovan, *The New Class*, London: Phaidon Press, 1954.

Djilas, Milovan, *Land without Justice*, New York: Harcourt Brace and Co., 1958.

Djilas, Milovan, *Conversations with Stalin*, London: Rupert Hart Davis Publishing, 1962.

Djilas, Milovan, *Montenegro*, London: Methuen & Co., 1964.

Djilas, Milovan, *Njegoš: Poet, Prince, Bishop*, New York: Harcourt, Brace and World, 1966.

Djilas, Milovan, *Memoir of a Revolutionary*, New York: Harcourt Brace Jovanovich, 1973.

Djilas, Milovan, *Wartime*, London: Secker & Warburg, 1977.

Djilas, Milovan, *Tito: The Story from Inside*, London: Weidenfeld & Nicholson, 1981.

Djilas, Milovan, *Rise and Fall*, San Diego: Harcourt Brace Jovanovich, 1985.
Djilas, Milovan, & Gace, Nadežda, *The Bosniak*, London: Hurst & Co., 1998.
Djokić, Dejan (ed.), *Yugoslavism: Histories of a Failed Idea*, London: Hurst & Co., 2003.
Djokić, Dejan, *Elusive Compromise: A History of Interwar Yugoslavia*, London: Hurst & Co., 2007.
Djonović, Ranko, *Ne pristajem! Vrijeme časti i beščašća u Crnoj Gori (1989–2013)*, Podgorica: Art Gloria, 2013.
Djordjević, Dimitrije, 'Migrations During the 1912–1913 Balkan Wars and World War One', in *Migrations in Balkan History*, Belgrade: Serbian Academy of Sciences and Arts, 1989.
Djuranović, Draško, 'Transition in Montenegro: Media', CEDEM Report No. 19, July–September 2003.
Djurković, Miša, 'Montenegro: Headed for New Divisions?' Conflict Studies Research Centre, UK Defence Academy, Balkans Series, 07/11, 2006.
Djurkovic, Miša, *Kraj i početak*, Belgrade: Stylos, 2006.
Djurović, Gordana, 'Evropski Put Crne Gore', *Matica*, broj 20, Godine 5, Winter 2004.
Doder, Duško, *The Yugoslavs*, New York: Allen & Unwin, 1979.
Donia, Robert, *Radovan Karadžić: Architect of the Bosnian Genocide*, Cambridge: Cambridge University Press, 2015.
Dragović-Soso, Jasna, *Saviours of the Nation: Serbia's Intellectual Opposition and the Revival of Nationalism*, London: Hurst & Co., 2002.
Dryzek, Richard, & Holmes, Leslie. *Post-Communist Democratization*, Cambridge: Cambridge University Press, 2002.
Durham, Mary Edith, *Through the Lands of the Serb*, London: Edward Arnold, 1904.
Durham, Mary Edith, *The Struggle for Scutari*, London: Edward Arnold, 1914.
Durham, Mary Edith, *Some Tribal Origins, Laws and Customs of the Balkans*, London: Allen & Unwin, 1928.
Dyker, David A., & Vejvoda, Ivan, *Yugoslavia and After: A Study in Fragmentation, Despair and Rebirth*, London: Pearson Education, 1996.
Džankić, Jelena, 'Transformations of Citizenship in Montenegro: A Context-Generated Evolution of Citizenship Policies', CITSEE Working Papers Series, March 2009.
Džankić, Jelena, 'Reconstructing the Meaning of Being Montenegrin', *Slavic Review*, Vol. 73, No. 2, Summer 2014, pp. 347–72.
Džankić, Jelena, *Citizenship in Bosnia and Herzegovina, Macedonia and Montenegro: Effects of Statehood and Identity Challenges*, Aldershot: Ashgate, 2015.
Ećo, Nusret, 'Bošnjaci u Crnoj Gori: integracija bez asimilacije', *Almanah*, 23–24, Podgorica, 2003, pp. 155–161.
European Commission (EC), 'Commission Opinion on Montenegro's Application for Membership of the European Union' (COMMUNICATION FROM THE COMMISSION TO THE EUROPEAN PARLIAMENT AND THE COUNCIL), Brussels, 9.11.2010 COM (2010) 670, {SEC (2010) 1334}.
European Commission (EC), 'Montenegro 2011 Progress Report, Brussels, 12.10.2011 SEC(2011) 1204 Final.
European Commission (EC), 'Montenegro 2014 Progress Report', Brussels, 8.10.2014, COM (2014) 700 Final.
European Commission (EC), 'Montenegro 2015 Progress Report', Brussels, 10.11.2015, SWD (2015) 210 Final.
European Commission (EC), 'Montenegro 2016 Progress Report', Brussels, 9.11.2016, SWD (2016) 360 Final.

European Community Conference (EC) on Yugoslavia, 'Statement by Lord Carrington to the parties at the tenth plenary session of the EC Conference on Yugoslavia', Brussels, 9 March 1992, Ref. BODA/1/1/3.
European Community Conference (EC) Yugoslavia, 'The Main Decisions of the Conference at Its London Session (August 1992), 26 August 1992, BODA/2/1/4.
European Community Conference (EC) on Yugoslavia, 'Background Briefing by Ambassador Geert Ahrens, Working Group on Ethnic and National Communities and Minorities', 6 October 1992, BODA/2/2/7/1.
European Stability Initiative, 'Montenegro: Rhetoric and Reform–A Case Study of Institution Building in Montenegro 1998–2001', Brussels 2001.
ECMI, 'EU Accession and Minority Rights in Serbia, Montenegro and Sandžak: Sandžak as Part of a Euro-Region?', ECMI Training Workshops, Kotor, 5–8 December 2002, ECMI Report No. 43, March 2003.
European Parliament (Directorate General External Policies of the Union), 'The Russian Economic Penetration in Montenegro', Briefing Paper, December 2007.
European Stability Initiative (ESI), 'Autonomy, Dependency, Security: The Montenegrin Dilemma', ESI Report, Podgorica & Berlin, 4 August 2000.
European Union Delegation to Montenegro (EUDM), 'Statement of the Delegation of the European Union to Montenegro Regarding the Recent Events in Podgorica', EUDM Press Release, Podgorica, 19 October 2015.
Fatić, Aleksandar, 'The Montenegrin Transition: A Test Case', *South East Europe Review*, Vol. 1, April 1998.
Federal Republic of Yugoslavia (FRY): Chief of General Staff of the Yugoslav Army/ STR. Conf. 615–10, 16 July 1998.
Fijuljanin, Muhedin, *Sandžački Bošnjaci*, Tutin: Centar za Bošnjačke Studije, 2010.
Fine, John V.A. Jr., *The Early Medieval Balkans*, Ann Arbor: University of Michigan Press, 1983.
Fine, John V.A. Jr., *The Late Medieval Balkans*, Ann Arbor: University of Michigan Press, 1987.
Friedman, Francine, 'The Muslim Slavs of Bosnia and Herzegovina (with reference to the Sandžak of Novi Pazar): Islam as National Identity', *Nationalities Papers*, Vol. 28, No. 1, 2000, pp. 165–180.
Gagnon, V.P., *The Myth of Ethnic War: Serbia and Croatia in the 1990s*, Ithaca, NY and London: Cornell University Press, 2004.
Gallacher, Tom, 'Identity in Flux, Destination Uncertain: Montenegro during and after the Yugoslav Wars', *International Journal of Politics, Culture and Society*, Vol. 17, No. 1, Fall 2003.
Garton-Ash, Timothy, *History of the Present: Essays, Sketches, and Dispatches from Europe in the 1990s*, London: Random House, 1999.
Glenny, Misha, *The Fall of Yugoslavia*, London: Penguin, 1993.
Glenny, Misha, 'Heading Off War in the Southern Balkans', in *Bosnia: What Went Wrong? A Foreign Affairs Reader*, New York, 1998, pp. 82–108.
Glenny, Misha, *The Balkans 1804–1999: Nationalism, War and the Great Powers*, London: Granta, 1999.
Glenny, Misha, *McMafia: Crime without Frontiers*, London: The Bodley Head, 2008.
Goati, Vladimir, *Elections in the FRY from 1990 to 1998: Will of the People or Electoral Manipulation?*, Belgrade: CESID, 2000.
Goati, Vladimir, *The Party Systems of Serbia and Montenegro*, Belgrade: CEDET, 2000.

Gordy, Eric D., *The Culture of Power in Serbia*, Pennsylvania: Pennsylvania University Press, 1999.
Gorgević, Vladan, *Crna Gora i Rusija*, Belgrade: Srpska Kraljevska Akademija, 1914.
Gow, James, 'Serbia and Montenegro: Small FRY, Big Trouble', RFE/RL Research Report, Vol. 3, No. 1, January 1994.
Gow, James, *The Serbian Project and its Adversaries: A Strategy of War Crimes*, London: Hurst & Co., 2003.
Goy, Edward Dennis, *The Sabre and the Song: Njegoš–The Mountain Wreath*, Belgrade: Serbian P.E.N. Centre, 1995.
Greenfeld, Leah, *Nationalism: Five Roads to Modernity*, New York: Harvard University Press, 1992.
Hadži-Jovacić, Dušanka (ed.), *The Serbian Question in the Balkans*, Belgrade: Faculty of Geography, University of Belgrade, 1995.
Hadžišehović, Munevera, *A Muslim Woman in Tito's Yugoslavia*, College Station, TX: A&M University Press, 2003.
Hall, Richard, *The Balkan Wars, 1912–1913: Prelude to the First World War*, London: Routledge, 2000.
Hamourtziado, Lily, 'The Bosniaks: From Nation to Threat', *Journal of Southern Europe and the Balkans*, Vol. 4, No. 2, 2002, pp. 141–156.
Harris, Robin, *Dubrovnik: A History*, London: SAQI Press, 2006.
Hastings, Adrian, *The Construction of Nationhood*, Cambridge: Cambridge University Press, 1997.
Hatcher, Peter J., *Partisan Wings: The Biferno Journal*, Miami, FL: Trente Nova Publishing, 1994.
Haug, Hilde Katrine, *Creating a Socialist Yugoslavia: Tito, Communist Leadership and the National Question*, London: IB Tauris, 2010.
Haynes, Rebecca, & Rady, Martyn (eds.), *In the Shadow of Hitler: Personalities of the Right in Central and Eastern Europe*, London: IB Tauris, 2011.
Headquarters of the Balkan Air Force, 'Report on the First Year of the RAF Liaison with Partisans', 12 December 1944, AIR 20/9035.
Headquarters of the Balkan Air Force, 'A History of the Balkan Air Force' July 1945, AIR/23/882.
Helmreich, Ernst C., 'Montenegro and the Formation of the Balkan League', *Slavonic Review*, Vol. XV, January 1937.
Helsinki Committee for Human Rights, 'Montenegro: Human Rights Practices 1993', Belgrade, 1993.
Helsinki obdor za ljudska prava u Srbiji, *Kovanje anitjugoslovenske zavere*, Belgrade: Svedočanstva, broj 26 2006.
Helsinki odbor za ljudski prava u Srbiji, *Dubrovnik: Rat za mir*, Belgrade: Svedočanstva, broj 24, 2006.
Hoptner, Jacob, *Yugoslavia in Crisis 1934–1941*, New York and London: Columbia University Press, 1962.
Human Rights Watch, *Human Rights Abuses of Non-Serbs in Kosovo, Sandžak and Vojvodina*, Human Rights Digest, Vol. 6, No. 6, May 1994.
Human Rights Watch, *Genocide, War Crimes and Crimes against Humanity: A Topical Digest of the Case Law of the ICTY*, New York: Human Rights Watch, 2006.
Humanitarian Law Center, *Spotlight on Human Rights Violations in Times of Armed Conflict, Serbia and Montenegro*, Belgrade: Slovograf, 1995

Ičević, Dušan, *Crnogorska nacija*, Belgrade: Forum za etničke odnose, 1998.
ICFY (David Owen's Papers), 'File: Political Sitrep 12/10/93–8/9/93, October 1992 to September 1993', D731 3/17 (1–2).
ICFY, 'Working Group on Ethnic and National Minorities: Sub-Group on Sandžak', Geneva, File: Sandžak/doc/G, 20 November 1992.
ICFY (David Owen's Papers), 'File: Monitoring Borders', September 1992 to July 1993, D731 4/4.
ICFY (David Owen's Papers), 'File: Political Sitrep 10/9/93–24/3/94, October 1993 to March 1994, D731 3/18.
ICFY (David Owen's Papers), 'File: CSCE', September 1992 to December 1993, D731 4/5.
ICFY, 'Letter from Ambassador Rey to Lord Owen, Mr Stoltenberg, Ambassador Masset, Ambassador Ahresn, Mr Ritz, Subject: Meeting with a Delegation of the Muslim National Council of Sandžak', Geneva, 20 January, 1994.
ICFY (David Owen's Papers), 'File: FRY', March 1993 to July 1994, D731 4/7.
ICFY (David Owen's Papers), 'File: Montenegro', October 1992 to March 1994, D731, 4/8.
ICFY (David Owen's Papers), 'File: Succession W.G.', November 1992 to August 1994, D731 4/25.
ICFY (David Owen's Papers), 'File: Minorities W.G., June 1993 to October 1993, D731 4/26.
ICFY (David Owen's Papers), 'File: Regional Issues/Neighbouring States', February 1993 to May 1994, D731 4/28.
Ingrao, Charles, & Emmert, Thomas A. (eds.), *Confronting the Yugoslav Controversies: A Scholar's Initiative*, West Lafayette, IN: Purdue University Press, 2009.
Institut Alternativa, 'The Case of the First Bank: Experiences for Supervisors and Other Decision Makers', Podgorica, June 2009.
Institut za savremenu istoriju, *Balkan posle Drugog svetskog rata: Zbornik radova sa naučnog skupa*, Belgrade: ISI, 1996.
International Conference on the Former Yugoslavia–ICFY (David Owen's Papers), 'File: Lord Carrington' D731/2.
International Court of Justice, Reports of Judgements, Advisory Opinions and Orders, 'The Application of the Convention on the Prevention and Punishment of the Crime of Genocide (Bosnia & Herzegovina v. Serbia and Montenegro)', Judgement of 26 February 2007.
International Crisis Group (ICG), 'Sandžak: Calm for Now', ICG Balkans Report, No. 48, November 1998.
International Crisis Group (ICG), 'Montenegro–In the Shadow of the Volcano', ICG Balkans Report No. 89, 21 March 2000.
International Crisis Group (ICG), 'Montenegro's Socialist People's Party: A Loyal Opposition?', ICG Balkans Report No. 92, Podgorica & Brussels, 28 April 2000.
International Crisis Group (ICG), 'Montenegro's Local Elections: Testing the National Temperature', ICG Background Briefing, 26 May 2000.
International Crisis Group (ICG), 'The Current Legal Status of the FRY, and of Serbia and Montenegro', Balkans Report No. 101, Brussels, 19 September 2000.
International Crisis Group (ICG), 'Montenegro: Settling for Independence'. ICG Balkans Report No. 107, Podgorica & Brussels, 28 April 2001.
International Crisis Group (ICG), 'Still Buying Time: Montenegro, Serbia and the European Union', ICG Balkans Report No.129, Podgorica & Brussels, 7 May 2002.
International Crisis Group (ICG), 'Serbia's Sandžak: Still Forgotten', Europe Report, No. 162, 8 April 2005.

International Crisis Group (ICG), 'Montenegro's Independence Drive', Crisis Europe Group Report No. 169, Brussels, 7 December 2005.
International Crisis Group (ICG), 'Montenegro's Referendum', Crisis Group Europe Briefing No. 42, 30 May 2006.
Internacionalni univerzitet u Novom Pazaru, *Sandžak juče, danas i sutra*, Grafokarton, Prijepolje, 2005.
Ilić, Predrag, *Srpska pravoslavna crkva i tajna Dahaua: mit i istina o zatočeništvu patrijarha Gavrila i episkopa Nikolaja u koncentracionom logoru Dahauu*, Belgrade, 2006.
Ilić, Angela, 'Church – State Relations in Present-day Serbia', *Religion in Eastern Europe*, XXIV, No. 6, December 2004.
Irvine, Jill, *The Croat Question: Partisan Politics in the Creation of the Yugoslav Socialist State*, Boulder: Westview Press, 1993.
Irvine, Jill, 'Introduction: State – Society Relations in Yugoslavia, 1945-1992', in Melissa K. Bokovoy, Jill A. Irvine, & Carol S. Liddy (eds.), State – Society Relations in Yugoslavia 1945-1992, London: Macmillan, 1997.
Jakšić, S, *Mitropolija Crnogorska nikad nije bila autokefalna*, Belgrade/Cetinje: Srpska pravoslavna crkva, 1991.
Jelavich, Barbara, *History of the Balkans* 2 vols, Cambridge: Cambridge University Press, 1983.
Jelavich, Barbara, & Jelavich, Charles, *The Establishment of the Balkan National States, 1804-1920*, Seattle and London: University of Washington Press, 1977.
Jelavich, Barbara, & Jelavich, Charles (eds.), *The Balkans in Transition: Essays on the Development of Balkan Life and Politics since the Eighteenth Century*. Hamden, CT: Archon Books, 1981.
Jovanović, Batrić, *Trinaesto julski ustanak*, Belgrade: NIRO, 1984.
Jovanović, Batrić, *Kosovo, inflacija, socijalne razlike*, Belgrade: Partizanska knjiga, 1985.
Jovanović, Batrić, *Crnogorci o sebi*, Belgrade: Narodna knjiga, 1986.
Jovanović, Batrić, *Rasrbljivanje Crnogoraca: Staljnov i Titov zločin*, Belgrade: Srpska škola kniga, 2003.
Jovanović, Batrić, *Rasrbljivanje crnogoraca–Duhovni genocid*, Belgrade: Srpska školska knjiga, 2003.
Jovanović, Jagoš, *Istorija Crne Gore*, Podgorica: CID, 2001.
Jovanović, Vladan, *Jugoslovenska država i južna Srbija: 1918-1929*, Belgrade: INIS, 2002.
Jovanović, Vladimir D., *Crna Gora: Kapija pravoslavja*, Podgorica: OKTOIH, 1994.
Jovanovich, William, *The Temper of the West: A Memoir*, Columbia: University of South Carolina Press, 2003.
Jović, Borisav, *Poslednji Dani SFRJ*, Belgrade: Politika, 1995.
Jović, Dejan, 'The Disintegration of Yugoslavia: A Critical Review of Explanatory Approaches', *European Journal of Social Theory*, Vol. 4, No. 1, 2001, pp. 101-120.
Jović, Dejan, *Yugoslavia: A State that Withered Away*, West Lafayette, IN: Purdue University Press, 2009.
Jovićević, Milan, *Montenegrin State and Dynastic Symbols*, Cetinje: National Museum of Montenegro, 2001.
Judah, Tim, *The Serbs: History, Myth and the Destruction of Yugoslavia*, New Haven, CT and London: Yale University Press, 1997.
Judah, Tim, *Kosovo: War and Revenge*, New Haven, CT and London: Yale University Press, 2002.
Jukić, Ilija, *The Fall of Yugoslavia*, New York and London: Harcourt Brace Jovanovich, 1974.

Kačavenda, Petar, *Balkan posle drugog svetskog rata: Zbornik radova sa naučnog skupa*, Belgrade: Institut za savremenu istoriju, 1995.
Kalezić, Danilo (ed.), *Kotor*, Zagreb: Grafički zavod Hrvatske, 1970.
Karchmar, Lucien, *Draža Mihailović and the Rise of the Chetnik Movement 1941–1942*, Vol. 2, New York and London: Garland Publishing, 1987.
Kardelj, Edvard, *Yugoslavia in International Relations and in the Non-Aligned Movement*, Belgrade: Socialist Thought and Practice, 1979.
Kardelj, Edvard, *Reminiscences: The Struggle for Recognition and Independence – The New Yugoslavia, 1944–1957*, London: Summerfield Press, 1982.
Keković, Vladimir, *Bijjezi vremena*, Podgorica: Crnogorska izdanja, 2012.
Keković, Vladimir, *25 godina poslije*, Podgorica: Crnogorska izdanja, 2014.
Kerner, Robert J. (ed.), *Yugoslavia*, California: University of California Press, 1949.
King, Robert, *Minorities under Communism: Nationalities as a Source of Tension among Balkan Communist States*, New York: Harvard University Press, 1973.
Kola, Paulin, *The Search for Greater Albania*, London: Hurst & Co., 2003.
Koprivica, Veseljko, *Amfilohijeva sabrana nedjela*, Podgorica: Vijesti, 1999.
Koprivica, Veseljko, *Naj Crna Gora: monografski leksikon*, Podgorica: Dan Press, 2002.
Koprovica, Veseljko, & Vojičić, Branko, *Prevrat '89*, Podgorica: Liberalni Savez Crne Gore, 1994.
Kordić, Mile, & Ašanin, Mihajlo, *Komitski pokret u Crnoj Gori 1916–1918*, Belgrade: Nova kniga, 1985.
Kostić, Kosta N., *Naši novi gradovi na Jugu*, Belgrade, 1922.
Kuković, Goran, & Racković, Dragan, *Velika narodna škuptina Srpskoj narodna u Crnoj Gori – Podgorica 1918 godine*, Berane: Srpski Kulturni Centar, 2006.
Kulić, Vladmir et al., *Modernism In-Between: The Mediatory Architectures of Socialist Yugoslavia*, Berlin: Jovis, 2012.
Kulišić, Špiro, *O etnogenezi Crnogoraca*, Titograd: Pobjeda, 1980.
Kusovac, Marko, 'Odnos Crne Gore i Rusije', *Matica*, zima 2013/proljeće 2014, pp. 53–72.
Lakić, Zoran, *Narodna vlast u Crnoj Gori 1941–1945*, Cetinje: Obod, 1981.
Lakić, Zoran, *Partizanska autonomija Sandžaka*, Belgrade: Stručna kniga, 1992.
Lampe, John, *Yugoslavia as History: Twice There Was a Country*, Cambridge: Cambridge University Press, 1996.
Lampe, John, & Mazower, Mark (eds.), *Ideologies and National Identities: The Case of Twentieth-Century Southeastern Europe*, Budapest: CEU Press, 2003.
Lampe, John R., & Jackson, Marvin R., *Balkan Economic History 1550–1950: From Imperial Borderlands to Developing Nations*, Bloomington: Indiana University Press, 1982.
Latković, Vido, *Petar Petrović Njegoš*, Belgrade: Nolit, 1963.
Lederer, Ivo, *Yugoslavia at the Paris Peace Conference*, New York and London: Yale University Press, 1963.
Lees, Michael, *The Rape of Serbia: The British Role in Tito's Grab for Power*, New York: Harcourt Brace Jovanovich, 1990.
Lindsay, Franklin, *Beacons in the Night: With the OSS and Tito's Partisans in Wartime Yugoslavia*, California: Stanford University Press, 1993.
Little, Alan, & Silber, Laura, *The Death of Yugoslavia*, London: Penguin Books, 1995.
Lješević, Čedomir, *Solanijada: Ili još jedan genocid nad Crnom Gorom*, Podgorica: NJP, 2005.
Lopandić, Duško, & Bajić, Vojislav. *Srbija i Crna Gora na putu ka Evropski Uniju: Dve godine kasnije*, Belgrade: Evropski pokret, 2003.

Lyon, James, 'Serbia's Sandžak under Milošević: Identity, Nationalism and Survival', *Human Rights Review*, Vol. 9, No. 1, 2008, pp. 71-92.
Maclean, Fitzroy, *Eastern Approaches*, London: Jonathan Cape, 1946.
Magaš, Branka, *The Destruction of Yugoslavia: Tracking the Break-Up, 1980-1992*, London: Verso Press, 1993.
Malešević, Siniša, *Identity as Ideology: Understanding Ethnicity and Nationalism*, London and New York: Palgrave Macmillan, 2006.
Marković, Slobodan et al., *Problems of Identities in the Balkans*, Belgrade: Anglo-Serbian Society, 2006.
Martinović, Dušan, *Cetinje: buntovno i revolucionarno*, Cetinje: Obod, 2003.
Matica Crnogorska, 'Crnogorski kao maternji jezik', *Godišnjak 1999-2003*, MCG: Cetinje, 2003.
Mazower, Mark, *The Balkans*, London: Weidenfeld and Nicolson, 2000.
McCarthy, Justin, *Death and Exile: The Ethnic Cleansing of Ottoman Muslims, 1821-1922*, Princeton, NJ: Darwin Press, 1995.
Memić, Mustafa, *Bošnjaci-muslimani Sandžaka i Crne Gore*, Sarajevo: OKO, 1996.
Memić, Mustafa, *Poznati Bošnjaci Sandžaka i Crne Gore*, Sarajevo: Matica, 1998.
Memić, Mustafa, *Bošnjaci (Muslimani) Crne Gore*, Bijelo Polje: Saznanja, 2002.
Memić, Mustafa, *Pojave prozilitizma u plavsko-gusinje kraju 1913. i 1919. godine*, Sarajevo: OKO, 2004.
Mihailović, Draža, *The Trial of Dragoljub-Draža Mihailović: Stenographic Records and Documents from the Trial of Dragoljub-Draža Mihailović*, Belgrade: Union of the Journalist's Associations of the Federative People's Republic of Yugoslavia, 1946.
Miller, William, 'The Founder of Montenegro', *English Historical Review*, Vol. 25, No. 98, April 1910.
Milović, Katalina, *La Montenegrina*, Cetinje/Podgorica: Matica Crnogorska, 2004.
Mitrić, Blagota, *Tragom identiteta: Državnog i ličnog*, Podgorica: Pobjeda, 2005.
Mitropolija Crnogorsko and Primorska, *Pravoslavje u Crnoj Gori*, Cetinje: Svetigora, 2006.
Mitropolit Amfilohije et al., *Duhovno i političko biće Crne Gore*, Nikšić: ETNOS, 2002.
Mitrović Andrej, *Serbia's Great War: 1914-1918*, London: Hurst & Co., 2007.
Mitrović, Ljubisa, & Eraković, Aleksander (eds.), *Sto dana koji su promijenili Crnu Goru*, Podgorica: Daily Press/Vijesti, 1997.
MNVS, 'Resolution: 28 April 1992, Novi Pazar, No. 54/92.
MNVS, 'Napomene uz memorandum o ospostavljanju specialnog statusa za Sandžak', Novi Pazar, June 1993.
MONSTAT (Republički zavod za statistiku), 'Popis stanovništva, domaćinstava i stanova 2003: Prva rezultati po opštinima, nascljima i mjesim zajednicama', Podgorica: MONSTAT, December 2003.
Montenegrin Ministry of Foreign Affairs, 'An Analysis of the Media Scene in Montenegro in the Year When Decisive Steps toward State Independence Are to Be Made', Podgorica 15 February 2005.
Morrison, Kenneth, & Roberts, Elizabeth, *The Sandžak: A History*, London: Hurst & Co., 2013.
Muslimansko nacionalno vijeće Sandžaka (MNVS), 'Resolution: 11 January 1992', Novi Pazar, No. 11/92.
NATO Press and Media, 'Statement by the Secretary General Following the Meeting of the North Atlantic Council', 12 April 1999, Press communique PR (1999) 058.
NATO Press and Media Service: Ministerial Meeting of the North Atlantic Council Held at NATO Headquarters, Brussels, on 15 December 1999, Press Communique M-NAC-2 (99) 166.

Nešović, Slobodan, & Petranović, Branko (eds.), *AVNOJ i revolucija: tematska zbirka dokumenata 1941-1945*, Belgrade: Narodna knjiga, 1983.
Nikčević, Želidrag, *Prava Srba u Crnoj Gori*, Belgrade: Focus, 2006.
Nikolaidis, Jovan, 'Multiculturalism in Montenegro and the City of Ulcinj', in Nenad Dimitrijević (ed.), *Managing Multiethnic Local Communities in the Countries of the Former Yugoslavia*, Budapest: OSI, 2001.
Njegoš, Petar Petrović, *The Mountain Wreath*, Translator - James W. Wiles, Introducer - Vladeta Popovic, London: Allen and Urwin, 1971.
Norris, H.T., *Islam in the Balkans: Religion and Society between Europe and the Arab World*, London: Hurst & Co., 1993.
NS/DSS/SNP, *Bijela knjiga: Referendum u Crnoj Gori 2006 - Zbornik dokumenata*, Belgrade/Niš: Narodna misao, 2006.
Oliver, Ian, *War & Peace in the Balkans: The Diplomacy of Conflict in the Former Yugoslavia*, London: IB Tauris, 2005.
Orlandić, Marko, *U vrtlogu*, Podgorica: Montenegropublic, 1997.
Orlandić, Marko, *Crnogorsko posrtanje*, Podgorica: Montcarton, 2005.
Orlandić, Marko, *O jednom vremenu i njegovim ljudima*, Podgorica: Montcarton, 2007.
OSCE/ODIHR, 'Republic of Montenegro: Presidential Election 5th and 18th October 1997, Final Report', 1997.
OSCE/ODIHR, 'Republic of Montenegro (Federal Republic of Yugoslavia): Parliamentary Elections 31 May 1998', Warsaw, 5 July 1998.
OSCE/ODIHR, Election Observation Mission Report, 'Republic of Montenegro (Serbia and Montenegro): Presidential Elections, 22 December 2002 and 9 February 2003, Warsaw, 3 April 2003.
OSCE, 'Assessment of the Referendum Law: Republic of Montenegro, Federal Republic of Yugoslavia', Warsaw, 6 July 2001.
OSCE/ODIHR, 'Referendum Observation Mission 2006, Republic of Montenegro (Serbia and Montenegro), Interim Report 1', Podgorica, 28 March - 20 April 2006.
OSCE Press Release, 'International Referendum Observation Mission: Referendum on State Status, Republic of Montenegro (Serbia and Montenegro), Podgorica, 22 May 2006.
OSCE/ODIHR, 'Republic of Montenegro: Referendum on State-Status 21 May 2006 - OSCE/ODHIR Referendum Observation Mission Final Report, Warsaw, 4 August 2006.
OSCE/ODIHR, 'Republic of Montenegro: Presidential Election', 6 April 2008, OSCE/ODIHR Election Observation Mission Final Report, Warsaw, 1 September 2008.
OSCE/ODIHR, 'Montenegro: Presidential Election' 7 April 2013 - Limited Election Observation Mission Final Report', Warsaw, 25 June 2013.
Owen, David, *Balkan Odyssey*, London: Victor Gollanz, 1995.
Pajović, Radoje, *Kontrarevolucija u Crnoj Gori: četnicki i federalistički pokret*, Cetinje: Obod, 1977.
Pajović, Radoje, *Crna Gora kroz istoriju*, Cetinje: Obod, 2005.
Pajović, Radoje, *Pavle Djurišić*, Podgorica: CID, 2005.
Palairet, Michael, 'The Culture of Economic Stagnation in Montenegro', *Maryland Historian*, No. 17, 1986, pp. 17-42.
Pavlović, Koča. 'Montenegrin Independence: Media Discourse', Paper presented at the Tenth Annual World Conference of the Association for the Study of Nationalities, New York, 14-16 April 2005.

Pavlović, Srdja, 'The Podgorica Assembly in 1918: Notes on the Yugoslav Historiography (1919-1970) about the Unification of Serbia and Montenegro', *Canadian Slavonic Papers*, Vol. XLI, No. 2, June 1999, pp. 157-176.
Pavlović, Srdja, 'Literature, Social Poetics and Identity Construction in Montenegro', *International Journal of Politics, Culture and Society*, Vol. 17, No. 1, Fall 2000, pp. 131-165.
Pavlović, Srdja, 'Understanding Balkan Nationalism: The Wrong People, in the Wrong Place, at the Wrong Time', *Southeast European Politics*, Vol. 1, No. 2, 2000, pp. 137-158.
Pavlović, Srdja. 'The Mountain Wreath: Poetry or a Blueprint for the Final Solution?', *Spaces of Identity*, Vol. 4, 2001.
Pavlović, Srdja, 'Poetry and History in Montenegro: Njegoš and the Construction of a Collective Memory', *Spaces of Identity*, Vol. 1, No. 4, 2002.
Pavlović, Srdja, 'Two Solitudes: Ethnic versus Civic in Contemporary Montenegrin Politics', 2002 *Moderne - Spezialforschungsbereich* @http:// www.gewi.kfunigraz.ac.at/moderne/heft7pa.htm
Pavlović, Srdja. 'Building Civil Society in Montenegro: Autocracy in the Making', Unpublished document, May 2005.
Pavlović, Srdja. 'Gradjansko društvo i kultura tranzicije', *Matica*, Number 21, Year 6, Spring 2005.
Pavlović, Srdja, 'Reckoning: The Siege of Dubrovnik and the Consequences of the "War for Peace"', *Spaces of Identity*, Vol. 5, No. 1, 2005.
Pavlović, Srdja, *Balkan Anschluss: The Annexation of Montenegro and the Creation of the Common South Slavic State*, West Lafayette, IN: Purdue University Press, 2007.
Pavlović, Srdja, & Dragojević, Milica, 'Peaceniks and Warmongers: Anti-War Activism in Montenegro, 1989-1995', in Bojan Bilić, & Janković Vesna (eds.), *Resisting the Evil: Post-Yugoslav Anti-War Contention*, Baden-Baden: Nomos Verlagagesellschaft, 2012, p. 146.
Pavlović, Srdja, & Živković, Marko (eds.), *Transcending Fratricide: Political Mythologies, Reconciliations and the Uncertain Future in the Former Yugoslavia*, Baden-Baden: Nomos Verlagsgesellschaft, 2013.
Pavlowitch, Stevan K. *A History of the Balkans 1804-1945*, London and New York: Lomgman, 1999.
Pavlowitch, Stevan K. *Serbia: The History behind the Name*, London: Hurst & Co., 2002.
Pavlowitch, Stevan K. *Hitler's New Disorder: The Second World War in Yugoslavia*, London: Hurst & Co., 2008.
Pejović, Čedomir, *KPJ u Crnoj Gori 1919-1941*, Podgorica: CID, 1999.
Pellet, Allain, 'The Opinions of the Badinter Arbitration Committee: A Second Breath for the Self-Determination of Peoples', *European Journal of International Law*, Vol. 3, No. 1, 1992, p. 185.
Perazić, Gavro, *Nestanak crnogorske države u Prvom svetskom ratu*, Belgrade: Vojnoistorijski Institut, 1988.
Perazić, Gavro, *Kuda ide Crna Gora*, Belgrade: Versal Press, 1999.
Perica, Vjekoslav. *Balkan Idols: Religion and Nationalism in Yugoslav States*, Oxford: Oxford University Press, 2002.
Perović, Jeronim, 'The Tito-Stalin Split: A Reassessment in Light of New Evidence', *Journal of Cold War Studies*, Vol. 9, No. 2, Spring 2007, pp. 42-48.
Petranović, Branko, *KPJ i društveno-političke promene u Jugoslaviji od AVNOJ-a do Ustavotvorne skupštine*, Vojvodina: Istoriski zapisi, 1971.

Petrović, Milić, F., *Pljevlja u dokumentima 1918-1941*, Belgrade: Pangraf, 2004.
Petrović, Ratislav, *Crnogorske ustaše*, Belgrade: Autor Agent, 2005.
Petrović, Ruža, & Blagojević, Marina, *Seobe Srba i Crnogoraca sa Kosova i iz Metohije*, Srpska Akademija Nauka i Umetnosti (SANU), Belgrade: Demografski Zbornik, 1988.
Petrovich, Michael Boro, *A History of Modern Serbia, 1804-1918*, 2 vols, New York and London: Harcourt Brace Jovanovich, 1976.
Pettifer, Kames, & Vickers, Miranda, *The Albanian Question: Reshaping the Balkans*, London: IB Tauris, 2009.
Pijade, Moša, *Izabrani govori i članci: 1941-1947*, Belgrade: Kultura, 1983.
Pinson, Mark, *The Muslims of Bosnia-Herzegovina: Their Historic Development from the Middle Ages to the Dissolution of Yugoslavia*, New York: Harvard University Press, 1993.
Popović, Milan, *Crnogorska alternativa: Neizvesnost promene*, Podgorica: Vijesti, 2000.
Popović, Milan, *Montenegrin Mirror: Polity in Turmoil (1999-2001)*, Podgorica: Nansen Dialogue Centre, 2002.
Popović, Milan, *Globalna prašina*, Podgorica: Vijesti, 2004.
Popović, Milorad, *Crnogorsko pitanje*, Plima/Digitas, Cetinje & Ulcinj, 1999.
Popović, Petar, *Crna Gora u doba Petra I i Petra II*, Belgrade: Kultura, 1951.
Poulton, Hugh, *The Balkans: Minorities and States in Conflict*, London: Minority Rights Publications, 1994.
Poulton, Hugh, & Taji-Farouki, Suha, *Muslim Identity and the Balkan State*, London: Hurst & Co., 1997.
Praxis International, 'Special Issue: The Rise and Fall of Yugoslavia', Vol. 13, No. 4, January 1994.
Radan, Peter. 'The Serbs and Their History in the Twentieth Century', in P. Radan, & A. Pavković (eds.), *The Serbs and Their Leaders in the Twentieth Century*, London: Ashgate Publishing, 1997.
Radio Free Europe (RFE) Research Background Report, 'Yugoslavia', No. 159, 13 July 1983, HU OSA 300-8-3: 86-3-280.
Radojević, Danilo, 'Autokefalna Crnogorska pravoslavna crkva', *Elementa Montenegrina hrestomatija (Crnogorska narod i srpska politika genocida nad njim)*, Zagreb, Vol. 1, 1990.
Radojevic, Danilo, *Iz povijesti hriscanskih crkava u Crnoj Gori*, Cetinje: CDNK, 2000.
Radončić, Šeki, *Crna kutija (2)*, Podgorica: Vijesti, 2003.
Radončić, Šeki, *A Fatal Freedom*, Belgrade: Humanitarian Law Center, 2006.
Radonjić, Radovan, *Tranzicije*, Podgorica: CID, 1998.
Radonjić, Radovan, *Politička misao u Crnoj Gori*, Podgorica: CID, 2006.
Radonjić, Radovan, *Socializam u Crnoj Gori*, Podgorica: Matica Crnogorska, 2013.
Radu, Michael, 'The Burden of Eastern Orthodoxy', *Orbis* Vol. 42, No. 2, Spring 1998.
Rakočević, Novica, *Crna Gora u Prvom svetskon ratu 1914-1918*, Titograd: Istorijski institut u Titogradu, 1969.
Rakonjac, Snežana, 'Mediji u službi rata – zaostavština TVCG', *Matica*, Podgorica, broj 50, ljeto 2012, pp.137-52.
Ramcharan, B.G. (ed.), *The International Conference on the Former Yugoslavia: Official Papers*, Vol. 1, The Hague: Kluwer Law International, 1997.
Ramet, Pedro, *Nationalism and Federalism in Yugoslavia 1963 - 1983*, Bloomington: Indiana University Press, 1984.
Ramet, Pedro (ed.), *Yugoslavia in the 1980's*, Boulder, CO: Westview Press, 1990.
Ramet, Sabrina, *Balkan Babel*, Boulder, CO: Westview Press, 1999.

Ramet, Sabrina, *The Three Yugoslavias: The Dual Challenge of State – Building and Legitimation among the Yugoslavs 1918 – 2001*, Bloomington: Indiana University Press, 2001.
Ramet, Sabrina, *Thinking about Yugoslavia: Scholarly Debates about the Yugoslav Breakup and the Wars in Bosnia and Kosovo*, Cambridge: Cambridge University Press, 2005.
Ramet, Sabrina (ed.), *The Independent State of Croatia 1941-45*, London and New York: Routledge, 2007.
Ramet, Sabrina (ed.), *Religion and Politics in Post-Socialist Central and Southeastern Europe: Challenges since 1989*, London: Palgrave MacMillan, 2014.
Ramet, Sabrina, & Adamovich, Ljubiša. S. (eds.), *Beyond Yugoslavia: Politics, Economics and Culture in a Shattered Community*, Boulder, CO: Westview Press, 1997.
Ramet, Sabrina, & Pavlaković, Vjeran, *Serbia since 1989*, Boulder, CO: Westview Press, 2006.
Ramet, Sabrina, & Pavlaković, Vjeran, *Serbia since 1989: Politics and Society under Milošević and After*, Seattle and London: University of Washington Press, 2006.
Raspopović, Radoslav, *Diplomatija Crne Gore 1711-1918*, Podgorica: The Historical Institute of Montenegro, 1996.
Rastoder, Rifat, & Kovačević, Branislav, *Crvena mrlja*, Titograd: Pobjeda, 1990.
Rastoder, Šerbo, *Janusovo lice istorije*, Podgorica: Vijesti, 2000.
Rastoder, Šerbo, *Političke stranke u Crnoj Gori 1919-1929*, Bar: Conteco, 2000.
Rastoder, Šerbo, *Uloga Francuske u nasilnoj aneksiji Crne Gore*, Bar: Conteco, 2000.
Rastoder, Šerbo, 'Muslimani/Bošnjaci: kako vam je ime?, *Almanah*, 23-24, Podgorica, 2003, pp. 27-38.
Rastoder, Šerbo, *Crna Gora u egzilu 1918-1925 (Kniga I)*, Podgorica: Almanah, 2004.
Rastoder, Šerbo, *Crna Gora u egzilu 1918-1925 (Kniga II)*, Podgorica: Almanah, 2004.
Rastoder, Šerbo, *Skrivana strana istorije: Crnogorska buna i odmetnićki pokret 1918 – 1929*, Cetinje: Obod, 2005.
Rastoder, Šerbo, *Šahovići 1924: Kad su vakat kaljani insani*, Podgorica: Almanah, 2011.
Ražnatović, Novak, *Crna Gora i Berlinske kongres*, Titograd: Istroijski institut CP Crne Gore, 1979.
Redžić, Enver, *Bosnia and Herzegovina in the Second World War*, London and New York: Frank Cass, 2005.
Research Institute for Military History (eds.), *Germany and the Second World War Vol. III: The Mediterranean, South-east Europe, and North Africa 1939-1941*, Oxford: Clarendon Press, 1995.
Roberts, Allen, *The Turning Point: The Assassination of Louis Barthou and King Alexander of Yugoslavia*, New York: St Martin's Press, 1970.
Roberts, Elizabeth. 'Montenegro', *The South Slav Journal* 20: 1-2 (75-76) Spring – Summer, 1999.
Roberts, Elizabeth, *The Realm of the Black Mountain: A History of Montenegro*, London: Hurst & Co., 2007.
Roberts, Walter, *Tito, Mihailović and the Allies 1941-1945*, Durham: Duke University Press, Durham, 1967.
Rodogno, Davide, 'Italian Soldiers in the Balkans: The Experience of the Occupation (1941-1943), *Journal of Southern Europe and the Balkans*, Vol. 6, No. 2, August 2004.
Ron, James, *Frontiers and Ghettos: State Violence in Serbia and Israel*, California: University of California Press, 2003.
Rondić, Dženan, 'Sandžak: A Geographical and Political Analysis', *South East Europe Review for Labour and Social Affairs*, Issue 1/2000, pp. 131-134.

Rotković, Radoslav, *Odakle su došli preci Crnogoraca*, Cetinje: Cicero, 2000.
Rudić, Vujadin. 'The Ethnic Structure of the Population in Montenegro', in Dušanka Hadži-Jovacić (ed.), *The Serbian Question in the Balkans*, Belgrade: Faculty of Geography, University of Belgrade, 1995.
Rudić, Vujadin, & Stepić, Milomir, 'Ethnic Changes in the Raška Region', in Jovan Ilić, Dušanka Hadži-Jovanačić, & Ivanka Grdović et al. (eds.), *The Serbian Question in the Balkans*, Belgrade: University of Belgrade Press, 1995.
Rusinow, Dennison, *The Yugoslav Experiment 1948-1974*, London: Hurst & Co., 1977.
Rusinow, Dennison, *Yugoslavia: Oblique Insights and Observations*, Pittsburgh: Pittsburgh University Press, 2008.
Russell, Alec, *Prejudice and Plum Brandy*, London: Michael Joseph, 1993.
Russinow, Dennison, 'Nationalities Policy and the National Question', in Pedro Ramet (ed.), *Yugoslavia in the 1980s*, Boulder, CO: Westview Press, 1988.
Samardžić, Slobodan, 'Democracy in Post-communism: The Case of Serbia', *Praxis International*, Vol. 13, No. 4, January 1994, pp. 405–415.
Šarkinović, Hamdija, *Bošnjaci od Nacertanije do Memorandum*, Podgorica: MNVS, 1997.
Schmidt, Fabian, 'The Sandžak: Muslims between Serbia and Montenegro', RFE/RL Research Report, Vol. 3, No. 6, 11 February 1994.
Schöpflin, George, *Nations, Identity, Power: The New Politics of Europe*, London: Hurst & Co., 2000.
Secretariat of the Conference on Yugoslavia: Working Group on Human Rights, 'Summary of the positions of the Montenegrin delegation related to the issues dealt with in CHAPTER II, TREATY PROVISIONS FOR THE CONVENTION, with an emphasis on part c) SPECIAL STATUS, Podgorica, 28 April 1992.
SEEMO, 'Southeast European Media Handbook 2005/06', SEEMO – IPI, Vienna, 2006.
Seton-Watson, R.W., 'The Question of Montenegro', *New Europe*, No. 14, London, 1 April, 1920.
Shoup, Paul, *Communism and the Yugoslav National Question*, New York: Columbia University Press, 1968.
Sjekloća, Veljko. *Krsto Popović: U istorijskoj gradji i literaturi*, Cetinje: Obod, 2001.
Škekić, Radenko, 'Politička previranja u Crnoj Gori 1996–1998. godine', *Matica*, Podgorica, broj 49, proljeće 2012.
Škerović, Nikola, *Crna Gora na osvitku XX vijeka*, Belgrade: Naučno delo, 1964.
Škrijelj, Redžep, 'Sandžacki Bošnjaci u Makedoniji', Internacionalni univerzitiet u Novom Pazaru, *Sandžak juče, danas i sutra*, Novi Pazar, 2005, pp. 245–282.
Škrijelj, Redžep, 'Osam i po decenija od zločina u Šahoviću i Vranešu', *Bošnjačka riječ*, Novi Pazar, 2009, godine IV, broj 13–16, January 2009, pp. 130–145.
Špadijer, Marko, & Roganović, Stanko, *Diplomatska poslanstva u Kraljevini Crnoj Gori*, Matica Crnogorska: Cetinje, 2004.
Špadijer, Marko, *Crnogorska raskršća*, Podgorica: Matica Crnogorska, 2007.
Srpska Pravoslavne Crkve, *Pravoslavje u Crnoj Gori*, Cetinje: Svetigora, 2006.
Stamatović, Aleksandar, *Istorijske osnove nacionalnog identiteta Crnogoraca 1918–1953*, Belgrade: Zips, 2000.
Stanković, Slobodan, *The End of the Tito Era: Yugoslavia's Dilemmas*, California: Stanford University Press, 1981.
Stavrianos, L.S., *The Balkans since 1453*, London: Hurst & Co., 2000.
Stephenson, Francis Seymour, *A History of Montenegro*, London: Harold & Son, 1916.
Stevanović, Vidosav, *Milošević: The People's Tyrant*, London: IB Tauris, 2004.
Tasić, Nikola, & Stošić, Dušica, *Migrations in Balkan History*, Belgrade: Narodna biblioteka, 1989.

Terzić, Velimir, *Slom Kraljevine Jugoslavije 1941*, Belgrade: Narodna knjiga, 1983.
The National Liberation Movement of Yugoslavia: A Survey of the Partisan Movement April 1941 – March 1944, P.I.C.M.E, June 1944, PIC/276.
Thomas, Robert, *The Politics of Serbia in the 1990s*, London: Hurst & Co., 1999.
Thomas, Robert, *Serbia under Milošević: Politics in the 1990s*, London: Hurst & Co., 2000.
Thompson, Mark, *A Paper House: The Ending of Yugoslavia*, London: Hutchinson Radius, 1992.
Thompson, Mark, *Forging War: The Media in Serbia, Croatia and Bosnia-Herzegovina*, London: Article 19, 1994.
Tito, Josip Broz, *The National Question*, Belgrade: Socialist Thought and Practice, 1983.
Todorova, Maria, *Imagining the Balkans*, Oxford: Oxford University Press, 1997.
Todorova, Maria (ed.), *Balkan Identities: Nation and Memory*, London: Hurst & Co, 1997.
Tomanić, Milorad, *Srpska crkva u ratu*, Belgrade: Medijska knjižara krug, 2001.
Tomašević, Bato, *Life and Death in the Balkans: A Family Saga in a Century of Conflict*, London: Hurst & Co., 2008.
Tomasevich, Jozo, *Peasants, Politics and Economic Change in Yugoslavia*, California: Stanford University Press, 1955.
Tomasevich, Jozo, *The Chetniks*, California: Stanford University Press, 1975.
Tomasevich, Jozo, *War and Revolution in Yugoslavia 1941–45: Occupation and Collaboration*, California: Stanford University Press, 2001.
Treadway, John D., *The Falcon and the Eagle: Montenegro and Austria-Hungary, 1908–1914*, West Lafayette, IN: Purdue University Press, 1983.
Treadway, John D., 'Engleski Crnogorac Aleksandar Divajn', *Alexandria*, Belgrade, Vol. 1, No. 7, 1988, pp. 14–20.
Treadway, John D., 'Anglo-American Diplomacy and the Montenegrin Question', *Occasional Papers*, Woodrow Wilson Centre, European Institute, East European Program, No. 26, April 1991, pp. 1–20.
Treadway, John D., 'Reflections on US-Montenegrin Relations', *Istorijski zapisi*, No. 3, 2010, pp. 9–29.
Trifunovska, Snežana, *Yugoslavia through Documents: From Its Creation to Its Dissolution*, Dordecht; London: Martinus Nijhoff, 1994.
Udovički, Jasminka, & Ridgeway, James, *Burn This House: The Making and Unmaking of Yugoslavia*, London: Duke University Press, 2000.
UN General Assembly (Security Council), 'Human Rights Questions: Human Rights Situations and Reports of the Special Rapporteurs and Representatives: Situation of Human Rights in the Former Yugoslavia (Note by the Secretary General), A/49/641/S/1994/1252, 4 November 1994.
United Nations, 'Final Report of the United Nations Commission of Experts Established Pursuant to Security Council Resolution 780: Annex XI.A – The Battle of Dubrovnik and the Law of Armed Conflict', S/1994/674/Add. 2 (Vol. V), 28 December 1994.
United Nations Economic and Social Council (UNESC), 'Situation of Human Rights on the Territory of the Former Yugoslavia: Special Report on Minorities', E/CN.4/1997/8, 25 October 1996.
United Nations Education, Scientific and Cultural Association (UNESCO), 'Report on the situation of human rights in the Federal Republic of Yugoslavia', E/CN.4/1998/15, 31 October 1997.
United Nations Education, Scientific and Cultural Association (UNESCO), 'Montenegro Earthquake: The Conservation the Historic Monuments and Art Treasures', Paris: UNESCO, 1984.

UN-ICTY Case No. IT-02-54-T, 'The Prosecutor v. Slobodan Milošević' (Witness Statement: B-1531), 04 November 2003.
UN-ICTY, Case No. IT-01-42, 'The Prosecutor v Pavle Strugar, Miodrag Jokić and Vladimir Kovačević (Amended indictment), 31 March 2003.
UN-ICTY Case No. IT-98-32/1-T, 'The Prosecutor v. Milan Lukić and Sredoje Lukić' (Prosecution final trial brief), 12 May 2009.
UN-ICTY, Case No. IT-01-42, 'The Prosecutor v Pavle Strugar, Miodrag Jokić and Vladimir Kovačević (Amended indictment), 31 March 2003.
UN-ICTY Press Release, 'Dubrovnik Indictment', The Hague, 2 October 2002, Doc. No. S.P/P.I.S/625.
UN Security Council (UNSC), 'Final Report of the Commission of Experts Established Pursuant to Security Council Resolution 780' (1992) United Nations Security Council S/1994/674 – 27 May 1992).
UNSC, 'Final Report of the Commission of Experts Established Pursuant to Security Council Resolution 780' (1992) United Nations Security Council S/1994/674 – 27 May 1992), Annex VIII part 1/10 Prison camps – 85. Višegrad.
United Nations General Assembly, 'Report of the Secretary-general Pursuant to General Assembly 53/35: The Fall of Srebrenica', 15 November 1999, A/54/549.
UNSC, Resolution 757 (Declaration of Imposition of Sanctions against the Federal Republic of Yugoslavia), 30 May 1992, BODA/4/1/12.
UN Security Council, 'Final Report of the United Nations Commission of Experts: Annex III – The Military Structure, Strategy and the Tactics of the Warring Factions', S/1994/674/Add.2 (Vol. I), 28 December 1994.
United Nations Development Program (UNDP), 'National Human Development Report: Montenegro – Society for All', UNDP/ISSP, Podgorica, 2009.
Urbačič, Ivan, 'The Yugoslav "Nationalist Crisis" and the Slovenes in the Perspective of the End of Nations', *Novi Revija*, No. 57, 1987.
Uvalic, Milica, *Serbia's Transition: Towards a Better Future*, London: Palgrave Macmillan, 2010,
Vasić, Miloš, *Atentat na Zorana*, Belgrade: Politika/B92, 2005.
Verdery, Katherine, *The Political Lives of Dead Bodies: Reburial and Post-Socialist Change*, New York: Columbia University Press, 1999.
Vickers, Miranda, *Between Serb and Albanian: A History of Kosovo*, New York: Columbia University Press, 1998.
Vladisavljević, Nebojša, *Serbia's Antibureaucratic Revolution: Milošević, the Fall of Communism and Nationalist Mobilization*, New York: Palgrave MacMillan, 2008.
Vojnoistoriski Institut, *Oslobidilački rat narodna Jugoslavije 1941–1945*, Belgrade: Druga kniga, 1965.
Vojska Jugoslavije, *NATO Aggression on Civilian Population and Facilities in Yugoslavia – Trace of Inhumanity: Yugoslavia, wartime spring of 1999*, Belgrade: 'Vojska', 1999.
Vucinich, Wayne S. (ed.), *The First Serbian Uprising, 1804–1813*, Boulder: Social Science Monographs, New York, distributed by Columbia University Press, 1982.
Vujadinović, Dragica, et al., *Between Authoritarianism and Democracy: Serbia, Montenegro, Croatia*, Belgrade: CEDET, 2003.
Vujadinović, Dragica, et al., *Between Authoritarianism and Democracy: Serbia, Montenegro, Croatia, Vol. II, Civil Society and Political Culture*, Belgrade: CEDET, 2005.
Vujović, Dimitrije, *Crnogorski federalisti 1919 – 1929*, Titograd: CANU, 1981.
Vujović, Milenko, *Istina o Srpstvu u Crnoj Gori*, Andrijevica: Nako Štampa, 2006.

Vujović, Svetislav, *Prenos i sahrana posmrtnih ostataka Nikole I Petrovića Njegoša*, Cetinje: Obod, 1994.
Vukadinović, Srdjan, 'The Status of Gypsies in Montenegro', *Philosophy and Sociology*, Vol. 2, No. 8, 2001: pp. 517–525.
Vukčević, Milan, *Crnogorska Dijaspora*, Podgorica: Centar za iseljenike Crne Gore, Grafotisak, 2006.
Wachtel, Andrew, *Making a Nation, Breaking a Nation: Literature and Cultural Politics in Yugoslavia*, California: Stanford University Press, 1998.
Wachtel, Andrew, 'Citizenship and Belonging: Literary Themes and Variations from Yugoslavia', CITSEE Working Papers Series, Working Paper 2010/12, University of Edinburgh, 2010.
West, Rebecca, *Black Lamb and Grey Falcon*, Edinburgh: Cannongate Books, 1942.
West, Richard, *Tito: The Rise and Fall of Yugoslavia*, New York: Carroll & Graf, 1994.
Wheeler, Mark, *Britain and the War for Yugoslavia 1940–1943*, New York: Columbia University Press (East European Monographs), 1980.
Whitney, Warren, *Montenegro: The Crime of the Paris Peace Conference*, New York: Brentano's, 1922.
Williams, Heather, *Parachutes, Patriots and Partisans*, London: Hurst & Co., 2003.
Woodward, Susan, *Balkan Tragedy: Chaos and Dissolution after the Cold War*, Washington, DC: Brookings Institution, 1995.
Žanić, Ivo, *Flag on the Mountain: A Political Anthropology of War in Bosnia and Croatia*, London: Saqi Books, 2007.
Zdravkovski, Aleksander, *Politics, Religion and the Autonomy Movement in Sandžak*, NTNU Doctoral Thesis, February 2017.
Zeković, Aleksandar, 'Primjeri diskriminacije Bošnjaka/Muslimana u Crnoj Gori', *Almanah*, broj 29–30, Podgorica, 2005.
Zekovic, Sreten (ed.), *Elementa Montenegrina hrestomatija (Crnogorska pravoslavna crkva)*, Zagreb: Crnogorski Federalisti, 1991.
Zeković, Sreten, *Nauk(a) o samobitnosti Crnogoraca V: Crnogorski autokefalni pokret*, Cetinje: Crnogorska prijestonica, 2003.
Zimmermann, Warren, *The Origins of a Catastrophe*, New York: Random House, 1996.
Živojinović, Dragoljub, *Crna Gora u borbi za opstanak 1914–1922*, Belgrade: Vojna knjiga, 1996.
Zlatar, Zdenko, *Njegos's Montenegro: Epic Poetry, Blood Feud and Warfare in a Tribal Zone*, New York: Columbia University Press (East European Monographs), 2005.

Newpapers and news agencies

Monitor (Podgorica), Vijesti (Podgorica), Pobjeda (Titograd/Podgorica), Dan (Podgorica), Dnevne novine (Podgorica), Bezbjednosti (Podgorica), MINA News Agency (Podgorica), Liberal (Cetinje), Borba (Belgrade), Vreme (Belgrade), Politika (Belgrade), Demokratija (Belgrade), Večerne novosti (Belgrade), NIN (Belgrade), Nedeljik (Belgrade), Dani (Sarajevo), Slobodna Bosna (Sarajevo), Oslobodjenje (Sarajevo), Nova Makedonija (Skopje), Globus (Zagreb), Institute for War and Peace Reporting (London), The Economist (London), The Guardian (London), The Times (London), AIM Press (Zurich), Deutsche Welle (Berlin), Radio Free Europe (Prague), Transitions and Transitions Online (Prague), Balkan Insight (Belgrade), BETA Press (Belgrade), Tanjug (Belgrade) & FBIS (Virginia).

Index

Note: locators with letter 'n' refer to notes.

Abazović, Dritan 158, 160
Abramović, Antonije 89–90, 211 n.48
Adriatic Sea 11, 16, 174 n.2
Agency for Electronic Communications (AEK) 164
Agreement on Minimum Principles for the Development of Democratic Infrastructure in Montenegro 74
Albania
   arms smuggling from 60
   Italian invasion and occupation of 10, 11, 12, 18
   and Montenegro border issue 5, 6, 12, 76–7, 99, 102, 134
   refugees in 99
Albanian community, Montenegrin 66–8, 123, 135, 139
Albright, Madeleine 96, 103
Alia, Ramiz 67
Allcock, John 24, 26
Alliance of Reform Forces for Montenegro (SRSCG) 39
Alliance of Reform Forces of Yugoslavia 39
All-Montenegrin National Synod 88–9
American Orthodox Church, Toronto 89
Annual National Programme (ANP) 134
anti-bureaucratic revolution 29–40, 58, 86, 147, 170, 198 n.35, 199 n.59
Anti-Fascist National Liberation Council of Yugoslavia (AVNOJ) 15, 18
'anti-Serb' policy 34, 44, 116, 125
ANVOJ 18
arms trafficking 60, 65, 67, 77, 135
Army of Republika Srpska (VRS) 63
ARS 115–16
Ašanin, Vladislav 72
Association of Montenegrins of America (AMA) 128
austerity measures 29–32, 34

Australia 128
Austria-Hungary
   BAF operations 19
   and Kolašin Conspiracy, 1909 5
   occupation of Montenegro 5–7
   Operation Punishment and 11
Autocephalous Montenegrin Orthodox Church 88–9, 90
Axis powers 11, 23

Babić, Božidar 46
Badinter Commission 50, 107
Bakarić, Vladimir 23
Balkan Air Force (BAF) 18–19
Balkans
   cigarette smuggling 106, 146
   Ottoman rule 11, 26
Balkan Wars 5, 56, 66
Banac, Ivo 5, 21, 22, 26, 174 n.2
Banjević, Branko 51
Bardhi, Mehmet 39, 67, 122
Bar to Belgrade railroad 23
Basara, Svetozar Arsić 32–3
Basariček, Djuro 9
Basque Country 131
Batrićević, Goran 142
Battle of Kosovo 84–5, 113
Battle of Mojkovac (*Mojkovačka bitka*) 6, 7
Battle of Neretva 15–18
Battle of Novšiće 56
Battle of Pljevlja 56
Bay of Kotor 11, 12, 18, 43, 44, 45, 89
Bečić, Aleksa 156, 163
Bećković, Matija 117, 125, 185 n.32, 194 n.75
Bećković, Olja 125
Belgrade
   coup 11, 16
   and Moscow frictions 21

Belgrade Agreement 106–8, 111, 118–19, 171
Belo orlovi (White Eagles) paramilitary group 62, 68, 198 n.34
Berlin, Congress of, 1878 3, 4, 56, 66, 113, 174 n.2
Biljarda, the 4, 89
Biroli, A. Pirzio 14
Bled Agreement 21
Bogdanović, Božidar 'Boba' 89, 98, 211 n.46
Bojić, Mehmedalija 8
Bojović, Božidar 77–8
Boka Mariner's Association (BM) 44–5, 191 n.25
Borba (daily) 23, 39, 47, 181 n.135, 183 n.11, 186 n.46
Bošković, Boško 56
Bošković, Husein 56
Bošković, Mašan 120
Bosnia & Herzegovina
  division of, between Croatia and Serbia 7, 10
  ethnic minorities 55, 58, 59, 60
  NATO peacekeeping forces in 70, 87
  war in 55, 60, 61, 63, 65, 69, 87, 106, 124, 170, 216 n.60
Bosniak Party (BS) 151, 152, 166, 231 n.3
Bosnian Serb Assembly 64, 87
Bosnian Serb Assembly of the Vance Owen Peace Plan (VOPP) 64, 87
Brajović, Ivan 153
Brajović, Radivoje 30
Brexit negotiations 173
Brković, Jevrem 89, 113, 115, 136–7
Brussels 118, 133, 141, 146
Bućin, Nenad 37, 45
Bulatović, Ilija 22
Bulatović, Kosta 33
Bulatović, Momir 36, 37, 38, 39, 42, 45, 46, 47, 48–52, 61, 65, 66, 67, 71–81, 89, 96, 98, 100, 103, 140, 156, 158, 171
Bulatović, Pavle 62, 63
Bulatović, Predrag 81, 93, 117, 123–4, 125, 129, 151, 154, 161
Bulgaria 5, 6, 10–11, 17, 21, 90
Burdžović, Rifat 'Tršo' 13, 34–5, 177 n.59

Bureau of the Bijelo Polje County Committee 22
Burzan, Dragiša 62

Carrington, Lord Peter 48
Carrington Peace Conference 107
Carrington Plan 48–9
Catalonia 131
Cathedral of Christ's Resurrection, Podgorica 86, 89
Catholics/Catholic Church 43, 44, 66, 68, 84, 87, 93, 96, 191 n.23
Central Bank 101
Central European Aluminum Company (CEAC) 143, 228 n.43
Cepurin, Alexander 157–8
Cetinje Bomb Affair, 1907 5
Cetinje monastery 4, 86, 87, 89, 91, 92, 149, 211 n.42
Chernozemski, Vlado 9
Chetniks *(Četnici)* 14–20, 56, 60, 89, 124, 169, 178 n.67
Chirac, Jacques 97, 106, 214 nn.17–18
Christmas Uprising *(Božićna ustanak)* 7, 8, 12, 176 n.29
Churchill, Winston 17
cigarette smuggling 71, 106, 138, 146–7, 216 n.61, 229 n.53
Čikić, Ibrahim 64
Clark, Wesley 97
Clinton, Bill 97, 214 n.18
'Code of Conduct' 116, 125, 126
Cohen, Lenard 100, 147
Cold War 57
Čolović, Božidar 42
COMINFORM crisis 21–3
Committee for the Liberation of Montenegro 12
Communist Party of Montenegro (KPCG) 22, 23
Communist Party of Yugoslavia (KPJ) 9, 13, 20–3, 25, 27, 31, 38, 85–6
Congress of Local and Regional Authorities of the Council of Europe (CLRAE) 129
Conversations with Stalin (Djilas) 23
Ćosić, Dobrica 53, 61
Council of Europe (COE) 134, 138, 222 n.38

Council of Regency 11
coup d'état 37, 163
Crawford, Charles 115
Crna ruka (Black Hand) organization 5
Crnogorstvo (Montenegrin-ness) 26, 88
Croatia
    fascism 42
    independence of 50
    Italian occupation of 177 n.53
    Montenegrin anti-Croat propaganda 41–53
    and Montenegrin border issue 45–6, 77
    multiparty elections 41
    Serb minority in 10, 41, 102
    war in 42–3, 45, 47, 51, 55, 58, 87, 170
Croatian Democratic Community (HDZ) 41
Croatian League of Communists (SKH) 38
Croatian National Guard (ZNG) 42, 43, 46
Croat Peasant Party (HSS) 9, 10
Croat Question 10
Cronjević, Ivan 4
Cuba 22
Cvetković, Dragiša 10, 11
Cvetković-Maček pact 10
Cvorović, Mitar 45, 46

Dačević, Milika Čeko 60, 61–2
Dachau concentration camp 85
Dakić, Radoje 30, 32, 33–4, 35, 185 n.35
Dan (daily) 80, 106, 115, 120, 126, 146, 152, 164, 205 n.46
Danilović, Goran 117, 124, 152, 163, 164
Dapčević, Peko 22
Dapčević, Vlado 22
Darmanović, Srdjan 36, 38
Dayton Agreement 65, 69
Deakin, Fredrick William 17, 18
Dedeić, Miraš 90, 91
De-Michelis, Gianni 48
Demirović, Idris 96
Democratic Alliance (DEMOS) 39, 152, 153, 159–60, 162, 172, 231 n.8
Democratic Alliance of Montenegro (DSCG/LDMZ) 39, 67–8, 74
Democratic Centre (DC) 142
Democratic Forum of Albanians 67
Democratic Institutions and Human Rights (OSCE/ODHIR) 118–19, 129

Democratic League of Montenegro (DSCG) 67–8, 74
Democratic Montenegro (DCG) 153, 156, 160, 163, 164, 166, 234 n.64
Democratic Opposition of Serbia (DOS) 103
Democratic Party (DS) 79, 103, 136, 217 n.66
Democratic Party of Socialists (DPS)
    approach to Kosovo war and Belgrade Agreement 95, 98, 101, 103–9
    and CPC–SPC conflict 91–3
    first five post-referendum years (2006–11) 133–50
    and media tensions 137
    official name change 40
    political crisis and protests against (2012–16) 151–67
    and referendum process 111–31
    split within 65–6, 68, 69–81, 171
Democratic Serb Party (DSS) 116–17, 122, 125, 135, 141, 144
Democratic Union of Albanians (DUA) 68, 74, 122, 136
Deripaska, Oleg 143
Devine, Alexander 8, 176 n.35
Dikić, Bratislav 163, 164
Dimitrov, Georgi 21
Dinosha, Ferhat 68, 136
Djilas, Milovan 13, 14, 17, 20, 21, 23, 26, 158
Djindjić, Zoran 79, 103, 111, 217 n.66
Djodjić, Lazar 35
Djukanović, Milo 37–40, 43, 45, 47–8, 49, 52, 62, 66, 68–81, 87, 90, 91, 95–8, 100–9, 111, 115, 117–18, 120–5, 127–8, 135, 136, 138, 140, 143–50, 153, 156, 158, 159–66, 171–3, 191 n.20, 194 n.73, 199 n.58, 201 n.85, 203 n.5, 203 n.8, 203 n.15, 204–5 n.33–34, 204 n.23, 204 n.26, 204 n.28, 205 n.40, 205 n.44, 205 n.46, 205 n.57, 206 n.64, 206 n.67, 206 n.69, 206 n.79, 212 n.56, 213 n.73, 213 nn.3–4, 214 n.9, 214 n.12, 214 n.18, 216 n.51, 216 n.60, 216 n.65, 216 n.83, 217 n.71, 218 n.84, 219 n.2, 221 n.26, 227 n.12, 227 n.28, 229 n.53, 229

n.57, 230 n.61, 233 n.28. *See also* Democratic Party of Socialists (DPS)
Djurišić, Pavle 14, 15, 19, 73, 81, 178 n.64, 178 n.67
Djurković, Miša 133, 220 n.9
Djurović, Gordana 134, 226 n.3
Dnevne novine (daily) 159
Drljević, Sekula 9, 12, 19, 113
drug trafficking 77, 147
dual citizenship 138
Dubrovnik campaign 43–53
Dukljan Academy of Sciences and Arts (DANU) 113, 115, 136

earthquakes 25
economy(ic)
 crisis 25, 28, 29–34, 40, 75, 143–5, 170
 growth 23, 143, 162
elections
 1907 5
 1920 9
 1990 39
 1997 74, 80
 2000 102
 2002 109
 2006 135, 143–4
 2008 138
 2013 152
 2016 162–7
electricity 30, 46, 120, 129, 143
Elektroprivreda Crne Gore (EPCG) 143
Elena, Queen 12
Elliot, William 18
Embattled Mountain, The (Deakin) 17
Euro-Atlantic integration 121, 133, 134, 140, 171, 173
Euro crisis 173
European Commission (EC) 118, 133, 134, 141, 167
European Community (EC) 46
European Community Monitoring Mission (ECMM) 64
European Court of Human Rights (ECHR) 150
European Parliament (EP) 129
European Stability Initiative (ESI) 98, 204 n.28

European Union (EU) 1, 2, 70, 95, 104–7, 118–20, 127, 130, 133–4, 137, 139, 140, 141, 142, 146, 148, 151, 155, 157, 161–2, 167, 169, 171, 173
Eurovision Song Contest 126–7
Evangelical Church 84
extremism 57–60, 62, 141, 156, 201 n.78

Facebook 153, 155
fascism 9, 10, 15, 42, 44, 46, 62, 113
Federal Republic of Yugoslavia (FNRJ) 2
Ferdinand, Franz, assassination of 5–6
Filaret, Bishop 149
Finci, David 50
First World War 11, 169
fishing industry 43
Five Year Plan, 1947 20
food supplies 6, 11, 34–5
For Better Living (DŽB) 80
foreign direct investment (FDI) 100, 135, 142–3
Fourth Reich 42
Franjić, Niko 146
Friends of Yugoslavia 25

Garašanin, Ilija 14
Garčević, Vesko 159
Gashi, Zeff 96
Gavrilo V 85
Gelbard, Robert 78, 203 n.8
Geneva Convention 53
Germany
 invasion of Montenegro 11, 15–19, 21, 56
 Montenegrin Albanians in 67
 post-reunification 42
 and Second World War 10–11, 18–19
Gligorov, Kiro 42
Golubić, Vidoje 64
Great National Assembly 7
Great Schism 93
Greece 5, 6, 11, 18, 21, 50, 86, 90
Green rebellion 8
gross domestic product (GDP) 24, 142–3
guerrilla conflict 6, 8
Gvozdenović, Dušan 88, 89

Hadžić, Harun 58, 59, 61, 64–5, 123
Hague, The 46, 48–53, 146

High Court of Montenegro 79, 166
higher education 24
Hitler, Adolf 11
Holbrooke, Richard 96
Holy Russian Synod 90
hospitals 4, 154, 179 n.87
Hoxha, Enver 67
Hrvatska banovina 10
Hrvatsko proljeće (Croatian Spring) 23–4
human trafficking 67, 109
Hungary 11, 21, 22, 23, 127, 177 n.53

Ilić, Pavle 27
illegal activities 65, 71, 77, 88, 103, 106, 120, 135, 137, 140, 146, 149, 226 n.11, 230 n.66. *See also* smuggling
independence referendum, 2006 1, 111–31
    anti-government protests and political crisis (2012–16) 151–67
    and constitution, 2007 137–41
    controversy over state symbols 112–14
    post-referendum (first five) years (2006–11) 133–50
    pre-referendum politics 116–20
    pro-independence and unionist campaigns 120–8
    referendum day, 21 May 128–31
    role of media 114–16
Independent State of Croatia (NDH) 41, 56
Indonesia 46, 57
industrial centres 20, 21, 22, 23, 25, 30, 75, 171
infrastructure 7, 23, 24, 66, 74, 75, 95, 96, 97, 160, 162
International Court of Justice (ICJ) 140
International Criminal Tribunal for the Former Yugoslavia (ICTY) 53, 64, 99, 111, 127, 149, 219 n.2
International Federation for the Rights of Man (IFRM) 52
International Monetary Fund (IMF) 29, 70, 142
International Security Assistance Force (ISAF) 134
Iraq 30
Irinej, Bishop 149
Islamic Community of Montenegro (IZCG) 57

Islamic Community of Yugoslavia (IZJ) 57
Italian Air Force 18
Italy
    annexation of Montenegro/Albania 11–19, 48, 56, 62, 98, 113
    fascist regime 9, 10
    illegal activities 71, 106, 138, 145–6
    and Second World War 10–11
Ivanović, Božina 34
Ivanović, Ivan 120
Izetbegović, Alija 39, 42, 58

Janjić, Ilija 96
Janjić, Janko 'Tuta' 64, 200 n.63
January coup (1987–90) 29–40, 41, 58, 77, 199 n.59
Jasenovac concentration camp 19, 86
Jehovah's Witnesses 84
Jeremić, Vuk 139–40
Jerusalem 11
JNA (Yugoslav People's Army) 20, 22, 42–7, 49–50, 53, 120
Jočić, Sreten 146
Jokić, Miodrag 46, 53
Jovanović, Arso 22
Jovanović, Batrić 33
Jovanović, Blažo 20, 22
Jovanović, Duško 115, 146
Jovanović, Obren 149
Jovanovich, William 181 n.127
Jović, Borisav 49, 52, 188 n.81, 194 n.61
Jovović, Mihailo 137
Jovović, Ranko 45
July uprising, 1941 14, 16

Kadić, Ranko 116, 125, 221 n.22, 229 n.49
Kalić, Mehmed 56
Kapičić, Petar 88
Karadžić, Radovan 63, 64, 87, 124, 192 n.32
Karadjordjević, Aleksander 84, 86, 92, 114, 176 n.29, 208 n.15
Karadjordjević, Petar 4, 7, 9, 13
Kardelj, Edward 21
Katnić, Milivoje 164–5, 166
Keković, Vladimir 33
Khomeini, Ayatollah 58
Kidrić, Boris 30, 32, 34, 35
Kilibarda, Novak 39, 42, 49, 74, 79, 89, 100

Kingdom of Serbs, Croat and Slovenes
  (*Kraljevina Srba, Hrvata i
  Slovenaca* – KSHS) 3, 7–9, 26, 56,
  84, 113, 169
Klapuh family murder 63–4
Klubaši (club members) 4–5, 25–6
Klub narodnih poslanika (Club of National
  Deputies) 4
Knežević, Milan 154, 161, 162
Knežević, Ratko 146, 147
Kočan, Esad 65
Kolašin Conspiracy, 1909 5
Kombinat Aluminijuma Podgorica (KAP)
  23, 143, 228 n.43
Komnenić, Petar 164–5
Kontić, Radoje 36, 37, 78, 80
Koprivica, Stanislav-Ćano 51
Korać, Žarko 124
Kosovo
  anti-bureaucratic revolution in 58
  autonomy 66
  declaration of independence, 2008
    138–41, 144
  Montenegrin concerns for 138–41
  Muslims in 58, 59
  riots/crisis 66–7, 81, 142
  Serbs and Montenegrins in 31–4, 66,
    170
Kosovo Liberation Army (KLA) 95,
  213 n.2
Kosovo Protection Force 158
Kosovo war, 1998–99 68, 95–109
Kostić, Branko 36, 37, 45, 49, 52
Koštunica, Vojislav 103–4, 116, 118, 124,
  212 n.68, 216 n.65, 217 n.71, 219
  n.2
Kovac, Radomir 64
Kovačević, Vladimir 53
Kragujevac, Serbia 5, 11
Kremlin 22
Krivokapić, Ranko 81, 125, 138, 150, 156,
  159, 160
krvavi božić (Bloody Christmas) 6
Kučan, Milan 42
Kuljača, Rajko 148

Land Assembly for the National
  Liberation of Montenegro and the
  Bay of Kotor (ZAVNOCG) 18

Land Assembly for the National
  Liberation of the Sandžak
  (ZAVNOS) 57, 196 n.12, 196 n.13
Law on Referendum 52, 119
Law on State Symbols and Statehood Day
  112
Lawson, Philip 19
League of Communists of Montenegro
  (SKCG)
  autonomy 24
  coup within 170
  economic crisis and January Coup of
    1989 29–41, 58
  and January movement 36
  official name change 40
  and SPC conflict 85–6
League of Communists of Yugoslavia
  (SKJ) 23, 24, 34, 35, 187 n.66
Lekić, Miodrag 151, 152, 156, 159–60,
  163, 172, 215 n.47, 231 n.2, 231
  nn.6–7
Lenin, Vladimir 22
Leper and Other Tales, The (Djilas) 23
Liberal Alliance of Montenegro (LSCG)
  44, 74
  anti-war activities 107–9, 170
  coalitions 107
  core objective 74
  downfall of 102
  leadership 51, 74, 80
  media reports 50
  pro-independence 80, 88
  referendum process 118, 120–2
Liberal Party (LS) 118, 142, 221 n.30, 231
  n.6
Lilić, Zoran 70–1
Lim-Sandžak brigade 15
Lipka, František 119, 130
Lovćen Brigade 19, 98
Lukić, Milan 62
Lukić, Sredoje 62
Lukovac, Branko 101, 107, 117–18, 120,
  122, 215 n.49
Lukšić, Igor 147–8, 149, 228 n.35

Macedonia 6, 9, 11, 14, 20, 50, 55, 66, 67,
  99, 140
Macedonian Orthodox Church 85
MacLean, Fitzroy 17, 18

Maček, Vladko 10
Mandić, Andrija 116–17, 124, 133, 134–5, 138–42, 154–5, 157, 160–1, 166, 220 n.13, 221 n.22, 221 n.24, 226 n.5
MANS (NGO) 152, 163, 230 n.62
Marković, Ante 39
Marković, Duško 147, 148, 165–6, 172–3
Marković, Mira 71, 203 n.12
Markuš, Jovan 33
Marović, Dragan 148
Marović, Svetozar 37, 38, 43–4, 70–3, 77, 92, 96, 100, 108, 147–8, 190 n.16, 203 n.4, 204 n.23, 227 n.12, 227 n.59, 230 nn.61–62
Martinović, Radoslav 97
Marx/Marxist theory 13, 22
Mašanović, Marko 9
Mathias, Thomas 19
Mazzolini, Stefano 12
media, role of Montenegrin 114–16, 125–30
Medojević, Nebojša 117, 138–9, 142, 144–7, 154
Mehonjić, Jusuf 56
Membership Action Plan (MAP) 134
'Memorandum on the Special Status of Albanians in Montenegro, The' 68
Merlin, Dino 161–2
Meštrović, Ivan 86
Mihailović, Draža 14–16, 19
Mijušković, Lazar 5
Milatović, Veljko 19
Milena, Queen 8, 149, 176 n.37
Milić, Pavle 33
Milić, Srdjan 141
Military Technical Agreement 99
Mills, George 18
Milošević, Slobodan
　and Žabljak Constitution negotiations 49–52
　anti-bureaucratic revolution 29–40, 58
　and DPS conflict 69–81
　and Kosovo war 96–104
　and Muslims/Bosniaks issue 64, 66
　rise to power 86, 170
Milutinović, Ivan 14, 32
Mićunović, Branislav 147
Mlada Bosna (Young Bosnia) 5

Moljević, Stevan 14, 19
Monitor (weekly) 44, 51, 64–5, 76, 102, 108, 115, 117, 128, 136, 153, 162
MONSTAT 111
Montenegrin Academy of Sciences and Arts (CANU) 24, 89, 113
Montenegrin Army 6
Montenegrin Assembly 4, 5, 35–7, 39, 45, 46, 48–9, 51, 62, 65, 70, 73, 76–8, 87, 92, 96, 107–8, 112, 137, 151, 155–6, 161, 164–6, 184 n.29, 193 n.58, 194 n.61, 195 n.92
Montenegrin Federalist Party (CFP) 9, 12
Montenegrin identity 24, 25–8, 56, 75, 84, 87
Montenegrin Intelligence Agency (ANB) 156, 160
Montenegrin Liberation Movement (COP) 100
Montenegrin Literary Paper (CKL) 115–16
Montenegrin Orthodox Church (CPC) 83–93, 136–7, 148–50, 171, 208 n.5, 209 n.23, 210 n.31, 211 n.49, 212 n.68, 230 n.66
Montenegrin Question 8, 101
Montenegrin state television (TVCG) 42, 73, 200 n.70
Montenegro
　census 111–12
　Constitution, 1905 4, 88
　Constitution, 2007 137–41
　dominant religion/religious communities 84
　ethnic minorities 55–68
　EU membership 133–4, 137, 139, 141, 142, 171, 173
　formal currency 51, 81, 101
　geographical characteristics and border issue 75–6
　language issue 113, 138
　NATO membership 134, 140, 158–9, 167, 171, 173
　state symbols 112–14
　tenth independence anniversary 1
　and Tito–Stalin split 20–2
　UN membership 134
　wars of expansion 3–11
　World War II (1941–45) 11–20

Montenegro: A Modern History (Morrison) 2
Montenegro Airlines 128
Montenegro (Djilas) 23
monuments 25, 113–14, 208 n.15, 227 n.28
Morris, Philip 106, 146
Movement for the Joint European State Union of Serbia & Montenegro 116, 221 n.23
Mugoša, Miodrag 137, 179 n.100
Muratović, Hakija 64
Muslimansko nacionalno vijeće Sandžaka (MNVS) 58–9
Muslim Brotherhood, Egypt 58
Muslim community, Montenegrin 55–66
Mussolini, Benito 17

Nacionalni stroj (National Alignment) group 156
Nacional (weekly) 106, 115, 146, 156
Narishkin, Sergey 161
Narodna sloga (NS) 74
NATO
  bombing campaign 87, 95–101, 171, 173
  Montenegro–Russia relations and 154, 156, 157–9, 162
Nazis 85
Nesterenko, Andrei 157–8
New Class, The (daily) 23
Nicholas, Tsar 4
Nikčević, Radomir 91
Nikčević, Vojislav 27
Nikolaidis, Jovan 67
Nikolić, Tomislav 124
Nikšić beer *(Nikšićko pivo)* 23
NIN (weekly) 33, 87
Njegoš: Poet, Prince, Bishop (Djilas) 23
Non-Aligned Movement (NAM) 57
non-governmental organizations (NGO) 89, 123, 129, 144, 152–3, 157, 163, 225 n.96, 230 n.62, 233 n.45
NOVA 144, 151, 152, 158, 159

Obradović, Milorad 97
Obraz (Honor) group 156
Observer, The 142

October protests/attacks
  1988 29, 33–7
  1991 49, 51
  2015 153–7, 158, 159
October Revolution 103
Operation Bullseye 16
Operation Eagle's Flight 135–6
Operation Korab 33
Operation Lim 64–5
Operation Punishment 11
Operation Radak 33
Operation Sabre 111
Operation Schwarz 17
Operation Storm 87
Operation Trio 15, 16
Operation Typical 17
Operation Weiss 16
Organisation for Security and Cooperation in Europe (OSCE) 76, 119, 124, 129, 130, 138, 152, 204 n.33, 217 n.76
Organisation of Independent Communists (ONK) 39
Orlandić, Marko 34
Orthodox CPC–SPC conflict 83–93, 148–50
OSCE/ODHIR ROM 119–20, 129
OSCE Parliamentary Assembly (OSCE PA) 129
Osvetnici (Avengers) paramilitary group 62
Ottoman Empire 3, 4, 5, 11, 26, 56, 75, 85, 88, 92

Pajović, Darko 153
Pajović, Radoje 20
Palestine 11
Panić, Milan 53
Paris 4, 95
Paris Peace Conference 8
Parliamentary Assembly of the Council of Europe (PACE) 119, 129
Partisans 14–23, 56, 88, 169
Partnership for Peace (PfP) 134
Party for Equality (SR) 39
Party of Democratic Action (SDA) 39, 58–9, 61, 64–7, 74, 123, 170–1, 188 n.83, 223 n.59
Party of National Equality (SNR) 59

Party of Serbian Unity (SSJ) 62
Pašić, Nikola 8
Patriarchy of Constantinople 90
Patrushev, Nikolai 166
Paul, Prince 10
Pavlović, Koča 152
Pavlović, Srdja 24, 27, 44, 46
Pejaković, Nikola 62
Pentagon 70
People's Liberation Movement (NOP) 15
People's Party (*Narodna stranka* – NS) 4–5, 39, 42, 45, 46, 49, 74, 77, 79, 80, 89, 100, 104–5, 108, 116, 122, 130, 135, 141, 144, 174 n.12, 188 n.82, 197 nn.27–8, 205 n.34, 208 n.13, 221 n.22
Perazić, Gavro 48
Perišić, Momčilo 96, 207 n.69
Perović, Gojko 149
Perović, Miodrag 'Miško' 51
Perović, Slavko 47, 51, 74, 80, 108, 118, 122, 155
Perović, Vesna 107
Petričević, Branko 22
Petrović, Danilo I 3–4, 8
Petrović, Nikola I 3–8, 12, 26, 66, 92, 113, 122, 176 n.37, 177 n.43
Petrović, 'Njegoš' Peter I 24
Petrović, Queen Milena 149
Petrović, Šako 4
Petrović dynasty 3–7, 12, 13, 92, 112–14, 169
Petrović 'Njegoš' Petar II 3, 11, 23, 26, 85–6, 89, 92, 150, 208 n.14
Piperović, Zoran 109
Plamenac, Jovan 8
Plavšić, Biljana 87
Plavska pobuna (Plav rebellion) 56
Pobjeda (daily) 37, 43, 44, 47, 51, 52, 57, 58, 73, 96, 114–15, 120, 126, 127, 129–30, 156, 158, 162, 164
Podgorica (Titograd)
    Allied bombings 19–20, 114
    and Belgrade agreement 95–109
    interethnic hostility 61
    protests 77–81, 120, 122, 124–30, 139–40, 151–67
    reconstruction 114
Podgorica Assembly (*Podgorička skupština*) 7, 8, 84–5, 114, 130, 169

Podgorica Lobby 79
Poland 10, 18, 21
police brutality 10, 34–5, 58, 60–6, 78, 79, 89, 92, 95, 97–8, 101–2, 105, 109, 125, 135, 149, 154–6, 158–9, 163, 165, 166, 188 n.77
Politika (daily) 32, 50, 57, 59, 126
Popov, Vladimir Nikolaevich 166
Popović, Krsto 7, 12, 19, 98, 176 n.29
Popović, Milan 100
Popović, Milorad 115
Popović, Predrag 116, 130
Positive Montenegro (PCG) 153
Princip, Gavrilo 5
pro-independence campaign 1, 79–80, 88, 93, 100, 105–6, 108, 115–18, 120–31, 136, 191 n.23, 211 n.40, 219 n.2, 223 n.51, 223 n.55
prostitution 109
Pukanić, Ivo 146
Putin, Vladimir 158, 159, 165

Račan, Ivica 38, 41
Račić, Puniša 9
Radić, Pavle 9
Radić, Stjepan 9
radio, Montenegrin 86, 137
Radio Televizija Crna Gora (RTCG) 43, 45, 52, 73, 77–8, 98, 115–16, 125–6, 153, 156–7, 160, 187 n.68, 190 n.14, 206 n.64
Radončić, Šeki 63
Radonjić, Radovan 34
Radović, Amfilohije (Risto) 86–93, 96, 117, 140, 149–50, 154, 209 n.17, 209 n.21
Radović, Miljan 31, 35–6
Radunović, Slaven 154, 157, 162
railroads 23
Rakčević, Žarko 46, 47, 52, 156
Rakočević, Branko 65
Ražnatović, Željko 'Arkan' 87
Ražnjatović, Željko 'Arkan' 60, 62
Ranković, Aleksander 22, 57
Rastoder, Šerbo 20, 26–7
Red Terror 14
Referendum day (21 May 2006) 128–31
Referendum Observation Mission (ROM) 119–20

Rehn, Elisabeth 66
Rehn, Oli 118
Religious Community of Montenegrins of Eastern Orthodox Confession 89
Republika (daily) 115, 116, 122, 126, 128
Revolution of the Logs 41
Roberts, Elizabeth 2, 26
Robertson, George 97
Roćen, Milan 148, 226 n.3
Rogozin, Dmitry 159, 234 n.46
Romania 6, 11, 21
Royal Air Force (RAF) 18
Rugova, Ibrahim 70
Russia
    constitution, 1905 4
    FDI into Montenegro 143, 157
    Ministry of Foreign Affairs (MFA) 158
    and Montenegro relations with NATO 154, 156–9, 161–4
Russian Military Intelligence 166

Šamardžić, Željko 161–2
Samardžić, Nikola 45, 118
sanctions 47, 53, 71, 75, 87, 106, 146, 157, 161, 170
Sandžak Question 64
Sarajevo 2, 5, 24, 50, 59–60, 101–2, 161–2
Šarić brothers 147
Sbutega, Don Branko 44
Scelsi, Guisseppe 106, 146
Schengen zone 134
Scutari 6
Second World War in Yugoslavia (1941–45) 18, 20–2, 56–7
Serbia
    Albanians in 66–8
    Chetniks in 14
    identity 83–93, 117, 124
    and Montenegro relations 4–11, 55–8, 71–81
    Muslim communities in 59–60, 64
    nationalism 26–8, 31–2, 63
    United States and 70
Serbian Academy of Sciences and Arts (SANU) 27
Serbian Autonomous Area (SAO) 124
Serbian Autonomous Region of Krajina (SAO) 41
Serbian League of Communists (SKS) 38

Serbian Orthodox Church (SPC) 83–93, 140, 149–50
Serbian People's Party of Montenegro (SNS) 117
Serbian Question 27
Serbian Radical Party (SRS) 9, 60, 62, 97, 99, 124, 198 n.35
Serbian Security Information Agency (BIA) 166
Serbian Volunteer Guard, The (SDG) 60
Serb Orthodox Youth Brotherhood 149
Šešelj, Vojislav 62, 68, 97, 99, 210 n.38
Seventh-day Adventist Church 84
Shia Muslims 58
Shirokov, Eduard Vladimirovich 166
Simović, Zoran 64
Sindjelic, Aleksander 164, 166, 235 n.73
Singapore 45
'6 January dictatorship' 9
Skenderović, Isad 64
Slobodna Bosna (weekly) 145
Slovenia
    borders 7, 19
    independence of 42, 50
    at UN Security Council 101
Slovenian League of Communists (ZKS) 38
Slovenian Territorial Defence Forces 42
smuggling 60, 67, 71, 77, 95, 102, 106, 138, 146–7, 216 n.61, 229 n.53
Soć, Dragan 116
Social Democratic Party (SDP) 59, 62, 74, 80–1
Social Democratic Party of Reformers (SDPR) 52
Social Democrats (SDCG) 153
Socialist Federal Republic of Yugoslav (SFRJ)
    disintegration of 2
    Montenegrin identity and 25–8
    Tito–Stalin split 20–2
    and World War II (1941–45) 11–20
Socialist People's Party of Montenegro (SNP)
    and DPS coalition 79–80, 104–9, 134–6, 143, 151, 153, 159–60
Socialist Republic of Montenegro 23–8
Solana, Javier 97, 105–7, 118, 119, 131
Šolević, Miroslav 32–3

Soros, George 70
Special Air Service (SAS) 101
Special Anti-Terrorist Unit (SAJ) 156
Special Operations Executive (SOE), British 16–19
Špegelj, Martin 120
sports and popular culture 1, 79, 114, 126, 127
Sredanović, Blažo 128
Srpstvo (Serbness) 26
St. Nicholas Day bombardment 49
Stability and Association Agreement (SAA) 133, 137
Stalin–Tito split 20–2, 23, 170
Stanišić, Jovica 146
Stanković, Ivica 164
Stanković, Ljubisa 38, 39
'state coup' controversy 162–7, 169
State Election Commission 152, 160
Steinberg, James 147
Stojadinović, Milan 9, 10
Stojčović, Gojko 90
Strugar, Pavle 53
Stuart, Bill 17
student protests 24, 33–6, 38, 66–7, 90, 157
Šturanović, Željko 138
Subotić, Stanko 'Cane' 106, 146
Sunni Muslims 58

Tadić, Božidar 36
Tadić, Boris 117, 130, 139–40, 144
Tadić, Ljubomir 117
television, Montenegrin 1, 37, 42, 52, 66, 73, 76, 98, 115, 125–7, 129, 137, 164
Terzić, Slavenko 117
theatre 4, 114
Titograd. *See* Podgorica
Titograd Municipality Committee 34
Tito–Stalin split 20–2
tourism 23, 25, 46, 47, 63, 100, 143, 157, 171
Treaty of San Stefano 56
Trieste 4
Tripartite Pact 10
Trsteno Affair 118, 122, 221 n.30
True People's Party (*Prava narodna stranka* – PNS) 5, 9
Trump, Donald 167

Tudjman, Franjo 41, 42, 53
Turco, Ottavio del 106, 146
Turkey 56, 64
Turković, Damjan 62–3, 65, 201 n.80
Twitter 153, 155, 231 n.8

Ugljanin, Sulejman 58–9, 64
Užice Republic (*Užička republika*) 15
UN General Assembly (UNGA) 140
unionist campaign 120–8
United Kingdom
    intervention in Montenegro 4, 48, 115, 139, 141–2
    and Kosovo war 101
    SOE mission 16–19
United Nations
    United Nations Charter 48
    United Nations Educational, Scientific and Cultural Organization (UNESCO) 45
    UN Security Council (UNSC) 101
    UN Security Resolution 757 53
United Opposition of Montenegro (UOCG) 52
United Reformist Action (URA) 152–3, 156, 158, 160, 162, 231 n.8
United States
    Congress 70, 95
    intervention in Montenegro 8, 18, 50, 70, 103–4, 139, 141, 146, 147, 167
    Montenegrin diaspora in 67, 128
University of Titograd 24, 32, 36
urbanization 23
Ustaša group 9, 41, 46, 47, 56, 86

Vance-Owen Peace Plan (VOPP) 64, 87
Varnava I 85
Velika narodna skupština Srpskog naroda u Crnoj Gori (Great National Assembly of the Serb People in Montenegro). *See Podgorička skupština* (Podgorica Assembly)
Velimirović, Mirko 163, 235 n.87
Venice Commission (VC) 119, 222 n.38
Viber 164
Vicković, Miodrag 107
Victor Emmanuel III 12
Vidovdan (St Vitus's Day) 5

Vijesti (daily) 108, 115, 126, 130, 136–7, 146, 164
visa-free travel 100–1, 134, 157
Vladike (Prince-Bishops) 3, 229 n.48
Vladisavljević, Nebojša 35, 36–7
Vlahović, Miodrag 38, 51, 116
Vojičić, Srdjan 137
Vreme (weekly) 70, 71, 72
Vučinić, Mirko 120
Vujanović, Filip 91, 101, 105, 108, 109, 138, 147–8, 152, 159, 166, 173, 231 n.6
Vukadinović, Vuko 34, 36
Vukčević, Radojka 117
Vukčević, Svetozar 34
Vukotić, Veselin 36, 37
Vuković, Miodrag 122
Vuković, Zoran 64

War for Peace propaganda campaign 41–53
Western Europe 10, 22, 95, 104
WhatsApp 164
White House 70
Whitney, Warren 8
World Bank 70, 142

Yoghurt Revolution 33
Youth Action Work (ORA) 23
Yugoslav Army 12, 35, 40, 42, 61, 78
Yugoslav Committee 7
Yugoslav Constitution 31
Yugoslavism 7, 9, 57, 79, 208 n.14
Yugoslav-Italian Friendship Society 10
Yugoslav Left (JUL) party 71
Yugoslav Navy 43, 46, 50
Yugoslav Secret Service (OZNA) 22

Žabljak Constitution 41, 50, 53, 195 n.92
Zagreb 7, 41, 44–5, 146, 191 n.22, 194 n.75
Zajedno protests 71–2
Žarković, Vidoje 32, 45, 183 n.1
Zavala case 148, 230 n.62
Zec, Milan 53
Zelenaši (Greens) 7, 26, 84–5, 169, 176 n.30, 210 n.38
Zeta film 120
Zetska banovina 9, 10
Zetski dom theatre 4
Živković, Miodrag 107, 109, 118
Zogović, Radovan 27
Žugić, Goran 102, 106, 216 nn.60–1